Miami Architecture

University Press of Florida

Florida A&M University, Tallahassee
Florida Atlantic University, Boca Raton
Florida Gulf Coast University, Ft. Myers
Florida International University, Miami
Florida State University, Tallahassee
New College of Florida, Sarasota
University of Central Florida, Orlando
University of Florida, Gainesville
University of North Florida, Jacksonville
University of South Florida, Tampa
University of West Florida, Pensacola

Allan T. Shulman · Randall C. Robinson Jr. · James F. Donnelly

Miami

ARCHITECTURE

An AIA Guide Featuring Downtown, the Beaches, and Coconut Grove

University Press of Florida
Gainesville
Tallahassee
Tampa
Boca Raton
Pensacola
Orlando
Miami
Jacksonville
Ft. Myers
Sarasota

15 14 13 12 11 10   6 5 4 3 2 1

Library of Congress Cataloging-in-Publication Data
Shulman, Allan T.
Miami architecture : an AIA guide featuring downtown, the beaches, and Coconut
Grove / Allan T. Shulman, Randall C. Robinson Jr., and James F. Donnelly.
p. cm.
Includes bibliographical references and index.
ISBN 978-0-8130-3471-3 (alk. paper)
    1. Architecture—Florida—Miami—Guidebooks. 2. Miami (Fla.)—Buildings, struc-
tures, etc.—Guidebooks. 3. Miami (Fla.)—Guidebooks. 4. Architecture—Florida—
Miami Beach—Guidebooks. 5. Miami Beach (Fla.)—Buildings, structures, etc.—
Guidebooks. 6. Miami Beach (Fla.)—Guidebooks. I. Robinson, Randall C. II. Donnelly,
James F. III. Title.
NA735.M398S58   2010
720.9759'381—dc22   2009047423

The University Press of Florida is the scholarly publishing agency for the State University
System of Florida, comprising Florida A&M University, Florida Atlantic University,
Florida Gulf Coast University, Florida International University, Florida State University,
New College of Florida, University of Central Florida, University of Florida, University
of North Florida, University of South Florida, and University of West Florida.

University Press of Florida
15 Northwest 15th Street
Gainesville, FL 32611-2079
http://www.upf.com

Miami Architecture Project

Randall C. Robinson Jr., Director

James F. Donnelly

Allan T. Shulman

Maps created by Ulises Peinado Eyherabide

Photography by Robin Hill and Thomas Delbeck

Project Manager: Rebecca Stanier-Shulman

Contents

THE CITY OF MIAMI   11

Randall C. Robinson Jr.

THE CITY OF MIAMI BEACH · 218

Randall C. Robinson Jr.

Maps

Foreword

A Place Unlike Any Other

Miami is like those treasure troves in Mesopotamia—when you start digging,
you find all the fads and fashions that have made America what it is in the
20th century. The whole city is one vast, wonderful tribute to the fact that,
in this part of the world, fantasy has the force of history.
T. D. Allman, *Miami, City of the Future*

When I was five, the family made a trip to see Grandfather, who lived
in Miami. During the long drive from Connecticut, my mind conjured
fantastic images of man-eating alligators; of perpetual sunlight; of white
sandy beaches where the aquamarine water was always warm and where a
population of sun-drenched residents had found their nirvana. Miami, for
me, was a dreamlike place where oranges and grapefruits were a fixture in
every man's yard, and where coconuts fell from trees as tall as skyscrapers
while their "milk" sloshed around just waiting for passersby to harvest its
goodness. Miami's natural world was as exotic as it gets, and that exoticism
inspired the fantasies of the men and women who made their homes and
their fortunes here.

Today, I find myself in a position to help preserve this very special place.
Yet in order to preserve Miami, we are challenged to define its uniqueness
within Florida and the nation. After all, how can a city built almost entirely
within the twentieth century justify its historic significance? What is historic preservation, and why does it matter in Miami?

Historic preservation is, first of all, a historical method. Conserving,
rehabilitating, restoring, and reconstructing the built environment all
contribute to the creation of useful primary sources for the study and interpretation of history. While the historic preservation movement in the
United States arose from motives of community pride and national pa-
triotism, by the fourth quarter of the twentieth century it had become an
important factor in the revitalization of American cities. The listing of the
Miami Beach Architectural District on the National Register of Historic

Places in 1979 is a leading example of this trend, and historic preservation in metropolitan Miami since then has often been linked with revitalization of the tourist industry and the strengthening and development of residential communities.

While historic preservation has played a role in many cities, the challenges and opportunities in Miami are unique. In recent development here, preservation has been used to establish context; it has contributed to our understanding of the city's significance in terms of its background and evolution.

Unlike the American cities that were settled by Europeans hundreds of years ago, Miami is a modern phenomenon. Besides the evidence that exists of the indigenous Seminole and Tequesta tribes, few references to the settlement of the region that would become Miami survive from the mid-nineteenth century, a time when pioneers faced unknown hardship to live in one of the world's most beautiful places. Miami's lack of a long shared history led to a disregard for the preservation of its seminal architectural pieces, especially because so many of the city's residents saved their allegiances for their states and nations of origin.

Miami has an established record of preserving landmarks, but more recently it has been reinforcing its identity through preservation of districts that represent identifiable layers of its history. For instance, Vizcaya (1916), an icon of Miami's fantasy architecture, was conveyed by its owners in 1952 to Miami-Dade County as a public museum in perpetuity. The Mediterranean Revival style that Vizcaya helped launch inspired the romantic theming of 1920s suburbs like Coral Gables that still capture the public's imagination. In 1973, Coral Gables became the first municipality in the county to adopt a historic preservation ordinance. Ralph Middleton Munroe's home, dubbed "The Barnacle" (1891) and a landmark of Miami's early settlement, was acquired by the State of Florida in 1973 as a Historic Site. Surviving districts of similar wood dwellings, including neighborhoods of bungalows, deserve protection as well.

It was the 1966 effort to preserve the magnificent Douglas Entrance in Coral Gables that touched off the modern preservation movement in Miami with the formation of the nonprofit Villagers. In 1973, realizing the need to increase interest in preservation in Dade County, the Villagers formed Dade Heritage Trust, which has become the largest preservation organization in Greater Miami. Also in 1966, iconoclast architects Denise Scott Brown and Robert Venturi began a series of visits to Miami Beach (originally to explore the architecture of Morris Lapidus), out of which emerged pleas for the preservation of the area's distinctive 1930s architecture. The hundreds of buildings in the Art Deco style make a cohesive neighborhood of Miami Beach's South Beach section. By 1976, activist Barbara Baer Capitman was leading the movement to preserve the area, an effort that would lead to its listing on the National Register in 1979. The urban renaissance of South Beach is one of the most exciting examples of urban revitalization through architectural conservation in the United States.

Miami's architectural themes are part of Florida's identity and its pedigree as a place. Moreover, these themes created urban ensembles that today are celebrated as districts in their own right. Today, historic preservation is more broadly accepted in planning circles, which recognize the imperative and challenge of keeping our history. Tourism—one of the economic engines that drives South Florida's economy—is preservation's greatest ally. No trip to Greater Miami would be complete without seeing Vizcaya; the hotels of South Beach; the city of Coral Gables; or the 1950s postwar Modern motels along Biscayne Boulevard, now branded as "Miami Modern," or "MiMo." The cities of Miami and Miami Beach have developed their own preservation cultures. Advocacy groups play a large role: Dade Heritage Trust watches over Greater Miami; the Miami Design Preservation League concentrates its efforts on South Beach; and newer organizations like DoCoMoMo Florida (Documentation and Conservation of Buildings, Sites and Neighborhoods of the Modern Movement), Save Hialeah Park, Friends of Miami Marine Stadium, and others broaden the agenda. Preserving Miami's history has enriched its identity and continues to reinforce the qualities that draw so many here.

Ellen J. Uguccioni
Historic Preservation Officer, City of Miami

Preface

Miami is a city of architecture. Perhaps that statement could pertain to any city, but here it acquires particular significance. Architecture is Miami's signature art form. Perched between natural ecosystems, Miami is an almost entirely man-made place. It is also a new city, barely one hundred years old. Within a short century, Miami has built itself and rebuilt itself, and in the process has defined itself. In this invented landscape, architecture, landscape design, and urban planning (or the lack thereof) have played a particularly important role in creating Miami's identity. We will concentrate on the architecture, while also touching on districts, parks, streetscapes, and other public spaces of the city. We hope the comments we provide will assist investigators of landscape and urban planning.

The goal of this guidebook project is to provide a broad overview of the core of the metropolitan area. Toward this end, it is important to look at the project as synthetic, curatorial, and narrative.

Greater Miami itself lacks synthesis, but this guidebook aims for cohesion, pulling material from diverse sources. We authors necessarily have our own collective and individual frameworks that shape our overall view of the subject. We hope this is an advantage, bringing different expertise and experience to bear on the wide scope of the built environment of Miami and Miami Beach. While Greater Miami is noted for the sheer quantity of artificially created landscape, we have limited ourselves for the most part to actual structures unless the dredging, filling, and planting were essential to the architecture being described. A number of excellent sources on the making of Miami and Miami Beach are available in contemporary literature.

Assembling a guidebook is also a curatorial task, requiring difficult choices. The desire to be comprehensive must be balanced with the need to keep such a book compact and useful. For example, we have not listed or described any private, single-family homes. We have given heightened attention to the buildings listed on the National Register and to structures listed as historically significant by Miami-Dade County and the cities of Miami and Miami Beach, though we have not included all of the items listed by these sources. We have tried to include those buildings that, singly or in a group, mark a change in the way architecture has been and continues to be practiced here. While we probably have failed to include many significant buildings, we have paid attention to those structures that have attracted attention in the media and those that have caused the public to think about architecture in new ways. Further, we have focused heavily on buildings that have defined or redefined the landscape of the city. These are not necessarily the best architectural specimens, nor the most historically significant ones, but rather are the ones that define the space of the city, the contours of an era or style, or that illustrate the sociocultural flavor that defines this metropolitan area. Miami has just completed another phase in its boom-bust cycle, making this an opportune moment for a snapshot of the city. Finally, though, we selected buildings that piqued our own curiosity. Time and again, we have wandered this intriguing landscape and asked, "What is that?" This book attempts to answer that question.

Finally, this is a narrative task, telling the story of Miami through its built environment even as it accretes new layers. We believe that buildings tell stories, and we have tried to share the story each building has to share. When these stories combined to tell of larger social, economic, and political changes, we have pointed to these. As a twentieth-century city, a crucible of demographic, cultural, and lifestyle trends, Miami certainly embodies many important larger themes; however, these remain outside the scope of this guidebook. Much work remains to be done interpreting Miami. We hope to stimulate not just more appreciation, but further research.

Miami Architecture: An AIA Guide Featuring Downtown, the Beaches, and Coconut Grove is the first part of Miami Architecture Project's overall guidebook. This edition focuses on Miami's metropolitan core: the cities of Miami and Miami Beach. The second edition will include the balance of this vast and diverse county. The guidebook is a work in progress. Please submit all questions, corrections, and comments to Miami Architecture Project at miamiarchitectureproject@gmail.com.

Miami Architecture

Miami
Architecture and the Invented City

Allan T. Shulman, FAIA

It has been said that Miami possesses more species of palm tree than any-where else in the world, yet few are native. The palm is an icon of Florida, symbol of the good life in the tropics. But the dream of a palm-studded city has been more than an Arcadian ideal; the exotic palm also suggests a world of fantasy and fabrication. Miami's creation in the everglade wilderness of Southeast Florida can never be separated from quixotic dreams that have defined the city's genesis and have strongly shaped its growth. In moments, Miami recalls an urban stage set, where man-made landscapes, imported flora and fauna, and especially architecture serve as the backdrop. Ironically, these artifices are its truest expression and the heart of an authentic identity. A dynamic tension between artifice and authenticity is Miami's central paradox, and the city's built environment has developed under its sway.

The elemental palm is thus a building block of the city, and a metaphor of its central paradox. Rustic wood dwellings, Mediterranean fantasies, and Modern architecture that runs the gamut from tropical minimalism to the unabashedly swank all spring from the same paradox. Miami is barely more than one hundred years old, yet its scenery has been entirely imagined and constructed in this period. In that construction, architecture has emerged as Miami's most exalted art form, its most prescient cultural product, and its most enduring image. This internationally prominent city of spectacle is unthinkable without its rich mixture of architectural expressions.

City of Constructed Identity

Miami came into being on the cusp of the twentieth century, in a land so sparsely populated and little understood it was referred to by botanist John Kunkel Small as the "land of the question mark." It was a fragile territory framed by coastal dunes and wetlands on one side and the Everglades river of grass on the other. Unfamiliar forests, pine rockland, and native hardwoods (hammocks) occupied its highlands.

By the turn of the twentieth century, however, Miami was at the confluence of powerful modern forces that would determine the shape of its development. Novel shipping, rail, and air networks made the once-remote location accessible, and then pivotal, as a hemispheric transit hub. New types of industry exploited Miami's status as America's subtropical garden: tropical fruit cultivation and, later, tourism and second-home construction drew on the nation's newfound wealth and appetite for leisure. The machine age shaped the city, supplying the dredge (that formed its landscape), the automobile (that choreographed its connectivity), and air-conditioning (whose advent helped convert it from seasonal resort to year-round city). Miami, as much as any other city, reflects the modern era's priorities, economies, technologies, culture, and arts. Although in many ways their antithesis, this leisure and resort metropolis complemented the industrial cities that were the modern era's other notable urban product.

Miami grew dramatically and famously from a wilderness to a metropolis, and its developers and architects used architecture to frame and dramatize the future development they envisioned. There was little tradition to guide them save the complex relationship with the city's natural environment—at once alluring and forbidding. Architects had to balance the dream of a richly foliated warm-weather paradise with the disproportionate intensity of Miami's heat, sun, rain, and mosquitoes, as well as with existential threats like hurricanes. Given the powerful role of the subtropical environment on the collective imagination as well as on the practicality of building, architecture naturally came to be influenced and even inspired by ideas about the climate and landscape.

In nearly every epoch of Miami's development, a regional approach to building emerged; these approaches constitute the city's architectural traditions. That they were not necessarily derived from history seems normal—the city was too new. Rather, each tradition was linked to ideas about place-making, and as often as not derived from the expectations of immigrants and tourists. Two recurrent landmarks of these expectations—tropicalism and Mediterraneanism—have played a particularly important role as frameworks for Miami's invented architectural traditions. Tropicalism catalogued Miami within the ecosystem of equatorial climates, and suggested links with other tropical areas (and consequently with a range of myths and implied exotica). Miami was celebrated as a laboratory of "tropicalism" within North America, and a demonstration of American culture in the tropics. Mediterraneanism, in contrast, established an associative bond with that region of the world whose rich cultural and historical essence imbued new developments with the perfume of civilization. That both tropicalism and Mediterraneanism were ideas, and not necessarily facts, of the existing landscape was of little importance. Miami's diverse architectural traditions were the more creative for having been synthesized from diverse European, American, Latin American, and even Asian antecedents. These traditions illustrate the paradox between artifice and authenticity. The degree to which they were successful at place-making is the measure of the city's constructed identity.

City of Layered Architectural Traditions

Miami's building traditions evolved rapidly, generated by periods of boom and swept away by each successive bust (only to be remembered in later booms). These boom-and-bust cycles have layered the city, and ultimately contributed to its complexity.

Miami's pioneers and early developers established its first tradition, a wood vernacular cobbled from sources as diverse as Florida's primitive Cracker homesteads, the bungalow, and even the Japanese pagoda. Light, airy, and well-ventilated, these buildings were well adapted to Miami's climate. The Barnacle (home of pioneer Ralph Middleton Munroe, 1891) and the Pagoda (Ransom Everglades School, 1902), both in Coconut Grove, are among the most remarkable of these early structures. Constructed of local pine and native oolitic limestone, raised off the ground to stay dry, they were sheltered by broad eaves and wrapping porches. More than rustic primitive huts, each was an evocation of cosmopolitan culture whose conscious and elegant blending of primitive and pastoral motifs was a demonstration of environmental fitness. These unassuming wood structures are landmarks of Miami's tropicalist identity.

Miami's accelerating urbanization in the 1920s demanded radically new types of formal representation. In Downtown Miami, skyscrapers sprouted in an eclectic range of commercial styles and stone-clad civic buildings exhibited a spectrum of Classical and Neoclassical designs. Even more significant, a new building tradition evolved here just as the Great Florida Boom was taking hold mid-decade. The "Mediterranean Revival" reflected the national popularity of Spanish Colonial architecture in the wake of the Panama-California Exposition in San Diego (1915), while also tapping a newfound appreciation for Florida's Spanish roots.

Mediterranean architecture was useful in this sunny resort city, as it suggested a romantic sensibility for beauty and pleasure, sublime dignity, and the picturesque (an implied contrast with Miami's stark newness as much as with what Rexford Newcomb has called North America's ingrained Protestant values and work ethic). Inaugurated in Miami at palatial private homes on Biscayne Bay like Villa Vizcaya (1914) and El

Jardin (1917), the style became vernacular in the countless small masonry and stucco homes organized around paved and landscaped patios. It introduced ideas like the outdoor living room and employed outdoor circulation systems like open-air loggias and theatrical exterior stairs. The Mediterranean Revival added urban gravitas to everyday buildings. It engaged a classical vocabulary of simple building forms pierced by arches, consoled doors and windows, and adorned with a rich palette of stone, tile, and ironwork. It drew from eclectic sources in the broad Mediterranean basin, often combining these to simulate the permanence and historical layering of an ancient civilization. Monumental structures like Downtown's Miami Metropolis Tower (today Freedom Tower, 1924) demonstrate the power of its architectural scenography to establish a bold identity for the city.

The Mediterranean Revival advanced the notion that architectural environments could be themed, not just at the scale of the building but at the scale of a district or even a city. Nearly all of Miami Beach's 1920s development was inspired by the Mediterranean mode, yet its urban potential was most clearly demonstrated at the Spanish Village on Espanola Way (1925). Garden-city suburbs like Coral Gables, Miami Shores, Miami Springs (Pueblo style), and Opa-locka (Arabian Nights) raised theming to a civic art. There, architectural theming was at the heart of a visually coherent infrastructure of boulevards, plazas, gateways, and monuments. Emblematic of a romantic, high style and urbane identity, the Mediterranean Revival became a recurrent theme in Miami's search for identity.

Architectural Modernism arrived in Miami in the 1930s, later than in most of the nation and, poignantly, in the heart of the Great Depression. Modernism appeared first in civic and commercial buildings, like the Collins Library (today Bass Museum, 1930) and Chrysler Building (1930) on Miami Beach. In contrast to the purist spirit that exemplified its polemical forms, Modernism operated in Miami on multiple and often contradictory levels. It brought a rational (even technological) approach to building type, functionality, and climate-appropriateness, yet it also integrated easily into the city's masonry and wood building traditions. It tempered the decorative exuberance of the Mediterranean Revival, yet brought with it new types of adornments: bas-relief panels, the rich use of native stone, etched and colored glassworks, decorative metalworks, and lighting effects. Further, the embellished and exuberant architecture of this period, acclaimed for its Art Deco and Streamline Moderne character, expressed a regional spirit in decorative work that depicted and thematized Miami's exceptional flora and fauna.

Modernism resonated strongly in this tolerant new city, and its use spread to hotels, apartment buildings, and even houses. The fullest expression of the period is found in Miami Beach, where L. Murray Dixon, Henry Hohauser, and a small group of like-minded architects designed most of the resort district of South Beach, and in the process defined a truly regional urban architecture. The integrity of their vision is at the heart of today's Miami Beach Architectural District.

After World War II, Modernism was redefined against a new context of technological progress, metropolitan growth, regionalism, and fashion. Postwar architects retained the Modernist principles codified in the early twentieth century, but interpreted them differently; a range of regional themes and novel building types distinguish Miami as a case study of Modernism in America. Office buildings illustrated the Modern virtues of transparency and functionality, yet their glass walls were screened with prominent sun-shading devices. Churches and synagogues expressed community and the modern iconography of spirituality using novel structural forms. Schools and universities meshed progressive educational ideals with regionally adapted building types that were so open-air they were nearly atmospherically transparent. Civic buildings based on the precepts of the Brutalists introduced porous megastructures with covered open-air plazas and expressed outdoor circulation. Miami's new Port Terminal (1959) was a pioneer in this regard, sheltering open-air concourses beneath giant airfoil roofs; similarly, the grandstands of the Miami Marine Stadium (1963) nestled beneath a spectacularly cantilevered sunshade of folded concrete planes.

Miami's postwar architects were visibly inspired by the modern world, yet many famously designed buildings for escape from its rational ideologies. Oceanfront resort hotels, Miami Beach's most visible institutions, projected unprecedented opulence in colossal eye-catching sculptural boxes that shouted extravagance and even decadence. The Baroquely curved white volumes of Morris Lapidus's Fontainebleau Hotel (1953) proudly announced a spirit of fantasist leisure that found full expression on the interior, where amoeboid rooms were astonishingly stocked with French-themed period furnishings. The exuberant sensibility of Modern resorts segued into residential towers, vertical suburbs of standardized units garnished with effusive entranceways, florid public interiors, and lavish poolside amenities.

Off the waterfront, in contrast, glamour and kitsch were jettisoned in favor of a quieter spirit. Neighborhoods of modest garden-apartment buildings reflected modern domestic leisure for the middle class and a comfortable urban lifestyle framed by communal values. The home, however, was the most important repository of regional consciousness and identity. Miami was a subtropic outpost of the American Dream. Using the single-family home as a laboratory of building type and lifestyle, architects like Igor Polevitzky, Rufus Nims, and Alfred Browning Parker creatively merged Modern forms with traditional ones, reaching back to the city's early vernacular traditions and even to a state of primitivism to create "tropical homes," an authentic expression of "Miami-ness."

Miami's fascination with Modern design faded in the late 1960s, mirroring national trends. The shift coincided with a decline in the city's nearly mythical reputation as a modish resort and paradisiacal, untroubled leisure city. Miami was transformed by its own aging, by immigration, and by an emerging consciousness of its complexity as a major American city. Historic preservation and environmental protection came to the forefront, revealing mounting concern over the devastation of both urban and natural environments. A boom in the 1980s countenanced a return to traditional architectural forms and expressions, reflecting the mounting popularity of Postmodernism. Mediterranean-inspired forms were popular again, even if at first this renewal had little of the fantasy, ingenuity, and artistry of Miami's 1920s Mediterranean Revival. Downtown Miami was one focus of boomtime development; the Miami-Dade Cultural Plaza (1980), one of the area's most important projects, housed a variety of cultural institutions in the trappings of a colonial Spanish fort. South Beach was another focal point; here, inspired by the context of a preserved South Beach, Art Deco and streamlined forms were reiterated in new buildings like the Police Headquarters (1987).

Miami's emergence in the 1980s as a pan-American city also forged a postmodern identity. One expression of Miami's emerging Latin American identity consolidated in the 1980s around a group of architects connected to the University of Miami School of Architecture—a group sometimes called the "School of Miami" or the Magic-Realists, and documented in Vincent Scully's *Between Two Towers*. Their inventive architecture borrows from antiquity, Spanish and Mediterranean traditions, and even Miami's vernacular. While it may be considered traditional in type and form, this architecture is romantic and vernacular in spirit, an expression of fantasy, craft, and the power of local contingency to inspire novel expressions.

The first decade of the twenty-first century has produced another massive boom in construction, one that is both varied in character and geographically widespread. In this resurgence, no single defining architectural style has emerged, but parallel (and often overlapping) streams can be discerned. A romantic resurgence of tropicalist Modernism and the ongoing investigations of the School of Miami are particularly notable. Equally significant, metropolitan Miami has approached its growth limits, accelerating the redevelopment of its urban core. Historic preservation projects, careful urban infill work, and the creative and adaptive use of urban centers constitute an ever-expanding field. The city is increasingly a palimpsest, where layer upon layer of development and civilization can be read.

City of Urban Diversity

From the air, Miami may look flat and undifferentiated. Yet it is a land of distinct landscape ecologies—the oceanfront strand, Biscayne Bay, the Everglades, forested hammocks and pinelands, and large stretches of landfilled wetlands interspersed with lakes and canals. Today, these environments have been subsumed into new and more complex urban landscapes that mix underlying geography with built environment, specialized character, ethnic and social identities, and a matrix of infrastructure. These environments are notable for their variety, diversity, and dynamism: prominent metropolitan centers and crossroads, older villages swallowed by the city, Miami's first suburban districts, which extend west and north from downtown, and the urban fantasyland along the beaches. The city remains a land of contrasts, a conflation of unalloyed pieces.

Miami's metropolitan landscapes and its beachfront resorts are the much-publicized façades of the city. As early as the 1920s, photographs of both sides of Biscayne Bay (Miami and Miami Beach) documented astonishing skyscraper silhouettes. Downtown Miami remains the region's dominant metropolitan center. Here, high-rise buildings break the tree canopy of the city to exploit the view potential of the waterfront; they define a memorable skyline even as they fail to bring commensurate benefits to the street. Although lacking the centrifugal force found in some older cities, Miami's compact Downtown has always maintained its central role as a business and civic center. The remnants of its prewar urban culture (large office blocks, arcaded commercial buildings, cinemas, department stores, and cross-block arcades) are relatively intact. Since World War II, commercial and residential extensions have stretched north (along Biscayne Boulevard), south (along Brickell Avenue), and west (along Coral Way).

South Beach in Miami Beach makes a second prominent urban façade. From the soaring overpass of Interstate 95 over the Miami River, Miami's other urban centers can be clearly identified: Coconut Grove, downtown Coral Gables, and even the new urban core evolving at the suburban crossroads of Kendall Downtown. Rather than centralizing, metropolitaniztion is actually reinforcing the diversity of this polycentric city.

In contrast to the character of these metropolitan centers, Miami boasts several small villages. Coconut Grove is Miami's oldest settlement, occupying areas of hardwood and pine forests raised on a limestone ridge that slopes down to Biscayne Bay. A mixed cast of pioneer settlers, industrialists, Bahamians, and bohemians forged its idiosyncratic identity. As the oldest part of the city, it is the most densely foliated, a haven for numerous early structures, many built of wood. A separatist counterculture has traditionally bred in this forested growth. In the 1980s, its village center grew into an important entertainment district. Although the Grove is unique, something of its character can be found in other early settlements, like Spring Garden and Lemon City.

Another early settlement is Overtown, lying northwest of Downtown. Overtown was home to Miami's black community, a result of racial segregation in this southern city. It originally mixed a wide range of uses and social strata in a relatively compact area: rich and poor, commercial, industrial, and civic landmarks could all be found here. Overtown was disrupted by the construction of Interstate 95 in the 1960s: the highway went right through its heart. Desegregation amplified the out-migration under way before World War II. The Midtown Exchange now divides the once-vibrant community into four smaller fragments. Prominent churches, schools, and historic sites punctuate the area.

A third characteristic landscape is found west and north of Downtown, in neighborhoods like Little Havana, Wynwood, Allapattah, and Little Haiti. These former residential suburbs and industrial districts, settled mainly in the 1920s, are being reinvented as dynamic urban districts in their own right. The generator of change has been demographic: the influx of immigrants from the Caribbean and Central and South America began with Cuban immigration in the late 1950s. Here is the heart of Miami's new transnational character, and a new type of Creole culture is being forged in these districts. Mixed areas of homes and small apartment buildings, interspersed with commercial fabric, define the area. The roads leading west to Coral Gables (Flagler Street, Calle Ocho, Coral Way)—fragments of Miami's gridiron of major arteries—are some of the main centers. These "boulevards" have taken on a civic character, increasingly defined not only by ethnic commercial establishments but also by monuments, parks, and new cultural institutions. No longer predominantly Cuban, these areas are still an incubator of the American Dream with many immigrant groups represented.

On the east side of Biscayne Bay are the beaches, America's "winter playground." Growing from Miami Beach, resort towns like Surfside, Bal Harbour, and Sunny Isles stretch northward along the Atlantic Ocean. These resort meccas were traditionally the center of a transient culture of hotels and motels, apartment hotels, restaurants, and clubs. Millions of tourists came to know them on holiday; many became permanent residents. They have developed into more than resorts. In the 1930s, Miami

Beach developed an urban skyline, and an urban density to match. It has subsequently become one of the metropolitan area's most important urban centers.

Resort fashions have varied greatly in the short history of Miami Beach. In the 1920s, grand hotels like the Flamingo and Fleetwood (now defunct) and the Blackstone were icons of the city; yet by the 1930s, the city was redefined by small- and medium-scaled hotels that offered a new more intimate scale of accommodations. After World War II, architect Morris Lapidus, along with Norman Giller and Melvin Grossman, revived the glamorous full-service resort as a type. The peripatetic Lapidus, who became a national figure, used Miami as a laboratory for his most experimental projects, and the lavish resorts he evolved here—often called "flabbergast hotels"—were branded "Miami" when they were emulated in the Caribbean and even in New York City. In addition to several large resort hotels, Giller pioneered a novel type of resort motel that sprang up at urban densities in Sunny Isles, but also along Biscayne Boulevard in Miami. In the 1950s and 1960s, Miami's leadership in the resort industry catapulted its resort specialists to the ranks of the busiest architectural firms in the nation.

Whatever the size, Miami's hotel and motel prototypes, and even its garden apartment–hotels, were so popular that they redefined the American resort experience. As stage sets for middle-class culture, celebrity, and even organized crime, they became evolving testaments to the nation's popular culture, its changing fashions, its social and cultural fault lines, and its financial well-being. Millions more came to know it through lavishly illustrated postcards, brochures, and magazine features, as well as through cameo appearances on television and in the movies. The Fontainebleau Hotel alone had appearances in movies as diverse as Frank Capra's *A Hole in the Head*; Jerry Lewis's *The Bellboy*; Frank Sinatra's *Tony Rome* and *Lady in Cement*; *Goldfinger*; *Midnight Cowboy*; and the more recent *The Bodyguard*. These films track the sociocultural role of Miami Beach itself, first as a glamorous paragon of luxury, then as a lascivious lair for high rollers, a time-worn anachronism, and, recently, as a reborn phoenix.

Media coverage has cemented Miami's brand, but it has also played a tangible role in shaping the city and its sense of place. During the nadir of Miami's popularity in the 1980s, the television show *Miami Vice* reformulated Miami's faded landscapes as urban chic, providing new impetus to recover and derive inspiration from them. The show's opening credits notably showcased Atlantis (1982), whose tall, thin residential tower, pierced in mid-slab by a landscaped sky-court, became an icon recognized as "Miami" around the world. The process continues today with recent visual confections like *Burn Notice* and *CSI Miami*. Miami's unusual landscapes, urban vistas, and architectural scenography are not just set-pieces of its discrete development patterns, but landmarks waiting to be synthesized into a larger urban identity.

City of Synthesis

Miami may be a place sprung from ripe fantasies, yet it has grown fast into a more complex city. In that growth, the city has creatively confronted the paradox of its origins, and constructed and reconstructed its traditions and environments. Fantasy still draws people to Miami, yet if the fantastical and exotic once singularly defined the city, today it is the mélange of architectural traditions and environments that seem more significant. The future of Miami rests on the hope of building a more complex identity from its many pieces, a new authenticity from its varied artifices. Miami is undeniably photogenic, yet during this image-making the overall urban environment has suffered a corresponding neglect. This city of spectacle, whose geographical, environmental, and cultural uniqueness has inspired so much iconic architectural work, must develop a parallel urbanism. The key to Miami's synthesis lies herein.

Few remarkable planning efforts were successfully realized in Miami in its first one hundred years. The city is still organized loosely by a minimal grid. Yet new master plans and infill development projects have multiplied. Efforts to weave together the city's disparate pieces are also under way, as new infrastructure like public transportation is planned. A recent parks master plan seeks to reintegrate Miami's pieces with one another, and with the surrounding ecosystem. In Miami, the citywide rezoning project Miami 21 seeks to shape future development to support pedestrian-friendly streets.

The search (conscious and unconscious) for a common architectural vernacular continues to temper Miami's polarities and its centripetal instincts. New styles, even avant-garde architecture, mix with local building traditions; historic preservation exists alongside invention; minimalism is juxtaposed against rich, embroidered glamour; and artifice flirts with authenticity. In many ways, Miami remains a terrain of contradiction that awaits complete synthesis. Yet there is much to learn from Miami's modern history and its suggestion of a process of knitting and fitting capable of assimilating the city's many complex elements. Traditionally, Miami has found its way by embracing its paradoxes.

The City of

Miami

Randall C. Robinson Jr.

The City of Miami was incorporated in 1896, following the extension of Henry Flagler's Florida East Coast Railway to the small settlement that had formed at the mouth of the Miami River. The city was established on land north of the river that belonged to Julia Tuttle, a widow from Cleveland, Ohio. Tuttle had offered half of her 600 acres to Flagler for the purpose of building a town if he would continue the railroad from its terminus at West Palm Beach. This mutually beneficial transaction transformed Flagler and Tuttle into the founding figures of modern Miami.

Tuttle had arrived in the Biscayne Bay wilderness a few years earlier, joining William and Mary Brickell, who owned the land on the south side of the river and ran a trading post. The Brickells also contributed a portion of their lands for the new town; the Brickell subdivision would become Miami's first posh residential area and later an important office and condominium corridor. Also in existence in 1896 were settlements at Little River, Lemon City, and Coconut Grove, all of which were incorporated into the City of Miami by 1925.

Miami saw enormous growth in the 1920s. Downtown, a skyline befitting a metropolis seemed to spring up overnight. Miami acquired the nickname "Magic City" for becoming a city without ever having been a town. Construction came nearly to a standstill, however, in September 1926, with the passing of a devastating hurricane. An ensuing real estate bust was exacerbated by the onset of the Great Depression. A revival of the regional economy in the mid-1930s, although more remarkable in Miami Beach, left its mark on Downtown's Flagler Street, which was partly rebuilt with modern buildings. Stepping off of Flagler, however, can be like stepping into pre-1926 Miami, even today.

Miami expanded by private initiative as a series of independent plats, roughly coordinated by an overall grid but urbanistically unintegrated. In 1921, councilman Josiah Chaille created the street-numbering system that divided the city and the county into four quadrants, with Miami

Avenue dividing east from west, and Flagler Street dividing north from south. The growth of the metropolitan area has turned Chaille's plan lopsided, creating northwest and southwest quadrants vastly larger than the northeast and the now relatively tiny southeast.

In spite of its East Coast location, Miami shares much in common with the railroad cities of the West. Its gridiron was laid out in the manner of a gold rush town, with little regard for the creation of civic spaces. With the exception of Biscayne Boulevard, little of the progressive urban vision of the City Beautiful movement was inscribed in the city's development (although prominent examples of City Beautiful's influence can be found in Miami's suburbs, like Coral Gables). Suburban towns sprouted all around the Miami core, each with its own identity, rendering a polycentric twentieth-century metropolis.

After World War II, Downtown and the city as a whole continued to grow as the region experienced unprecedented growth. The commercial streets of Little River, Allapattah, Edison/Liberty City, and Riverside/Little Havana are lined with functional modern storefronts. Several important office buildings were constructed Downtown in the 1950s and 1960s; corridors of suburban office buildings began to radiate from the city center, along Brickell Avenue, Biscayne Boulevard, and Coral Way. By the 1960s, new expressways lessened the importance of the city proper, and Miami's core declined. Street riots in the 1980s dealt crippling blows to the remaining economic viability of nearly all but the city's waterfront neighborhoods.

In the wake of the riots of 1980, a new Miami arose propelled by an influx of transnational capital, as well as by immigration, particularly the striving Cuban exile community, which came into its own two decades after its abrupt arrival in the city. Miami's image was transformed with a new skyline, yet the boom of the 1980s benefited Downtown and suburban areas, bypassing the city's inland neighborhoods. Although far younger than countless other cities that have suffered from capital flight to the suburbs, Miami did not escape the same fate and the resultant urban decay.

Downtown Miami, by design and by geography, has managed to remain the dominant center of the metropolis. Planning assured that the seat of county government and a nucleus of cultural facilities were established there in the 1980s. Miami's proximity to Latin America and the Caribbean has provided a niche market for Downtown retail. The city's bayfront and riverfront have benefited from a new generation of condominium tower development. Although many larger, older cities lost their downtown department stores, Macy's remains a fixture on Flagler Street, which remains Downtown's "Main Street." The county and federal courts also anchor the city center in commanding quarters.

At the beginning of the twenty-first century, the City of Miami had a population of 362,470 within a land area of 35.5 square miles. It is the seat of Miami-Dade County, which covers an area of 1,945 square miles and is home to 2,253,362 residents. In addition to its main land area, the City of Miami includes Port Island (formerly Dodge and Lummus islands), home to the Port of Miami-Dade. Also included is the greater part of Virginia Key, which provides the city proper with a location for a sewage-treatment plant and an ocean beach, as well as wetlands teeming with wildlife.

For all its newness and wealth, Miami proper ranks among the nation's poorest cities. A constant stream of immigrants, of every economic level, at once fuels and challenges the adolescent city's multicultural milieu. As the city begins its second century, however, efforts to renew and redevelop the decayed urban fabric are proving successful. The charms of close-in neighborhoods such as Edgewater, East Little Havana, Wynwood, and Buena Vista are being revived by a vibrant mix of immigrants and a generation of Miamians that is returning from the suburbs. After much controversy and political horse trading, in 2009 the City of Miami passed a major milestone when it replaced its established Euclidean zoning system with Miami 21, a form-based code developed by Duany Plater-Zyberk & Company. Miami 21 codified the trend already emerging in Miami toward a return to human-scaled urbanism.

A

City of Miami: Downtown, Brickell, and the Islands

This area comprises the downtown core of Miami and its extensions, north into Park West and south along the Brickell Corridor. The mainland portion is bounded by Biscayne Bay on the east, I-95 on the west, I-395 on the north, and the entrance to the Rickenbacker Causeway on the south. This section also encompasses the Miami River, the Port of Miami, and Virginia Key. It was in this area that the city was founded, and it has continued to play a central role in the cultural and economic life of the region.

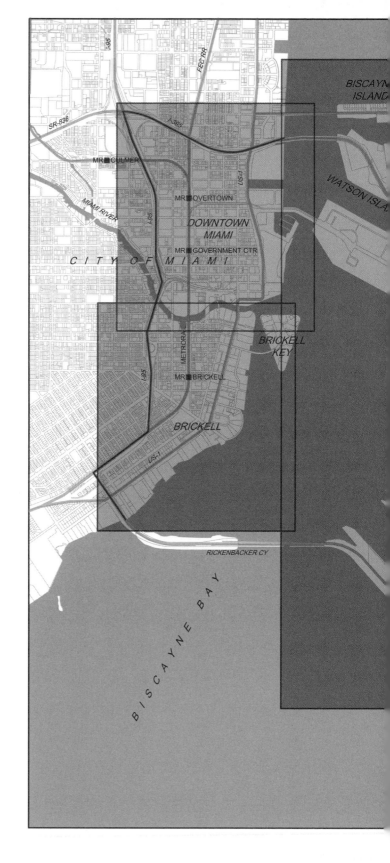

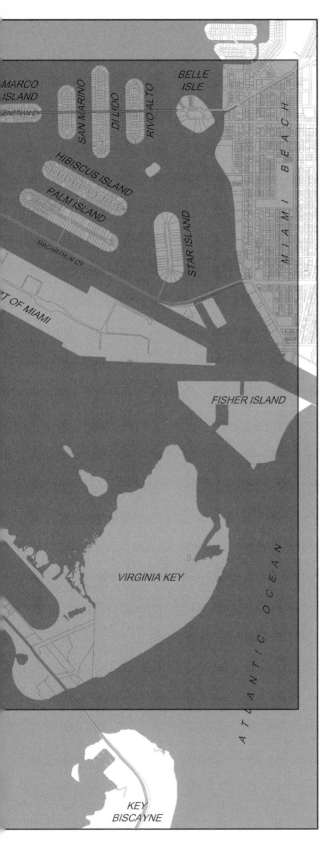

A. City of Miami:
Downtown, Brickell,
and the Islands

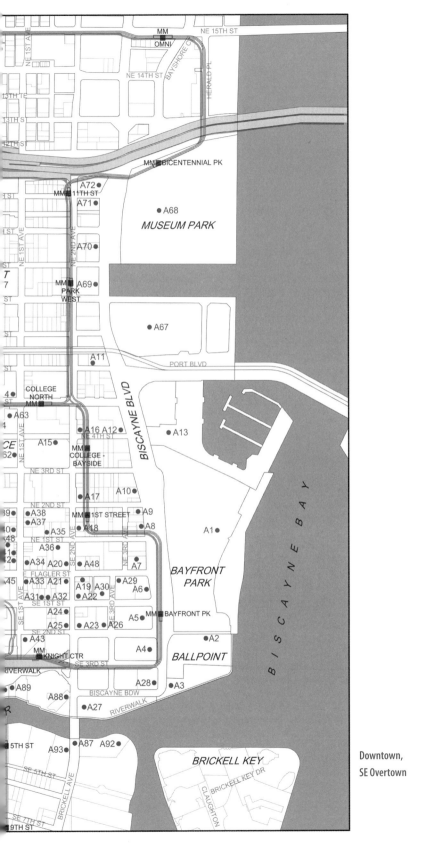

Downtown,
SE Overtown

Bayfront Park   A1

Metromover: Bayfront Park

East side of Biscayne Boulevard between Chopin Plaza and Bayside
Warren Henry Manning, Landscape Architect, 1926
Isamu Noguchi, 1982–94
Modifications: Curtis + Rogers Design Studio, 2009

Once the location of Miami's principal bayfront hotels, the lower portion of Biscayne Boulevard has historically formed the city's principal urban façade. Facing the boulevard is Bayfront Park, the city's front yard and most important civic space. After World War II, the area evolved from a resort to business character; the latest trend has produced several significant residential buildings.

Planning for today's Bayfront Park began in the early 1920s. When the City of Miami acquired a narrow strip of land along the bayfront from the Florida East Coast Railway, Boston-based landscape architect Warren Henry Manning was hired to design a relatively passive park with a yacht basin at one end. Manning's design—influenced by the work of the Olmstead firm, for whom Manning had worked—was picturesque, with meandering paths and flower beds featuring tropical planting and a rock garden that (somewhat incongruously) still survives. Subsequently, a band shell, a convention facility, and a public library were added, creating a more active space. The contention between active and passive uses of the waterfront site persists to the present day. Among the noted architects and planners involved in proposals for Miami's "front porch" have been Walter DeGarmo; Konstantinos Apostolos Doxiadis; Pancoast, Ferendino, Grafton; Edward Durell Stone, Jr.; Alfred Browning Parker (Miamarina); and Isamu Noguchi, upon whose design the current park is based.

Like much of the region's landscape, Bayfront Park was actually dredged up from the shallow bay bottom. Formerly the location of docks and slips serving Downtown Miami, the area was reformulated as a park in 1924, literally becoming a front yard to the procession of skyscraper hotels that quickly crowded the west side of Biscayne Boulevard during the Great Florida Land Boom of the 1920s. In between, Biscayne Boulevard was expanded into a grand processional avenue with rows of royal palm trees leading from Henry Flagler's Royal Palm Hotel, at its south end, north to the Miami News and Metropolis Building, now Freedom Tower (A11).

As the civic heart of Miami, Bayfront Park has been the object of various redevelopment schemes, most never completed. However, a 1968 plan by Miami architect Alfred Browning Parker and Edward Durell Stone Jr. was partially realized; it called for mixed-use commercial nodes at the north and south ends. The marina portion was renovated in 1971 according to Parker's plans and renamed Miamarina. Parker's marina design featured an octagonal glass restaurant pavilion, now the Hard Rock Café. In the 1980s, a limited revamping of Manning's original design was realized by sculptor Isamu Noguchi, and Miamarina became the centerpiece of Bayside Marketplace (A13).

Highlights of the 32-acre park include the Baywalk promenade and the Pepper Fountain, which replaced the public library at the terminus of Flagler Street; a 2,400-seat amphitheater; Noguchi's sculpture *Slide Mantra*; a laser tower; and several monuments and memorials. The Torch of Friendship, which celebrates Pan-American unity, and a smaller amphitheater (including a memorial to the space shuttle *Challenger*) face directly on the boulevard at the park's northern and southern borders. While offering significant assets, the park feels somewhat removed from the city, with its berms (concealing the large amphitheater) and a 50-foot grassy verge permitting bleachers to be erected for the defunct annual Orange Bowl Parade and Grand Prix auto races. Inexplicably, the wide granite-paved walkway extending Flagler Street to the bay as designed by Noguchi offered no shade, making it and its benches inhospitable for most of the year.

In 1986, the Brazilian landscape architect Roberto Burle Marx was invited to develop the master design plan for Biscayne Boulevard from Flagler Street north to the planned performing arts center. The plan combines amorphous colored paving designs and extensive landscaping in the median. The most recent iteration of a downtown master plan, prepared by Zyscovich Architects, calls for narrowing Biscayne Boulevard to increase the size and quality of the park. As of this writing, Bayfront is receiving a facelift, with the amphitheater already completed.

Ball Point

An assemblage of towers occupies what was once the southern end of Bayfront Park, at the important junction of the Miami River with Biscayne Bay. Located mainly on landfill, the site once included a marina as part of the park master plan by Walter Manning. Later filled, it functioned as a waterfront parking lot for decades. During the 1930s, the area came under the control of Ed Ball, director of the du Pont family interests in Florida; it would henceforth be known as Ball Point. The site figured prominently in quixotic prewar and postwar plans for a Pan-American Convention Hall and Exposition Center. Still empty in the 1960s, it then figured in strategies to extend Bayfront Park to the mouth of the Miami River, and for the development of a complementary riverfront park. Development for commercial uses started in the 1980s.

Miami Center   A2

Metromover: Bayfront Park

325 South Biscayne Boulevard
Pietro Belluschi, 1980

Miami Center's 34-story Intercontinental Hotel and 36-story Edward Ball Office Building ushered in the 1980s transformation of the Miami skyline. Although the scheme was only partially completed (of the four towers originally projected, only two were built), the built portions form, along with the nearby Wachovia Financial Center (A4), One Biscayne Tower (A6), and the New World Tower (A8), the symmetrical stair-step profile that became the subject of countless postcards and newscast backdrops, essentially the symbol of the city through the turn-of-the-twenty-first-century building boom.

Pietro Belluschi's design matched bold tower forms with opulent finishes. Miami Center is clad entirely in travertine, the stone extending even into the hotel's soaring interior atrium and extensive array of public spaces. Belluschi directed that the travertine panels be placed in relation to one another exactly as they had existed in their natural state, but in an embarrassing construction faux pas, the panels were placed in a random pattern.

A2 and A4

In spite of this, the crisp towers present a visage of luxurious precision, their sheer volumes fitting solidly in the context of Belluschi's body of work, which includes Portland's Equitable Savings and Loan Building of 1945–48 and the travertine-clad Juilliard School of 1966 at New York's Lincoln Center. The hotel faces Chopin Plaza and Bayfront Park with a suitably grand porte cochere. Unfortunately, with two rows of almost uninterrupted angled parking and scarce landscaping, Chopin Plaza seems insufficiently street- or plazalike. The office tower faces west to Biscayne Boulevard with a monumental arcade at ground level. The roof of the pedestal joining the two towers serves as the recreational open space of the hotel, and has a swimming pool, tennis courts, and a picturesque garden with meandering paths.

One Miami
A3

Metromover: Bayfront Park

335 South Biscayne Boulevard
Arquitectonica, 2005

One Miami occupies the 3-acre southern portion of Ball Point, comprising
the knuckle that joins Biscayne Bay to the north shore of the Miami River.
The site was to have been developed in 1980 with two travertine-clad towers as part of the adjacent Miami Center project (A2). Twenty-five years
later, One Miami filled the empty lots with two long residential towers and
a 4-story commercial annex fronting South Biscayne Boulevard. The annex
houses a restaurant and the corporate headquarters of the project's developer, the Related Group, which maintains an art gallery in the complex. The
two staggered slabs rise 45 stories, tied together by 12 stories of parking
deck. The subtly prismatic character of the lower buildings plays across the
edges of the towers, an effect accentuated by the jagged lines of the varied
roof parapets.

At One Miami's base, fronting both Biscayne Bay and the Miami River, is
Art Walk, the connecting segment between the Miami River Greenway project and the Biscayne Bay Walk. When complete, Art Walk will feature public
art in a landscaped promenade as part of a continuous sequence of public
waterfront spaces.

Wachovia Financial Center
(Southeast Financial Center)
A4

Metromover: Bayfront Park

200 South Biscayne Boulevard
Skidmore, Owings & Merrill, 1985

Built for Southeast Bank, the serrated profile of the 55-story Wachovia
Financial Center dominated the Miami skyline from its completion in 1985
until the topping out of the Four Seasons (A114) in 2002. Southeast (previously First National Bank of Miami), the city's preeminent financial institution since pioneer days, chose Edward C. Bassett of Skidmore, Owings &
Merrill's San Francisco office to design what would be its last headquarters.
The site sat just across SE Second Street from its existing headquarters in
the First National Bank Building (A5). The granite-clad office tower's novel
sawtooth, trapezoidal floor plates offer a primary façade to each of the site's
three major vantage points: the MacArthur and Rickenbacker causeways
to the southeast and northeast, and the city to the west. Parking is housed
in a separate 16-story building just to the west. Clad in perforated precast
panels, the parking structure combines commercial space and a grand
bank lobby on its lower levels with an athletic club on the top floor. The
glass-sheltered palm court between the two buildings is one of Downtown
Miami's finest public open spaces, its animated nature further enlivened by
the periodic passing of the Metromover on its south side.

One Bayshore Plaza (First National Bank Building/Southeast Bank Building)   A5
Metromover: Bayfront Park

100 South Biscayne Boulevard
Weed Johnson Associates, 1957
Retrofit of pedestal: 1988

Designed for First National Bank of Miami (see previous and subsequent headquarters [A34, A4]), 100 South Biscayne was the first major new office building built in Downtown since the A. I. DuPont Building in 1939, and filled a prestigious slot at the south end of Miami's bayfront skyline. The decision to keep the new headquarters Downtown indicates the urban core's symbolic importance even as suburban growth challenged its dominance in the postwar years.

Following postwar trends in commercial architecture, the steel-framed tower was raised over a block-long pedestal that provided ample room for parking, retail space, and a banking lobby. Facing Biscayne Boulevard, the pedestal presented a sheer marble façade that intentionally obscured the 3-story bank lobby, which opened north to SE First Street and south to SE Second Street. Behind it, the 600-car parking garage was concealed by a grid of blue aluminum struts. Above, the slender 15-story tower captures views to Biscayne Bay and the Miami River. Broad cantilevered precast-concrete sunshades, calibrated to protect the south, east, and north façades, are the tower's defining feature.

When the bank moved to new headquarters (now the Wachovia Financial Center) in the mid-1980s, an extensive renovation made the building more pedestrian-friendly. Windows were cut into the pedestal's Biscayne Boulevard façade, and a spacious shopping arcade was carved from the banking hall, reviving Downtown's pre–World War II arcade tradition. The arcade connects SE First Street with SE Second Street, aligning with the plaza of the Wachovia Financial Center (A4) across SE Second Street, while also providing an entrance from the boulevard. As part of the effort to introduce night lighting to the Downtown skyline, touched off by the popularity of International Place (A43) and the Miami Line (A96), the edges of the tower's sunshades were lined with continuous white neon in the 1990s.

A6

One Biscayne Tower   A6
Metromover: Bayfront Park

2 South Biscayne Boulevard
Gutierrez-Latimer and Fraga & Associates, 1973

At 38 stories, One Biscayne Tower dominated the Miami skyline from its completion until the arrival of the Wachovia Financial Center (A4) and Miami Center (A2). Its bulky presence in the skyline reflects the evolution of office building design in the 1970s. In contrast to the narrow profile of 100 South Biscayne Boulevard (A5), its greater volume reflected the larger floor plates required by contemporary office planning. The office floors are wrapped in dark glass, reflecting (like the New World Tower [A8]) a more technological approach to solar control. Moreover, the building is structurally expressive. The glass curtain wall is vertically sliced by sculpted white concrete piers that flare outward where the office tower meets the parking garage and at the top. The pedestal's clearly expressed ramped parking garage, finished in exposed cast concrete and occupying nearly a third of the tower's full height, is a visible if brutal manifestation of contemporary parking requirements.

One Biscayne turns its tower to Biscayne Boulevard, while its lobby opens to the cross streets. This cross-block lobby, along with the building's unusual below-grade shopping arcade, extends a local tradition of interior arcades connecting streets.

50 Biscayne Boulevard   A7
Metromover: Bayfront Park

Sieger-Suarez Architectural Partnership, 2005

The undulating crown feature of 50 Biscayne, and the robust, twisting columns that play against the crisp rectilinearity of the tower's projecting floor plates, introduce the sort of whimsy normally associated with beachfront architecture to the Bayfront Park high-rise ensemble. The figural patterns and colors of Roberto Burle Marx's sidewalk paving design along Biscayne Boulevard seem to have inspired elements of the façade. Similar patterns run up the walls of the parking garage, and appear along the columns and even on a central window panel near the top of the building. In the window panel, the mural is comprised of a colored inner layer of the triple-layer glass system, giving the appearance of opacity, yet allowing residents to view outward. The technique was used a second time, with the mural in shades of white, to add thickness to the balconies, without compromising outward views. The undulating crown feature is actually the roof of the mechanical equipment housing. The void at the tenth-floor level houses a sky-lobby, pool deck, and related amenities.

A7

New World Tower (100 Biscayne Tower)   A8
Metromover: Bayfront Park

100 North Biscayne Boulevard
Rader & Associates, 1964

Brainchild of developer Jose Ferré, the ambitious New World Tower was for a time Miami's tallest building, and its first modern tower to mix office and residential uses. It was also the first commercial skyscraper built entirely of reinforced concrete, a demonstration perhaps, since Ferré's Maule Industries was Miami's premier concrete provider. At 30 stories, it far exceeded the 18-story First National Bank Building (A5) of 1957, and it topped the Dade County Courthouse (A53) by 16 feet, holding the title of Miami's tallest building until it was edged out by Suntrust International Center (A29) in 1969. It employed a "piggyback" use principle: while the lower floors were for offices, its top 9 stories were originally built as apartments, served by a separate entrance and lobby, an early attempt to transform Miami's central business district into a twenty-four-hour neighborhood. While the luxury apartments managed to attract some prominent Miamians, the idea was far ahead of its time, and the residential idea was abandoned. Subsequently, the upper floors were converted to office use.

A8

The New World Tower's dark curtain wall was the first in Miami to use tinted, heat-resisting glass, thus not requiring the tropicalizing sun-protection devices that were a common feature of office building design in the 1950s. Similar to the Bacardi Building (C19), its slender shaft featured an east-facing glass curtain wall sliced by continuous marble-clad piers rising the building's full height. Its north and south façades are contrastingly solid, while, in a cost-cutting measure, the west façade has solid spandrels and bare concrete piers.

Ferré originally intended to build his "New York–style" skyscraper at the more prominent intersection of Biscayne Boulevard and Flagler Street. (That site later became the location for One Biscayne Tower (A6), Miami's tallest during the 1970s and early 1980s.) Ferré's son Maurice, Miami mayor in the late 1970s and early 1980s, would follow in his father's city-building footsteps, presiding over the construction boom that transformed Downtown in the 1980s.

Riande Continental Hotel (Miami Colonial Hotel)   A9
Metromover: Bayfront Park

146 Biscayne Boulevard (146 North Bayshore Drive)
1926

Originally the Miami Colonial Hotel, the Riande Continental is among the last of the hotels that once formed an almost continuous façade along Bayfront Park. The 16-story structure was reclad with a curtain wall of glass and aluminum, although it still remains, in its size and proportions, a quint-essentially 1920s structure.

A9

Everglades on the Bay   A10
Metromover: College/Bayside

250 Biscayne Boulevard
Fullerton Diaz Architects, 2008

The twin telescoping residential towers of Everglades on the Bay rise 53 and 57 stories, certainly tall but foiling in subtle ways the gargantuan cubic character of Miami's more recent bayfront skyline. The towers, at right angles from each other, have the formal, stepped massing and sky-scraping verticality of 1920s Art Deco. Core elements project past the roof to provide sculptural effects. The project is very large, containing a total of 860 residential units that rise from an 8-story pedestal containing extensive ground-floor retail-restaurant space. All of the retail spaces face the street, and the pedestal is notably lined along its street frontage with townhouse units. The roof of the pedestal comprises a nearly 2-acre amenity deck with multiple swimming pools and water features.

A10

Freedom Tower (Miami News   A11
and Metropolis Building)
Metromover: Freedom Tower

600 Biscayne Boulevard
Schultze and Weaver, 1924
Renovation: Rodriguez and Quiroga Architects, 2003

Constructed as the Miami Daily News Tower to house the offices and print-ing plant of the now-defunct *Miami News*, the Freedom Tower is a monu-ment of Florida's 1920s boomtime Mediterranean Revival architecture, a style inspired by Bertram Goodhue's 1915 Panama-California Exposition in San Diego. Along with the Biltmore Hotel and Miami Beach's late Roney Plaza Hotel, it was one of three tower structures in Miami-Dade County by the New York firm of Schultze and Weaver modeled on the Giralda Tower of Seville, Spain. A fourth building inspired by the Giralda Tower was the original 617-room Everglades Hotel (1925), designed and built by the Fred F. French Company of New York, the designers of Manhattan's Tudor City complex, among others. The 1925 hotel was replaced by the contemporary Everglades on the Bay project (A10) a few blocks south.

While the original Giralda Tower was constructed over centuries and provides an architectural narrative in stone from the time of the Moors to the Baroque era, Schultze and Weaver liberally blended these epochs into a hybrid style unique to 1920s South Florida. The extravagantly ornamented main entrance comprises native quarry keystone cast and colored to imitate the travertine used for ornamental details. Above, picturesque stucco detailing lends rich complexity to the tower and its surmounting lantern. Behind the tower is the gabled shed that once housed the printing presses.

The newspaper occupied the tower until 1957, when it relocated to a new plant along the Miami River. In 1962, the General Services

A11

Administration leased the building for use as the Cuban Refugee Center, and it became affectionately known as the "Freedom Tower," a name that endures today. Renovations to convert the base into a Cuban American museum were undertaken, and although the museum never materialized here, the space continues to be well used as an exhibition venue. The building was donated to Miami-Dade College in 2008.

First United Methodist Church   A12
Metromover: College/Bayside

400 Biscayne Boulevard
Walter Baggesen and Sons (church member), 1980

The current church was born of the merger, in 1966, of two Downtown congregations, Trinity Methodist Episcopal Church and White Temple Methodist Episcopal Church. The combined church bucked contemporary trends and chose to locate Downtown, taking a prominent site on Biscayne Boulevard at the north end of Downtown's assemblage of bayfront towers.

Designed as a religious and community center in the heart of a commercial district, the main elements of the church (worship, school, music, library, social, and administration areas) pivot around a central patio. The main entrance from Biscayne Boulevard is through the patio, and mementos of both old churches are arranged there, including cornerstones, the cross that stood atop White Temple, and stained-glass windows from Trinity.

Along Biscayne Boulevard, the low-slung body of the ancillary spaces, accentuated by a long ribbon window, is punctuated on its south side by the sanctuary and a tower. The trapezoidal shape of the sanctuary structure betrays the formal predilections of postwar Modernists. Its Modernist spire, a four-way illuminated cross, is made of intersecting concrete fins, and supports a suspended electronic carillon simulating a chorus of thirty-nine bells. Its sanctuary features stained-glass windows brought from the earlier churches. The whole seems designed to be viewed from the car, an exception to the monumental scale of adjacent residential and commercial buildings.

A13

Bayside Marketplace and Miamarina   A13
Metromover: College/Bayside

401 Biscayne Boulevard
Miamarina: Alfred Browning Parker, 1971
Bayside Marketplace: Benjamin Thompson & Associates, 1987

The Rouse Company's Quincy Market in Boston and, more directly, Harborplace in Baltimore were the models for Miami's waterfront "festival marketplace." Beginning in the 1970s, Rouse's successful development and management formula brought retail back to ailing downtowns by adapting the suburban mall experience. With considerable controversy, Bayside was built within Bayfront Park, around its existing marina. The marketplace consists of two 2-story retail and restaurant pavilions parallel to the bulkhead line, joined by a curved double-height unenclosed space for vendor carts reminiscent of an open-air market. The L-shaped complex wraps the land side of Alfred Browning Parker's Miamarina of 1971. With the addition of a giant neon guitar and other embellishments, Parker's existing octagonal glass restaurant pavilion was transformed into Bayside's Hard Rock Café. The marina has been a traditional point of departure for fishing and sightseeing excursions. Bayside's restrained yet colorful architecture alludes to the metal-roofed market sheds of the former British West Indies. A planned marine museum and aquarium were never realized.

Central Baptist Church A14
Metromover: College North

500 NE 1st Avenue
Dougherty and Gardner, 1926

A14

With its gleaming gold-leafed cupola, Central Baptist Church marks the northern edge of Downtown Miami. Thomas Jefferson would recognize the architectural intent here, which is reminiscent of his own Monticello and its Palladian forebears. This four-sided temple of reason and restraint with its symmetrical elevations tells, perhaps, of a desire for rational order in a frantic time. The congregation was first organized in 1896, along with Miami itself, and this structure replaces an earlier 1901 sanctuary.

Although its monumental Neoclassical grandeur is harshly offset by the Metromover guideway along its south flank, the church's composition, craftsmanship, and fine detail help it bear the insult with grace. Adaptations to climate include the use of the deep porticos and the high ceiling in the sanctuary. The building houses several church functions and is divided by an internal circular core with an ambulatory running its perimeter, and a series of rooms extending from the corridor to the exterior walls. On the first floor are the dining hall and maintenance facilities. The sanctuary takes up the central core of the second, third, and fourth floors, surrounded by classrooms, choir rehearsal rooms, study rooms, and a library. The sanctuary comprises a particularly imposing space. A row of Corinthian columns between arched openings rises from the balcony to recessed coffered vaults with large circular windows. The projecting 270-degree balcony adds seating for a total of 2,500, making this one of the largest Downtown auditoriums. The stained-glass windows in the social room on the lower floor are from the 1901 building.

Abutting the church to the north, a sympathetic addition was added in 1946.

Mitchell Wolfson New World Center Campus, Miami-Dade College

In the 1970s, Alvah Chapman, chairman of Knight Ridder Newspapers, then parent company of the Miami Herald, *and other leaders of the Non-Group, the unnamed center of power in mid-twentieth-century Miami, sought a concept they hoped would revitalize Downtown Miami. Hank Meyer, pioneering public-relations guru and the man who famously branded Miami Beach in the 1950s, presented the idea of Miami as the "New World Center," the golden buckle of the Western Hemisphere. Under this conceptual shelter, several projects were planned and brought to fruition: the New World Center*

Campus of Miami-Dade Community College, a New World section of Bicentennial Park on the bayfront, the New World Symphony on Miami Beach, and the New World School of the Arts in Downtown Miami.

The burgeoning New World Center Campus provides Downtown with a constant stream of activity throughout the day and evening hours and contributes to the community and its culture as the site of the annual Miami Book Fair International, the nation's largest book fair.

A15

Buildings One and Two (Buildings 1,000 and 2,000)   A15

Metromover: College/Bayside

Miami-Dade College, Mitchell Wolfson New World Center Campus
300 NE 2nd Avenue
Ferendino, Grafton, Pancoast, 1971

Now named Buildings One and Two, the first structures of the Wolfson Campus built in the cast-concrete syntax that Ferendino Grafton Spillis Candela had pioneered at the college's south (Kendall) and north campuses. Building One belies an initial fortresslike impression with an open tropical vocabulary that includes large open portals to the surrounding plazas and a full-height skylit atrium open to the exterior at various levels. In recognition of its public, educational function, the diagonal siting sets it apart from the surrounding fabric. Its placement close to NE Second Avenue affords a generous plaza on NE First Avenue that acts as a forecourt for the grand Neoclassical U.S. courthouse (A40) to the west. The pedestrianization of NE Fourth Street between First and Second avenues, named Kyrkiades Plaza, fosters a lively campus atmosphere in the heart of Downtown Miami. Building Two fronts the north side of Kyrkiades Plaza with a façade that reinterprets the arcaded commercial buildings of early Miami in a handsome modern vocabulary. The ground floor is set back behind an arcade that stretches the entire block face, while the second-floor fenestration is protected from the sun by a layer of operable metal louvers.

Robert McCabe Building (Building 3,000)   A16

Metromover: College/Bayside

245 NE 4th Street
Bermello Ajamil & Partners, 1992

The Robert McCabe Building, on the east side of NE Second Avenue and separate from the original core of the Wolfson Campus, was the first Miami-Dade College building whose architectural commission was based on a competitive selection process. (Previously, college buildings on all Miami-Dade College campuses were designed by Ferendino, Grafton, Pancoast, or its successor firms.) The Robert McCabe Building continues the pattern of the grand, open-air public interiors achieved at Building 1,000. The building remains faithful to the Tropicalist ideals of porosity and ventilation. Here,

however, the architect's Brutalist Modern surface program is displaced by
a Postmodern foil, including the suggestion of gables, tripartite massing,
and contrasting courses of rough and smooth blocks colored a deep red.
A monumental staircase is the star of the building's soaring interior court,
punctuating a north-south pedestrian passage, bifurcating the block, and
providing the campus a face on Fifth Street. Building 3,000 is easily visible
behind the First United Methodist Church on Biscayne Boulevard, which it
complements strikingly well (A12).

Metropolitan Building   A17
Metromover: College/Bayside

201 NE 2nd Avenue
John Bullen, 1925

A typical, yet distinct 2-story representative of Miami's Mediterranean
Revival style as interpreted in commercial architecture. Closely related in
style and function to the old Saks Fifth Avenue, its relative across the bay
at 701 Lincoln Road (F18), this structure recalls early Downtown and offers
ground-floor retail frontage with space for offices or living quarters above.
It conspires sotto voce with the viewer: "Let's pretend; let's pretend we are
somewhere in Spain or Italy." Wide eaves respond to the climate and the
whimsy of the decorative elements presents a fantasy image of the tropics.

Congress Building   A18
Metromover: First Street Station

111 NE 2nd Avenue
Martin Luther Hampton, 1923
16-story addition: Martin Luther Hampton, 1925
Residential rehabilitation: Adolfo Albaisa, 1999

A18

The expanding aspirations of Miami's 1920s boom are preserved in the very
body of this building, composed of two separate buildings constructed
three years apart. The first building was a three-bay, 5-story structure. In
1925, when Miami raised its height limitation, 16 additional stories were
constructed by straddling the original 5-story structure with two additional
bays of 17 stories constructed as a north wing. The truss system supporting
the addition is placed through the sixth and seventh floors and is connected
to a column system attached to the earlier portion of the building. The
trusses, clad in stucco, are legible on the south façade.
    Typical of the period, the Congress Building's ornamental program in-
cludes an eclectic mix of early twentieth-century revivals. The first 5 stories
are clad in limestone, and five double-height bays are topped with arched
windows at the base. In contrast to the decorated base, the upper stories
are relatively austere, Neoclassical in style, and clad in gleaming white-
glazed ceramic tile. More recently, the Congress Building has figured in the
development of a residential community in Downtown Miami; its commercial spaces have now been converted to residences.

A19

La Época (Walgreens)   A19
Metromover: First Street Station

200 East Flagler Street
Zimmerman, Saxe and McBride, 1936

La Época Building, originally a Walgreens drugstore, and the A. I. DuPont Building (A20) diagonally across the intersection, illustrate the wide range of American Modern architecture in the 1930s. Where the DuPont Building has the formal gravitas, vertical articulation, and Art Deco ornament of a modern civic landmark, the striking, streamlined horizontality of La Época bears the functionalist influence of the International style. Its stark platonic forms impart an almost factorylike appearance, an imagery perhaps favored by the drugstore chain because of associations made between progress and hygiene at the time. The continuous banded windows, a trademark of the International style, were remarkable for 1930s Miami. The interior is arranged around an impressive 3-story atrium. While few of the interior details and finishes remain, save for the fine double stairway and its railings, this endures as one of the grandest retail spaces in Miami.

A. I. DuPont Building   A20
Metromover: First Street Station

169 East Flagler Street
Marsh and Saxelbye, 1937

After South Florida's economic bust in 1926, Downtown Miami saw little construction until after 1935, explaining why there are so few buildings in the Art Deco style. Miami's economic recovery, however, was signaled by the proliferation of modern buildings on Miami Beach and the construction of the A. I. DuPont Building in Downtown Miami. Built for the headquarters of Florida National Bank, and named after its founder, Alfred I. du Pont, the 17-story DuPont Building was the first Downtown high-rise built since the completion of the Dade County Courthouse in 1928. Similar in massing to the Ingraham Building (A22), the building employs modern styling. The limestone-clad tower displays the stripped and flattened classicism of 1930s Depression Moderne, with a black granite–clad base and public interior spaces that offer a wealth of Art Deco ornamentation. Beneath the DuPont Building's Modern aspirations lies a tripartite massing scheme derived from Beaux-Arts principles. In another dichotomy, the base of the building is oriented toward Flagler Street, while the tower presents its primary façade to the east.

   A brass escalator connects the lobby to the mezzanine bank lobby, a strategy also used at the Mercantile Bank Building in Miami Beach (F12), its smaller-scale Art Deco counterpart. The second-floor banking hall is one of the most ornate spaces in Downtown Miami. The high ceiling comprises primary and secondary beams embellished with painted motifs providing a narrative of the city's history. The polished brass elevator doors feature reliefs of flamingos, pelicans, herons, and ibises.

Olympia Theater at Gusman Center   A21

Metromover: First Street Station

174 East Flagler Street
John Eberson, 1926
Renovation of theater: Morris Lapidus, 1972
Renovations: R. J. Heisenbottle Architects, 1989-95
Conversion of offices to residential use: Victor Morales, 1995

A21

The Olympia Theater and Office Building was built by Paramont Enterprises on the site of the earlier open-air Airdrome Theater. Paramont selected John Eberson, creator of the "atmospheric" theater concept, as architect. Atmospheric theaters created the illusion of an open-air amphitheater in an exotic setting under a starry, moonlit sky with drifting clouds. At the Olympia, considered one of Eberson's finest, the setting is an Italian garden, closed in on three sides by the walls of a castle. Among the Olympia's distinctions, the theater was the first in the South to be designed with air-conditioning. The mixed-use building included an office tower on Flagler Street. Purchased by the Gusman family, the cinema was renovated into a performance theater in 1972 by Morris Lapidus and then in 1975 donated by Maurice Gusman to the City of Miami. The Olympia has served as the venue for an array of the city's cultural offerings including ballet and modern dance, classical music, and several film festivals. In the 1990s, the tower was converted by the City of Miami Parking Authority, its owner, into affordable housing using tax-credit financing, the first such conversion in Downtown Miami.

The exterior of the building is unique in Miami for its use of pressed brick and Flemish-inspired decoration. The tower, clad in buff-colored brick, is relatively simple except for the richly detailed frieze along the parapet, which rises to form a Flemish scroll pediment over the three center bays of the north façade. Directly below is the decorative theater marquee, which has been restored several times, most recently in 1999. The simplicity of the tower façades is in contrast to the theater façade on NE Second Avenue. Seven windows with double Flemish scroll pediments and wrought-iron grilles rise above the first-story storefronts, illuminating the theater lobby. The roofline is broken by further Flemish scroll pediments. In a crowning gesture, the center pediment projects outward, supported by four brackets.

A product of Miami's 1920s boom era, the Olympia remains Miami's most elaborate theater and, along with the Tampa Theater in Tampa, also of 1926, one of only two atmospheric theaters to survive in Florida.

A21

Ingraham Building

Metromover: First Street Station

25 SE 2nd Avenue
Schultze and Weaver, 1926
Renovation: Rodriguez Khuly Quiroga, 1990

The Ingraham Building was built by the Model Land Company, the real estate division of the Florida East Coast Railway, as a memorial to James E. Ingraham, former president of the Model Land Company and a Miami pioneer. Ingraham, in conjunction with William Brickell and Julia Tuttle, persuaded Henry Flagler to extend his railway from Palm Beach to Miami, thus laying the groundwork for the development of the city. Only thirty years after the city's founding, Schultze and Weaver's opulent design reflected the economic optimism of the 1920s as well as a progressive early vision of Miami as a center of business and commerce. Typical of the big-city, mid-rise office Palazzí of the turn of the twentieth century, its Renaissance architectural features reached upward to fulfill contemporary commercial purposes. The lifting of height restrictions in 1925 allowed the building to rise to a majestic 12 stories, divided into a three-part Classical composition of base, main body, and bold, projecting cornice.

The Ingraham Building offers decorative details and luxurious finishes both inside and out. The building exterior is distinguished by its Indiana limestone cladding, rustication that diminishes with height, and wide, prominent eaves with polychrome rafters. An elaborate double-height archway at the main entrance creates a dialogue with the equally grand Gusman

A22

Center (A21) across SE Second Avenue. The ornate lobby features a vaulted ceiling with gilded accents. Engaged Doric columns supporting a full entablature encircle the main lobby space and lead to the elevator lobby, also finished in limestone and marble. Polished brass elevator doors are adorned with palm tree bas-reliefs and the building's initials. The exquisite materiality extends to the marble-lined corridors of the upper floors. The Ingraham Building has remained virtually unaltered during its history.

Ingraham Parking Garage   A23
Metromover: College/Bayside

225 SE 2nd Avenue
Steward & Skinner Associates, 1950

In a portent of the ascent of the private automobile in the decades after World War II, the Ingraham Parking Garage, built to serve the 1920s Ingraham Building, was one of the first major buildings built Downtown after the war. Typical of some early postwar commercial buildings, its ribbons of concrete and stucco reference the Streamline Moderne style popular in the 1930s. Though it is most prominent facing Second Street and the corner of Second Avenue, note its marquee signage facing SE Third Street.

As cars became an increasingly important fact of urban life in postwar America, Downtown office buildings sought to adapt. The resulting boom in urban parking garages produced functional structures that fit into constrained Downtown sites. Although less innovative than some of its contemporaries, the Ingraham Garage is, along with the A. I. DuPont Building Garage, one of the last of the early multilevel garages Downtown.

Huntington Building   A24
Metromover: Knight Center

168 SE 1st Street
Louis Kamper with Pfeiffer and O'Reilly, 1925

With Miami's 1920s boom ending abruptly in 1926, the city did not see an Art Deco skyscraper until the arrival of the A. I. DuPont Building (A20) in 1937. However, the trend toward stylistic simplification and modern iconography began much earlier. The Huntington Building's suggestion of structural expression, through the employment of continuous vertical piers and spandrel panels, contrasts with the flat walls and punched openings of contemporaries, like the nearby Ingraham Building. However, the building does not lack in detail. The thinner of its alternating piers is crowned by busts of knightlike figures. Mask and urn ornaments dominate the third-floor cornice. (Winged griffins, part of the original composition, were later removed.)

A24

The Huntington Building was part of a grand scheme by developer Frederick Rand to create a "Fifth Avenue of Miami" along Second Avenue. Although it never attained the name-recognition of Brickell Avenue or Biscayne Boulevard, the street saw the construction of some of Downtown's finest 1920s and 1930s skyscrapers, including the Ingraham and DuPont buildings.

A25

Americas Center (Bay Towers)   A25

Metromover: Knight Center

150 SE 2nd Avenue
Morris Lapidus and Associates, 1966

Americas Center is notable for the use of sun grilles years after reflective
thermal glass made them technically unnecessary. In fact, the finely detailed
grilles are part of a second skin projected some 2 feet from the glass building wall. The rear façade sports narrow vertical stairwell windows that create
a rhythmic, Op-Art effect. The relatively opaque stairwell, in turn, bisects
the rear façade of ribbon windows. As at Lapidus's Ainsley Building (A42),
a glass-walled penthouse with a folded-plate concrete parapet crowns the
tower.

Atrium (Pan-American Bank Building)   A26

Metromover: Bayfront Park

150 SE 3rd Avenue
Carl H. Blohm and Charles P. Nieder, 1953
Residential Rehabilitation: Denis Arden, 2004

Facing the corner of SE Third Avenue and SE Second Street, the Pan-
American Bank Building would have fronted the Pan-American convention
hall planned directly to the south. The building's austerely expressed façade
was entirely clad with cast stone, with details in serpentine Italian marble.
The U.S. Coast Guard, U.S. State Department, and banks were among the
first tenants. The Pan-American Bank, on the ground floor, originally had the
largest safe-deposit vault door in the South. As an affirmation of postwar
commercial necessity, an auto tunnel through the structure led to four teller
windows. Today the building has been converted to residential lofts.

DuPont Site

*The north bank of the mouth of the Miami River is one of Miami's
most historic and contested sites. Once marked by burial mounds and
later by Fort Dallas, the site was chosen by Henry Flagler for his Royal
Palm Hotel, at the southern terminus of his Florida East Coast Railway
network. Acquired by DuPont interests after the demolition of the
Royal Palm in the 1930s, it has been the site of some of Miami's grandest urban visions, including plans for a Pan-American convention hall
and exposition center by B. Kingston Hall (1936) and by Robert Law
Weed Associates (1948). It was for this envisioned complex, which
extended to Ball Point, that a spur of Miami's North-South Highway
(now I-95) to NE Second Avenue was built, obliterating acres of
Downtown real estate and cutting off the river from Downtown west
of SE Second Ave. From the 1930s until the turn-of-the-century building boom, most of the centrally located site has been used as surface
parking lots.*

Epic Miami Hotel and Residences   A27

Metromover: Knight Center

300 Biscayne Boulevard Way
Revuelta Vega Leon, 2006

After the demolition of the Royal Palm Hotel in 1930, the only structure of
the many proposed to actually rise on the site was the DuPont Plaza Hotel
(1957), which stretched along the riverfront side of the parcel. DuPont Plaza
was demolished to make way for Epic, the master plan of which includes
two nearly identical waterfront towers. Only the first part of the complex,
occupying the western half of the site, has been completed. The redevelopment of the site has allowed for a key segment of the Riverwalk to be built,
connecting the Knight Center with Ball Point and the Bay Walk.

On top of a pedestal that largely fills its site, the 54-story Epic tower tilts
toward the southeast in order to capture a straight line of views to the bay.
Toward the water, the tower façade is bowed, with a curtain motif in the
glass railings meant to represent the bow of a motorboat. In addition to
residences, Epic is home to Kimpton Hotel Miami.

Metropolitan Miami   A28

Metromover: Bayfront Park

Met One
300 South Biscayne Boulevard
Nichols Brosch Sandoval & Associates, 2006

Met Two
355 SE 2nd Avenue
Nichols Brosch Sandoval & Associates, 2008

While Epic occupies the former site of the DuPont Plaza Hotel, Metropolitan
Miami, or Met, sits on 6 acres that had been devoted to surface parking for
decades. Met's master plan calls for an integrated cluster of office and residential buildings, a hotel, and a vertical mall. The project as designed comprised more than 1,100 residential units.

The 40-story, L-shaped Met One building wraps the corner of South
Biscayne Boulevard and Biscayne Boulevard Way and exploits diagonal
views to the bay at the corner. One missed opportunity was a decisive connection to the Palm Court of the adjacent Wachovia Financial Center (**A4**),
which would have expanded that space to the Miami River.

Planted at the southwest end of the complex, Met Two comprises two
tapered towers housing office space and a hotel. Its 14-story podium houses
ballrooms, meeting spaces, and retail, as well as a 1,500-car parking garage.
Facing west toward the James L. Knight Center (**A88**), the 42-story Marquis
Hotel (Hotel Beaux Arts) will have 376 hotel rooms. Facing east is a 47-story
office tower comprising nearly 700,000 square feet.

As originally designed, Met Three is planned to have a slender shaft rising 817 feet high, surpassing the Four Seasons Tower (**A114**) as Miami's tallest. Met Square will be the commercial accompaniment to the Metropolitan
project. Conceived as a vertical mall, its 4 stories are designed to house retail
space, movie theaters, and restaurants.

A29

SunTrust International Center (Amerifirst Savings and Loan)

A29

Metromover: Bayfront Park

1 SE 3rd Avenue
Connell, Pierce, Garland & Friedman, 1969

By the late 1960s, the growth of First Federal Savings and Loan at 100 NE First Avenue (A40) required the construction of a new headquarters. In order to promote the revitalization of the business district and reinforce its identity within the community, the savings bank decided to locate its new headquarters Downtown. The resulting 32-story tower, along with adjacent One Biscayne Tower (A6) and the New World Tower (A8), defined the Miami skyline of the 1970s. First Federal, the nation's first chartered federal savings and loan association (1933), was aptly renamed Amerifirst in 1979 and occupied the building until its demise in the national savings and loan debacle of 1986-91.

Like the other two towers, SunTrust celebrates verticality but carries the theme the furthest, and its division into base, middle, and top reflects the influence of the Classically proportioned late midcentury Modernism of architects like Edward Durell Stone and Philip Johnson. Its bronze-anodized window frames and dark bronze–glass curtain walls are subsumed by a rhythm of marble piers in two widths, the wider of the two rising uninterrupted to support the signage parapet. The triangular piers actually taper from the base to the top, giving the building a taller appearance. Originally slated to be exposed concrete, they were redesigned to be clad in highly polished white "Lasa Ortles," with the intention that the marble retain its brilliance over many years. Its soaring verticality is best appreciated from SE Third Avenue, where the center portion of the parking garage is camouflaged by the tower cladding, allowing the piers to extend full height. Of note on the interior are the modular light sculpture in the lobby, whose 1,400 bulbs are mounted in a three-dimensional grid of black chromed tubes, and the surrounding concourse clad in cioccolato travertine walls and Botticino marble floors.

Plaza Building

A30

Metromover: First Street

245 SE 1st Street
Igor Polevitzky, 1955

The low-slung Plaza Building broke with the tall massing and stone or brick skin of Miami's prewar commercial buildings. It is a structure seemingly calibrated to the horizontal mobility of the suburbs yet firmly anchored in its central urban location. Its façade—no doubt inspired by the work of Le Corbusier and Brazilian Modernist architects, and by the iconic Ministry of National Education and Public Health in Rio de Janeiro—employed a system of concrete brise-soleils set in an egg-crate grillage of concrete fins. A mansard roof and stone cladding, added more recently, dilute the building's Modernist aesthetic, yet the solar shading is a powerful evocation of Miami's postwar concern with evolving a tropicalist architecture.

A30

Langford Building   A31
Metromover: Knight Center

121 SE 1st Street
Hampton and Ehmann, 1925

Built for the Miami Bank and Trust Company at the peak of the 1920s boom, the Langford Building is notable for its rigorous Neoclassical ornamentation and for its monumental 2-story projecting arcade. Though it is rather modest in size, its precise masonry work and façade provide visual interest along the block.

Royalton Hotel   A32
Metromover: Knight Center

131 SE 1st Street
Pfeiffer and O'Reilly, 1924

Front portion: 1926
Rear addition: 1927
Rehabilitation: Beilinson Gomez Architects, 2006

The Royalton Hotel rose during the 1920s boom, a monument to Downtown Miami's aspirations as a tourist destination. After years of neglect and unsympathetic alterations, it reopened as transitional housing for the formerly homeless, with much of its original Neoclassically inspired ornamentation and rich surfaces covered up. These features have been uncovered and restored in the latest renovation. The Royalton's arcade, similar to the one next door at the Langford Building (A31), which had been enclosed and turned into retail spaces after the advent of air-conditioning, was also restored. The original floor plans containing 100 hotel rooms were retained for the new transitional housing units, a fortuitous convergence of original and current programmatic requirements. The original windows, on the north, east, and west façades, were retained and restored as they were found to satisfy fire rating standards at the time of the renovation.

100 East Flagler Street   A33

Metromover: Knight Center

Fraga & Associates, 1973

Originally built as the Bank of Miami, this modest tower's pronounced
verticality is accentuated on its west façade by full-height, high-relief ceramic murals designed by Jose Maria Gual Barnades of Studios Raventos
in Barcelona. Described by the *Miami Herald* during its construction as
the largest ceramic artwork in the United States, the mural measures 1,834
square feet.

Flagler First Condominium   A34
(First National Bank)

Metromover: Knight Center

101 East Flagler Street
Mowbray and Uffinger, 1922
North Tower: H. H. Mundy, 1926
Residential rehabilitation: Roberto M. Martinez Architects, 2005

Flagler First Condominium is an office-to-residential rehabilitation encom-
passing two buildings from Miami's 1920s boom years. The building was
constructed as the headquarters of First National Bank of Miami, founded
in 1902. The bank's history would become intertwined with that of Miami
itself. Its founder and longtime president, Edward C. Romfh, became mayor
of Miami during the frenzied boom of the 1920s and, as a private citizen, he
led the city through the hard times of the bust. First National was the only
Miami bank to survive the economic crises touched off by the hurricane of
1926 and stock market crash of 1929. Under the bank's evolving name, this
and subsequent headquarter buildings would leave a defining architectural
legacy for the city.

When the 10-story building opened in 1922, the *Miami Herald* described
it as Miami's most modern building. In contrast to its contemporaries, 101
East Flagler was more frank in the expression of its steel skeleton structure
and greater use of glass, a design vocabulary pioneered in Chicago skyscrapers of the turn of the twentieth century. The tower's ornamental program is divided into base, middle, and top. The base consists of imposing
3-story pilasters topped by Doric capitals. Reddish brick walls are accented
with gold brick and copper-clad mullion accents.

The taller and thinner tower next door on NE First Avenue appears to
have been built as an addition to 101 East Flagler not long after the latter's
completion. While the north building's ornamental program is plainly distinct and handsome in its own right (note the double-height arched entry
portal), the matching floor levels provide the best indication that it was a
well-disguised addition.

After decades of neglect and unsympathetic alterations, the building
has been restored to its 1920s appearance, and adaptively used as a condominium with 91 units and ground-floor retail.

A34

Dade Commonwealth Building   A35

Metromover: First Street

139 NE 1st Street
Henry LaPointe, 1925

The Dade Commonwealth Building opened in 1925 as a 15-story building, but it lost its upper seven floors in the 1926 hurricane. In the 1930s, sale of the structure fetched $27,000, a tiny fraction of the $1.25 million it cost to build. It was one of the first Downtown buildings to hold an elevator, and during the 1940s the Miami Public Library occupied two floors. Its robust ornamentation includes carved eagles on the cornice. Doric pilasters rising from behind the eagles on the cornice support a projecting parapet crowned by Corinthian urns. Henry LaPointe is better known as the designer of Casa Casuarina (E31) on Miami Beach.

Shoreland Arcade   A36

Metromover: First Street

120 NE 1st Street
Pfeiffer and O'Reilly, 1925
Flagler Street façade renovation: Robert Law Weed, 1939

A36

The Shoreland Arcade was built by the Shoreland Company, developer of Miami Shores, Biscayne Boulevard, and the Venetian Causeway. The arcade was the pedestal of a 20-story building designed to be built in two phases (a relatively common practice during the 1920s and 1930s in Miami and Miami Beach). The bust of 1926 prevented the second phase from being built. Plans to increase the height were revived in 1944, when Robert Law Weed designed a 9-story addition. Like the original proposal, this one was not completed.

Unrealized plans notwithstanding, the Shoreland Arcade is a grand vestige of Miami's Roaring Twenties. Each of the eight arched bays of the NE First Street façade is flanked by stylized pilasters embellished with masonry medallions that feature symbols relating to Florida history. The rich ornamentation combined with materials like Indiana limestone, granite, and terrazzo extend into the interior. The arcades designed to connect NE First Street with Flagler Street and NE First Avenue constituted one of the building's most important features. Cross-block arcades were once an important feature of Downtown's urban network of spaces. The latter two entrances have been turned into retail spaces, leaving only the NE First Street entrance accessible as a dead-end arcade.

As designed, arcades leading from the three entrances converged on an elevator lobby at the center of the block. The ceiling of the arcade features elaborate coffers, and the floor is a rare combination of mosaic tile work set within terrazzo. The scale of the interior reflects usage for the larger building that was never constructed. The elevations at 115–121 East Flagler Street and NE First Avenue were modernized by Weed in 1939 and later altered, erasing the presence of the arcade on those streets. This writing finds the interior in an alarming state of near ruin, reminiscent of many of the early arcades of Paris that now serve as gritty garment factories.

Capital Lofts at the Security Building (Security Building, Capital Building)   A37
Metromover: First Street

117 NE 1st Avenue
Robert Greenfield, 1926
Residential rehabilitation: Rodriguez and Quiroga Architects, 2006

Unlike some its contemporaries, the Security Building was built all at one time in 1926. At 16 stories and 225 feet, it was one of the more imposing structures in the city at the time of its construction. Its most distinctive feature, a faux mansard roof topped by an eight-sided tower, is Downtown's single contribution to the Second Empire style, an attempt to identify Miami with established commercial capitals of the time. As such the Security Building is the most ornate and lavish skyscraper from the 1920s boom. The principal façade is clad in granite and off-white terra-cotta, while the upper stories and copper mansard roof are a feast of ornamentation. The base is embellished with 3-story-high pilasters supporting an entablature bracketed by granite lion heads. In 2008, the Security Building was transformed into a loft-style residential building, and the façades restored to their 1920s grandeur. Even with the recent wave of high rises that have risen to the east, the Security Building still cuts a distinctive silhouette on the Downtown skyline.

Gesu Church   A38
Metromover: First Street

118 and 130 NE 2nd Street
Orin T. Williams, 1925

The Gesu Church is managed by the Jesuits, and the Baroque decorative tradition of their Roman churches is expressed here in the interior, but encased in a spare and simplified Mediterranean Revival exterior. The interior decoration, in fact, was not completed until the 1950s. The church houses Holy Name parish, established in 1896 as the first Catholic congregation in Miami. Henry Flagler donated the land for the first church, and the corner-

A37 and A38

stone for the present church was laid on the same site in 1920. The building is distinguished by a monumental triple-arched portico, crowned by a robust tripartite bell tower with triple decorative arches in both the central and side towers. The deep, arcaded portico as well as the high ceiling in the sanctuary respond well to Miami's climate. Of note, Belen Jesuit High School in Havana, alma mater of Fidel Castro, had its first American home in the school building that stood to the east of the rectory until 1984.

Hahn Building   A39
Metromover: First Street

140 NE 1st Avenue
George Pfeiffer with Gerald O'Reilly, Associate Architect, 1921

The 2-story Hahn Building is a sober counterpart to the Mediterranean-style Metropolitan Building; its fine Neoclassical decoration was intended to distinguish the building from its boomtime cohort. The second story of the building once contained apartments, and an open-air shaft situated in the center of the west elevation provided some degree of ventilation to the spaces found on that floor.

Pfeiffer helped organize the Florida chapter of the American Institute of Architects and served as its president. The firm also designed the Shoreland Arcade (A36) and the Biscayne Building (A51).

Old U.S. Post Office and Courthouse   A40
Metromover: First Street

100 NE 1st Avenue
Oscar Wenderoth, 1912
Addition: Robert Swartburg, 1948
Renovation: Architectural Design Consultants, 2002

The first major federal building built in Miami housed a post office, courts, offices, and a weather bureau until the completion of the U.S. Courthouse at 300 NE First Avenue (A62) in 1931. With its restrained Classical composition and cladding of Indiana limestone, the building was an impressive high-style addition to the young city and was touted as the most modern federal building south of Washington, D.C. Its monumental pilasters, arched openings, balconies, and enriched entablature lend an air of dignity and grandeur befitting a government institution, while its truncated, hipped roof of clay tile and wide eaves respond to the Miami climate. The handsome building design was a prototype built around the country. One notable sibling is the nearly identical Old Pasadena Post Office, 1913, an anchor of Pasadena, California's Beaux-Arts civic center.

A40

In 1937, the building became the home of First Federal Savings and Loan Association, the first federally chartered savings and loan association in the country. In 1948, the bank added an L-shaped structure to the west and north. Robert Swartburg's sympathetic postwar addition facing First Street on the west carries the theme. At some point in the building's history, the original arcade facing First Avenue was filled in. First Federal was headquartered in the expanded building until the construction of its subsequent trademark tower at 1 SE Third Avenue (A29) in 1969. The bank continued occupying the building as a branch office until 1990. In 2002, the building underwent a major renovation, restoring several original features.

Ralston Building   A41

Metromover: First Street

40 NE 1st Avenue
August Geiger, 1917

From 1917 until the completion of the 10-story McAllister Hotel (which once stood on the site of 50 Biscayne [A7]) at the beginning of the next tourist season, the Ralston Building, at 8 stories, was Miami's tallest building. The *Miami Daily News and Metropolis* referred to the Ralston as a semi-skyscraper and, in a special section entirely devoted to the building, professed "that whatever the future may bring, the Ralston Building is the pioneer sky-scraper of this city and will be so recorded in the building and business his-tory of Miami, it makes no difference how many skyscrapers may be erected during the golden years of prosperity and progress yet to come with their overflowing cornucopias of riches."

John Orr of Miami is credited with designing the molded stucco orna-mentation described as Italian Renaissance. Recently introduced oil-based paints produced vivid hues of "golden buff" and "ultra-marine blue" in the stucco walls. One feature that rarely ever again appeared in Miami skyscrap-ers was a roof garden. The *Metropolis* advertised vistas of the "surrounding country for many miles, the Everglades and the Ocean . . . for 25¢."

R. W. Ralston, the developer, was able to lease the entire building before it opened. He and his brother would go on to develop the community of Sunny Isles.

Foremost Building (Ainsley Building)   A42

Metromover: Knight Center

14 NE 1st Avenue
Morris Lapidus, 1952

The 15-story Ainsley Building was the first post–World War II office build-ing built in Downtown Miami, and one of two Downtown office buildings by Miami's iconoclast Morris Lapidus. The architect of the Fontainebleau Hotel applied his distinctive Modernist vocabulary to this office building in a somewhat restrained yet expressive manner. While the building's east fa-çade employs a finely detailed glass curtain wall, the south façade features a play of cantilevered traylike projections that add depth and emphatic horizontality to the Flagler Street façade. Reminiscent of Mies van der Rohe's Concrete Office Building Project of 1923, the trays here serve to shade the windows from Miami's intense sunlight. Lapidus went on to explore decora-tive sun-shading devices in other office buildings, including the nearby 150 SE Second Avenue (1966) (**A25**) and the Meridian Office Building on Miami Beach (1961) (**F37**). Ironically, he rarely applied the same concern to his iconic hotels. A penthouse, set back on all four sides, with continuous windows shaded by a folded-plate metal canopy, adds a crowning, sculptural touch and offers sweeping views in four directions. However, to the pedestrian, Lapidus's touch is most evident in the tilted entrance canopy and in the canted tray walls.

A42

Bank of America Tower at International Place   A43
(Centrust Tower, Miami World Trade Center)
Metromover: Knight Center

100 SE 2nd Street
I. M. Pei & Partners, 1987

Commissioned by the Centrust Corporation, this distinctive telescoping
47-story tower rises just north of the Miami River. This exquisite and costly
monument, including the fine art within, was a factor in the bank's demise
and subsequent transfer to the Resolution Trust Corporation. It remains a
distinctive element of Miami's skyline, especially at night, when the building
is variously lit in emblematic colors of the season. The tightly constrained
site required that the lighting system be placed on the roofs of neighboring
structures.

   Facing southeast, the quadrant-shaped layers of the upper structure descend to an elaborately conceived terrace over the 10-story parking garage

A43

the building shares with the Knight Center (**A88**). The terrace level includes a marble-lined sky-lobby whose plate-glass windows open to landscaping, a reflecting pool, and a sweeping view of the city. Below, the parking garage structure is faced with taut aluminum screens that mimic the horizontal striations of the curtain wall above. Facing northeast, the building's flat chamfered walls fall sheer to the ground. Where they meet, the opposing radiused and chamfered façades are neatly resolved in a folded connection. Metromover (**A59**), the driverless elevated public transportation system that links major points Downtown, passes through the base of the building, depositing commuters at a station that occurs within. Conversely, a helicopter pad on the roof, a symbol of the go-go 1980s, has been abandoned.

Macy's (Burdines)   A44
Metromover: Miami Avenue

2–22 East Flagler Street
E. L. Robertson and J. R. Weber, 1936
Addition and Annex: E. L. Robertson and J. R. Weber, 1946

Burdines, Miami's enduring hometown department store, was a fixture in this vicinity since 1898, two years after Miami's incorporation. Parts of the existing store date from the 1920s and were expanded during Flagler Street's heyday in the late 1930s and 1940s. In 1936, the easternmost 100 feet of the building along East Flagler Street received a modern façade of ribbon windows with inset panels of glass and glass block. In 1946, the lot just to the west was acquired and an addition following the same design as the 1936 building was built. In the same year, a second addition, in the same architectural vocabulary, albeit in a different color stone, was built across Miami Avenue and connected to the main store by a three-level bridge.

A44

The mainly opaque building walls are smooth and curved at the corners, an exhibition of the Streamline Moderne popular in the years before and immediately after World War II. Limestone cladding and finely detailed fenestration were appropriate to the store's flagship status at its construction. However, even before Burdines was subsumed into Macy's, the Downtown store was no longer the flagship of the chain. Yet, in contrast to most other cities that have lost comparable flagship department stores in the face of capital flight to the suburbs, this retailer's continued existence here is indicative of the relative viability of Downtown Miami. As at many other southern retail establishments, the lunch counter at Burdines was the site of a "sit-in" protesting and eventually defeating the segregationist policies of that time.

Woolworth Building   A45
Metromover: Miami Avenue

44 East Flagler Street
1924

A45

As Miami's commercial main street, Flagler Street was a popular shopping destination and home to a range of five-and-dime stores. McCrory, S. H. Kress & Co., and F. W. Woolworth, as well as Walgreens and Liggett's Drugs, all built distinctive buildings. More than just stores, five-and-dimes functioned as social centers, with lunch counters that made convenient meeting points for shoppers.

The F. W. Woolworth store offers a distinctive Art Deco façade of terra-cotta panels and tiles. The Woolworth lunch counters figured prominently in the civil rights movement in Miami, with one action by the Congress of Racial Equality (CORE) famously occurring at the Flagler Street Woolworth store.

Whaling Wall #78 Florida's Marine Life   A46
Metromover: Miami Avenue

0–100 block of SE 1st Street (south façade of Macy's building)
Wyland, 1998

A46

The environmental artist Wyland has painted life-sized whale murals on at least one hundred walls around the world. These "Whaling Walls," dedicated to the protection and preservation of cetaceans, feature various species of whales and dolphins. *Whaling Wall #78* is more than 265 feet long and 70 feet high, filling the back wall of the Macy's Building. The Metromover passes directly in front, momentarily transforming its cars into aerial submarines.

Seybold Building   A47
Metromover: First Street Station

30–44 NE 1st Street
Kiehnel and Elliott, 1921; upper 8 stories: 1925
Flagler Street arcade entrance: Robert Law Weed, 1939

A phased expansion, fueled by hopes of prosperity and new height regulations in 1925, transformed the Seybold Building, named for one of Miami's earliest entrepreneurs, into one of Downtown's grandest boom-era structures. The building's first 2 stories were constructed in 1921, and the top 8 in 1925. Two years after this expansion, the top of the Seybold offered enough space and distance from other tall buildings to make it the weather observatory for the area. This lasted until 1939, when a 17-story building to the east blocked the winds and forced a move. The 2-story arched entrance portal is an open invitation to the immense retail arcade within. The archway and the colonnade of engaged columns stretching from the third to the tenth stories are the centerpiece of an architecturally rich block face.

The original arcade was later extended in 1939 through to Flagler Street, where it presents a modern façade. With some three hundred jewelers, it houses one of the world's largest jewelry centers.

A48

South side of NE 1st Street between Miami Avenue and NE 1st Avenue

A48

Metromover: First Street Station

76–78 NE 1st Street (Hill Building)
1906

60–68 NE 1st Street (Real Estate Building)
1913

56–58 NE 1st Street (Walker-Skagseth Food Stores)
1920

Seybold Building
30–44 NE 1st Street
Kiehnel and Elliott, 1921; upper 8 stories: 1925

International Jewelry Center (McCrory's)
22 NE 1st Street
1936

2–14 NE 1st Street
August Geiger, 1934

With the Seybold Building (A47) as its center, this block is an architectural feast from end to end. Moving from east to west, and chronologically as well, at the corner with NE 1st Avenue stands the former Hill Building, the oldest on the block. This Masonry Vernacular structure received its Mediterranean Revival appearance sometime in its long history. Next at 60–68, the former Real Estate Building provides a vernacular representation of early Miami's arcaded buildings. Next door, but with its arcade displaying an exquisite three-dimensional Art Deco ornamental program, stands the former Walker-Skagseth Food Stores. The Art Deco frontage was part of a 1930s remodeling to the original 1920 structure.

On the opposite side of the Seybold Building stands the International Jewelry Center at 22. The center is carved from a McCrory's store that fronted Flagler Street with a Modern Classical façade. In 1936, a rear addition was added with a richly ornamented off-white terra-cotta façade facing First Street. Completing the block is a streamlined 2-story building that features thin horizontal bands of black Vitrolite across contrasting light-colored stucco on its upper story.

Seminole Hotel (Iroquois Hotel)   A49
Metromover: First Street Station

53 East Flagler Street
1906

Most hotels in Downtown Miami were lined up along or just behind
Bayfront Park. In contrast, this modest hostelry, constructed before the park
was envisioned, was located in the heart of Flagler Street, Downtown's main
commercial thoroughfare. The main lines of the building are still visible today, although the attached arcade that sheltered the sidewalk and provided
a spacious terrace on the second floor (once a tradition among Downtown
commercial buildings) has been removed. The building's corbelled parapet
and pilastered façade are among the oldest extant structures in Downtown
Miami.

Bonnie McCabe Hall,   A50
New World School of the Arts
Metrorail/Metromover: Government Center

25 NE 2nd Street
1956
Expansion and adaptive use: Rodriguez Khuly Quiroga, 1990

Housed in a former Bell South switching station, this facility for the New
World School of the Arts offers a series of lofts, used as classrooms, studios,
and offices, as well as rehearsal, performance, and exhibition spaces. The
school, whose name capitalizes on Miami's 1980s-era cultural initiatives,
offers art, theater, dance, and music study. Open to both high school and
college students, it is a partnership of the Miami-Dade County School Board,
Miami-Dade College, and the University of Florida. The school also occupies space at its original home completed in 1987, at NE Second Street and
Fourth Avenue.

The school added three stories to the top of the building in 1990, and
these are clearly identifiable on the façade by large glass-block panels.
Behind their translucent walls, dance and drama studios, as well as a
200-seat black-box theater, occupy the eighth floor. The building's bright
colors were meant to establish the school's identity within the (more) sober
architecture of the city's commercial core.

McCabe Hall connects via a pedestrian bridge to 36 NE Second Street,
also originally a Bell Telephone facility. Built in the 1920s, it features the sort
of traditional brick architecture common in the South but seldom seen in
Miami.

Biscayne Building   A51
Metromover: Miami Avenue

19 West Flagler Street
Pfeiffer and O'Reilly, 1925

Downtown's westernmost boomtime skyscraper was built to house Miami's
first bank, Bank of Biscayne. Organized with the help of Henry Flagler, it did
not survive the bust of 1926. Typical of the period, the building was built in

two stages with the first five floors being completed first. Eight stories were added the following year. Ornamental highlights include the third-story cornice above egg-and-dart ornamentation and compassed arched windows on the top floor. Colossal arched openings in the 3-story base of the building were unfortunately filled in.

After World War II, local developer Shepard Broad, for whom the Broad Causeway is named, had his office here. Besides creating the town of Bay Harbor Islands in the late 1940s, Broad was credited by David Ben-Gurion as being a founder of the Jewish state.

A52

City National Bank (Industrial National Bank or Miami Industrial Bank)   A52

Metromover: Miami Avenue

25 West Flagler Street
Edwin T. Reeder Associates, 1956

Built to house the headquarters of Miami's Industrial National Bank, this originally 5-story building was designed for expansion, a vote of confidence in the city's commercial and industrial future. This optimism was warranted as the planned expansion was realized. In midcentury fashion, the building's façade expresses the polarity between the office plates and its functional core. The former are almost entirely glass, the building screened on its upper floors by a second skin of gold-anodized aluminum grilles whose intersecting hexagonal grid throws patterns of light and dark into the interior. The core, on the other hand, is constructed of precast concrete panels. Its original midcentury color scheme, aqua-tinted concrete accented by blue and gold Italian tiles, has been covered.

Dade County Courthouse   A53

Metrorail/Metromover: Government Center

73 West Flagler Street
A. Ten Eyck Brown with August Geiger, Associate Architect, 1925
Restoration of Courtroom 6–1: MC Harry & Associates, 2006

The first courthouse on the site was built in 1904 and was expected to meet the county's needs for fifty years. Only twenty-one years later, after considering several locations, it was decided to build a new courthouse on the same site. The older courthouse continued in use as the new one rose around it.

Upon its completion, the 28-story Dade County Courthouse was hailed as the tallest building south of the Washington Monument, giving credence to Miami's claims of being the Magic City that was never a town. It was lighted at night and visible across great distances from land and sea. The courthouse was designed to house the county courts and Miami City Hall, including administrative offices and jails for both government entities. The choice of the Neoclassical style was popular and in keeping with contemporary ideas that the workings of the judiciary and government were a solemn business to be housed in the dignified manner of the ancients. An eclectic selection from Classical styles is presented: Doric columns on the base, engaged columns with Egyptian-style capitals on the secondary base, and a Greek temple front with decorated pediments just below the

A53

3-story top, whose ziggurat form is reminiscent of the ancient mausoleum of Halicarnassus. The choice of a skyscraper met the desire for a modern building as well as the county's and city's needs for expansion. Modern conveniences included parking camouflaged under the terrace base, and a battery of eight high-speed elevators, some with specifically programmed access routes.

In 1954, the Miami City Hall moved out of the building and Downtown to its current location at the former Pan American seaplane terminal in Coconut Grove (**B54**). The jail, originally located in the upper floors, was moved in 1961 to the county's new civic center along the Miami River, and in 1984 the county administrative offices moved to the Stephen P. Clark Center (**A57**), leaving the county judiciary as the sole occupant of the building.

Mostly civil cases are heard here, including disputes about the preservation of buildings; criminal cases are adjudicated at the more secure Gerstein Building in the civic center adjacent to the jail (**D1**). In 2008, Courtroom 6-1, the scene of many landmark trials, was painstakingly restored to its 1920s grandeur. Turkey buzzards often roost on the tower; local cynics say the birds are the unlamented spirits of lawyers who practiced here and passed "unshriven, unhouseled, and unanealed."

A54

Claude Pepper Federal Building   A54

Metrorail/Metromover: Government Center

51 SW 1st Avenue
Steward & Skinner Associates, 1964

The 18-story tower of the Claude Pepper Federal Building is located in the civic complex that developed around the Dade County Courthouse at the west end of East Flagler Street. Originally, the site was intended for a Downtown city hall, a project unrealized to this day. Steward & Skinner's plan for a fully integrated civic center complex several miles up the river, on the site of the former Miami Country Club, instead freed the area for other uses. The federal office building bolsters the Downtown civic center, yet the massing of the tower turns an ambivalent narrow side wall toward the main façade of the Dade County Courthouse. Its long principal façade looks west, probably in deference to the planned Pan-American concourse once projected to be built over the alignment of the Florida East Coast Railway tracks. Today, it faces a tangle of Metromover tracks and an open space that functions as a bus transfer station, but that would make an excellent plaza.

The building's nearly windowless ground floor is clad in granite, while the tower projects over, resting on piers sheathed in stainless-steel sleeves and forming a wrapping loggia. The loggia is cut by the glass entry lobby on the west side. The slab façade is monumentalized with a severe alternation of precast concrete panels, some blank and others with windows. Each precast concrete panel is faceted, giving the building a strong and satisfying texture, as well as powerful shadow lines. An abstracted cornice hides machine rooms on the roof.

Miami-Dade Cultural Plaza   A55

Metrorail/Metromover: Government Center

101 West Flagler Street
Philip Johnson and John Burgee Architects, 1980

Philip Johnson reconciled his own 1970s vintage Postmodernism with South Florida's Mediterranean Revival architectural traditions in his design for the Miami-Dade Cultural Plaza, housing the main library, the Historical Museum of Southern Florida, and the Miami Art Museum. Similar to the use of the style in the 1920s to endow Florida with far more of a Spanish Colonial heritage than it had, Johnson's Cultural Plaza gave Miami its own Spanish Colonial fort, echoing those in Havana, San Juan, and Cartagena.

What the complex lacks in street presence is made up by the illusion of an acropolis created by its namesake elevated plaza framed by the upper floors of the three cultural facilities. While the complex has never fulfilled expectations of a Lincoln Center–like activity generator for the Downtown, the plaza is a fine ceremonial and celebratory space providing respite from the grit and hubbub of a Downtown planned without any aspirations to civic grandeur. In the stark, utilitarian manner of a fort, the plaza is devoid of landscaping, and unfortunately also of the capacity to support large works of public art, as it doubles as the roof for a warren of facilities serving the three institutions. Surrealist glimpses to the surrounding towers animate the otherwise sleepy space. Yet, Johnson's spare use of Spanish and Italian motifs, including a geometric paving pattern, creates an air of dignity and timelessness under the big Miami sky, which is brought into play by the elevated nature of the open space. Beyond the illusion, or because of it, the architects were able to fit more programs onto the site than is apparent. The rampartlike base of the complex houses more of the three facilities than is expressed in the separate structures that frame the upper-level plaza.

All three facilities open to the plaza, not to the street. This strategy was meant to activate the plaza but instead emphasizes detachment from the city. A bridge connecting the plaza to the Stephen P. Clark Center was an avatar of the kind of planned multilevel pedestrian connectivity that might have activated the plaza, but that never developed in Downtown. Nevertheless, the grand entrance stairs carved into the south side of the complex, ascending from Flagler Street, provide the Cultural Plaza with a suitably dramatic arrival experience. The adjacent ramped loggia with parallel cascade are quite exquisite, and built on a tradition of indoor-outdoor circulation that distinguishes Miami.

The public library contains the only suitably grand public interiors in the complex. Its 2-story rotunda, at the main entry, creates a spacious lobby. Artist Ed Ruscha transformed text into surface art along its walls. His *Words without Thoughts Never to Heaven Go* (1985) offers the words of Shakespeare floating in a continuous 360-degree frieze around the oculus of the rotunda. Ruscha also designed a related series of lunettes featuring language fragments that adorn interior archways. As of this writing, the Miami Art Museum is planning to depart the complex for new quarters designed by Herzog and DeMeuron in Museum Park.

Museum Tower   A56
Metrorail/Metromover: Government Center

150 West Flagler Street
Spillis Candela & Partners, Inc., 1983

The 28-story Museum Tower office building, so named because of its location across Flagler Street from the Miami-Dade Cultural Plaza, marks the west end of Downtown's Flagler Street "canyon." The tower appears as a sheer glass volume gently cradled between precast concrete bookends that rise full height. The glass volume steps inward at the top to create a tapering effect and conversely inward at the bottom to allow for a sheltered plaza space. The structural gymnastics are made visible through the use of an exposed 3-story truss that transfers the building load outward. From the plaza, a double-height passageway—which aligns with the grand stairway of the Cultural Plaza across Flagler Street—cuts through the base of the tower, connecting to SW First Street. This building is a Modernist take on the cross-block arcades that once thrived Downtown.

A55 and A56

Stephen P. Clark Center   A57
Metrorail/Metromover: Government Center

111 NW 1st Street
Hugh Stubbins Associates, 1984

Miami-Dade County's government structure is not easily discerned from the buildings that house its seats of governance, nor from their respective locations. For instance, Miami City Hall is not Downtown, but rather in the former Pan American seaplane terminal in Coconut Grove (B54). The 30-story Stephen P. Clark Center, seat of county government, is a dominant

A57

feature on the Downtown skyline. Unincorporated Miami-Dade County has a municipal form of government and, as such, qualifies as the largest "city" in the county, far more populous than the City of Miami. The region was also one of the first, in 1957, in the United States to adopt a metropolitan governance charter, putting broad authority, including many functions normally handled at the state level, in the hands of an expanded county government, given the name Metro-Dade.

When time came for the planning of a county hall to serve Metro-Dade, a new master plan was developed that called for the erection of facilities for both county and city in a governmental campus on the western edge of Downtown. Over the years, the State of Florida, the Miami Police Department, as well as the county government and its major cultural institutions, have built facilities in the area, while the Miami City Commission has found it difficult to vacate its tranquil Bayshore location (**B54**) for Downtown.

The completion of the Stephen P. Clark Center along with its integrated Metrorail and Metromover stations represented a quantum leap in the development of Downtown Miami, and helped to maintain its political and symbolic status as the dominant center of the metropolitan area. While the buff-colored tan limestone structure may appear intimidating (the banded windows of its chiseled tower give the impression of dark slits allowing only those inside to peer out), it succeeds in making government accessible to the citizenry. Like Hugh Stubbins's Citicorp Tower in New York City (1978), the tower is hoisted over a broad public concourse. Between the Metrorail/Metromover station and the tower is a spacious, glass-enclosed atrium animated by the constant pedestrian activity generated by the county administration, the county commission, the rail stations, cafés, and accessory retail. Before September 11, 2001, this glass-covered open space flowed almost imperceptibly into the lobby of the office tower. On the opposite south side, the tower is entered from a plaza on NW First Street, but not before passing under the spaceshiplike county commission chambers, which project outward from the tower at the mezzanine level. The bridge connecting the chambers to the tower slides through a colossal 3-story colonnade, rising several stories to support the tower.

The office floors are arranged in an open plan allowing natural light from the continuous banded windows to reach deep into the interior. This is made possible, in part, by the placing of the elevator banks at opposite ends of the tower, and by keeping the floor plates relatively narrow.

To the west of the tower is a park, a key feature of the governmental campus master plan. The park comprises lawns, groves, and fountains, and features an outdoor sculpture and fountain designed by sculptors Claes Oldenburg and Coosje van Bruggen: *Dropped Bowl with Scattered Slices and Peels*. Oranges and diversity, fractures and patterns—these were the images that came to the artists as they contemplated their charge and the site. It would be "disorder at the foot of order." Unfortunately, disorder within the county building since 1990 has often kept the fountain from operating.

Metrorail Government Center Station   A58

Metrorail/Metromover: Government Center

101 NW 1st Street
Cambridge Seven Associates with Edward Durell Stone, Jr., 1982

Slated as the intermodal hub of Dade County's mass transit system, this station was also integrated into the design of the Stephen P. Clark Government Center. Its structure includes a multilevel viaduct running roughly over the alignment of the Florida East Coast Railway tracks, approximately at the location of Miami's historic central railroad station. The viaduct carries trains for Metrorail's Green Line on its upper level and the Metromover loop just below. Perpendicular to the main viaduct, and running just north of the Clark Center's atrium, is an unused platform reserved for a future east-west line. A bus station one block south completes the intermodal picture.

Since it opened in May 1984, Government Center Station has been an important hub of activity, with passengers transferring between Metrorail and Metromover, and riders spilling down stairs and escalators into the spacious concourse beneath the Clark Center's skylit atrium.

The Metrorail station area is relatively typical of the station prototype developed by Harry Weese. Its principal decoration is the exposed structure, made of concrete double-tees supported on large transverse beams, with cutouts for skylights. Glass block, quarry tile, and stainless steel provide durable accents. The station consists mainly of an open structural framework, part of a strategy to maintain open sight lines and positive ventilation, while allowing commuters excellent views. Escalators float between levels, while stair and elevator towers provide solid accents. Flanked by these towers, an egg-crate screen constructed of oblique concrete panels terminates the axis of NW Second Street from the east and forms a rare accent along the longitudinal flank of the station.

Metromover   A59

Spillis Candela & Partners, Inc., with Westinghouse Electric Corp.'s
Transportation Division, 1986

Expansion: North Leg—Parsons, Brinckerhoff, Quade and Douglas, 1989;
South Leg—Post, Buckley, Schuh and Jernigan, 1990

Metromover was the first application of an automated, rubber-tired people-mover system to an urban setting, and the first integration of a people mover with heavy rail. The idea was to distribute Metrorail riders at nine Downtown stations. The electric trains stop at stations at ninety-second intervals, completing the Downtown loop in about ten minutes. Each of its twelve cars has a capacity of 155 passengers.

The initial line looped 1.9 miles around Miami's Downtown on an elevated guideway. The Downtown loop provides a touristic panorama of the city, gliding through a variety of buildings and public spaces. Between 1989 and 1990, an additional 2½ miles, and twelve additional stations, were added in north and south extensions. The north extension travels parallel to Biscayne Boulevard, passing Bicentennial Park and the Omni area. The southern extension crosses the Miami River and travels parallel to Brickell Avenue, serving the office corridor in this area.

Like Metrorail, the design of the Metromover stations finds inspiration in the concrete architecture of Washington, D.C.'s Metro stations, most specifically in the vaulted walls of that system's underground stations. Because Miami-Dade's public transport does not run underground, the vaults have been raised up to shelter the Metromover's aerial platforms, where they float on elliptical concrete columns. As in the Washington system, the canopy is coffered, and escalators float to the granite-paved upper platforms. White ceramic tile covers the walls and the elevator shafts. The weight and massivity of the concrete frame is offset by these lighter touches, except in the Miami River stations, where the platforms are thrust up more than 75 feet on massive concrete scaffolds.

A60

Miami Police Department Building   A60

Metrorail/Metromover: Government Center

400 NW 2nd Avenue
Lester Pancoast and Allan Poms with Bouterse Fabregas, 1976

Miami's Police Department headquarters employs Brutalist-inspired architecture to monumental effect. Much like its local counterpart, the Miami Beach City Hall (F34), the building's sculpted massing, with cutaway voids at the corners, reveals its structure as well as identifiable functional areas, and creates pools of shade on its ample terraces. The exterior walls mix banded areas of red clay tile with exposed concrete, precast wall panels with an aggregate finish, and precast panels with hooded openings for windows. On its west side, a parking garage facing I-95 repeats key details of the police station.

Rohde State Office Building   A61

Metrorail/Metromover: Government Center

401 NW 2nd Avenue
Russell Partnership, 1978 (Phase I); 1985 (Phase II)

The Rohde State Office Building's two triangular towers, connected by a common lobby with entries facing the site's northeast and southwest street corners, result from the successful effort made to preserve and embrace a grove of mature, mostly native trees along NW Second Avenue. The building complex includes a rich network of public spaces, including a pedestrianized block of NE First Court between the south tower and the adjacent parking garage. This pedestrian network, along with the complex's multiple orientations, seems designed for the Downtown governmental campus that has only partly materialized. The façades make a formal distinction between pedestal and tower, with distinct concrete egg crates that seem inspired by the work of Rudolph, Sert, and others. These egg crates exhibit the kind of regular and repetitive Modernist solution one might anticipate in a government administration center. Yet, the attention to sun protection, deep-set windows on the upper floors, and projecting vertical planes between windows on lower floors make it a fine complement to the Miami Police Department across Second Avenue.

A61

Federal Justice Center

Three federal judicial and law enforcement facilities and one federal jail fill most of the four square blocks between NE First Avenue and NW First Avenue, and between NE Third and NE Fifth Streets. The justice center incorporates and extends a pedestrianized section of NE Fourth Street, which begins one block east at Miami-Dade College's Wolfson Campus. It is also terminated by the formal entrance axis of the Wilkie Ferguson block. Incorporated into the Federal Detention Center, along Miami Avenue, is the historic Chaille Block, Miami's only surviving block of structures from before 1920.

David W. Dyer Building (Old U.S. Courthouse)   A62

Metromover: College North

300 NE 1st Avenue
Paist and Steward with Marion Manley, 1931
Expansion: Spillis Candela & Partners, Inc., 1983

A62

The U.S. Courthouse is a monumental civic pile and the nucleus for the development of the Federal Justice Center. Completed in 1933, it replaced the previous U.S. Post Office and Courthouse at 100 NE First Avenue (A40). Miami's grandest Neoclassical structure, the courthouse is unusual for employing the full expression of the style rather than the stripped modern Classicism that was customarily used in public buildings by 1930. The raised basement and entry terraces are faced in granite. Spandrel panels between the first and second story on the principal east façade represent scenes of Florida history. The courthouse bears a familial resemblance to Coral Gables City Hall, a collaboration of Paist and Steward with Denman Fink, using a similar material vocabulary four years earlier.

   Directly off the main lobby is an open courtyard with a 2-story gallery on the north, south, and west sides. The columns of the gallery rest on a band of red granite. The principal courtroom presents a mural by Denman

Fink, *Law Guides Florida Progress*, and was the site of the celebrated Kefauver Committee hearings on organized crime in the 1950s.

An addition by Spillis Candela & Partners expanded the building to the west in 1983. Typical of the firm's work, the addition employs concrete to render a tropical Modernism of bold faces and large openings. The addition is U-shaped in plan, allowing for a second courtyard space in what became a full-block building. The U-shape also allowed for the preservation of much of the west façade of the original. The rhythm of the window bays continues that of the original. The southwest corner of the addition is cut diagonally, creating a street corner plaza to mark a new principal entrance for the enlarged building.

As was done at Miami-Dade College campus, across NE Second Avenue, the block of Fourth Street between the buildings of the Federal Justice Center has been closed to traffic and adapted as a pedestrian mall. The eastward view corridor is made dramatic by the artfully designed pedestrian bridge for the incarcerated to travel between the jail and the courtrooms of the Dyer Building. Beyond the bridge, the view is terminated by the towering glass-enclosed central space of the Wilkie D. Ferguson, Jr. Courthouse.

James Lawrence King Federal Justice Building   A63
Metromover: College North

99 NE 4th Street
Rodriguez Khuly Quiroga, 1996

The 12-story Lawrence Federal Building is a good neighbor to the 1933 courthouse across Fourth Street. To wit, the base of the Lawrence Building takes its cues from the massing of the 1933 courthouse, continuing its cornice levels and suggesting Classical pilasters in its sandblasted and tinted precast concrete panels. The panels include crushed coquina stone aggregate to respond to the richness of the keystone-clad 1933 building. A bowed green curtain wall rises from behind the central bay beginning at the recessed seventh floor. The central portion of the top three floors on the Second Avenue façade is punctuated by a 3-story colonnade articulated with pilasters and green curtain wall between them. The building stands on a 3-foot-high granite-clad podium that rises up to form the monumental entry portico. With its simple Neoclassical reliefs and green accents recalling aged copper, the building recalls such early Miami skyscrapers as the Congress (A18) and First National Bank Buildings (A5).

Federal Detention Center (FDC) Miami   A64
Metromover: College North

33 NE 4th Street
Wolfberg Alvarez & Partners, 1994

The Federal Detention Center looks as dour as any jail should as it faces the rest of the campus. Quite surprisingly, though, it presents a feast of intricate gold metallic ornamentation on the central portion of the north façade, which stair-steps to narrow the building at the top. The ornamented central portion is bookended by the sober end wings, which taper as they reach the street.

Chaille Block   A65

Metromover: College North

401–477 North Miami Avenue
1914–19
Renovation: Wolfberg Alvarez & Partners, 1994

A65

The Chaille Block comprises the restored façades of pre-1920 structures that
have been incorporated into the base of Federal Detention Center, facing
Miami Avenue. The five buildings are exceptional examples of Miami's early
accommodation to the semi-tropical climate, using balconies, canopies, and
extended arcades providing shelter to pedestrians. Due to in part to security
concerns, the block's continuous storefronts are closed to the street, making
it only a visual artifact, albeit a fine one.

Wilkie D. Ferguson, Jr. United States   A66
Federal Courthouse

Metromover: Arena/State Plaza

400 North Miami Avenue
Arquitectonica with Hellmuth, Obata + Kassabaum, 2006
Flutter: Maya Lin, 2005

A66

The Wilkie D. Ferguson Courthouse, one of a recent crop of architecturally
noteworthy federal courthouses nationwide, has brought Arquitectonica's
playful form-making and Modernist verve to the forlorn northern edge of
Downtown. This latest construction at the western edge of the judicial complex is an elaborate statement that contrasts the twenty-first century with
the 1933 Dyer Building without sacrificing the earlier building's immersion in
a particular time and place.

Occupying a two-block-size parcel, the Ferguson Courthouse is actually
two buildings connected by a glass-walled "breezeway." The plan arrangement acknowledges the block of Fourth Street that was vacated to as-
semble the parcel and is gentle in its interruption of the street grid, allowing
the shaft of space to flow beneath the full-height glass circulation space. A
cone-shaped atrium in the central glass volume rises full height and breaks
through the roof in a form reminiscent of a nautical smokestack. The varied
window patterns reflect interior functions, from offices to courtrooms, and
give the building's extensive glass walls a pleasing texture.

Built after September 11, 2001, the building was subject to newly strin-
gent security requirements; thus its generous setbacks and intervening
landscape features that throw up a well-designed protective barrier. With
landscape architect Curtis + Rogers, Maya Lin, artist of the seminal Vietnam
Veterans Memorial in Washington, D.C., created the undulating lawn surrounding the towers, a work called *Flutter*. Perhaps recalling the saw grass
of the Everglades, the expansive lawn provides a soothing respite from
Downtown's hard concrete context.

AmericanAirlines Arena   A67

Metromover: Freedom Tower

601 Biscayne Boulevard
Arquitectonica with Heinlein Schrock, 1999

Only a decade after its completion in 1988 at NW First Avenue and Seventh Street, the Miami Arena, a centerpiece of the redevelopment of Park West, was considered obsolete. (The disused structure was eventually demolished in 2008.) A process was set in motion to site and build a new venue for the arena's primary user, the Miami Heat basketball team. The selection of the former Florida East Coast Railway docks, on the bayfront between the Port Bridge and Downtown's last deepwater slip, ignited controversy and civic discussion about the proper use of waterfront open space.

While the large building blocks postcard views of the Freedom Tower from the bay, Arquitectonica's design for the AmericanAirlines Arena rises to its location. The sweeping curves of the arena's smooth white skin project upward in a manner suggestive of ship sails. Multicolored lighting effects and digital tickers announce events, striking a note of big-city flash. In response to demands that the waterfront remain active and open to the public, the arena is surrounded by a series of terraces providing views of the bay and city, as well as ancillary structures including a practice court for the Heat, a restaurant, and a television studio. Yet to be built is a planned pedestrian bridge over Port Boulevard connecting to Bayside Marketplace (A13), as well as a planned park and soccer field on the empty waterfront parcel to the east.

A67

Museum Park and Museum Park High-Rise Group

Spurred by the planned development of two new museums in Bicentennial Park, and the park's rechristening as "Museum Park," new development has sprung up on the opposite (west) side of Biscayne Boulevard. Four roughly contemporary towers fill part of the unbuilt frontage along this stretch, nearly fulfilling the postwar vision of an urban façade stretching from the Miami River to the MacArthur Causeway and almost joining the skyscraper groups of Downtown and Omni. These towers are the first major redevelopment in the Park West area since the 1980s. Each at least 50 stories tall and comprising a mix of flats and 2-story lofts, they offer a startling new scale to the façade of Biscayne Boulevard's park frontage. Each building is distinct, but they are connected by a consistent vocabulary of floor-to-ceiling glass walls, projecting balconies, and spacious amenity decks over parking.

Museum Park (Bicentennial Park)   A68
Metromover: Eleventh Street

Edward Durell Stone, Jr., 1972
Cooper Robertson, Urban Planners, 2007

The site of Bicentennial Park remained for many years part of the port established in 1900 by Peninsular & Occidental (P&O) Steamship Company; the
land was occupied at that time by wharves, piers, and railroad sidings. In the
late 1960s, the port was relocated, partly in an effort to modernize, but also
in order to respond to the needs of real estate interests who saw Biscayne
Boulevard as an important and emerging frontage to the city. The new port
moved to Dodge Island, a newly created island in the middle of Biscayne
Bay, in 1968.

The site of Miami's original port was then transformed into a park as
part of the celebration of the country's bicentennial. Landscape architect
Edward Durell Stone Jr. designed a picturesque landscaped park, densely
planted, its edges defined by irregular coves and plazas that exploited strategic viewpoints to Biscayne Bay.

However, lacking a real focus as well as connection to the boulevard,
and most importantly an adjacent residential population, the park soon fell
into disuse. It was occasionally used as a site for the Miami Grand Prix. The
new design by Cooper Robertson presents a more formal and hierarchical
plan, integrating museums and various activities around a large green.

Marina Blue   A69
Metromover: Park West

888 Biscayne Boulevard
Arquitectonica, 2008

Nautically inspired, Marina Blue's 52- and 58-story conjoined towers form an
L-shaped slab that billows toward Biscayne Bay. The sleek and boldly curved
tower faces bowlike sails; undulating glass walls and balconies face the pedestal office and retail space, making reference to the water and adding to
the nautical imagery. The green south tower, which momentarily terminates
the axis of northbound Biscayne Boulevard, appears suspended over the
sky-lounge atop the garage. In spite of its dynamics, the complex retains a
monumental aspect, reinforced by its connection to the ground-floor plaza
created by Roberto Burle Marx's exuberant paved sidewalks.

900 Biscayne   A70
Metromover: Park West

900 Biscayne Boulevard
Revuelta Vega Leon, 2008

900 Biscayne presents a broad and undulating front toward Biscayne
Boulevard. The massing evokes the architect's signature tower forms, which
mix the volumetrics of broad curves and straight segments. Sixty stories
high, the façade is broken by vertical piers and a nearly continuous wrapper
of balconies. The amenity deck sits on the west side of the building; a small
hole in the tower façade opens it to bay views.

A69–A72

10 Museum Park   A71
Metromover: Eleventh Street

1040 Biscayne Boulevard
Oppenheim Architecture+Design, 2007

Within the bayfront ensemble, 10 Museum Park is marked by its slender profile and open structural armature. At 50 floors, it is also the smallest tower
in the group. Chad Oppenheim repeats here the exoskeletal design first
proposed by him and Walter Chatham at Ice (unbuilt) in nearby Edgewater.
Five 10-story structural modules are modulated by staggered balconies that
produce a refined rhythm and texture. The frame of the highest module
bypasses the top floor of the building to address the skyline. The pedestal
of the building is offset from the tower, allowing the tower to come to the
ground and emphasize the independence of the base. The boulevard-front-
ing pedestal is designed to include a ground-floor restaurant and outdoor
café. The east-facing units in the building are double-height apartments.

Marquis   A72
Metromover: Eleventh Street

1100 Biscayne Boulevard
Arquitectonica, 2006

At 66 floors (700 feet tall), Marquis is one the city's tallest buildings. It comprises 306 apartments over the 56-unit RockResort boutique hotel spa and
restaurant space.
    The volume of the tower is a blue-tinted glass prism whose powerful
vertical thrust is balanced by the horizontal lines of its projecting balconies.
In plan, the tower comprises interlocking parallelograms that create variation in the form. The alternation, especially along corners, between 1- and
2-story units provides further visual interest.
    The Marquis's twelfth-floor amenity deck, termed the "water garden," is
an interesting variation from the standard tower-over-pedestal type. Three-
story townhouse units surround the deck, providing a sense of enclosure
and urbanity to these often bland rooftop spaces. An 8-story vertical slot
in the tower façade at the water garden level opens to the bay. The slot
contains a lap pool, whose clearly expressed volume projects onto Biscayne
Boulevard.

Park West

Since the 1930s, the southeast portion of Miami's historic black neighborhood, Overtown, was coveted for an expansion of the Downtown business core. Attempts to relocate the black community from this area had no small part in the siting of I-95 and its Midtown Expressway Interchange (A86), which physically destroyed the area, disconnecting east from west and north from south. Between the railroad tracks and Biscayne Boulevard was the industrial hinterland of the old Port of Miami. With the completion of the highway and the relocation of the port in the 1960s, this 240-acre district stretching from Biscayne Boulevard to I-95 was reconceived as "Overtown—Park West," formalized in a new-town-in-town concept based on Miami's Neighborhood Comprehensive Development Plan of 1976. The plan focused on the strategic importance of this area in connecting the historic Downtown with the Omni district, and in connecting Overtown with Bicentennial Park and Biscayne Bay.

The centerpiece of the Park West plan was the Miami Arena (now demolished), and a mixed-use urban core of retail and apartment buildings centered around the Ninth Street Rambla (A73). Only one block of the Rambla was completed, flanked by two apartment complexes. Although the area saw a flurry of activity in the 1980s, no overall sense of neighborhood or community has developed here, partly for lack of critical mass. A nearby product of the same urban renewal effort is the 4-story Poinciana Village, a condominium development. Its companion 11-story tower, and matching Odessa project, connected by a plaza also designed by Wallace Roberts & Todd, were never built. Housing by community development corporations didn't fully materialize. Since the late 1980s, the area saw little development until the construction of towers fronting Museum Park in the early years of the twenty-first century. Unfortunately, the large scale of the nearby NAP (A77) has adversely altered the scale of Ninth Street.

The Park West station of the Metromover offers potential to connect the neighborhood to the city.

Ninth Street Rambla   A73

Metrorail: Historic Overtown/Lyric Theatre
Metromover: Park West

100 block of NW 9th Street
Wallace Roberts & Todd, 1992

Inspired by the ramblas of Barcelona, Spain, the Ninth Street Rambla followed a master plan by Wallace Roberts & Todd and was designed to connect Bicentennial Park with the planned Historic Overtown Folklife Village on the west. One block of a Barcelona-style streetscape with a wide paved median was completed between Arena Towers and Biscayne View Towers. To the west, just across the railroad track, but a psychological distance away, African-inspired motifs have been used in the blocks adjacent to the Lyric Theater.

The Towers at Park West (Arena Towers)   A74

Metrorail: Historic Overtown/Lyric Theatre
Metromover: Park West

800 North Miami Avenue
Bermello, Kurki, Vera with Windsor/Faricy, 1989

The Towers at Park West comprises 376 rental units in two high-rise stepped buildings framing a multideck parking structure. Much to the chagrin of city planners, the complex ignored the street, largely defeating its purpose of fostering a vibrant neighborhood.

Park Place by the Bay (Biscayne View Towers)   A75

Metrorail: Historic Overtown/Lyric Theatre
Metromover: Eleventh Street

915 NW 1st Avenue
Rodriguez Khuly Quiroga with Stull and Lee, 1989

Across Ninth Street, in a 180-degree turn from the design of the Towers of Park West, Park Place by the Bay has 463 units in a single enormous slab surrounded by a low-rise pedestal of shops and townhouses. This more successful urban complex hides its parking garage and shelters an attractive and protected amenity court. While the Towers at Park West cynically turned its back on the neighborhood it was built to revive, Park Place was far ahead of its time with its base of glassy townhouses facing the harsh streets that have yet to rise up to its example.

Cisneros Fontanals Art Foundation   A76

Metrorail: Historic Overtown/Lyric Theatre
Metromover: Eleventh Street

1018 North Miami Avenue
1936
Adaptive use: Rene Gonzalez Architect, 2005

Converted from a former boxing gym into a cultural institution, Cisneros Fontanals Art Foundation (CIFO) is one of a number of innovative arts-related institutions that have sprouted north of Downtown Miami since the 1990s. CIFO was established by Ella Fontanals Cisneros and her family in 2002 to "foster cultural exchange among the visual arts." On the interior, CIFO's raw open space serves rotating exhibits. Exhibitions focus on contemporary Latin American artists.

Renovations to the structure, originally built in 1936, included opening the interiors and refacing the building. The building addresses the street with a 4,800-square-foot tile mural, which transformed the nearly blank street façade into a trompe l'oeil that is best appreciated from a distance. More than two hundred colors of 1-inch glass mosaic tiles (about 1 million in total) create an abstraction of a bamboo jungle, or rather a manipulation of the image of one. The collage features layered bamboo stalks and other tropical foliage. The mural merges into the ground plane of the forecourt parking area, accented by clumps of real bamboo, suggesting that it, too, is a virtual garden. The mural is an installation, set on 4 × 4 aluminum panels, to ease removal and transfer.

NAP of the Americas (TECTOTA: Technology Center of the Americas)   A77

Metrorail: Historic Overtown/Lyric Theatre
Metromover: Park West

50 NE 9th Street
Bermello Ajamil & Partners, 2004

Centered on the high ground in Park West, this full-block, fortresslike box bristling with geodesic domes on its roof houses the nation's fifth carrier-neutral Tier-1 Network Access Point. The structure manages and provides access to the intense traffic traversing north and south along the hemispheric information byways that meet in Miami. An orchestrated tour sequence for NAP visitors leads from the center's Network Operations Center through the technical bays, where state-of-the-art equipment hums.

Southeast Overtown

Overtown is really the earliest of Miami's distinct neighborhoods, the product of a segregated time when African Americans were not permitted to live in places of their choosing. First called "Colored Town," Overtown was also "over" the Florida East Coast Railway tracks that came from the north to the Downtown Miami station near West Flagler Street and NW First Avenue. Not an independent municipality, Overtown's boundaries are the product of community consensus and are generally stated to run north from Fifth Street to Twenty-second Street, and east from NW First Avenue to NW Seventh Avenue. Overtown perhaps reached its population peak in the 1940s, and it remained the center of Miami's African American business, entertainment, and religious activities into the 1950s, when desegregation provided new opportunities for the black middle class and new highways cut the original neighborhood into pieces. The following entries are in what has officially become known as Southeast Overtown. Other parts of Overtown, across the I-95 and I-395 elevated expressways, are covered in sections B and C. Much of the neighborhood simply disappeared to make way for the Midtown Expressway Interchange (A86).

In 2009, a Miami city commissioner representing the Overtown area took advantage of her "swing vote" position on the Marlins stadium project to extract hundreds of millions of dollars to meet Overtown's needs. One hopes this funding will be the catalyst that will realize the full potential of ongoing revitalization efforts such as the dream of an Overtown Folklife Village centered on the transformed Lyric Theater. Like Harlem to black New Yorkers, Overtown has a symbolic significance to South Florida's African American community that outstrips the limited personal contact an individual might have with the neighborhood.

Remaining to tell Overtown's story are several buildings reflecting aspects of Overtown's once leading role in Miami's African American community: a theater, several churches, a private home, and some municipal structures.

Lyric Theater   A78

Metrorail: Historic Overtown/Lyric Theatre

819 NW 2nd Avenue
ca. 1913
Restoration: Beilinson Gomez Architects, 2000
Restoration, addition: R. J. Heisenbottle Architects with Judson Architect, 2003

There are few architectural reminders of the once flourishing life of Overtown, the historic heart of Miami's African American community. The Lyric Theater is a notable exception. It is located in what was once the center of an important entertainment and nightlife district known between the world wars as "Little Broadway." Famous African American performers frequented Overtown's theaters and clubs, often in the hours after performances in the grand hotels on Miami Beach. After all, they could perform in Miami Beach hotels, but they could not stay in them. Built about 1913 by Gedar Walker, the Lyric was designed to function for both movies and theater. It comprised a simple rectangular plan, with a decorated front on Second Avenue that included an arched parapet and Corinthian columns framing arched windows. The entrance was recessed into the front wall, creating an unusual covered outdoor foyer.

The theater was restored in 2000; several years later, an undulating glass-enclosed addition opened on the north side of the historic theater, itself opening to a broad tree-shaded, brick plaza on the Ninth Street right-of-way. The addition provided the theater with a state-of-the-art ticket window, café and food-service facilities, back-of-house spaces, an elevator, and the double-height gathering space visible from the street. A grand floating staircase is the main visual feature of the new space. Canted curving glass walls and slanted mullions make a freeform gesture to the plaza, while the new elevator tower facing the street is clad in masonry and recalls the design of the vertical side bays of the theater.

A78

Greater Bethel A.M.E. Church   A79
Metrorail: Historic Overtown/Lyric Theatre

245 NW 8th Street
John Sculthorpe, 1927, completed 1943

A79

The African Methodist Episcopal Church housed the first Downtown Miami black congregation, organized in March 1896 even before the incorporation of the city in July of that year. The current building dates from 1927, when the Mediterranean Revival style was in vogue. The front of the structure faces south and the two stairways leading to the sanctuary level from the street lend dignity to the façade. One of several landmark churches in Overtown, Greater Bethel remains a center of Miami metropolitan African American life.

Mt. Zion Baptist Church   A80
Metrorail: Historic Overtown/Lyric Theatre

301 NW 9th Street
William Arthur Bennett, 1928, completed 1941

This Baptist tradition congregation was organized in Miami in September 1896, shortly after the incorporation of the city. The first structure was a palmetto-thatched shack, but eventually a wood-frame structure was built on today's site. Hurricane damage in 1926 and, perhaps, the relative prosperity of the 1920s appears to have encouraged the congregation to attempt a significant building.

For many Miamians, the square tower of Mt. Zion Baptist, easily visible from the northbound lanes of I-95, is what they know of Overtown's architecture. Upon closer examination, the building's design makes use of a long porch and vestibule to alleviate the challenges of a semi-tropical climate. Rev. J. R. Evans, a significant figure in Miami's troubled racial history, was pastor of this congregation from 1918 until 1947.

A80

A81

New St. John Baptist Institutional Church (St. John's Baptist Church)   A81

1328 NW 3rd Avenue
McKissack and McKissack, 1940

The Art Deco architecture of St. John's is one of the only examples of the style in Overtown, and the architects, McKissack and McKissack, were African Americans from Nashville, Tennessee. The interpretation of Modernism here is quite distant from the whimsical tropical Deco of Miami Beach, and the building does not do much to accommodate Miami's semi-tropical climate.

Rev. J. W. Drake led this congregation from 1912 until 1951 and was involved in the initial planning and development of Liberty Square, the New Deal housing project for African Americans and the first public housing project in Florida.

New Providence Lodge No. 365   A82

Metrorail: Overtown

937–939 NW 3rd Avenue
1954

This building was built by Miami's African American Masons as their lodge at a time when the freemasons were still a segregated society. A jurisdiction covering Florida, Belize, and Central America for the exclusive membership of black men in these areas was incorporated in 1912. The Overtown lodge was issued its charter in 1917 and has worked together with the neighborhood to uphold dignity and achieve equity.

The design of the lodge temple has symbolic references to the organization including the three boxed windows on the second floor, evoking the plans for King Solomon's temple. These windows also represent the three conferrals of degrees. The square and compass, symbols of the Masons, appear on the main door. Stones around the door represent the quarries that provided the material for Solomon's temple.

D. A. Dorsey House   A83

Metrorail: Historic Overtown/Lyric Theatre

250 NW 9th Street
ca. 1913
Reconstruction: 1995

This is the reconstructed home of a significant figure in Miami's African American history, Dana. A. Dorsey, who is popularly acknowledged as Miami's first black millionaire. Dorsey, who came to Miami as a carpenter with Flagler's railroad in 1897, purchased substantial property in Overtown and became wealthy as the black population grew and Miami expanded in the first two decades of the twentieth century. While contemporary figures might challenge the assertion, historians believe that Dorsey put together the most comprehensive real estate empire ever amassed by an African American in Miami-Dade County history. Dorsey at one point owned what is today Fisher Island, formed in 1905 by the creation of Government Cut, which sliced off the southern tip of Miami Beach's main island. This simple wood-frame house, reconstructed in 1995 by the Black Archives History and Research Foundation of South Florida, reflects Dorsey's history as a carpenter, but gives no hint of his extraordinary life in Miami.

Overtown Youth Center   A84
Metrorail: Historic Overtown/Lyric Theatre

450 NW 14th Street
Cohen Freedman Encinosa, 2001

The Overtown Youth Center and the 1940 St. John's Church (A81) make an interesting pair inside the tight curve of the I-95 north to I-395 east ramp. One is perhaps the entire city's finest church in the Art Deco style, wrapped in a muted yellowish brick. Next door, the Youth Center's simple volume, comprising an eye-catching metal shed roof and bright saturated red and orange walls, seems to respond to the new context of the expressways with jabbing elbows. Richness is added to the composition by the use of natural stone.

The Overtown Youth Center was the vision of local real estate developer Martin Z. Margulies. Through the Margulies Foundation, he built the Overtown Youth Center with the support of Miami Heat basketball star Alonzo Mourning with the goal of creating a haven for the children in Overtown. Opening in early 2003, the center is a state-of-the-art facility. The center co-locates academic and recreational activities in a safe environment, working with children, families, and schools from second grade through high school.

Under the shed roof can be found a gymnasium with a full-size indoor basketball court, locker rooms with showers, classrooms, computer lab with T1 connection, and other facilities. In addition, the center is adjacent to a public park with access to athletic fields, a swimming pool, and a public library.

Perhaps the center's siting, as if it puts Southeast Overtown's best foot forward to the Midtown Expressway Interchange (A86), is a sign of much-needed healing between the neighborhood and the expressway.

X-Ray Clinic   A85
Metrorail: Historic Overtown/Lyric Theatre

171 NW 11th Street
1939

There is evidence that the design of this building was the product of a drawing teacher at Booker T. Washington High School by the name of Barker. In context, the simplicity of this modest Streamline Moderne structure masks the complexity of its origins. When the building was constructed, African Americans could not be X-rayed at Miami's hospital. Dr. Samuel Johnson, an African American physician and native of Miami, opened the clinic to meet this need. The building can stand as a tribute to all the black professionals who lived and worked in Overtown in the days of segregation to make it a self-sufficient community.

A85

Midtown Expressway Interchange   A86

Interchange of I-95, I-395, and Dolphin Expressway
Wilbur Smith & Associates, 1956-1959

Together with the paths of I-95, I-395, and the Dolphin Expressway, this four-level interchange is infamous in mid-twentieth-century American urban history as an example of urban renewal as "Negro removal." Planned and proposed in 1956, construction began in 1959 and continued throughout the 1960s. Eighty-seven acres of homes, stores, and other neighborhood facilities, approximately bounded by NW Tenth Street to NW Fifteenth Street, NW Third Avenue to NW Seventh Avenue, were eliminated by the construction of the interchange. The project destroyed Overtown's sense of place, but not its symbolic meaning to generations of black Miamians.

As the surrounding urban fabric attempts to heal the scar, this interchange in the heart of the city would make a fine candidate for decorative night lighting and other types of public art in the many open spaces between its ramps.

Miami River

The Miami River is a largely natural watercourse, originally connected to the Everglades through a cut in the limestone ridge that separates the "river of grass" from the Atlantic Ocean. Humans have inhabited the banks of the Miami River for many thousands of years. North and west of Downtown, the Miami River runs through some of Miami's earliest neighborhoods. Many residential and institutional architectural styles from the first four decades of the twentieth century are represented as well as a few survivors from the nineteenth century.

Also north and west of Downtown, the Miami River remains an industrial center and transportation avenue. While fewer in number in recent years, the river has been home to a large selection of maritime industries: commercial fishing, boatbuilding, and boat-repair facilities, freight loading, and transshipment areas. These businesses have been confronted with rising real estate prices and residential encroachment, and their future is in doubt. There is every likelihood that the residential towers now lining the mouth of the river will eventually extend north and west along its banks.

A87

Brickell Avenue Bridge   A87

Metromover: Knight Center

Brickell Avenue at the Miami River
Jorge L. Hernandez, Rafael Portuondo and Mike Sardinas, 1993
Manuel Carbonell, Sculptor

The Brickell Avenue Bridge is a critical link in the commercial fabric of the city. It connects the historic Downtown north of the Miami River with the newer Brickell business corridor. It is a traditional bottleneck, once aggravated by the poor functioning of the old red drawbridge that commanded the entrance to the heavily trafficked Miami River. Public pressure led the

Department of Transportation to arrange a competition, resulting in the selection of a winning design by Jorge Hernandez, Rafael Portuondo and Mike
Sardinas. The new bridge returns in many ways to Miami's premodern tradition of civic representation. The Classical motivation of its abutments and
templelike pilothouse contrasts favorably with the disorder of surrounding
office buildings and hotels in tight proximity. Notably, the bridge trans-
mits a narrative of the city's early history, presenting a statue of a Tequesta
Indian, and reliefs of figures like Miami pioneer Julia Tuttle, railroad magnate
Henry Flagler, and Everglades activist Marjory Stoneman Douglas.

James L. Knight Center/Miami Convention Center/Hyatt Regency Hotel   A88

A88

Metromover: Knight Center

400 SE 2nd Avenue
Ferendino Grafton Spillis Candela, 1982

With renewed interest in Downtown real estate in the 1980s, the City of
Miami, University of Miami, and Hyatt Regency partnered to build this mul-
tipurpose entertainment, cultural, and convention complex on the north
bank of the Miami River, at the foot of the Brickell Bridge. The project took
inspiration from the 1970s San Antonio riverfront development; indeed, one
of the best parts is the landscaped promenade along the river, an early attempt to create a fully functional Riverwalk. Notwithstanding the intention
to create a vibrant civic center, the I-95 ramps on the north side of the complex cut it off from the Downtown core. Adding to the lack of street presence, the building is set back, elevated beyond landscaping and a vehicle-
dominated entrance. The complex remains strangely isolated, a marginal
presence within the dense fabric of Downtown's central business district.
Perhaps the completion of the Riverwalk will reinforce the center's ties to
the surrounding city.

The James L. Knight Center was financed by the Knight Foundation, and
named in memory of *Miami Herald* publisher James Landon Knight. Each element of the three-part complex (hotel, conference/convention center, and
Continuing Education Center) is clearly legible. The key element of the complex is the pie-shaped, 4,686-seat concert hall and theater. Its curved cast-
concrete walls sweep from the river to SE Fourth Street, where a grand stair
cascades to the street. The Convention Center includes a 28,000-square-
foot Riverfront Exhibition Hall. Both are owned by the City of Miami. Above
the convention center, the University of Miami's James L. Knight School
of Continuing Education occupies two floors, including the 500-seat Ashe
Auditorium and 117-seat Miami Lecture Hall.

The 612-room Hyatt Regency Hotel is perched in front of, and over, the
convention center. Its 19-story, Z-shaped slab and egg-crate façade are set at
a 45-degree angle to the city, framing the wide porte cochere and entrance
drive that face SE Second Avenue. The atrium lobby is dominated by a massive Yaacov Agam sculpture. Greenhouse windows look onto the southeast-
facing pool deck.

Parking for the complex is provided in the garage of the Bank of
America Tower. The parking garage, accessible via a glass-enclosed pedes-
trian walkway beneath the I-95 ramps, and designed by Ferendino Grafton
Spillis Candela, provides the pedestal for I. M. Pei's Miami World Trade
Center, now the Bank of America Tower (A43). As originally built, lush land-

scaping along the walkway kept pedestrians walking between the parking garage and the center completely unaware they were walking under the expressway ramps.

A89

Royal Palm Cottages   A89

Metromover: Riverwalk

Fort Dallas Park, 60–64 SE 4th Street
1897–99
Moved to current site: 1980

This was one of thirty similar cottages built by Henry Flagler, the owner and builder of the Florida East Coast Railway and thus the man who put Miami on path to development as a great city. Built to house the management at Flagler's Royal Palm Hotel, located north of the mouth of the Miami River, the houses were known as the Royal Palm Cottages. The house is a 2-story balloon-frame structure with a gabled roof. Famously durable Dade County pine was one of the building materials, but the rest was brought in by the newly established railway. The cottages, including this one, were once a few blocks away, near SE First and Second streets, where International Place (A43) now stands. This structure was saved and moved to the riverfront, where it stands out of place and out of time, the last marker in Downtown Miami of its pioneering years as a railroad town.

Red M at Riverwalk Station   A90

Metromover: Riverwalk

Riverwalk Station at SE 4th Street
R & R Studios (Roberto Behar and Rosario Marquardt), 1996

Red M serves as an entranceway to the Riverwalk Metromover station, but addresses the city at large. Installed under the Art in Public Places program and constructed of concrete and masonry and finished in stucco, the bold *M* can be construed to imply many meanings: "Miami," "Metromover," "magic," or even "memory." A clock perched in the entranceway connects to the memory of railway stations. For an *M* it is big, but it provides a human-scale counterpoint to the giant station, which is lifted nearly 8 stories above the Miami River.

A90

Riverfront   A91
Metromover: Third Street or Riverwalk

Mint
92 SW 3rd Street
Revuelta Vega Leon, 2008

Wind
350 South Miami Avenue
Revuelta Vega Leon, 2007

Ivy
90 SW 3rd Street
Revuelta Vega Leon, 2008

Occupying a 13.5-acre site along the Miami River between the Metrorail
viaduct and South Miami Avenue, Riverfront is one of Downtown's most
ambitious if introverted planned developments. The master plan called for a
gated community of six apartment towers organized astride a grand central
boulevard with retail spaces, restaurants, cafés, and office condos facing the
parking pedestals on the lower floors. Employing descriptions like "urban
oasis," "sanctuary" and "city within a city," it aims at privacy in the Downtown
realm. Yet, the complex opens expansively to almost 900 feet of riverwalk,
which expands toward the central boulevard, offering trees, pools, and a
relief from Riverwalk's minimum 50-foot mandated width.

    Only three of six towers have been built, all designed by Revuelta Vega
Leon. Each tower contains 500 to 600 units, and rises from 41 to 56 stories
above the river. The planning emphasizes a spatial grandeur in striking relief
with the intimate scale of the river. Nevertheless, the assemblage of new
towers marks an emphatic return of development to the river since the construction of the ramps connecting I-95 to NE Second Avenue.

Miami Circle   A92
Metromover: Fifth Street

South bank of the Miami River near Brickell Avenue and SE 4th Street

The Miami Circle is Miami's earliest man-made structure, dating back 1,700
to 2,000 years. The circle comprises a ring of twenty-four holes cut into the
bedrock, shaped and carved to allow perhaps for the placement of wooden
or other ephemeral posts upholding a structure. It was during the excava-
tion in 1998 for a new high-rise condominium project on the site that the
Circle was rediscovered. Extensive archaeological work has yielded a trove
of stone axes and bone implements.

    A pitched battle ensued among the developer, preservation advocates,
the city, the county, and the state over the final disposition of the Circle.
Eventually, an enormous sum of public money was spent to acquire the site,
but little effort was exerted to make it accessible to the public. However,
in 2009, the State of Florida, in partnership with the Historical Museum of
Southern Florida, announced plans for a public park that would include the
site and provide pedestrian access. New residential towers, a product of the
Miami's latest building boom, loom over the site.

Rivergate Plaza (Capital Grille Building)   A93

Metromover: Fifth Street

444 Brickell Avenue
Morris Lapidus, 1971

Rivergate Plaza is a functional office block set on a broad lifeless plaza over-looking the Brickell Bridge and Miami River. As the northernmost building on Brickell, it functions as a gateway in two directions: to the Brickell area from Downtown, and to the river from the bay. Unfortunately, the building performs neither function well, a product of the inability of the suburban type to come to terms with a complex urban site. Although it aspired to pro-vide a public plaza at the landfall of the Brickell Bridge, the space provided is not at the river level, but on a raised plaza over the building's parking deck. The move is clumsy. Yet here, a decade prior to the completion of the James L. Knight Center (A88), was the beginning of the Miami Riverwalk.

A94

NeoVertika   A94

Metrorail/Metromover: Brickell

690 SW 1st Court
Revuelta Vega Leon, 2006

The 36-story, L-shaped tower wraps the corner between the Miami River and Metrorail corridor, with each face exhibiting a mix of flats and maisonette-style units. The egg-crate façade, articulated at every other floor, reduces the apparent bulk of the structure. Metrorail's Miami River Bridge, still quite high at this point, passes along NeoVertika's east front. The juxtaposition gives context to the rail, while animating the building's pedestal garage frontage.

Latitude   A95

Metrorail/Metromover: Brickell

185 SW 7th Street
Arquitectonica, 2007

Located along the Miami River, on the site of the old port customs house (location of the fictional Organized Crime Bureau headquarters in the televi-sion series *Miami Vice*) and an old PT boat works, this project site controls the river frontage along a straight segment between two bends.

   This dense mixed-use complex includes a residential tower and an office tower. The two structures are tied together at their base by an integrated pedestal, but exhibit distinct architectonics. The residential tower, Latitude on the River, is raised over its pedestal by pilotis at the level of the amenity deck. It is an undulating block that twists and folds for better exposure and orientation. In contrast to the more rationalized façade of NeoVertika, it is an expressionistic statement. Woggle-shaped core elements, identified in a vibrant chartreuse color, penetrate from the ground, through the ame-nity-deck level, and up to the roof. Unlike some of Arquitectonica's more famous buildings, the units are not flow-through. Latitude One, a 22-story, 230,000-square-foot office building, rises just to the south. It features a mainly gridded façade with a cutaway glass corner.

Latitude's pedestal faces the river with a ground-floor restaurant and townhouses with broad staggered balconies above. The entry plaza is an interesting agglomeration of loggias and patios that sort traffic and open byways to the river from SW Seventh Street. The grand archway forms a covered space for outdoor dining. The old customs house is to be reconstructed and used as a retail/restaurant space. Tall awnings shade and exaggerate the loggias. Sculptural elements adorn the walls above the loggias.

Miami Line A96

Metromover: Fifth Street

Rockne Krebs, 1984

The neon installation along both sides of Metrorail's Miami River viaduct, by Washington, D.C.–based Rockne Krebs, is an early product of Miami-Dade's Art in Public Places program, and is one of the city's most visible public art projects, as well as a landmark in the field of "aesthetic illumination." Originally 300 feet in length, the multicolored line was expanded to more than a quarter mile. A monumental work of minimalist means, it exploits "light's ephemeral nature" as civic art, an expression of vibrancy appropriate to a modern city. Krebs was a pioneer in light sculpture, known for large-scale urban and environmental works. In Miami, he merged his own interest in laser and neon light with the city's distinct color and light traditions (as evidenced on South Beach).

Miami-Dade's public-art ordinance, adopted in 1973, emphasized commissioned creative works over acquisition. Metrorail was a primary target of the public-art ordinance. Lighting has since become a perennial interest in Miami. Organizations like Light up Miami continue to promote exterior lighting on Downtown's buildings and infrastructure.

A96

Brickell

Brickell

*Brickell Avenue is the financial center of Miami and, in many respects,
the financial center of the Caribbean and Latin America. Brickell Avenue
is also the spine of a continually developing neighborhood of residential
high-rises that follows the bay shore to the Rickenbacker Causeway. The
Brickell neighborhood contains Miami's oldest-known human construction and a venerable residential district, but it is also home to many
representative structures of the go-go 1980s boom, and its turn-of-the-
twenty-first-century equivalent.*

*The Brickell family was among Miami's earliest Euro-American pio-
neers. The first Brickells, William and Mary, came to the Miami area in
the 1870s. Their trading post was set back a few yards from the mouth
of the Miami River on the south bank, near Fifth Street and Brickell
Avenue. The Brickells traded with the Miccosukee and Seminoles, who
had hidden unconquered in the Everglades after the Third Seminole War
(1855–58) and had only begun to emerge again as the nineteenth century ended. The Brickells' extensive real estate holdings extended south
along Biscayne Bay from the Miami River to today's Coconut Grove.*

*Between 1910 and 1919, the Brickells laid out a subdivision with broad
avenues divided by landscaped medians. By the 1920s, winter estates
lined both sides of Brickell Avenue. In the 1950s and 1960s, Brickell experienced a new surge of growth that transformed its waterfront estates for
commercial and residential uses. Brickell figured along the new trajecto-
ries of Miami's postwar expansion, its generous estates offering ample
land for new suburban office buildings and residential towers. The trend
southward was accentuated by changes in banking legislation that
transformed Miami into an important pan-American financial center in
the 1970s. Brickell was at the heart of these transformations.*

*Although it offers pedestrians little more than rich landscaping, this
quarter of high-rise commercial and residential buildings is increasingly
a mixed-use neighborhood with a range of functions and services.*

*The Brickell Avenue corridor is divided into the North Brickell office
section, Brickell Key, an island city-within-a-city at the end of SW Eighth
Street, the South Brickell residential section, and the heterogeneous
West Brickell section.*

Icon Brickell and Viceroy Hotel   A97

Metromover: Fifth Street

495 Brickell Avenue
Arquitectonica, 2008

The vast scale and complexity of Icon Brickell make this one of the most ambitious projects attempted in Miami. The project comprises more than 1,600
apartment units and a 148-room hotel in three large towers connected by a
single pedestal with offices, retail spaces, and parking. This condensed urban
package is sited at the foot of the Brickell Bridge, wedged between the Miami
Circle archaeological site (**A92**) and the rather magnificent First Presbyterian

A97

Church (**A98**). Although very large, the project deftly organizes its towers to mitigate their effect from both within the complex and without.

Two of the three towers, 57 stories each, are residential. The third, at 50 stories, contains the Viceroy Resorts and Residences, which has its own rooftop restaurant, lounge, and pool. Clever disposition of the three towers preserves views. Also adroit are the tower walls, combining glass and concrete frames, which reduce the apparent scale of the building and impart a sense of lightness to an otherwise heavy structure. The towers are joined by the 15-story base, which almost fully occupies its site. The pedestal roof, almost 140 feet above the street, comprises a 2-acre landscaped deck whose centerpiece is a 300-foot-long pool. At the entrance, 22-foot-tall columns inspired by Easter Island's Maori sculptures and signed by Philippe Starck provide a monumental entrance.

First Presbyterian Church   A98
Metromover: Eighth Street

609 Brickell Avenue
Lester W. Geisler, 1949

From 1898 to 1947, the congregation of the First Presbyterian Church met in a church or chapel built by Henry Flagler at the corner of Southeast Flagler and Third avenues. The current building includes a replica of the interior of the original Flagler Chapel, with its Tiffany stained glass windows.

500 Brickell Avenue   A99
Metromover: Fifth Street

Arquitectonica, 2005

Number 500 Brickell forms a tall rectilinear slab slit at its center with a vast multistory court, a grand gesture that goes far beyond Arquitectonica's earlier sky-court at the Atlantis (**A120**); rather, this aperture is designed to be

A99

understood as a monumental portal. The 90-foot-wide, 30-story-high covered void separates the nearly identical 42-story towers with the intention that together the composition serves as a frame, or gateway, to the Brickell district. Below the void, the towers are connected by the continuous parking pedestal. Above, they are connected by a roof. The roof is constructed of a space frame pierced by a circular oculus, which frames views to the sky from the circular pool 300 feet below. The main pool and amenity deck are raised from their usual location on top of the parking garage to the top of the buildings, exploiting the roof acreage of the conjoined towers.

The pedestal continues the theme of perforation. It contains two levels of retail and a 930-car parking garage on continuously sloping ramps that are hidden by large perforated precast-concrete wall panels ventilated by 700 oculae colored in a gradient blend of colors. The colors are achieved by uniquely painted metal grating in each opening. The kaleidoscopic effect is a monumental Op-Art mural.

Northern Trust Bank   A100
Metromover: Eighth Street

700 Brickell Avenue
Morris Ross Architect, 1971
Ground-floor renovations: Sackman 2, 1994

The headquarters of Northern Trust Bank, one of Miami's foremost private banks, was established when Boston-based Northern Trust acquired Miami's Security Trust Company in 1971. The building dates from this time, expressing the buttoned-down world of private banking. Its crisp modern façade has dark glass walls (without visible mullions) that are shaded by strongly projecting plates of white concrete at each floor. The banding of dark glass and white structure creates a boldly graphic effect. An elegant detail: the slab edges are cut by a horizontal reveal.

A100

701 and 777 Brickell Avenue   A101
Metromover: Eighth Street

701 Brickell Avenue
Hellmuth, Obata + Kassabaum, 1984

777 Brickell Avenue
Hellmuth, Obata + Kassabaum, 1980
Renovation: Thompson Ventulett Stainback, 1993

701 Brickell is clad in polished russet-colored granite and silver reflective glass, and until the completion of Icon Brickell it served as iconic entry marker into the luxe Brickell corridor from the messy vitality of Downtown across the river. At 450 feet, it was one of the tallest buildings in Miami upon its construction in 1986, but has since been dwarfed by taller buildings in the surrounding Brickell Financial District. Originally named the Lincoln Center, it has housed the Bank of America since 2004. Its exposed columns of rectangular concrete piers costumed in shiny, polished chrome cylinders continue the Miami tradition of spiking structural elements with purely visual effects.

This complex was among the first Brickell developments to install a public baywalk. Facing Brickell Avenue, however, the two towers together are remarkable for the yawning entry/exit into their shared circulation and parking system, centered between them opposite the intersection with SW Seventh Street. The experience of approaching the complex by car is fraught with conflict, as one is not sure whether to luxuriate in such well-designed thoroughfares or despair of the wholly autocentric cityscape. Anyone who braves the windswept, sheer-walled plaza space leading to the bay between the towers is rewarded with pleasant, sloping lawns with views of the bay and *Aquila*, a graceful sculpture by John Raimondi.

Brickell Key

As Brickell Avenue grew in importance as an extension of the Downtown core in the 1960s and 1970s, Claughton Island, originally a spoil bank near the mouth of the Miami River, became an attractive development opportunity. Hong Kong–based Swire Properties became the major property owner on the island in the 1970s. The island was subsequently renamed Brickell Key, to trade on the cachet of the Brickell address. Swire brought Brazilian architect Oscar Niemeyer to Miami to prepare plans for the island's development. Niemeyer's initial project featured a swarm of serpentine tower blocks housing offices and residences, whose curved surfaces offered panoramic views. While Niemeyer's plan was eventually jettisoned, the concept of an island of towers remained.

Today's formidable cluster of office, residential, and hotel towers implies urbanity from a distance, but the development is clearly a product of late-twentieth-century land planning and its reliance on the automobile, gated communities, and single-use zoning. The ground plane is dominated by curved roadways, parking garages, and ramps leading to lavish, heavily landscaped arrival platforms. To its credit, the plan called for a public walkway that now rings the entire island, providing spectacular views of the city, port, and bay.

Brickell Key Bridge Illumination   A102

Metromover: Eighth Street

Brilliant Lighting Design, 1997, 2000

Metal halide and CFL fixtures create a glittering entrance along the 900-foot-long Brickell Key Bridge.

Asia   A103

900 Brickell Key Drive
J. Scott Architecture, 2001

As if in response to the dramatic towers on the north side of the mouth of the river, Brickell Key's relatively bland skyline has sprouted the monumental Asia. And perhaps as a gesture to Swire Properties' Hong Kong roots, the condominium tower sports an East Asian–inspired ornamental program. The base of the tower is especially imposing as a 10-story gap nearly the size

A103

of an entire floor plate provides a soaring space for the pool level, at approximately the third floor. The enormous gap flows north to open directly onto the Miami River, asserting the building as an integral part of the ensemble, including Icon Brickell, Epic, and One Miami, around the mouth of the river. From a distance, and perhaps most novel of all, the tower's curved pitched roof element recalls the architecture of the Far East.

Mandarin Oriental   A104

500 Brickell Key Drive
RTKL Architects, 2000

In contrast to the mostly bland mix of towers that inhabit Brickell Key, the Mandarin Oriental Hotel forms a broad, sweeping swoosh, a logo-inspired crescent that rises like a wedge to the north. The curve billows out toward the water, giving the hotel's sequence of public rooms panoramic views westward toward Downtown and the Brickell waterfront. At the north end of the arc, centered on the approach from the Brickell Key Bridge, is a freestanding, copper-clad restaurant structure designed by Tony Chi Associates. The hotel's banquet and ballroom facilities are in a separate building northeast of the hotel. They are connected by a bridge that frames a cloistered entry court centered on an elliptical pond.

A104

Courvoisier Center I and II   A105

Courvoisier Center I
501 Brickell Key Drive
Nichols & Associates, 1985

Courvoisier Center II
601 Brickell Key Drive
J. Scott Architecture, 1988

A105

Managing to appear climatically adapted, inspired by Caribbean vernacular, and contemporary all at the same time, Courvoisier Center I and II's stepped massing, recessed windows, and disengaged piers add a distinguished touch to the largely placeless appearance of Brickell Key. Note how the contrasting spandrels appear as brise-soleils and how such a Modernist allusion can go so well with sloping roofs. Perhaps if Corbusier had worked in the Bahamas it might have looked something like this. These paired office buildings were among the very first structures on the island. If only the many residential buildings that came later harmonized so well with their subtropical locale.

One Brickell Square   A106

Metromover: Eighth Street

801 Brickell Avenue
Skidmore, Owings & Merrill, 1984

The 28-story One Brickell Square office building was designed as one of three towers in the 1980s, but it was not until the turn-of-the-century residential building boom that the build-out occurred with the construction of the Plaza on Brickell residential towers, designed by Nichols Brosch Wurst & Wolfe. The office building is aging well and holds its own against the two

A106

more recent towers. Its white skin and lightly tinted green glass play well in the Miami sun. The windows recall the classic tripartite Chicago windows of early skyscrapers in that city, the headquarters of Skidmore, Owings & Merrill, while horizontal planes suggest brise-soleils to shield the Miami sun. The base of One Brickell Square is notable for the space frame rising three stories and whose columns alternate with the trunks of sabal palms to create a uniquely urban subtropical hypostyle effect. Note the stair-stepping pattern, both vertical and horizontal, of the wider north and south façades. The pattern is revealed as a flat ziggurat form facing east. At the opposite end, facing Brickell Avenue, the ziggurat is expressed in vertical form, narrowing to one bay where it comes closest to the avenue. At the base of the central bay, a gigantic round window adds a dramatic touch at street level.

A107

Four Ambassadors   A107

Metromover: Eighth Street

801 South Bayshore Drive
T. Trip Russell and Associates, 1968

Development of the Brickell Avenue corridor as an extension of the Downtown core south of the Miami River gained momentum with the construction of the Four Ambassadors, a mixed-use development of four identical residential and hotel towers joined by a retail concourse. While the mixed-use nature of the development provides activity throughout the day and evening, the complex welcomes the automobile while challenging the pedestrian. Typical of the period, the lobby level concourse connects to an expansive deck overlooking Biscayne Bay, yet maintains its distance from the water and its neighbors; to wit, it presents a major interruption in the Brickell area baywalk.

A108

Helm Bank (Citizens Federal Savings and Loan Bank)   A108

Metromover: Tenth Street/Promenade

999 Brickell Avenue
Morris Lapidus, 1972

The multifaceted walls of the 12-story Helm Bank tower, rendered in alternating vertical bands of stucco and mirrored-glass curtain wall, illustrate a new and more expressive type of office tower. Designed to house the headquarters of Citizens Federal Savings and Loan Bank, the idiosyncratic massing expresses corporate identity, while the compact plan emphasizes oblique views up and down Brickell Avenue. The twelfth-floor penthouse with wrapping balcony is clearly expressed as the cockpit of this podlike spaceship.

Projecting from the tower base, the ground-floor banking lobby is a smaller-scaled polygonal glass pod, a reiteration of the geometry of the tower. Its concrete fins frame prismatic glass sections with mullions angled like the flèche of an arrow.

Consulate of the Dominican Republic   A109

Metromover: Tenth Street/Promenade

1038 Brickell Avenue
Petersen and Shuflin Architects, 1954

An isolated reminder of Brickell Avenue's early postwar scale, the front of this 2-story consulate building mixed brick and stucco walls with a decorative wood screen of louvered persianas. This low-slung composition of vertical and horizontal planes recalls the residential style of Frank Lloyd Wright.

Colonnade Plaza (Mutual of Omaha Building)   A110

Metromover: Financial District

1201 Brickell Avenue
Minoru Yamasaki with Houston, Albury, Baldwin and Parish, 1967

The monumentality of this corporate Parthenon for insurance giant Mutual of Omaha powerfully demonstrated Brickell Avenue's symbolic role as Miami's new business center. Raised on a plynth that concealed the below-grade parking lot, its slender columns rise 8 stories to carry the structure's penthouse floor, where precast concrete grilles form a scalloped fascia around the building. The explicit interplay of columns and beams echoes the colonnades surrounding Classical Greek temples. Recessed into the structural system, solar bronze glass walls with dark frames intersecting in curved fillets surround the main office block. Brickell Bank, once housed in the first floor, touted the building as the first Downtown suburban banking facility in Miami.

A110

J. W. Marriott/Mellon Bank   A111

Metromover: Financial District

1109 Brickell Avenue
Nichols Brosch Sandoval & Associates, 2000

This multiuse complex was the first large new infill project on Brickell Avenue since the boom of the 1980s. Notably, it included the first major hotel to locate in the heart of the city's financial district. The building improved on its through-block predecessors by presenting formal urban frontages on both Brickell Avenue and Brickell Bay Drive.

1221 Brickell Avenue   A112

Metromover: Financial District

Harwood K. Smith & Partners, 1986

The 27-story 1221 Brickell Building is remarkable for its innovative use of glass curtain wall and lighting effects that employ strips of neon. Mirrored-glass walls on the two street façades rise and step back, framing a dramatic corner shaft of ebony-black glass that sheathes the elevator bank and its battery of five glass elevator cabins. The differences in glass quality produce interesting effects. The elevators, which swoop up and down, provide one of the best rides in town, and complement the horizontal trajectory of Metrorail. The building comes alive at night, when ten "electric blue

A112

pinstripes" running the full height of the corner elevator shaft are illuminated. Note the address numerals carved from slabs of polished white marble, with water cascading over them, at the base of the chamfered elevator
bank. With its extensive use of neon, mirrored glass, and metal surfaces and
luxuriant use of marble, 1221 Brickell is the epitome of Miami's 1980s *Miami-
Vice*–flavored boom.

Banco Espiritu Santo   A113

Metromover: Financial District

1395 Brickell Avenue
Kohn Pederson Fox Associates with SB Architects and Swanke Hayden Connell
Architects, 2004

The American headquarters of the Portuguese Espiritu Santo banking family is a well-crafted statement of transnational finance. The Brickell Avenue
façade presents a fine-grained glass curtain wall subtly inflected with a
concave scallop to suggest a 30-story arch. In the manner of the St. Louis
Gateway Arch, the move is intended to symbolize Miami's role as a gateway
to the south.

The 36-story building stacks 203 guest rooms of the Conrad Miami hotel over 116 condominium apartment units, both of which sit on top of the
300,000-square-foot office building, 12-story parking garage, and ground-
floor retail block. The lobby is an interior street running east-west, connecting the different uses of the building. Two separate entrances, for offices on
one side and for residential and hotel on other, distribute circulation. A sky-
lobby at the twenty-fifth floor serves as the hotel's lobby, restaurant, lounge,
and "Level 25," the bar. While the parabolic arch of the office building makes
one grand gesture facing west, the multistory window of the hotel atrium,
facing east, marks an equally important statement. An interesting feature is
the glass-bottom pool over vehicular drop-off.

A113

Four Seasons   A114

Metromover: Financial District

1425 Brickell Avenue
Gary Edward Handel & Associates with Bermello Ajamil & Partners, 2003

The Four Seasons tower, rising 70 stories above Brickell Avenue, is the tallest American building south of Atlanta, and the tallest residential tower
south of New York. It rises in a smooth, tapered shaft, which is divided along
its entire height into separate south and north skins to break the mass of
the tower. Constructed entirely of reinforced concrete with post-tensioned
slabs, the tower is supported by caissons 6 feet in diameter that run 140 feet
deep into bedrock. One of Miami's most spacious amenity decks, this one
2 acres large, is situated atop the 6-floor, 934-space parking garage on the
building's east side. Venerable landscape architect Dan Kiley designed the
gardens.

A114

　　　The Four Seasons Hotel occupies floors thirty through forty, and 184
apartment units occupy the balance to the seventieth floor. Below, the base
of the building comprises an office block, retail space, and a spa facility,
with an 80-foot waterfall in the main lobby. A separate lobby on the seventh floor, featuring Fernando Botero's *Seated Woman*, serves the rest of the
building.

Infinity at Brickell   A115

Metrorail/Metromover: Brickell
Metromover: Financial District

1300 South Miami Avenue
Borges + Associates with Adache Group Architects, 2008

Projected to occupy nearly a full block off Coral Way, Infinity at Brickell was
designed as a two-tower mixed-use project that joined residential units and
offices. The first part of the combo, the residential tower, stands alone now.
Its 52 floors rise 630 feet above the street.

　　　Infinity's 13-story pedestal is unapologetically solid. In contrast, the
mass of its tower is broken by a graphic system of horizontal balcony trays,
vertical fins, expressed core elements, and two-story units that add further
complexity. These features are sculpted to dissipate the powerful size of the
building.

Brickell Bay Office Tower   A116

Metromover: Tenth Street/Promenade

1001 South Bayshore Drive
Luckman Partnership, 1985

In contrast to the host of towers that sprouted on the Brickell corridor in the
1980s, the 32-story Brickell Bay Office Tower tried neither to hide its parking
garage nor to pretend it didn't exist. Instead, the parking levels provide the
pyramidal base from which the relatively thin slab of the tower arises. The
dramatic effect is heightened at close proximity by the plantings draping
from planters on the garage-level parapets of the stair-stepping garage
levels. On the street side, the garage splits into two prongs, like the front
legs of a sphinx reaching for the sidewalk, forming the vehicular entry and

A116

exit into the garage, as well as a lavishly appointed pedestrian arrival court rising as high as 9 stories, between the prongs of the garage. The seamless interweaving of automobile and pedestrian arrival sequences is exemplary and unfortunately rare in 1980s Brickell architecture. Inside, a wide corridor leads to the elevators and a retail arcade facing Biscayne Bay and an early portion of the baywalk.

The tower is notable for its contrasting façades. The broad north and south faces are solid with punched openings, cradling, but seemingly not touching, the narrow east and west ends of sheer mirrored glass with creases and wedges where the two wall types seem to only nearly meet.

Dr. Jackson's Office   A117
Metromover: Financial District

190 SE 12th Terrace
1905
Moved to current site: 1917

This Neoclassical wood-frame building, with barrel-tiled roof, sits like Willy Loman's house on the set of *Death of a Salesman*, besieged by surrounding modernity and postmodernity. The building originally stood at Flagler Street and NE Second Avenue in Downtown Miami and was moved to this location in 1917. Originally the office of Dr. James Jackson, Miami's pioneer physician and namesake of Jackson Memorial Hospital, the building now houses the offices of the Dade Heritage Trust. The trust works to preserve the architectural, cultural, and environmental heritage of Greater Miami through restoring landmarks, working with the media and community leaders, publishing books and magazines, and presenting tours and historic programs such as its Dade Heritage Days signature month-long event each spring, as well as programs for schools.

A117

South Brickell

While upper Brickell Avenue's mansions were replaced by office buildings beginning in the 1950s, lower Brickell has maintained a distinctly residential character. Some of the mansions in this area live on as clubhouses for the condominiums that have grown around them.

The Babylon   A118
Metromover: Financial District

240 SE 14th Street
Arquitectonica, 1982

Although its folded ziggurat façade breathes the spirit of Postmodern styling, the Babylon is an urbane study in modern apartment design. Seemingly derived from French architect Henri Sauvage's experimental stepped buildings of the early twentieth century, the building's profile provides continuous open-to-the-sky balconies at almost every floor. As conceived by Sauvage, the terraces are sun-filled and healthful, a critique of the stacked

A118

balconies of most multifamily dwellings. Wedge-shaped in relationship to its pie-shaped lot, the building's mass is broken in the center by a courtyard, allowing each apartment a frontal façade as well as generous side views. The Babylon's nearly freestanding frontal stucco walls, brightly colored, pierced by taut rectangular windows, and connected by long runs of horizontal pipe railing, are decidedly modern. The main façade's keystone base conceals a level of underground parking, exposed on the other three sides through supporting pilotis. The Babylon occupies a place in Arquitectonica's first generation of innovative residential buildings. Unlike the Imperial, Palace, and Atlantis, however, the Babylon is low-scaled, with only 15 apartments of varying sizes. It has been dwarfed and rendered anachronistic, much like Dr. Jackson's office two blocks away, by the enormous buildings that now tower around it.

Palace, Villa Regina, and Imperial   A119

Metromover: Financial District

Palace
1541 Brickell Avenue
Arquitectonica, 1981

Villa Regina
1581 Brickell Avenue
William Dorsky Associates, 1982

A119

Imperial
1627 Brickell Avenue
Arquitectonica, 1983

These three buildings, built within four years, create a characteristically Miami ensemble. The 42-story Palace and 31-story Imperial, both designed by Arquitectonica, established (as the firm's name would suggest) an architectonic playground of form and color. The Palace was the first of the firm's characteristic thin-slab towers, and when finished was the tallest condominium in Miami. Organizationally, it comprised three elevator cores with only two apartments per elevator on each floor, allowing floor-through apartments. Raised on a podium that concealed parking beneath and that served as an entry court to the monumental porte cochere (the allée of royal palms is the remnant of an earlier mansion, Palm Court), the tower was a graphic collage of curtain wall, concrete, and masonry. Its main slab was a concrete supergrid framing recessed balconies, intersected with a smaller stepped structure painted a contrasting red. Townhouses in the manner of Viennese architect Adolf Loos front the parking garage on the water's edge, a first at the time and now commonly required. An organic roofline defines the rooftop penthouse, while geometric figures punctuate the building's long walls. The porte cochere literally slices through the building mass.

To the south, the Imperial similarly rises from a podium. Here the main graphic device is the polarity between the continuous white masonry balconies of the south side and the floating red masonry wall of the north side.

Between the two Arquitectonica structures is Villa Regina, designed by Cleveland architect William Dorsky, also the architect of the Plaza Venetia on North Bayshore Drive. Overshadowed by its more graphically powerful neighbors, Villa Regina was transformed in 1984 by Israeli artist Yaacov Agam into one of the artist's "fractured rainbows." Requiring three thousand gallons of paint and contemporary with the paint gymnastics that were transforming Miami Beach's Art Deco hotels, the surface treatment fails to lift the building to the level of its neighbors to either side. Together, however, the three provide a succinct snapshot of Miami's roaring 1980s.

A120

Atlantis   A120

2025 Brickell Avenue
Arquitectonica, 1982

Indelibly fused into popular memory by virtue of its appearance in the opening credits of the 1980s television series *Miami Vice*, the Atlantis's playful imagery blended the lighthearted approach of Miami Beach's Modernism at midcentury with the ornamental shorthand of Postmodernism to the scale and dimension of a new generation of high-rise construction. A central element of its monumentality was the brash use of form and color, once legible at great distances across the skyline. Here, at least from the high-speed viewing platform of I-95, such brashness is transformed into what critic Paul Goldberger has called a "noble act of public benefit."

A signature element is the building's thinness and length, resulting from an organizational plan that included multiple elevator cores; most of its 96 apartments thus open to both north and south exposures. The building's most famous and photogenic feature was the sky-court, a multistory void cut through the building and populated with representative symbols of leisure and whimsy: a whirlpool, a palm tree, and a red spiral stair framed by a wavy yellow wall. The 20-story structure was clothed on one side by reflective glass curtain wall, and on the other by a supergrid of blue masonry that screens the south-facing terraces. Atlantis was built on the site of the Mitchell-Bingham Residence. (Mary Tiffany Bingham was the sister of Louis Tiffany.) That original Shingle style house was maintained at the base of the tower as a clubhouse for the building.

Santa Maria

A121

Metromover: Financial District

1643 Brickell Avenue
Revuelta Vega Leon, 1997

Although it sits parallel to the street and the shoreline of the bay, flouting the number-one rule of waterfront tower siting, Santa Maria makes up for it with its simple vocabulary of white cladding and lightly tinted green glass wrapping the memorable tower form comprised of multiple cylinders in a soaring tripartite arrangement. The design concept of the pristine white cylinder was initiated at the earlier, nearby Bristol Tower by Fullerton Diaz Revuelta, and carried to its full 51-story realization at Santa Maria. Of note is the design of the balconies, which allows for unimpeded views from apartments, but with a small lip parapet to add thickness and provide solidity to the tower surfaces. Crowning the tower is the fitness center, enclosed in double-height glass.

A121

The name "Santa Maria" comes from the name of the mansion originally built on the property and that now serves as a clubhouse.

Brickell Place

A122

1865–1925 Brickell Avenue
Fraga & Associates with Melvin Grossman, 1975

The largest residential compound on Brickell Avenue, Brickell Place is a campus of four towers and bayfront townhouses built over and around the extensive platforms of low-rise parking decks. The development formula, amalgamating high-rise housing (for middle-class retirees, mainly), substantial recreational amenities and largess, was pioneered by Grossman a decade earlier in the palisades along Collins Avenue and West Avenue in Miami Beach. Here, the complex is set back behind a private fronting road, and the towers are staggered to preserve their views. They are grouped to share two circular porte cocheres with integrated planting islands. Along Biscayne Bay, townhouses create a waterfront edge to the garage decks (an improvement on the typical South Florida waterfront development of the period), stepping from the pool and tennis court level to a generous baywalk and marina.

Brickell Townhouse

A123

2451 Brickell Avenue
Steward & Skinner Associates, 1961

This first generation of Brickell high-rise apartment buildings included this 21-story specimen, built of steel and precast-concrete wall panels and financed by the FHA. When completed, the Y-shaped tower occupied only 7 percent of its 9-acre site, a necessary concession to zoning restrictions in the Brickell estates district that prescribed a maximum building height of thirteen stories. Following a common practice, lower lot coverage was used to make up for taller height. The surroundings, of course, have since been built up to far greater heights and densities. Unfortunately, the building's low parking decks do much to divorce it from the street.

One International Place (Brickell Station) A124
Metrorail/Metromover: Brickell

829 SW 1st Avenue
Hatcher, Zeigler, Gunn & Associates, 1985

The first major commercial project built in coordination with the arrival of the Metrorail in the Brickell area, the 30-story Brickell Station building eschewed both Downtown and the Brickell banking corridor and is located facing the Metrorail, a block north of the Brickell Avenue Station. The mixed-use project was originally planned with 26 floors of offices and 6 floors of condominiums, in addition to retail shops, a health club, café, and gourmet restaurant. It stood solitary until development of the Miami River and West Brickell corridors began to catch up. The tower is octagonal in plan, with handsome reflective green glass façades. In a distant echo of Art Deco, the banks of curtain wall on the angled façades rise to a reverse stair-step, crystalline, sculptural effect. The glazing of the tower's two street façades comes down to street level, providing camouflage for the opaque parking pedestal. The main entry is at the tower's southwest corner, facing the combined Brickell Metrorail and Metromover stations.

A125

Joe Moretti Apartments A125
Metrorail/Metromover: Brickell

201–219 SW 10 Street
1948

Joe Moretti Apartments, managed by the Miami-Dade Housing Agency, is one of the few postwar public housing projects organized according to Garden City planning principles. This 96-unit complex is planned as a miniature village of modest garden apartments. A central avenue bisects the assemblage longitudinally, and multiple streets run laterally. The buildings are simple square blocks, 2 stories tall, with individual stoops for the ground-floor units and open staircases to those on the second floor. The styling, like the building type, tends to the prewar, with modernized pilasters and cornice treatments, and with casement windows below projecting eyebrows. In their rigorous planning repetition and unalloyed modern aesthetic, these buildings are reminiscent of early twentieth-century Modernist housing proposals. Fanciful triangular cutouts in the parapet walls add levity.

Fire Station No. 4 A126
Metrorail/Metromover: Brickell

1000 South Miami Avenue
H. H. Mundy, 1923

Fire Station No. 4 is notable for its fine 1920s Mediterranean Revival architecture and, as a restaurant and bar in the growing Brickell area, for demonstrating the viability of adaptive use of designated buildings.

Mary Brickell Village

A127

Metrorail/Metromover: Brickell

900 South Miami Avenue
Wolfberg Alvarez & Partners, 2003

Spanning two blocks from SW First Avenue, across Miami Avenue, to Brickell
Plaza, the 2-story Mary Brickell Village brings a semblance of humanity and
pedestrian scale to the anonymous canyons of the Brickell corridor. Sited
across from the Brickell Metrorail station and planned to include a supermarket and a residential tower, it has the potential of being more than just
another festival marketplace.

First Miami High School

A128

Metrorail/Metromover: Brickell

140 SW 11th Street
1905
Rehabilitation: R. J. Heisenbottle Architects with William Medellin, 2009

The building currently in Southside Park at SW Eleventh Street and SW First
Avenue is an addition to the first Downtown Miami school building located
on NE First Avenue near Third Street. It was added in 1905 and dedicated to
the education of high school students, the first in Miami-Dade County. By
1911, the small structure was overwhelmed by the demand, and the building was moved south of the Miami River, where it served as Southside
Elementary until 1914. From 1914 until its rediscovery by Miami historian
Thelma Peters in 1983, the role of the building in Miami's educational history
was forgotten. In 2003, the bungalow structure was moved to its present
site in a public park to escape the demolition that would have awaited it
had it been left in private hands. In March 2009, the rehabilitated building
was reopened as a community center.

Jose Marti Building (Edificio Marti)

A129

Metrorail/Metromover: Brickell

801 SW 3rd Avenue
Tripp and Skrip, 1964

A129

Built in the wake of the substantial Cuban influx into Miami to house small
offices for Spanish-speaking and pan-American businessmen, Edificio Marti
was also the first building to explicitly face the North-South Expressway
(now I-95), under construction at the same time. Its blank west wall, facing
the highway viaduct and entrance ramps, is transformed into an urban canvas by Coconut Grove artist Fran Williams's ceramic mural of the Cuban flag.
The flag faces west along SW Eighth Street, the Tamiami Trail, which would
soon be known as Calle Ocho—the centerline of Miami's Cuban diaspora.
The Jose Marti Building's upper floors cantilever over its first floor, creating
a covered walkway on the ground floor. Of note, the 3-story building was
erected almost entirely from prefabricated components.

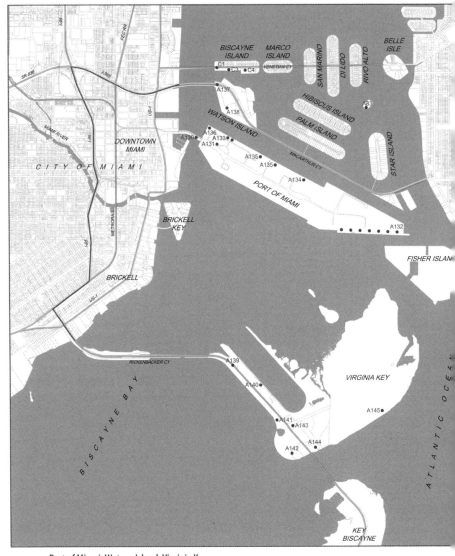

Port of Miami, Watson Island, Virginia Key

Dante B. Fascell Port of Miami-Dade

Miami's Dodge Island port and ocean terminal complex on Dodge and Lummus islands, initiated in 1959, replaced the city's first port along Biscayne Boulevard. Established in 1900 by the Peninsular and Occidental (P&O) Steamship Company, this port and its operations eventually conflicted with real-estate development concerns along Miami's valuable bayfront. While never an important heavy cargo port (like Port Everglades in Fort Lauderdale), it quickly established itself as a significant clean-cargo transshipment port and, more importantly, the "Cruise Capital of the World."

Prominently located on two connected artificial islands (Dodge and Lummus) in the center of Biscayne Bay, the linear port is a highly visible center for commerce and travel. Though cruise ships dock along both the port's north and south sides, those facing the MacArthur Causeway and the islands beyond provide one of the city's most unforgettable cinematic backdrops. Cargo ships dock mainly on the south side, where twelve cranes provide a skyline that complements the towers of Miami Beach and Downtown Miami.

Dodge Island Port Bridge Illumination   A130

Metromover: Freedom Tower

Brilliant Lighting Design, 1997
Bridge completed 1993; lighting completed 1997

The design for illuminating the Dodge Island causeway to the Port of Miami called for accenting the 1,200-foot-long Port Bridge's tall, chamfered piers. After extensive trials, sixty floodlights and metal halide lamps were trained on the narrow ends of the piers, an effect calculated to dramatize their elegant radiused corners and flared tops. The strong blue light is especially evocative when seen from the MacArthur Causeway, creating a luminous middle ground to Miami's skyline, a mirror of Rockne Krebs's Miami Line on the Metrorail bridge across the Miami River (**A96**).

Port Headquarters Building   A131
(World Trade Center Miami)

1001, 1007, and 1015 North America Way, 1967
Addition: Post, Buckley, Schuh and Jernigan, 1982

The Port of Miami Headquarters complex is located near the east abutment of the port bridge, and clearly conveys the two phases of its construction. In the first phase, two low wings were built around a central landscaped courtyard. The buildings housed administration offices, steamship agents, shipping lines, foreign consulates, and offices like U.S. Customs. The 2-story buildings had walls of oolitic stone, glass, and aluminum curtain wall (with blue spandrels) and perforated concrete block. The walls are set in between projecting roof and floor slabs; in an interesting detail, the ground-floor slab is raised up off the ground, creating the impression that the building floats. Projecting sunscreens protect the south-facing windows. The buildings

A131

are connected by a wonderful serpentine covered walkway on steel pipe columns.

In the second phase, a new administration tower was built over the center courtyard. Its 2-story mass rendered in raw concrete is held aloft on 2-story high pilotis; only the center core comes down to the ground. The addition floats over the complex and patio like the bridge of a ship, a virtual cockpit commanding views of the port stretching to the east.

A132

Port Gantry Cranes   A132

The port of Miami's twelve gantry container–handling cranes are a part of the urban landscape of Miami, Miami Beach, and Biscayne Bay. Operating on six 1,000-foot wharves, the cranes include three diesel-powered shuttle booms (early 1980s), three luffing/high-profile cranes (late 1980s), four ZPMC-types (1985, the first in the United States), and two super post-panamax cranes (2005), among the largest cranes in operation in the world.

A133

Passenger Terminals   A133
John Andrews, 1968

In response to early criticism that the port complex design seemed too prosaic, the development of the passenger terminals was opened to a limited competition, with the intention that they be developed separately as a world-class architectural attraction. The final design, by John Andrews, was a brilliant response to the structure's visibility, as well as a radical reinvention of the port terminal type. In particular, Andrews reorganized ship embarkation and disembarkation, creating a monumental transportation machine for the burgeoning age of cruise ship travel.

Andrews's design employed two prototype modules that were repeated along the port's 2,500-foot-long wharf. The first module was the terminal, a raised, air-conditioned lobby space connecting the street with telescoping walkways into the ship. These were trapezoidal in plan, and their corners were marked by cylindrical towers. The second module comprised large open hangars running parallel to the pier, where luggage was unloaded, sorted, and inspected. These hangars were covered by airfoil roofs formed of concrete double-tees. Elevated gangways from the terminals allowed passengers to connect into this area. The system, inspired by air-terminal design, split the disembarkation of passengers from the offloading of their luggage and other cargo, allowing both to occur simultaneously.

The serial repetition of the monumental terminal and hangar forms, punctuated by numerous switchback stairs and telescoping walkways, were an expression of both function and movement, as well as the kind of Brutalist "New Monumentality" then in vogue for public infrastructure.

Cruise Terminals B and C (Carnival Terminals)   A134
Post, Buckley, Schuh and Jernigan, 1992
Renovation and expansion: Bermello Ajamil & Partners, 1995

When completed in the 1990s, these new terminals for Carnival Cruise Lines extended the port's original alignment of cruise ship terminals farther to the east, to an area formerly occupied by storage sheds. The calibration of gangway access points, which sail over existing adjacent sheds to connect into the ships at suitable intervals, makes apparent the increased size of contemporary ships (when compared to the spacing of gangways in the earlier Andrews terminals).

Cruise Terminals D and E   A135

BEA, 2007

The port's two most recent additions were designed to accommodate the newest megavessels, carrying up to 5,000 passengers each. Their wing-like roof structures, made of steel trusses carried on tensile cables from tall masts, seem a contemporary interpretation of Andrews's nearby airfoils, which similarly opened toward the north. Here, however, the hangars are sheathed in glass. The result is an airy structure that dematerializes at night.

In Terminal D, Shan Shan Sheng's *Ocean Waves I and II* (2007) is a two-part series of suspended glass sculptures conceived to echo the ocean waves. In Terminal E is Dixie Friend Gay's *Ephemeral Everglades* (2007), an homage to the flora and fauna of Florida's "river of grass" comprising original paintings interspersed with digitally printed murals and reliefs of tropical flowers.

Cruise Terminals F and G   A136
(Royal Caribbean Terminals)

John Andrews, 1968
Redevelopment: BEA, 1999

The western end of Andrews's original terminal complex was renovated in 1999, adapting the existing structure to the requirements of the latest generation of cruise terminal facility. The adaptation reveals little of the original facility to the water; new walls of glass line the pier, and tentlike Teflon-coated membranes create a new roof for the terminal. The structure is illuminated at night, making a virtual lantern toward the bay. However, the terminal is remarkable on the inside for its airy spaces and creative reuse of the original building. New mobile gangways systems and conveyor belts move and sort luggage for quick delivery to cabins. Hot air is directed up-ward through the tents, a passive cooling strategy. The lobby wall features Lydia Rubio's *All Night Long, We Heard Birds Passing*.

MacArthur Causeway Bridge Illumination   A137
(Magenta Mood over Miami)

Metromover: Eleventh Street

Brilliant Lighting Design, ca. 1999

With shorter spans, more columns, and a less elegant column pro-file ("Hammer Tee Piers," in highway parlance), the illumination of the MacArthur Causeway's 1,700-foot-long Downtown bridge followed a con-trastingly more simple formula than found on the Dodge Island Port Bridge. Metal halide and fluorescent lighting provides a gentle magenta glow from below, while lamps mounted on the bridge parapets provide glittery accents.

A138

Miami Children's Museum   A138

980 MacArthur Causeway
Arquitectonica, 2003

"Play, learn, imagine, create!" proclaims the museum's Web site, and the four processes begin before one enters the front door that faces Government Cut and the Port of Miami cruise ship docks. In concept, the Miami Children's Museum (MCM) building recalls the four elements: earth, air, water, and fire. In execution, the exterior shell of the structure is a combination of cones, pyramids, and planes rising to a wavy parapet, inviting the visitor to try to imagine what might be inside. The structure's gymnastics, which derive partly from its tilt-up construction method, animate this very visible site. The practicalities of the site require the visitor to circumnavigate the building before entering it, and the learning begins with that action.

Virginia Key

Virginia Key (along with Key Biscayne and Miami Beach) is part of the chain of barrier islands separating Biscayne Bay from the Atlantic Ocean. The Norris Cut passage between Virginia Key and Fisher Island to the north was created by a nineteenth-century hurricane; Bear Cut between Virginia Key and Key Biscayne to the south and east appears on the earliest European maps.

A139

Rickenbacker Causeway   A139

William Lyman Phillips, 1947

The 4-mile Rickenbacker Causeway, including the mainland approach and areas for fishing, bathing, and boat launching along its length, was designed by William Lyman Phillips, Miami-Dade County's preeminent landscape architect of the 1930s and 1940s, responsible for the design of many New Deal facilities throughout Greater Miami.

Ralph Middleton Munroe Miami   A140
Marine Stadium

3501 Rickenbacker Causeway
Pancoast, Ferendino, Grafton, Skeels and Burnham, 1963

With its dramatically cantilevered, folded-plate concrete roof, Miami Marine Stadium demonstrates the incipient prowess of concrete construction in elaborating a civic tropical architecture. The stadium compares with a generation of concrete sports facilities designed in Europe and South America, although this facility was the first of its kind when completed. (Its gravity-defying gesture of thin, cantilevered concrete roofs was at one time matched in Weed Russell Johnson's now-defunct National Airlines Nose Hangar Building [1957] at Miami International Airport.) The site design and program are part of the necklace of public amenities developed along the Rickenbacker Causeway. It included more than 240 acres, forging in the landscape the 5,300-foot-long aquatic basin for boat races and water-skiing competitions. The simple palette of exposed concrete, block, and

A140

stucco makes for an elegant sculptural object. Its cantilever design placed
the roof's supporting posts well to the rear of the stands, so unobstructed
views are available from most seats. The location on Virginia Key provides
a memorable location for waterborne events with Biscayne Bay and the
Miami skyline serving as backdrop. A concerted local preservation effort has
resulted in the inclusion of the stadium on the National Trust for Historic
Preservation's 11 Most Endangered Historic Places.

Miami Seaquarium   A141
4400 Rickenbacker Causeway
Steward & Skinner Associates, 1954
Geodesic Dome: Charles McKirahan and Buckminster Fuller, 1960

A141

Replacing Miami's first aquarium in Miami Beach, the Miami Seaquarium
was one of a network of attractions constructed to exploit tourists' thirst for
exotic flora and fauna in this outpost of "subtropical America." It was also
a major thematic attraction, designed to bolster tourism in Miami and to
increase toll revenue on the Rickenbacker Causeway (A139). The 55-acre attraction occupies a spectacular location on the southwest tip of Virginia Key,
providing views of Biscayne Bay and Downtown Miami.

The construction of more advanced aquatic theme parks in the intervening years, such as Sea World near Orlando, makes the Seaquarium's 1950s
vintage plant seem quaint today. However, when completed it was one of
only three large-tank oceanariums in the United States, and a technological feat of marine architecture and showmanship. State-of-the-art metal
tanks, glass, paraplastics, rubber, and paint made it possible for the visitor
to plumb ocean depths. The axial site design is based on World's Fair models

familiar to the architects, who had designed Florida's exposition exhibits before World War II. Later additions like the geodesic Golden Dome over the sea lion show arena reinforce the appearance of a futuristic World's Fair on the sandy shore of Biscayne Bay. Other futuristic additions, like a monorail that circled the site, have since been removed.

Along with the Miami Marine Stadium (**A140**) across the causeway, the Seaquarium, with its Golden Dome, makes Virginia Key home to a very small, yet outstanding, collection of institutional midcentury Modern architecture.

University of Miami Rosenstiel School   A142
and National Oceanographic & Atmospheric
Administration (NOAA) Building
Rosenstiel School of Marine and Atmospheric Science
4600 Rickenbacker Causeway

Alexandrine duPont Collier Building
Marion Manley, 1952

Gilbert Hovey Grosvenor Building
Steward & Skinner Associates, 1957

Doherty Marine Science Center and Commons
Pancoast, Ferendino, Grafton, 1966

Science Administration Building
Abramovitz/Kingsland, 1985

The southeast end of Virginia Key comprises a 16-acre oceanographic research and educational complex straddling both sides of the Rickenbacker Causeway and opening to Bear Cut. Taken together with the Seaquarium and Marine Stadium, it represents an impressive infrastructure of marine and aquatic facilities tied to the causeway park system.

The University of Miami's Rosenstiel School of Marine and Atmospheric Science occupies the west side of the causeway. The facility is dedicated to the study of oceans and the atmosphere where the tropical and temperate zones meet. Founded in 1943, the school was established on its 6½–acre Virginia Key campus in the early 1950s.

The modest 2-story Collier Building by architect Marion Manley is a survivor of the school's early development. Originally two of these small laboratories on stilts lined Bear Cut. Manley's work here is not far from her better-known VA housing structures at the university's Coral Gables campus. To the west is Ferendino Grafton Spillis Candela's large Doherty Marine Science Center. Originally built for NOAA, its waterfront façade includes the type of concrete egg-crate window wall the firm popularized in the 1960s, and is similar in spirit to the firm's contemporary work for Miami-Dade College. Here, the egg crate is broken by a projecting concrete stair. On the causeway side is the campus's largest facility, the Science Administration Building. This low-slung and vaguely nautical structure, with a south-facing bay window, comprises two stories of laboratories, library, and administration spaces raised over parking. It opens broadly through recessed walls of dark glass to a continuous arcade that surrounds the building. Its white walls contrast with the red-painted guardrails to graphic effect.

NOAA/Atlantic Oceanographic and Meteorological Laboratory (AOML)   A143

4301 Rickenbacker Causeway
Ferendino Grafton Spillis Candela, 1972

NOAA/National Marine Fisheries Service Southeast Fisheries Science Center   A144

75 Virginia Beach Drive
Pancoast Ferendino Grafton Skeels Burnham, 1964

On the east side of the causeway are the facilities of NOAA, including the
Atlantic Oceanographic and Meteorological Laboratory (AOML) and the
headquarters building for the organization's Fisheries Service. The Fisheries
building is a functional L-shaped block that opens a court to the beach. Its
wall treatment notably varies, with textured solid end walls facing southwest, screenblock facing east, and ribbon windows along its long façades.
NOAA's Atlantic Oceanographic & Meteorological Laboratory Building, just
to the north, is far more sophisticated. Its vaguely Corbusian vocabulary,
probably influenced by the Convent of La Tourette (1957–60), has a central
laboratory block flanked with detached office wings that are lifted high
above the ground on pilotis. The office wings have a fine-grained grid of
concrete window frames with deeply recessed glass. Ramps and stairs penetrate into the building from the northeast. On the northwest, the building
is elevated above a small pond.

A144

Virginia Key Beach Park   A145

4020 Virginia Beach Drive, at 3861 Rickenbacker Causeway
1945

Historic Virginia Key Park first opened in August 1945 as a beach for African
Americans after a civil rights protest at another county beach. Prior to the
completion of the Rickenbacker Causeway in 1947, the only way to reach
Virginia Key was by boat. Still, African Americans living in Overtown and
Liberty City found their way to Virginia Key since it was, after all, the only
ocean beach legally available to them. After the beaches of Miami-Dade
County were integrated, Virginia Key fell into disuse and finally was closed
by the City of Miami in 1982.

In 1999, an interracial group of citizens, joining together in response to
insensitive development proposals for Virginia Key, began the long process
of seeking its designation as a historical resource and its restoration for contemporary use.

In 2002, the original Virginia Key Beach site was placed on the National
Register of Historic Places. The park was reopened in February 2008 to
mark an important place and time in Miami's complicated history of race
relations.

The concession-stand structure at the center of the park seems to have
drawn upon the skills acquired during World War II in the use of prefabricated concrete structures. In 2009, the original carousel, restored, reopened
for business.

City of Miami:
Southwest and Coconut Grove

This section encompasses the vast area south of the Dolphin Expressway and west of I-95 almost to the orbital Palmetto Expressway. It comprises the city's oldest settlement, Coconut Grove, which predates the creation of Miami. It also includes dense residential neighborhoods like East and West Little Havana and part of Overtown, close to Downtown. The rest is composed of single-family neighborhoods such as Shenandoah, the Roads, Silver Bluff, and Flagami. The area includes urban centers as well as important commercial corridors like Coral Way and Calle Ocho (SW Eighth Street), Flagler Street, and Twenty-seventh Avenue.

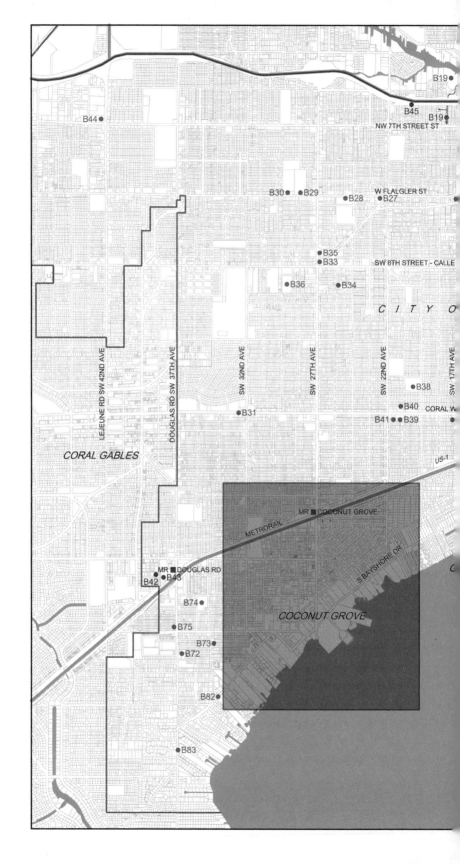

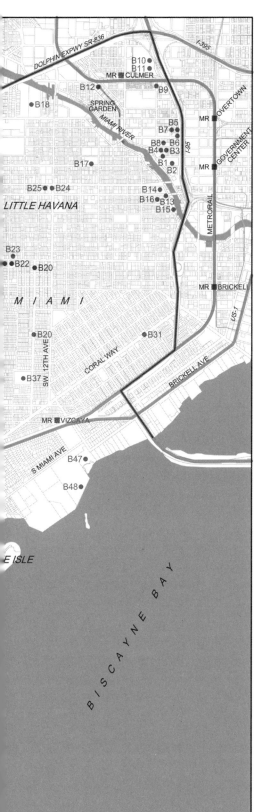

B. City of Miami:
Southwest and
Coconut Grove

Lummus Park

Named after J. E. Lummus, the City of Miami's second mayor, the Lummus Park area was platted in 1909, following the creation of Lummus Park that same year. The park was Miami's first, and the catalyst for the development of the surrounding area into a desirable residential neighborhood.

Stretching two blocks eastward from the river to the ramps of I-95, the park became an open-air museum of Miami history when the Fort Dallas Barracks (B2) and the Wagner Homestead (B1) were moved here. Since 2005, much of the area has been included in the Lummus Park Historic District.

B1

Wagner Homestead   B1

Lummus Park, approx. 404 NW 3rd Street
1855–88
Relocated: 1979
Exterior renovation: R. J. Heisenbottle Architects, 2000

The Wagner Homestead is probably the oldest home still intact, if not in place, in Miami. Originally built on Wagner Creek, upriver to the northwest, the building was relocated to allow for the construction of Metrorail and moved here by the Dade Heritage Trust in 1979, utilizing Community Development Block Grant funds. The oldest parts of the structure are made of hand-hewn wood; milled lumber was used for later additions and repairs. The Third Seminole War was raging when William Wagner erected this building. While North American history books typically picture pioneers and homesteaders on the Great Plains of the West, southeast Florida was also a nineteenth-century frontier and battleground, and William Wagner was one of the earliest and most successful settlers.

B2

Fort Dallas Barracks   B2

Lummus Park, approximately 404 NW 3rd Street
ca. 1844
Disassembled, relocated, and reconstructed: 1925
Exterior renovation: R. J. Heisenbottle Architects, 2000

Even older than the Wagner Homestead (B1), Fort Dallas Barracks was constructed from bearing walls of oolitic rock. Formerly located near SE First Avenue and the Miami River, the building was moved to its current location piece by piece in 1925, when the local chapter of the Daughters of the American Revolution undertook what was, perhaps, the first historic preservation action in Miami history. First a slave quarters built by William English in 1849 and then a barracks for the U.S. Army soldiers fighting in the Third Seminole War, 1855–58, the barracks is one of Miami's three relics of a dark and bloody time when Florida's history was riven by the clash of red, black, and white.

Today, this building is a peaceful reminder of Osceola's fighting words at the beginning of the Second War: "Am I a Negro, a slave? My skin is dark, but not black! I am an Indian, a Seminole. The white man shall not make me black. I will make the white man red with blood, and then blacken him in the sun and rain, where the wolf shall gnaw his bones and the buzzard shall live on his flesh" (Sprague, *The Origin, Progress, and Conclusion of the Florida War*).

Temple Court Apartments   B3

431–439 NW 3rd Street
Edward A. Nolen, 1918
Rehabilitation: R. J. Heisenbottle Architects, 2002

B3

The Temple Court Apartments, an example of residential architecture in Miami's first decades, illustrates the Masonry Vernacular style. This style was used extensively in the early twentieth century, predating the better-known and more flamboyant Mediterranean Revival; while most Masonry Vernacular buildings constructed in Downtown Miami are long gone, a number survive in the Lummus Park Historic District.

The west or left wing of this structure is the older part, built around 1914; the east, or right, four-story wing was added around 1918. Both structures are masonry boxes with concrete floor slabs. The many porches, probably used for sleeping, are a characteristic response to Miami's hot, humid climate. In 2003, the apartments were rehabilitated to serve as subsidized housing for the elderly.

Scottish Rite Temple   B4

471 NW 3rd Street
Kiehnel and Elliott, 1922

Well before the 1925 Exposition Internationale des Arts Decoratifs in Paris that gave Art Deco its contemporary name, and even before *National Geographic* magazine enthralled the world with an account of Tutankhamen's tomb in 1923, Scottish Rite Masonry laid the cornerstone for this building in October 1922. Employing abstracted and stylized decorative elements from Egyptian and European history, and a simplified form of Neoclassicism, Kiehnel and Elliott's design was an early harbinger of Modernism in Miami. The two-headed eagles on the entablature above the façade's four Doric columns are symbols of the Scottish Rite, and the number is that of this lodge. The pyramidal roof, based loosely on the mausoleum of Halicarnassus, was a popular motif for civic temples, and was also used to crown the Dade County Courthouse (A53).

B4

B5

Camillus Health Concern Clinic and Administrative Facility   B5

336 NW 5th Street
Rodriguez Khuly Quiroga, 1997

Evidence of urban healing along the scarred edges of I-95 are multiplying north of Downtown, where the highway's construction divided neighborhoods and generated fields of emptiness. A small, thoughtful campus of facilities for Miami-based Camillus House, anchored by a clinic and administrative facility, is an example. Born out of the needs of Cuban refugees in 1960 and founded by the Little Brothers of the Good Shepherd, Camillus House—named for St. Camillus, patron saint of the sick and poor—is a humanitarian services organization that provides care for the destitute. The new clinic and administrative facility give a civic and architectural face to the organization's activities for the homeless in Miami.

The Camillus facility faces both NW Fifth Street and I-95. From either vantage, the focal point is a corner tower wrapped in glass, aluminum, and precast concrete walls and containing the main stair and elevator core. The gesture is an efficient one: the core provides a recognizable focus to the highway, but it also functions as a sound attenuation gesture. Behind is the 3-story clinic and administration structure whose straightforward façade features Modern Classical styling, including a double-story Modernist Monumental order of window openings connecting the first and second floors (the Camillus Health Concern Clinic). Above, the smaller square windows identify the administrative offices. The complex is entered through the recessed slot between the tower and clinic block, where a ground-floor plaza opens to the street.

Camillus Somerville Apartments   B6

471 NW 3rd Street
Rodriguez and Quiroga Architects, 2000

As part of the Camillus House complex, Somerville Apartments comprise 48 units of permanent supportive housing for formerly homeless women with children, some in low-rise townhouses and others in a 7-story block on the property's north side. The low- and mid-rise structures are organized around a patio space. The taller building's top floor features a community room and terrace, the better to exploit breezes and Downtown views. The enclosed patio is screened from the street by a barrel-vaulted portal. At its center is a baked enamel metal mural celebrating Brothers to the Rescue, the Miami-based humanitarian organization whose purpose is to assist and rescue *balseros*, refugees attempting to flee Cuba by raft.

YWCA Headquarters of Greater Miami-Dade   B7

351 NW 5th Street
Bermello Ajamil & Partners, 1993

This playful structure, plainly visible from I-95, houses the Greater Miami YWCA headquarters and day-care center. The building includes office space and five day-care classrooms for preschool children, with each element of the design articulated in separate volumes and bright colors.

400 block of NW 4th Street   B8

Miami River Park Apartments	G. P. Michner House
445 NW 4th Street	436 NW 4th Street
Albaisa Architects, 2001	1914
Orlando Apartments	Burr Apartments
458 NW 4th Street	342 NW 4th Avenue
1921	1924
T. P. Way House	Frank J. Pepper House
450 NW 4th Street	326 NW 4th Avenue
1914	1922
E. S. Lyne House	
444 NW 4th Street	
1918	

The south side of the 400 block of NW Fourth Street included in the Lummus Park Historic District comprises a fine collection of early wood-frame houses. Soon after it was announced that a high-rise, affordable housing project would be built on the north side of the block, preservationists mobilized to assure that the new construction would complement the existing group. As the affordable housing was federally funded, mandatory appropriateness reviews gave the local preservation community sufficient leverage to achieve this goal.

The scrutiny resulted in a reasonably good neighbor to the historic buildings. While the tower and parking garage of the Miami River Park Apartments dwarf the historic buildings, the inclusion of small gabled-roofed "houses" projecting from the set-back façade of the parking garage effectively mitigates the disparity. The size and rhythm of the projecting units send a strong signal of respect from the high-rise to its smaller-scaled neighbors.

Southwest Overtown

The Southwest quadrant of Miami's Overtown neighborhood (described in more detail in section A) includes some important historic civic landmarks. The area is cut off from the rest of Overtown by the Midtown Expressway Interchange (A86).

Black Police Precinct and Courthouse   B9
Metrorail: Culmer Station

1009 NW 5th Avenue
Walter DeGarmo, 1950
Addition: 1957
Renovation: City of Miami Capital Improvements, 2008

When it was built, this building was known as the Colored Police Precinct Station; the name was later changed to the Negro Precinct Station. Today it is known as the Black Police Precinct and Courthouse. The building fell into disuse when the African American officers and court personnel stationed here were integrated into the City of Miami's law-enforcement systems, starting in 1963. Miami's 1896 charter called for a separate "Colored Town." Civic facilities like the Black Police Precinct and Courthouse reflected the complex interplay between progress and bias in the segregated city. Having a black police force and courthouse was progress; denying them a role in policing the entire city was segregation. So controversial was the role of these black patrolmen that the training of the first five was carried out in secrecy.

The design of the building demonstrates how a skilled architect like DeGarmo could depart from the historicist styles that had made him famous in Coral Gables and Miami Beach and create a functional yet noble Modernist structure. In its simplicity, the Black Police Precinct and Courthouse resembles the Dorsey Memorial Library (C41) by Paist and Steward.

B10

Booker T. Washington High School   B10
(Booker T. Washington Middle School)
Metrorail: Culmer Station

1200 NW 6th Avenue
Robert Bradford Browne Architects in a joint venture with Steward & Skinner Associates, 1966
Addition: MC Harry & Associates, 2001

It is hard to exaggerate the significance of this site to Miami's African American community. Here the original Booker T. Washington High School was built in 1927. "Booker T." was the first "colored" high school with a twelfth grade in South Florida. The original building was demolished in the 1960s during conversion to a middle school. Robert Bradford's Browne's 1966 building is uncharacteristically traditional for this Modernist architect, likely a reaction to the site's importance.

In the 1990s, Miami's African American community advocated for the restoration of "Booker T." as a high school, and, in 2000, the process of conversion from middle to high school began. The renovated 1966 buildings are closest to the Midtown Expressway Interchange (A86), on the east side of the site, and the historic Chapman House (B11) is on the northeast side of the site. The entryway to the original 1927 Booker T. Washington High School is preserved in the center of the campus.

B11

Dr. William A. Chapman House   B11
Metrorail: Culmer Station

526 NW 13th Street
ca. 1923

This was the home of Dr. William Chapman, a prominent black physician. Chapman had an office and pharmacy at 219 NW Eighth Street and could, at that time, easily walk between home and work. Today, the expressways have divided much of Overtown from this site, making the trip to central Overtown a roundabout journey. Before desegregation, Overtown encompassed all socioeconomic strata; this Masonry Vernacular house is a reminder of the affluence that existed here. Occupied by Chapman family members until at least 1983, this home operates today as an educational center.

Spring Garden

Designated as a local historic district in 1997, Spring Garden lies generally between NW Eleventh Street and the Miami River and from the Seybold Canal to NW Twelfth Avenue. Picturesque access is available by way of the NW Seventh Street Bridge over the canal.

Spring Garden was proposed and advertised in 1919 as an exclusive suburb, and the properties were developed over the next twenty years in a variety of residential architectural styles. The neighborhood also boasts a copious tree canopy. The area declined after World War II; its recent renewal derives strength from access to Metrorail, and its central position between Downtown and the Civic Center/Jackson Memorial Hospital complex.

Hindu Temple · B12
Metrorail: Culmer Station

870 NW 11th Street
August Geiger, 1920

This home in the guise of a Hindu Temple was inspired by an earlier movie set at the same location. The principal façade faces the Seybold Canal, and is best viewed from across the turning basin at the north end of the canal.

B12

Little Havana

Little Havana is centered on SW Eighth Street (Calle Ocho), and bounded on the north by the Miami River and S.R. 836/Dolphin Expressway; on the west by Twenty-second Avenue; on the east by Interstate 95 (Fourth Avenue); and on the south by SW Ninth Street between SW Twelfth to SW Twenty-second Avenue, and SW Eleventh Street east of SW Twelfth Avenue to I-95. The neighborhood is divided into East Little Havana and West Little Havana by Seventeenth Avenue, the eastern portion comprising multifamily buildings and the western portion comprising mainly single-family homes.

Little Havana was first an agricultural area, prospering after the coming of the railroad to Miami in 1896. During and after World War I, it developed into a residential suburb of Miami. After 1959, the whole area became the location of first arrival for the Cuban diaspora. Today, while most of the businesses remain in the hands of Cuban Americans, the residential population is largely made up of people from other parts of Latin America, especially Nicaragua.

The northeastern section was once called Riverside, and became an early Miami Jewish neighborhood from the 1920s through the early 1950s. Like South Beach, East Little Havana can be understood as a "museum of the streets" containing buildings from several eras of the early twentieth century: Bungalow, Mediterranean Revival, Art Deco, Streamline Moderne, and postwar Modern. The area is close to the Brickell Avenue Financial District, and large-scale residential developments, hoping to cater to that workforce, have begun to pop up. Unfortunately, most of East Little Havana does not enjoy protection against demolition.

B13

Miami River Inn   B13

118 SW South River Drive
1908–18

Among the nine buildings that comprise the Miami River Inn property
are the six that constitute the South River Drive National Register Historic
District. This district provides a rare view into Miami's first decades of development and the early history of the Miami River. The buildings are typical
examples of early twentieth-century Frame Vernacular architecture in Miami
and, with the possible exception of 437 SW Second Street, probably served
as boardinghouses from the outset. The boardinghouses provided accommodations to working-class tourists and workers lured by the attractions
and industries along the river. Typical of the period and place, most are
without stylistic reference or applied ornamentation. They are characterized by balloon-frame construction, clapboard siding, hipped or gabled
roofs pierced by large dormers, double-hung windows, and prominent
front porches. Unique in the district are the three second-story plank walkways that connect the buildings facing SW First Street to the SW First Street
Bridge, which was completed in 1929.

Neolofts   B14

10 SW South River Drive
Revuelta Vega Leon, 2004

When completed in 2004, Neolofts was the first major apartment house
built on the Miami River in at least twenty-five years. Its 20-story tapered
slab faces the river on its narrow side, where projecting balconies supported
on wide circular columns spread like wings.

Jose Marti Park   B15

351 SW 4th Street
Wallace Roberts & Todd, 1985

Named for the liberator patriot of Cuba's nineteenth-century War of
Independence, this small riverfront park marks the boundary between Little
Havana and Downtown Miami. It occupies the site made famous in the af-
termath of the 1980 Mariel Boatlift, when it became Tent City, a temporary
holding area for Cuban refugees.

The park's design was the result of a competition whose objectives were
to serve the East Little Havana community and create a space that represents Cuba in America. The park comprises several pavilions, water features,
and even a school, which are distinguished by their pink stucco walls, tile
roofs, and Baroque parapets that make reference to colonial Havana, but
that also mesh well with the Mediterranean Revival architecture of Little
Havana. The park features a monument by Rolando Lopez Dirube that
consists of a long wall inscribed multiple times with the word "sembrar" (to
plant), a reference to the writings of Jose Marti. Located at a bend of the
Miami River, the park sits in the shadow of I-95's Miami River Bridge, which
soars overhead. It runs along the river, creating an initial fragment of the
evolving Riverwalk that will one day stretch uninterrupted to Biscayne Bay.

B15

Warner Place B16

111 SW 5th Avenue
Reputed to be George Pfeiffer, 1912

Built as the home and shop of Miami's first florist, exquisite detailing and craftsmanship make Warner Place one of the finest Neoclassical Revival buildings in Greater Miami. Its prominent portico and lavish proportions recall the architecture of southern antebellum estates. The wraparound porch and extensive use of French doors and balconies adapt it to the local climate. Originally, the business operated on the ground floor, with the family living quarters above. The building was rehabilitated for office use in the 1980s. Its largely intact interior features a wealth of intricate woodwork and provides an excellent picture of well-to-do life in early Miami.

Dr. Rafael Peñalver Clinic B17

971 NW 2nd Street
Rolando Silva, 1998

A pillar of the East Little Havana community, the Dr. Rafael Peñalver Clinic is a tribute to the legacy of the man who opened the way for thousands of Cuban exile physicians and health professionals to practice in the United States. A lighthearted folly that defies categorization, the outside of the building borrows from the Mediterranean, the Moorish, and the Postmodern. Behind the colorful façade, the clinic was designed to create a peaceful and nonthreatening environment for visitors and staff.

Robert King High Towers B18

1403 NW 7th Street
Pancoast, Ferendino, Grafton, Skeels and Burnham with Smith and Korach, 1963
Community Building: Ferendino Grafton Spillis Candela, 1973

New priorities at the Miami Housing Authority in the 1960s produced one of Miami's finest Modern ensembles and a watershed in public housing for the

B18

elderly. Robert King High Towers, named for the city's mayor, represented an adventurous foray into high-rise architecture and tower-in-the-park planning.

A fully realized example of modern site planning, the campus was laid out in harmony with existing vegetation and the topography of its unusually rolling, prime riverfront site. The south end is covered by a canopy of live oaks while another grove of native trees commands the crest of the slope overlooking the river. Floating in this picturesque greensward, the staggered slab of the 13-story tower, a superblock, looks southeast to capture trade winds.

The apartment block is divided into three segments joined by two prominent elevator cores. The apartments face northwest and are accessed by open galleries with views of the Miami skyline to the southeast. The west face of the superblock is dominated by the floor-to-ceiling, operable metal louvers of the apartments. The floor plates project outward several feet beyond the west face to provide sun protection and, along with the detached piers, suggest porches or corridors where none, in fact, exist. The galleries are faced with individual panels of aggregate river rock, appearing to float between the piers of the east façade. The fire escapes parallel to each elevator core and at the ends of the superblock are faced in concrete panels, molded to form roughly textured vertical ribbing. Continuous vertical ribbon windows create subtle separation of the planes encasing the fire escapes.

The campus also includes an administration building and riverside recreation and community buildings connected to the superblock by covered walkways. The latter two command sweeping views of the Miami River and the arcing bridge of the Dolphin Expressway. The recreation building is arranged around an open patio with a broad covered terrace open to the river view.

B19

Lawrence Park Canal and E. G. Sewell Memorial Park   B19

NW 17th Place/NW 18th Avenue between NW 7th Street and Dolphin Expressway
W. A. Williams, 1921–22

The Lawrence Park Canal, designed as the centerpiece of the eponymous subdivision, is imbued with both grand intentions and myth. Located on the former General Samuel Lawrence estate (1897–1911), the canal was created by developer W. A. Williams, who, in order to bring water to his proposed residential subdivision, cut an inland waterway through the oolitic limestone ridge along the south side of the river in 1921–22. On the south side, in a grand civic gesture, streets line the canal with homes fronting the water. On the north side, the canal snakes through Sewell Park and joins the Miami River. In the 1960s, the Dolphin Expressway traversed the site, cutting it in two.

Another part of the site's history relates to its caves on the north side of the expressway, which likely began as solution holes (holes in limestone caused over many decades of acid leaching from fallen leaves). General Lawrence developed the area around the caves as a Japanese garden, and Williams planned to expand it as a sunken garden. Williams also planned a series of metal arches crossing the waterway that would be lighted at night. Enlarged over the years, the caves were the backdrop of Robert F. Hill's production of *Robinson Crusoe*, filmed here in 1922. They later entered the realm of local lore as "Seminole Caves" and "Pirates Cove."

Cuban Memorial Plaza and Boulevard   B20

SW 13th Avenue between SW 8th Street and Coral Way
SW 13th Avenue (West Moreland Park Boulevard): 1912
Eternal Torch of Brigade 2506: 1971
Cuban Memorial Plaza: Albert Perez, 1976
Cuban Memorial Boulevard renovation: City of Miami, 2005

B20

While Miami's street grid is often basic and provides little in the way of civic flourish, early subdivisions such as Miramar, Brickell, and West Moreland Park featured broad avenues with wide, planted medians. SW Thirteenth Avenue, originally West Moreland Boulevard, was one of these, connecting the major arterials of SW Eighth Street (also known as the Tamiami Trail) and Coral Way. What is interesting here is the way the Cuban exile community has shaped street life and new types of public space within Miami's rather elementary grid.

In the late 1950s, as the first wave of Cuban exiles began to settle in the area, the intersection of Calle Ocho and Thirteenth Avenue became the closest thing to a town square for the growing immigrant community. By 1971, the Eternal Torch of Brigade 2506 memorial, a tribute to those who lost their lives in the 1961 Bay of Pigs invasion, went up. In 1976, a plaza was created around the torch on the northern end of the avenue's median and became known officially known as Cuban Memorial Plaza.

Seven memorials to Cuban independence and aspirations for democracy stretch along the four northernmost blocks of the boulevard. Over the years, the torch has been joined by a statue of the Virgin Mary and memorials to Cuban independence fighters from the nineteenth century, as well as journalists from the twentieth. Among the memorials is a mature ceiba, or kapok tree, which is sacred to practitioners of the Afro-Cuban Santeria religion. Often candles and melted wax cover its massive sprawling roots.

In 2004, the City of Miami embarked on a program to turn the entire fourteen-block stretch from Calle Ocho to Coral Way into a linear park featuring a broad meandering walkway down the middle of the median. The plan, which called for the removal and replacement of many invasive, exotic, but mature trees, caused an uproar when the trees began coming down. In a compromise, many of the mature exotics were retained as part of the new, denser, native tree canopy. In 2005, Hurricane Wilma toppled several of the shallow-rooted non-native ficus trees, helping to accomplish the original intentions of city planners.

Tower Theater   B21

1508 SW 8th Street
Henry J. Lawrence, 1926
Renovation: Robert Law Weed, 1931
Renovation: Bermello Ajamil & Partners, 1997

The Tower Theater began as a Mediterranean Revival building in 1926, but was modernized by Robert Law Weed in 1931. Weed gave the theater its Art Deco appearance, one of the first of its kind in Miami. It includes a sky-piercing finial and a Modernistic marquee and box office. In 1997, the theater was restored to its 1931 appearance and is today managed by Miami-Dade College as a venue for film and live performances.

B21

Maximo Gomez Mini-Park–Parque Domino   B22
South side of SW 8th Street at 15th Avenue
1976
Expansion: Perez Associates Architects with Laura Llerena, Landscape Architect, 2002

East of the Tower Theater is Maximo Gomez Mini-Park, known popularly as Parque Domino. Similar to the evolution of Cuban Memorial Plaza at SW Eighth Street and Thirteenth Avenue (B20), the site had earlier acquired significance as a popular gathering place. Cuban immigrants had long congregated here to play dominos, and, in 1976, the City of Miami formalized the space. Maximo Gomez Mini-Park includes domino tables, shade structures, and trees. A mural added later celebrates the 1994 Summit of the Americas in Miami with representations of the chief executives of the attending nations.

In 2002, the park was renovated and expanded across the 700 block of Fifteenth Avenue, creating a plaza between the existing mini-park and the Tower Theater. The colorful paving pattern of the pedestrianized Fifteenth Avenue right-of-way celebrates the distinctive place dominoes hold in Cuban culture. The wavy-edged planter wall along the base of the Tower Theater features a brightly colored depiction of rural Cuba by the Curras Brothers, legendary local ceramicists.

The plaza is the site of the popular Viernes Culturales, or Cultural Fridays, live performances that have been instrumental in the revitalization of Calle Ocho as an evening entertainment destination.

Latin Quarter Specialty Center   B23
1475 SW 8th Street
Rodriguez and Quiroga Architects, 2004

Developed by the East Little Havana Community Development Corporation, this 6-story structure is one of the best of recent attempts to create humanly scaled urban infill along Calle Ocho. The mixed-use building has retail on the ground floor behind a streetfront arcade that wraps from Calle Ocho to Fifteenth Avenue. Parking is concealed on floors two and three behind a 3-story street façade whose window grouping derives from Classical hierarchies (on the second floor the parking level comprises the top of the large streetfront arches). Apartments occupy the three set-back upper floors. The corner tower and an internal courtyard are part of a newly synthesized language of urban architecture based on Miami's traditions.

Walgreens (Firestone Building)   B24
1200 West Flagler Street or 1201 SW 1st Street
1929
Renovation: Brown Demandt Architects, 2002

B24

This 3-story building, once a model Firestone Tire outlet, features an 84 × 36 foot neon sky-sign and a broad roof that cantilevers over surrounding sidewalks and parking areas. The Firestone sign, the largest in Florida, was reputedly visible from Biscayne Bay, several miles away. The roof originally sheltered open-air bays for tire changes.

The Firestone Building was for a short time an object of preservation activism, briefly but prominently appearing on Dade Heritage Trust's list of most-endangered buildings. Plans to demolish the building were eventually abandoned in favor of its retrofit as a Walgreens store. The ability to keep the building's massive rooftop signage helped convince the drugstore chain to restore the building. (A similar compromise was realized at the former Woolworth's in Miami Beach (**H12**), where Walgreens restored the building and converted its storefront into art windows). A few letters of the Firestone signage were reconfigured to spell "Walgreens."

1236 West Flagler Street   B25
1941

This service station is a Nautical Moderne folly making the most of a quirky wedge site along the Flagler corridor. Most notable is its Art Deco lantern, which rises from the bull-nosed corner of the building and is lit from vertical glass-block panels.

B25

Plaza de la Cubanidad   B26
Southwest corner West Flagler Street at 17th Avenue
Miami-Dade County Office of Community and Economic Development (Jorge Morales), 1984
Sculptor: Tony Lopez

Taking advantage of a kink in West Flagler Street where it crosses Seventeenth Avenue, the Plaza de la Cubanidad was created as part of a county street-beautification project. The plaza honors the heroes of the fight for Cuban independence from Spain in the nineteenth century. The focal point is a bronze sculpture consisting of overlapping rectangles of various sizes to approximate the outline of the island. The sculpted bronze rectangles depict the faces and acts of the patriots. The sculpture projects from a glass-tile water wall. The sculptor, Tony Lopez, was later sought out to work on the Miami Beach Holocaust Memorial (**F42**).

To the right of the water wall is a quote from José Martí, himself a patriot and poet, that reads "las palmas son novias que esperan" (the palms are lovers that await). To mirror the sentiment, the ensemble is adorned with six royal palms, native to Cuba and southern Florida, for each of Cuba's six traditional provinces. More recently, the basin of the water wall became home to a poignant memorial in the shape and size of a toy boat. It commemorates the 1994 sinking of the ship *13 de Mayo* by Cuban forces as it attempted to transport refugees to freedom.

B26

B27

City of Miami South District Police Substation   B27

2200 West Flagler Street
Rodriguez Khuly Quiroga, 1990

The Little Havana district police station raises a civic and monumental presence on its triangular site. The building's two office wings pivot off a 2-story, drumlike lobby volume placed at the corner. The building uses a simple palette of masonry, stucco, and opaque and clear green glass. The glass makes transparent the workings of the station, and gives this Classical type a Modern face. The allusion to the Classical is appropriate as the station is sited on the only radiating, six-way intersection in Miami. Developed in 1915 as the main street of Glen Royal, the Glen Royal Parkway cut a powerful diagonal from the intersection of Flagler Street and SW Twenty-second Avenue to the northwest, while Beacom Boulevard mirrors it to the southwest.

Miami Senior High School   B28

2450 SW 1st Street
Kiehnel and Elliott, 1928
Renovation: Zyscovich Architects, 2008

Miami Senior High School is one of the city's most distinctive Mediterranean Revival landmarks. Other grand buildings in this style (like the Freedom Tower [A11] and Coral Gable's Biltmore Hotel) evoke the late Renaissance with allusions to Neoclassicism. Contrastingly, the high school recalls the Byzantine, Moorish, and pre-Renaissance epochs of the Mediterranean region.

The school is sited appropriately off Flagler Street beyond a half block–sized greensward named Colombia Park. The school's central pavilion with its broad façade and crenellated parapet appears like a Mudéjar palace rising from the West Little Havana neighborhood. From the central pavilion extend wings that in turn end in smaller tower pavilions and connect via covered arched walkways to gabled wings facing Twenty-fourth and Twenty-fifth avenues. The building features a grand entrance of three arched portals befitting a Gothic cathedral. Fronting Twenty-fifth Avenue, the imposing double-height entrance to the gymnasium is marked by massive faux columns with intricate Byzantine capitals.

Delayed for over a year by the hurricane of 1926, the high school opened at this location in 1928. This is the fourth location of Miami's earliest secondary school; the earliest is preserved at 140 SW Eleventh Street (A128).

Dade County Auditorium   B29

2901 West Flagler Street
Steward & Skinner Associates, ca. 1953

This 2,500-seat auditorium was designed to serve small conventions, concerts, lectures, and full stage presentations. For many years, it was the Miami-Dade County venue for Florida Grand Opera. Until the completion of the performing arts center in 2006 (C15), it was a main venue for the performing arts in Miami. Large entrance foyers on both ground and balcony level extend across the face, with large windows onto Flagler Street.

Saint Michael the Archangel   B30

2987 West Flagler Street
Murray Blair Wright, 1964

B30

Saint Michael the Archangel Church bears a distinct resemblance to Alfred Preis's 1961 USS *Arizona* Memorial in Pearl Harbor. In fact, the "bow tie" building shape was a popular motif in midcentury Modern architecture. Preis's idea that the design of the memorial signified initial defeat but ultimate victory must have resonated with Murray Blair Wright as appropriate to evoke the death and resurrection of Christ. The metaphor is successful here. While the church at first appears stark and without any of the reassuring traditional elements of Christian religious architecture (with the exception of a thin cross rising from its broad, flat façade), the interior is welcoming and voluminous. The front face of aggregate panels contrasts with the smooth concrete side walls and roof.

Light enters the interior through vertical rows of narrow offset rectangular stained-glass windows in shades of red, gold, and off-white as well as full-height windows on its sides. A chapel projects from the rear of the church, giving it a secondary façade to the parking area, and groves of carefully sited, tall, thin Veitchia palms mark the low point of the building volume on the north and south sides.

The front façade is punctuated by a concave entrance alcove, whose side walls of oolitic rock relate the church to rectory next door with its extensive use of the stone. The rectory is housed in the grand 1920s Brightman Estate, which was purchased for its current use in 1964. The estate brought with it a colorful history of its own that had little to do with religious endeavors.

Coral Way Historic and Scenic Road   B31

SW 22nd Street from SW 37th Avenue to SW 12th Avenue and SW 3rd Avenue from SW 12th Avenue to SW 15th Road
Dade County Parks, 1929
Public Works Administration (PWA) and Works Progress Administration (WPA), 1935

B31

The magnificent tree canopy of false banyan trees (*Ficus altissima*) in the median of Coral Way dates back to a county road-beautification program of the late 1920s. In 1929, the trees were originally planted in the road's swales because the streetcar line of the Coral Gables Rapid Transit Company ran down the middle of the street. In 1935, after the streetcar line was abandoned, the WPA and PWA removed the rails and moved the trees from the sides of the street to a newly created median. Although visitors marvel at the tree canopy that spreads from curb to curb, the *Ficus altissima* is a smaller relative of the true banyan (*Ficus bengalense*), a fine specimen of which can be seen off Old Cutler Road at the north end of Fairchild Tropical Garden.

Gas Station (Southland Super Service Station)   B32

1700 SW 22nd Street (Coral Way)
Lester Avery and Curtis E. Haley, from a prototype by Russell T. Pancoast, Architect, 1938

B32

The last remaining gas station based on Russell Pancoast's 1930s prototype for the Gulf Oil Company, this one is clearly distinguished from today's standardized models. Two canopies and a single-story service wing spring from a taller central block. The stripped-down Mediterranean Revival styling of these basic structures includes arched openings and hipped and gabled roofs clad in clay tile. The complex and its styling are leavened by the lyrically mechanomorphic "spring" column and by the Art Deco corbelling that supports the canopies. The device conveys the impression of a piston in compression.

B33

InterAmerican Plaza (Twenty-seventh & Eighth Building)   B33
701 SW 27th Avenue (Unity Boulevard)
M. E. Valls, 1976

Although residential high-rises have popped up along Twenty-seventh Avenue to the south, InterAmerican Plaza remains the tallest object on the skyline of the expanse between Downtown Miami and Downtown Coral Gables, the Dolphin Expressway, and Coconut Grove. It occupies the entire trapezoidal block bounded by SW Eighth Street, Twenty-seventh Avenue, SW Seventh Street, and the diagonal Beacom Boulevard. Its original name, the Twenty-seventh & Eighth Building, reflected its key location.

An unusual approach to Miami's routine tower-over-pedestal type, the building's massive retail and parking pedestal is carved at its center to create a large patio. Stores are oriented toward the patio while the introverted complex accordingly turns a cold face toward the busy intersection of SW Eighth Street and Twenty-seventh Avenue. Opaque glass walls, beneath a garage structure that bellies out over the sidewalk, meet the pedestrian. The 14-story tower is thrust high over the patio on an independent structural scaffold of concrete columns and beams. The resulting interior concourse, centered on the core of the tower, is animated by pedestrian bridges and automobile ramps. Light and air enter through the gap between the tower and pedestal, and plants and trees thrive in the perpetual penumbra. The tower block has chamfered corners that bracket an egg-crate grille of precast-concrete window frames.

B34

Duany Plater-Zyberk & Company Offices   B34
1023 SW 25th Avenue
Duany Plater-Zyberk & Company, 1990

The offices of Duany Plater-Zyberk & Company (DPZ) occupy a renovated aircraft engine repair shop in a residential district of Little Havana, just south of SW Eighth Street (Calle Ocho). The building achieves a monumental presence against its foil of small homes and garden-apartment buildings that surround it. The formal façade has just a single large portal framed by loose curtains, revealing a foyer painted in Pompeian red. The structure's scale and expression achieve the sort of balance between civic and residential identities popular in the 1930s (manifest, for example, in Miami Beach at the U.S. Post Office on Washington Avenue (E61) or Fire Station No. 2 on Pinetree Drive (F56).

The interior space is organized around a linear atelier, lit by tall industrial windows on its south side and open to a walled court used for parking. In back is a skylit atrium, which forms a central and more introverted meeting place. A later residential building on the south frames a parking court and provides meeting rooms for the firm's frequent design charrettes.

InterAmerican Campus, Miami-Dade College   B35

627 SW 27th Avenue
Campus design, adaptive reuse, and expansion: Rodriguez and Quiroga Architects, 2000

On a busy crossroads in the heart of Little Havana, Miami-Dade College's InterAmerican Campus is a rather introverted campus serving international students. The development strategy notably favored infill development over the creation of an architectural icon. At one corner, the complex incorporated Connell, Pierce, Garland and Friedman's 1963 Inter National Bank building, which was fully renovated and given a new skin. New buildings developed around it, largely filling the block. The process of accretion generated several plazas of different size and orientation at the interior of the complex. The largest (Courtyard of the Americas) is a U-shaped area ringed by flagpoles, and opens to SW Seventh Street. Where the courtyard meets the street, a single-story community classroom provides a threshold. The courtyard appears to center on the tower of InterAmerican Plaza, which rises to the south. Another patio runs east-west, connecting SW Twenty-seventh Avenue with the new parking garage to the east. Here, overhead canvas sun shades cool the patios. Bordered or bisected by covered loggias, these patios become tight social spaces. Another virtual courtyard, roofed and clerestoried, comprises the college's multistory computer facility, which is wrapped by faculty offices. The building skin combines natural tone precast concrete and gray aluminum panels, and projecting solar shades add texture.

George A. Smathers Plaza   B36

940 SW 29th Court or 935 SW 30th Avenue
Robert Bradford Browne Architects, 1967

Named for Florida's U.S. senator George A. Smathers and following the success of Robert King High Towers (B18), this complex translates the tower-in-the-garden residential type to public housing for the elderly. Located just south of SW Eighth Street, it was an element of urban renewal plans in Little Havana. The fenced complex relates poorly to its surroundings, but its towers are a rare and dignified example of Brutalist architecture in the service of public housing.

The complex comprises three structures: a 13-story tower with 100 units; a 6-story low-rise building with 82 units; and a community center offering social services and recreation. The three structures, along with shuffleboard courts, occupy only 10 percent of the 6.7-acre lot; the balance of the property was originally filled with orange groves as well as oak and jacaranda trees. Citrus blight and the ravages of Miami's hurricanes have rendered the current site bleakly open. The housing is set on low plinths of concrete and earth, with wide walkways in between. Plans by the Miami-Dade Housing Authority to further develop the site, including a 1991 plan to add density, remain incomplete.

B36

The building forms result from a Brutalist application of cast-in-place concrete, an approach undoubtedly influenced by the work of Paul Rudolph and Hans Scharoun as well as the architecture of British New Towns. The structures are articulated in plan with deeply recessed slots that let light into the elevator lobbies, and splayed walls that expand the space of the rooms. All units are cross-ventilated through vertical ribbons of glass. The concrete was tinted green with the intention that it would weather to eventually mesh with the surrounding landscape.

Coral Way Elementary School   B37

1950 SW 13th Avenue/Cuban Memorial Boulevard
August Geiger, 1936

B37

The Public Works Administration (PWA) constructed this building as a
New Deal stimulus to Miami's sagging economy and to meet the needs of
a recently expanded population. Works Progress Administration (WPA)–
sponsored artists contributed the decorative elements inside and outside;
the result is a flourish of Art Deco ornamentation on this otherwise traditional building. The school's tree-filled courtyard with a fountain in the
center is one of the best open public spaces in Miami, and is surrounded by
open porticos that link the classrooms.

Shenandoah Middle School   B38

1950 SW 19th Street
August Geiger, 1942

Shenandoah Middle School, a New Deal–sponsored project like Coral
Way Elementary School (B37), replaced an older 1926 building on the site.
Shenandoah is a museum magnet school, with a curriculum that centers
around projects for students and teachers that take advantage of Miami's
museums as educational resources. Much of the original building, except
for the imposing front façade featuring open-air porticos linking the classrooms, has been modified.

2100 Block of Coral Way

*Beginning in 1974 with the installation of WLTV Channel 23, a
Spanish-language television station, in the 2103 Coral Way Building,
this block of Coral Way was refashioned as a Latin media center, a
"Madison Avenue South" of Spanish-language broadcasting. The result is a tight cluster of small and medium-sized office buildings along
the tree-lined thoroughfare. The site is located strategically, midway
between Coral Gables, Downtown Miami, and the Brickell Avenue corridor. Although WLTV has moved (after its merger with Univision), the
area still includes WSCV–Channel 51, WCMQ Radio Alegre, and WSUA,
Radio Suave. The elegant concrete buildings exude the spirit of Latin
American Modernism.*

Coral Plaza Office Building   B39

2100 Coral Way
Ruben Travieso, 1985

Set up on a broad plaza, the 7-story 2100 Coral Plaza Office Building has an
expressive armature of cast-in-place concrete interwoven with ribbons of
flush-glazed dark glass. Each building face has articulated spandrels, disengaged circular columns, and projecting bay windows. On the south side,
the windows are sheltered by eyebrows. Music from Radio Suave wafts from
loudspeakers on the plaza during the day.

21/22 Center   B40
2103–2105 Coral Way
J. M. Hevia, 1982

The 8-story 21/22 Center, whose cast-concrete Modernism derives from the Latin American variety, is a composite of several structures. On the east end, at the corner of Twenty-first Avenue, the lobby is tucked in below a dark-tinted curtain-walled tower block. An adjacent component sandwiches five floors of parking between a ground-floor retail concourse and two levels of offices on the upper levels. The parking garage has an efficient staggered section, avoiding exposed ramping systems. It cantilevers over the wide sidewalk creating a Modernist arcade that protects from sun and rain.

2150 Coral Way   B41
Johnson Associates, 1978

Predating the similar 2100 Coral Way Building, this 8-story office block features a cast-in-place concrete façade with projecting window bays framing dark ribbons of glass. It is softened with curved corners, deep recesses, and built-in planters. Elevators run in an exposed shaft on the east side of the building.

Miami Green   B42
Metrorail: Douglas Road

B41

3150 SW 38th Avenue
Behar Font & Partners, 2009

The prowlike glass walls of this tall and compact office building make it a landmark presence along U.S. Highway 1 and the Metrorail corridor, as well as a Modernist standout among Mediterranean Revival–inspired neighbors. Located just in front of the Douglas Road Metrorail station, Miami Green is one of the first commercial structures in the city to incorporate (and brand its identity on) the sustainability practices of the U.S. Green Building Council's Leadership in Energy and Environmental Design (LEED) standards. The LEED-certified building is oriented to increase the efficiency of its partly shaded green-glass walls, and circulation is organized to maximize light and exposure in the offices. The 13-story building projects over ground-floor loggias and horizontal bands of glass, and projecting fins rise on two sides of the building in a tapered and projecting way. A multistory parking garage is imbedded in the building volume, and a roof deck occupies the top level.

B42

Miami-Dade Water and
Sewer Department Building   B43
Metrorail: Douglas Road

3071 SW 38th Avenue
Rodriguez and Quiroga Architects, 1999

This headquarters for the county's Water and Sewer Department adds a sober and well-proportioned piece of public infrastructure along the Metrorail corridor. Constructed inexpensively of tilt-up concrete panels, the façade achieves a substantial sophistication by the use of stripped-down Classicism

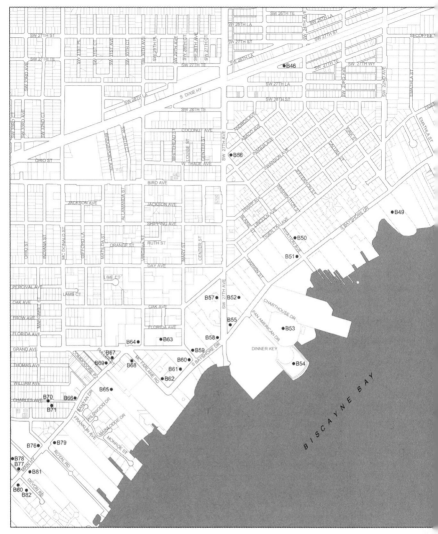

Coconut Grove

in sync with Coral Gables Mediterranean Revival. The window treatment of the first two floors was joined to create a Monumental order, while simple punched openings articulate the floors above. The center of the building inflects to identify the entrance. A 735-car garage, serving and feeding directly into the Douglas Road Metrorail station, is just behind.

Ocean Bank Building   B44

780 North Le Jeune Road
George Peon, 1982

B44

This multiuse urban complex close to Miami International Airport, at the busy intersection of Le Jeune Road and NW Seventh Street, creates a dynamic suburban center in the heart of the city. The self-contained megastructure comprises offices, a shopping arcade with cinema and patio areas, a palm court, and a cafeteria sheltered by a space frame. Set back behind fronting lawn, fountains, and plaza, the building inflects toward its open courtyard along Le Jeune Road. The complex, sheathed in dark blue tinted glass, glows blue at night. A front loggia of Carrera marble creates a rich contrast.

MDX Dolphin Expressway Toll Plaza   B45

Eastbound lanes of the Dolphin Expressway west of 17th Avenue
Bermello Ajamil & Partners, 2007

The winglike canopy shelters a toll plaza along the Dolphin Expressway, framing passage eastward and views of Downtown. Six toll-booth lanes sit beneath the front portion of the wing while the two AVI lanes pass under its angled outrigger, supported by steel cables from two hexagonally shaped pylons located at the north side of the structure.

Coconut Grove

Coconut Grove is Miami's oldest tourist destination and predates the founding of the city. At first, it was home to Bahamians and North Americans who earned their living from farming and the sea, but, by 1883, the Peacock family had opened a hotel in today's Peacock Park at the suggestion of Commodore Ralph Middleton Munroe. The Peacock Inn attracted many of Munroe's associates and friends from the Northeast who sought relief from winter or the ravages of tuberculosis. Munroe's community of writers, naturalists, sailing enthusiasts, and intellectuals set a tone for the Grove that remains observable today, even in the face of gentrification and development, more than one hundred years later. Like Munroe's self-built home, the Barnacle, the Grove's architecture demonstrates attention to the tropical environment.

During the 1960s, the commercial center of Coconut Grove became the heart of counterculture in Miami, and artists and bohemians claimed it as their own. Beginning in the 1980s, the Downtown Grove was redeveloped as an upscale shopping, dining, and entertainment destination. The eventual rise of South Beach and the development of other entertainment destinations throughout Greater Miami have challenged its popularity.

B46

2424 South Dixie Highway   B46

Metrorail: Coconut Grove

2424 South Dixie Highway
Mateu Architects, 1984

One of the few buildings to celebrate the overlay of South Dixie Highway's diagonal trajectory with Miami's north-south gridiron, the building is a wedge-shaped, or "flatiron," structure. Recalling the nautical architectural imagery of the 1930s while responding to the high-speed mobility of the highway, the building can be understood as a collage of two elements: prow and body. The prow comprises a bullnose that is lifted off the ground, and that achieves its full expression at the third floor, where it is rendered in glass block and wrapped by a continuous balcony of nautical railings. The body is a stepped block whose two stories of office space, over ground-floor parking, are expressed in ribbons of squarish windows and stucco. The line of royal palms, in cube-shaped masonry planters, reinforces the rhythm of the fenestration when viewed at 45 mph. An exterior stairway on the back side lends further movement to the façade.

On one hand, this structure is a highly visible landmark, designed to command views from the opposite lines of moving traffic and from the Metrorail. On the other, it is scaled to the adjacent residential neighborhood, mediating disparate urban conditions.

Vizcaya and the Vizcaya Farm Village   B47

Metrorail: Vizcaya

2351 South Miami Avenue
F. Burrell Hoffman; Paul Chalfin, Associate Architect; Diego Suarez, Landscape Architect, 1914
Restoration and glass roof over courtyard: David Wolfberg, 1978-1989

Forged from a landscape of coastal mangroves and native hammock, Vizcaya blends a network of natural ecosystems and refined formal gardens as the backdrop for an immensely extravagant villa. The project was initiated by James Deering, industrial magnate of International Harvester farm machinery, who initially purchased 130 acres of land from the Brickell family. The site soon grew to 180 acres, including a working farm on the west side of South Bayshore Drive, and required over one thousand workers to build, making it the most important construction project of its time. Deering was encouraged and supported in this endeavor by Paul Chalfin, a classically trained architect whose duties extended to escorting Deering through Europe on a kind of grand tour. Hoffman, a New York architect formerly with the New York firm of Carrere and Hastings, and Diego Suarez, a Colombian architect and landscape specialist, were soon hired to prepare plans.

Villa Vizcaya comprises a central courtyard around which loggias connect four corner towers, lending the structure its fortified appearance. The influence of the Italian Renaissance in both the home and gardens was pervasive, although native materials were used throughout. The house addressed the surrounding landscape differently on each of its four sides.

B47

Arriving from the west through the dense hammock, a gateway sets up a
formal linear approach that slopes down to the entrance court. From the
house, Suarez laid a parterre garden sweeping southward along axial lines.
The south garden builds toward a casino planted atop a forested mound,
and oblique axes cross the mound toward the site of a former lake, now the
site of Mercy Hospital. On the east, the house opens to a paved plaza overlooking Biscayne Bay and a small island in the shape of a ceremonial stone
barge moored to the seawall. The barge and bay frontage are bracketed by
curving jetties terminated by domed pavilions. Of the four sides, the north
is the most private, allowing the hammock to press close to the house. Here,
a small swimming pool tucks into a grotto beneath the structure.

In 1952, the Deering heirs donated the property to Miami-Dade County
for use as a museum. Beginning in 1978, the County Parks Department
considered covering Vizcaya's central courtyard in order to air-condition
the museum, with the stated intent to preserve its many precious objects.
During the 1980s, the roofing project created considerable controversy, but
a pyramidal bronze glass roof over the courtyard was nonetheless completed in 1986.

Ermita de La Caridad   B48

3609 South Miami Avenue
Jose Perez Benitoa, 1971
Additions: Felipe de Leon and David Cabarrocas after the design of Jose Perez Benitoa,
1994

B48

This conical, slightly parabaloid chapel honors the patroness of Cuba. The
effort to create the shrine began in 1966 with the donation of the land on
the shore of Biscayne Bay by then Archbishop Coleman Carroll. After a
fund-raising effort mainly among exiles, the shrine was dedicated in 1973.
In 2000, the shrine was designated a National Shrine by the U.S. Conference
of Catholic Bishops. The shape of the 90-foot-high chapel corresponds with

the shape of the statue of Our Lady of Charity; thus pilgrims are symbolically invited to enter the heart of the Virgin. Six columns within the chapel
represent the six traditional provinces of Cuba.

A mural behind the statue of Mary, by artist Teok Carrasco, depicts the
history of Cuba with an image of Mary and the baby Jesus at its center, representing the centrality of Christ in Cuban history.

Two wings housing offices, a gift shop, and other ancillary spaces were
eventually added in a design sympathetic to the original.

Kennedy Park   B49
2400 South Bayshore Drive

This heavily used 29-acre facility, in one of the precious few public waterfront parks in Miami, is named for former Miami mayor David Kennedy. It
represents the core of a long-planned expansion of Coconut Grove's waterfront for public purposes.

Bayview Plaza   B50
3225 Aviation Avenue
Baldwin Sackman & Associates, 1985

This small office building is remarkable for its simple, but finely detailed,
use of lightly tinted glass and white-clad masonry. The pattern of crystalline
step-backs creates terraces and provides a memorable ornamental dimension to the building mass.

B50

SBS Tower (General Development Center)   B51
2601 South Bayshore Drive
Bermello, Kurki, Vera, 1987

This development would be an unremarkable Brickell Avenue escapee were
it not for the townhouses that camouflage the parking garage on Tigertail
Avenue. They were added in response to neighborhood demands. One
wishes the same demand had been made of the Ritz-Carlton façade on
Tigertail three blocks to the south.

Grand Bay Plaza   B52
2665–2669 South Bayshore Drive
Nichols & Associates, 1982

The Grand Plaza Hotel can be clearly identified by its stair-stepping terraced
profile rising from Bayshore Drive like a Mayan pyramid. The design of the
office tower, in the same vocabulary of dark-tinted glass and buff-colored
masonry as the hotel, is more restrained. The slender tower slab is distinguished by its more subtle stepped massing and projecting full-height
banks of uninterrupted glass, which house end offices with 180-degree
views of the Coconut Grove bayfront. Note the dramatic bright-orange
metal sculpture, *Windward*, by Alexander Liberman, in the drop-off area.

B52

Dinner Key

Dinner Key occupies a key position geographically and historically in the necklace of parks and civic facilities following Bayshore Drive along Coconut Grove's waterfront, an exception to the more pervasive privatization of Miami's waterfront. Today, it comprises roughly 117 acres, including Miami's city hall, an exhibition center, hangars used for boat storage, the extensive Grove Key Marina, restaurants, and large parking areas. On the south, Seminole Boat Ramp and Kenneth Myers Park separate Dinner Key from Peacock Park. On the north, public access runs as far as Monty's; the Biscayne Bay Yacht Club, Coral Reef Yacht Club, and U.S. Sailing Center block waterfront access to nearby Kennedy Park.

Once an island, Dinner Key was developed as a naval air station during World War I, and commissioned as a U.S. Coast Guard air station in 1932. After Miami's plans to construct a new air and seaport at Virginia Key were abandoned in the early 1930s, Pan Am established its marine air terminal here in 1934. Pan Am's facilities were extensive, comprising a state-of-the-art terminal, ramps, and seaplane hangars to support its hemispheric network of flying clippers. Pan Am and its Coconut Grove seaplane base made Miami a center of aviation, literally an "Air Gateway between the Americas."

Pan Am eventually relocated to Pan Am Field on NW Thirty-sixth Street, now subsumed into the grounds of Miami International Airport. The U.S. Coast Guard left Dinner Key for Opa-locka in 1965. Miami then purchased the Pan Am terminal for use as its city hall; marina facilities have subsequently expanded into the former seaplane hangars. Two restaurants have developed along the water's edge.

Today, much of the site contains parking lots, and a bayfront walkway remains incomplete. The complex is centered on Pan American Drive, which creates a formal approach to Miami's city hall. A series of master plans, including plans by Bermello, Kurki, Vera and Bradshaw, Gill, Fuster and Associates (1996), and more recently by Sasaki Associates, have sought to make sense of Dinner Key's diverse facilities.

Old U.S. Coast Guard and Pan Am Hangars   B53

Biscayne Bay Yacht Club
2540 South Bayshore Drive
1923

Miami Watersports Center (U.S. Coast Guard Station at Dinner Key/Virrick Gym)
2600 South Bayshore Drive
1930

Merrill-Stevens Hangars
2640 South Bayshore Drive
1923

B53

This group of hangars, once containing repair space, shops, and storerooms for Pan American Airlines' flying clippers as well as for the U.S. Coast Guard, has been adaptively used for a variety of purposes. The Biscayne Bay Yacht Club occupies one of Pan Am's 1923 hangars. Next door, a former U.S. Coast Guard hangar was converted to a boxing gym dedicated to Coconut Grove activist and housing advocate Elizabeth Virrick. A variety of marine storage uses occupy the balance of the structures.

B54

Miami City Hall (Pan American Seaplane Base and Terminal Building)   B54

3500 Pan American Drive
Delano and Aldrich, 1933
Renovation: R. J. Heisenbottle Architects, 2001

The Miami City Hall sits incongruously not in Downtown Miami, but in Coconut Grove, on the shores of Biscayne Bay. It occupies Delano and Aldrich's storied Pan American Seaplane Base and Terminal Building, once a nexus of the pioneering airline's hemispheric route network. Built to serve the airline's fleet of clipper ships, essentially flying boats, the seaplane base expressed the spirit of modern aviation in its architecture. The white cubic structure was flanked by lower wings providing expanded wraparound observation decks around the second-floor dining rooms and suggesting an airplanelike appearance. Throughout the interior and on its main façade, friezes depicted stylized airplanes, Pan Am's winged globe insignia, and the motif of a rising sun. Its center was a 2-story hall whose focal point was a 10-foot-diameter, rotating globe recessed into the floor.

The terminal was highly functional, able to simultaneously accommodate four separate aircraft via covered canopies; and, with its battery of hangars to the north, it became a model for Pan Am's future seaplane bases, including the Marine Air Terminal at New York's LaGuardia Airport, with which it bears a strong familial resemblance. The use of multiple gangways, in particular, innovated the future interface of airplanes and terminals.

The Miami City Hall has occupied the structure since 1954. While the commission chamber, conference rooms, and commissioners' offices fit poorly into the originally open and airy structure, a 2002 restorative renovation accommodated the current use more sensitively into the historic interior, exposing many original features. The original winged clock of the main ticketing hall is still plainly visible above the commission dais. The globe (relocated to the Miami Science Museum) has been recalled in the lobby floor as a circular tile mosaic.

B55

Office in the Grove   B55

2699 South Bayshore Drive
Kenneth Treister, 1973

Perched on tall green berms overlooking the intersection of Twenty-seventh Avenue and South Bayshore Drive, the elegant block of the 9-story Office in the Grove tower speaks to the evolution of Coconut Grove as a modern business center. Its compact form set amid suburban greenery and art in a waterfront location meshes business culture with the Grove's more relaxed lifestyle.

The architectural solution responds to the unusual siting of the building. Grass berms, crisply set on battered concrete plinths and capped with a concrete planter, hide three floors of parking, a solution that discards the standard parking pedestal of Miami's urban condition. Taking advantage of the sloping site, the three levels of the garage are entered from different directions, so no interior ramps were required.

The pentagonal tower block rises above on concrete pilotis. It forms a prowlike mass oriented toward the Dinner Key marina on one side, and toward NE Twenty-seventh Avenue on the other. At the top of the building, double-height open portals on the east and west side provide commanding balconies. Its façades are defined by the orderly repetition of narrow pre-cast-concrete window frames. The precast units are colored in warm, glare-cutting hues of sand. Bronze-tinted glass is deeply set within each frame, providing sun and hurricane protection, and raking the tower mass with a rich texture of shadows. On the north side, the block is slit along its full height with a wedge that opens to the entrance and core of the building. In contrast to the repetitive precast units, the wedge is framed by rougher cast-in-place concrete.

Treister's characteristic mix of architecture and art is on display here as well. A bronze sculpture of birds nesting at a fountain stands at the entrance. Florida's flora and fauna are cast into features of the lobby, including bronze sculpted elevator doors and interior panels, carved mahogany front doors, and a 16-foot-high mural.

Grove Forest Plaza B56

Metrorail: Coconut Grove

2937 SW 27th Avenue
Gifford House, 1903
Robin Bosco/Architects & Planners, 1983

Grove Forest Plaza would be just another low-rise office building along Twenty-seventh Avenue were it not for the fact that it is built around the 1903 Gifford House. The structure began as a grapefruit-packing plant in the late nineteenth century. It was renovated into a house in 1903 by Dr. John Gifford, a physician and one of America's first foresters. It is an exceptional example of the oolite-clad pioneer homes referred to locally as coral rock houses. In 1967, seminal Florida Modernist architect Alfred Browning Parker purchased the house for his son Derrick's use as a studio and living quarters.

After much debate among city planners, the community, and the developer, the developer of the office building was allowed to build a slightly larger building in return for the restoration and incorporation of the Gifford House into the project. Note how the office building relates to the house through the inclusion of glass gable details and the grounding of the building in a solid masonry base.

Ritz-Carlton Coconut Grove B57

3300 SW 27th Avenue
Nichols Brosch Sandoval & Associates, 2002

At great distances, the mansard roofs of the Ritz-Carlton cut a romantic silhouette on the skyline of Coconut Grove. Its triangular site is just north of the Grove's historic center, and its two towers, 22 stories each, float in landscaped decks over concealed ground-level parking and are staggered to maintain clear lines of sight. The south tower contains condominium apartments while the north tower has hotel and condominium hotel rooms. They appear nearly identical and share two common entrances from SW

27th Avenue. Shared amenities are located on the west side, backed up to Tigertail Avenue, where unfortunately they present a nearly blind block-long wall.

Coconut Grove Bank   B58

2700 South Bayshore Drive
Weed Johnson Associates, 1960

The first office building along South Bayshore Drive, Coconut Grove Bank is a tower-over-pedestal type adapted to an open, landscaped site. Here the pedestal is not the usual parking garage, but rather a low-slung glass banking lobby with glass walls set in beneath a projecting fascia that wraps the structure. The pedestal slides beneath a squat, square office tower, which is wrapped by vertical concrete fins and giant brise-soleils clad in blue-and-white patterned ceramic tiles. Like Office in the Grove (**B55**), the siting takes advantage of the escarpment that runs along the shore of Biscayne Bay. The hilltop parking area is connected directly to the main entrance and banking lobby on the second level via a pedestrian bridge.

Grove Towers   B59

2843 South Bayshore Drive
James Deen, 1982

This residential tower has a more sculptural form than its numerous contemporaries. Deen, who earlier concocted the concave trylon tower at Palm Bay (**C91**), here goes convex, assembling the building of bundled cylindrical volumes with fully wrapping balconies. An interior atrium rises the full height of the structure. With only four residences per floor, each unit has panoramic views toward Miami, Coconut Grove, or the bay. The unfortunate removal of a distinctive scalloped relief pattern on the parapet has diminished the sculptural effect.

Yacht Harbor   B60

2901 South Bayshore Drive
Kenneth Treister, 1975

Kenneth Treister married his richly ornamented Brutalism with modernist Minimalism to sublime effect in this residential tower built into the slope of the escarpment that runs along the bay from the Miami River to South Dade. The eighteen-story Yacht Harbor forms a veritable Treister campus along with Mayfair in the Grove (**B63**) and nearby Office in the Grove (**B55**). This slab-type building is tapered to a point on both narrow ends, resulting in an elongated, hexagonal form. Deep and fully wrapping balconies are interrupted by floor-to-ceiling living-room windows forming full-height prismatic bay-window shafts. Wood and brass produce a nautical feeling in the building lobby. Celebrating the tower's siting on the escarpment, Treister anchored the building to ground with a series of terraces formed by sloping panels of his trademark concrete rich in relief. Beyond the terracing, the building is meant to rise from the type of informal, naturalistic vegetation for which Coconut Grove is popularly known.

B61

Woman's Club of Coconut Grove   B61

2985 South Bayshore Drive
Walter DeGarmo, 1921
Renovation: R. J. Heisenbottle Architects, 2008

The Woman's Club of Coconut Grove was founded as the "Housekeeper's Club" in 1891, five years before the incorporation of the City of Miami. The simple structure, distinguished by its oolitic limestone–clad porch with broad arched openings, is one of few remaining from preboom days in Miami. Rising behind the wrapping porch is a taller stuccoed volume housing the club's meeting space.

Coconut Grove Branch Library   B62

2875 McFarlane Road
Original library: 1901
Addition: T. Trip Russell and Associates, 1963

The direct descendant of Miami's oldest library, founded by the Pine Needles Club (predecessor of the adjacent Woman's Club of Coconut Grove) in 1895, the first Grove library was commissioned by settler Ralph Munroe and constructed in 1901. The Grove library was later incorporated, first into the City of Miami Library System (1957), and then, into the Miami-Dade Public Library System (1969). In spite of its affiliation with the larger regional system, this branch has maintained and reinforced a strong local identity.

B62

The old Coconut Grove Library is a simple gabled structure, clad in native oolitic rock, and has the appearance of a small village school or church.

Next door, T. Trip Russell's 1963 project reinterpreted the historic library's high pitched roof, sheltering a new pavilion below a pyramidal roof that undoubtedly took inspiration from the nearby Barnacle (**B65**). Raised on coral rock walls that appear to grow from the rock ledge of Silver Bluff, the library's main reading room is a vaulted space wrapped with glass walls and a continuous exterior wood verandah. The verandah's canted walls, cantilevered from the rock base and faced in lapped siding, suggest a nautical motif. The original library has been fully reconstructed. The grounds contain the oldest marked grave in Miami-Dade County—that of Eva Munroe, the first wife of Commodore Munroe, who died in 1882 at their camp along the Miami River.

The World of Mayfair   B63

B63

The development of Mayfair at the north end of Coconut Grove's traditional center reflected the urban center's 1970s-1980s drift toward a regional shopping, leisure, and arts district. The carefully conceived and articulated urban complex integrates a hotel, private club and spa, department store, shopping center, and two subterranean parking levels across two-and-a-half blocks, spanning Rice Street (now Mayfair Lane). While the project is densely urban, it also was a product of zoning codes that imposed height limits in the Coconut Grove village center, prohibiting towers and encouraging midrise development with a mix of uses.

The overall complex is unified by consistent decorative and artistic themes. The architect, Kenneth Treister, was committed to the integration of architecture and the arts. Drawing on the idea of the Grove as an arts center, and with an intent to humanize a large urban structure, he conceived an architecture that mixes modern architecture with eclectic decorative themes based on Mediterranean and Latin American traditions. The resulting efflorescence of detail has been much admired and critiqued over the years.

In contrast with the orthogonal character of the main structures, the detailing of various areas tends toward artisanally worked organic forms and details. Wall surfaces are encrusted with a variety of floral designs sculpted in concrete and stucco in a modern version of Art Nouveau. Mosaic patterns made from fragments of tile embroider walls and benches. Lamps and decorative sculptures are forged of copper with a patina of age. Other ornamental accents include quarry keystone, screens of Brazilian ipe, polished brass, stained glass, painted murals, fountains, and large areas planted with ferns.

The structures are rather introverted; yet, the vision of a dense and low-scaled urban commercial core was a significant step in urban design terms and inspired several nearby projects, including CocoWalk (**B64**).

Mayfair in the Grove (Mayfair East)
2911 Grand Avenue
Kenneth Treister with Antonio Cantillo, 1979

Mayfair in the Grove, on the corner of Mary Street and Grand Avenue, was the first Mayfair component to be completed. Originally built as a luxe, 3-level mall, it has evolved to serve a variety of functions. When completed, it was touted as a new model of in-town mall based on "cultivated elegance." Developed by architect Kenneth Treister, partly in collaboration with developer Edward J. DeBartolo, it proposed a European-type shopping experience that mixed lushly landscaped plazas and courts, fountains, art, and sculpture with luxury shops, sidewalk cafés, and amenities like valet parking. Built around atria over two levels of underground parking, the mall forms a pedestrian arcade linking Florida Avenue with Grand Avenue.

Although visually engaging, the complex has been recurrently described as cacophonous. Mayfair struggled as a high-end retail destination. With the completion of the extroverted CocoWalk next door in 1990, a new commercial paradigm based on popular eateries and entertainment took hold. In 1994, a 10-screen movie theater and Planet Hollywood–themed restaurant were brought in to try to increase occupancy and energize the mall. As of this writing, Mayfair in the Grove incorporates retail, gallery, and office uses.

Mayfair West and Mayfair Lane
Kenneth Treister with Antonio Cantillo, 1984

Just west of Mayfair in the Grove, the complex expanded in 1984 with the construction of a custom Burdines department store; its merchandise was initially specially selected to fit the upscale Mayfair's concept. Farther west, Rice Street was redeveloped as Mayfair Lane, creating additional retail spaces around a pedestrian mall. Part of Mayfair Lane was designed to access the parking garage in Mayfair West. Although privately owned, the street has a public character, paved with a variety of tile mosaics, and inhabited with fountains, benches, and decorative urban furnishings.

Mayfair House Hotel
3000 Florida Avenue
Kenneth Treister with Antonio Cantillo, 1983–85

Mayfair House Hotel occupies the western side of the Mayfair complex, with 5 levels comprising 185 rooms, retail space, restaurants, and an outdoor café. Zoning incentives resulted in the creation of a basement theater/auditorium that doubles as a ballroom.

Like Mayfair in the Grove, the hotel features a complex spatiality based on a series of multilevel patios. Here, the architecture seems more stylistically restrained, yet the full extent of Treister's vision is also still intact. There are two interconnected patios, one of which is covered by a skylight. Each is surrounded by lushly planted galleries, sculpture, and abundant wood trim. The galleries provide access to the rooms yet share the space of the multistory atria. Brass-framed glass elevators rise from the interconnected fountains that run along the floor of the patios.

The façade is more permeable than its neighbors, owing to the residential character of the upper floors. The exterior walls are a sculpted armature of concrete with a Gaudiesque treatment of infill materials. Copper screen panels, portraying a bird and a butterfly, fill two high corner panels. Wood-slatted garden trellises screen the private balcony of each room, and showers of bougainvillea spill into the street. The entrance is through the cutaway corner on Florida and Virginia streets; given the building's scale, the lobby is unexpectedly intimate.

CocoWalk B64

3015 Grand Avenue
John Clark/D. I. Design, 1989

CocoWalk was not the first building of its size in Coconut Grove, but its intense, outward disposition and location at the heart of the Grove's village center marked a milestone in the area's development. It launched dozens of imitators in South Florida and beyond; even suburban shopping malls have sprouted CocoWalk-like appendages complete with Mediterranean arcades and curbside cafes.

Like Mayfair before it, CocoWalk is a mixed-use complex with plenty of public space, bountiful ornamentation, and concealed parking. The site sits at an even more advantageous location, at the junction of Grand Avenue, McFarlane Road, and Main Highway. Zoning controls limited the height to 50 feet, so the complex is mid-rise, tying into the scale of Mayfair and linking it to the heart of the village.

In contrast with Mayfair, CocoWalk was based on a more popular (and eventually more enduring) entertainment formula. The project takes some inspiration from Disney, and its architectural formulas, which make shallow allusion to Miami's Mediterranean Revival traditions, seem principally intended to distract and animate. Of note are the outdoor spaces, which, partly sheltered yet open to the street, work well. Almost every public area of the complex is open-air, and a variety of terraces, including a large outdoor bar above the center pavilion, illustrate the commercial potential in Miami of indoor-outdoor spaces.

In a valiant gesture, a storefront was located at the termination of the Florida Avenue view corridor. Unfortunately, it is stranded between the parking garage and loading zone entries.

Barnacle B65

3485 Main Highway
Ralph Middleton Munroe, 1891
Raised to make 2-story building: 1908

For a pioneer, Ralph Middleton Munroe was an elegant figure, and so was the house he built for himself on the shores of Biscayne Bay in Coconut Grove—an aestheticized merger of Bungalow with Florida Cracker architectural vernacular.

Munroe, a sailing buff, had visited the area as early as 1877. He decided to make the fledgling town his permanent home in 1889 and acquired bayfront land that was partially covered in native hardwood hammock. He first completed a small boathouse at the water's edge and lived on its second floor while he designed and constructed the main house. Munroe's knowledge of boat building has surely influenced both structures.

B65

The main house, surrounded by a wrapping veranda on three sides, has a squarish plan whose rooms were arranged four-square around an octagonal central dining room. It was sheltered by a pyramidal roof vented at the top, creating a chimney effect from the dining room below. Raised off the ground, the bottom of the structure was also fully vented. Although strong, the structure was light; when the need to expand it arose, it was innovatively raised and a new ground floor added below. Munroe can be considered a founder of Coconut Grove, having encouraged its early development and having named the post office in 1884. In addition to his reputation as a boat designer, he became known as an amateur photographer of the natural environment.

Coconut Grove Playhouse   B66
2500 Main Highway
Kiehnel and Elliott, 1926
Renovation: Alfred Browning Parker, 1955

B66

The Mediterranean Revival–style Coconut Grove Playhouse was originally
a movie palace, designed in 1926 by Kiehnel and Elliott. Only nine years
earlier the firm had designed and built El Jardin (**B80**), the nearby home of
John Brindley that is often considered the first real synthesis of the style.
The theater, conceived to be Miami's largest, was turned over to Paramount
Pictures before completion. The auditorium was wrapped on its street sides
by several stories of commercial space, capitalizing on its prominent urban
frontage. A top floor of residential penthouses was also included. The theater was not a success, closing in the 1930s.

   Renovations in 1955 by Alfred Browning Parker converted the cinema
into a full performing arts theater, Miami's first. Parker added a second,
smaller stage near the entrance, a mezzanine in the main hall, and a variety
of backstage workspaces. Over time, the theater became one of the most
important playhouses in the South. The building is currently abandoned,
but plans call for the renovation of the structure and the introduction of a
smaller series of theater boxes within the complex.

3430 Main Highway (Bank of Coconut Grove)   B67
Walter DeGarmo, 1923

This single-story former bank building manages a quite monumental entrance. Note the richly ornamented door surround.

Saint Stephen's Episcopal Church
and Day School   B68
3439 Main Highway
Cloister: 1919
William E. Tschumy, 1959
Expansion: Jorge L. Hernandez, 2001
Expansion: Briley & Associates, 2008

B67 and B69

Saint Stephen's Episcopal Church was founded in 1910, and its first structure was completed in 1912. In 1919, a cloister was added, leading from the
original Mission-style church to Main Highway. Unfortunately, the original
church was demolished in 2009.

   A new church building designed by William Tschumy and reminiscent
of the work of Frank Lloyd Wright was completed in 1959. More recently, the
campus has been further expanded.

Peacock Plaza and Anthony Arcade   B69
3436–3468 Main Highway
From a plan by John Erwin Bright, 1925

Intimately scaled and well-suited to the climate, Peacock Plaza and the
Anthony Arcade are among the few remaining structures of the town plan
for the area by Philadelphia architect John Erwin Bright.

West Grove

Coconut Grove has traditionally been divided between white and black sections; the division is marked roughly by Thirty-second Avenue. While the "white" Grove's fortunes have fluctuated, it remains an upscale area. The "black" Grove, also known as West Grove, contains some poorer areas. While its commercial arteries have suffered from economic disinvestment, many of West Grove's residential areas retain the intimately scaled West Indian charm that once characterized the pregentrified "white" Grove.

Charles Avenue   B70
Between Douglas Road and Main Highway

Here on Charles Avenue, once the hub of the Grove's Afro-Bahamian immigrant community, is a nineteenth- and early twentieth-century assemblage that is a virtual village. In addition to housing, there are civic institutions like the library, fraternal societies, churches, and a cemetery.

E.W.F. Stirrup House   B71
3242 Charles Avenue
E.W.F. Stirrup, 1897

Ebenezer Woodbury Franklin Stirrup was a Bahamian carpenter who migrated to the United States seeking work in 1888. Eventually, he built and settled in this house in 1897 and occupied it until his death in 1957. Stirrup and his wife, Charlotte Jane, built over one hundred homes, mostly for their fellow Bahamians to rent and, eventually, to buy. While these simple homes, some of which may still be found on Charles Avenue, were built in styles from the islands, Stirrup's home has been described as a "Gabled-Ell," with two gabled rooflines perpendicular to each other.

B71

Macedonia Baptist Church   B72
3515 Douglas Road
1948

This very early congregation was formed in 1894 as a church for persons of African descent, as Miami's race relations plunged into the abyss of racial segregation at the end of the nineteenth century. Previously, whites and blacks had worshipped together at the Union Chapel. The earlier building was at 3500 Charles Avenue. Across the street is the Coconut Grove Cemetery, established in 1913 as the final resting place of black Miamians. It reflects the Bahamian style preferences of many of those who are buried here.

Christel Episcopal Church   B73
Christ Episcopal Church   B73
3481 Hibiscus Street

Though the date of construction is unclear, the congregation was founded
in 1901 and was led by Father Theodore Gibson, community activist, civil
rights leader, and Miami city commissioner. The oldest church in Coconut
Grove in its original location (on land donated by E. W. F. Stirrup), it is also
arguably the most picturesque. It, and its setting, transport the visitor to the
Bahamas or a Caribbean isle.

Elizabeth Virrick Park   B74
Metrorail: Douglas Road

Plaza and Oak streets
Kenneth Treister, 1963

B73

Virrick Park, dedicated to Coconut Grove activist and housing reformer
Elizabeth Virrick, was developed in the early 1960s to serve residents of the
West (black) Grove. Kenneth Treister conceived the park as a "community
focal point" for neighborhood residents, a type of town square. To frame
and shelter activities in the park, he sculpted a series of biomorphic mushrooms, creating an organic architectural environment. The mushrooms are
scattered within the park's tree canopy, and among the shuffleboard courts,
horseshoe pitching, sandboxes, playgrounds, and dance areas that defined
its active recreation.

B74

   It was in this park that the architect first developed the Expressionist architecture he would later use in the Gumenick Chapel at Temple Israel (C36),
and at the World of Mayfair (B63). The mushrooms were constructed using
ferro-cemento, a technique in which concrete is sprayed over a flexible armature of steel reinforcing rods and wire mesh. The resulting thin shells had
a variety of uses in Miami. The park is as much a personal expression as a
work of civic architecture.

Grand Island   B75
Metrorail: Douglas Road

3705 Grand Avenue
Eric Vogt, ca. 2004

Filling in the northwest corner of the West Grove's main intersection,
Grand Island is a fine contribution to ongoing efforts at local revitalization.
Drawing on Mediterranean, vernacular, and elements of pure fantasy, the
building's tower elements assert the intersection's importance.

B75

Saint Hugh Roman Catholic Church   B76
3460 Royal Road
Murray Blair Wright, 1961

Saint Hugh is one of the most beautiful of the postwar crop of "praying
hands"–type churches. To create its soaring roof, twenty-eight glue-
laminated beams of Arkansas pine were assembled in pairs over pyramidal
concrete supports. The beams support wood planking more than 3 inches
thick. Oolitic rock walls surround the lower sanctuary, and leaded-glass windows cap the narrow ends.

B76

B77

Plymouth Congregational Church   B77
3429 Devon Road
Clinton Mackenzie, 1916

In spite of its secluded location on Main Highway, this small church hints at the urban potential of Spanish-themed architecture. Its façade fronts a simple stone plaza, or "parvis," flanked by low walls terminated by stone pavilions at either end. Known as the "Church in the Garden," the ensemble is embraced by landscaping on either side.

The church sits on land procured by George Spalding and George E. Merrick, future developer of Coral Gables, and its construction was originally funded by the sale of part of this land to a group of retired admirals, bestowing on the adjacent subdivision its name, Admiral's Row.

Merrick sent New York architect Clinton MacKenzie to study in Mexico before designing the church. Indeed, the design is an early example of Mission-style architecture in Miami, and is rumored to be based on a Mission church in Mexico. The original structure was built of Miami oolite by a single mason, Felix Rebom, who achieved its aged and weathered appearance using primitive tools. The main door, of hand-carved walnut and oak, is a real antique: three hundred years old, it was procured from a monastery in the Pyrenees Mountains.

Robert Law Weed executed renovations and expansions in 1947, and transepts were added in 1954. Classrooms, offices, and a fellowship hall were built adjacent to the original church and frame an open courtyard.

First Coconut Grove School House   B78
3429 Devon Road
1887
Relocated: 1970

Perhaps the simplest expression of a regional vernacular architecture, this building was constructed as a Sunday school near the Peacock Inn on

B78

McFarlane Road and Mary Street, and served as the forerunner of Plymouth Congregational Church (B77). Lumber salvaged from wrecked ships was used to construct the single-story, 1-room structure. Its roof was gabled and its walls were built in the board-and-batten style. In 1889, it was rented to the school board for the area's first public schoolhouse. In 1970, it was donated to the church and moved to its current site. Restorative work has included the removal of many additions and the reinstallation of the original bell.

Ransom Everglades School   B79

3575 Main Highway
Pagoda: Green and Wicks, 1902
Band Cottage/Paul C. Ransom Cottage: 1909; Restoration: Rocco Ceo, 2001

Established by Paul Ransom in 1895, the Adirondack-Florida School was the nation's first two-campus migratory school. After World War II, the Adirondack campus at the Meenagha Lodge in Upstate New York was sold, and the Coconut Grove facility was renamed Ransom School. In 1974, the school merged with nearby Everglades School to become Ransom Everglades School.

Since the 1960s, the campus has expanded with new buildings that alluded to both the bayside location of the campus and the vernacular architecture of the historic Coconut Grove area. Large windows, overhangs, and porches to shade interiors from the sun are featured, while the frequent use of limestone relates other local historic structures. The campus has grown building by building as the school's needs have evolved, creating a central quadrangle that is the center of student activity. Circulation among most areas of campus traverses this space shaded by mature live oaks and royal poincianas. A historic cannon salvaged from an English shipwreck at the bottom of Biscayne Bay sits centrally located in the quadrangle; students decorate it regularly for sporting events and other occasions.

The Pagoda is the most important and only remaining building associated with the early history of the Adirondack-Florida School. A 2-story rectangular structure, the wood-frame building sits high on the coastal escarpment, raised above the ground on Miami oolite piers. The building features a double-hipped roof and walls of vertical board-and-batten siding. The second story rests on the truncated hipped roof of the larger first story, vaguely recalling an East Asian pagoda. Facing the bay on the northeast and southeast corners are two verandas, one of which was converted to a sleeping porch. Fenestration includes both double-hung sash and wood casement windows. The Pagoda's many windows, the high ceiling in the main room, the verandas, and its position on the escarpment along the bayshore make it superbly adapted to the climate. Today it is surrounded by modern classroom buildings built since the 1960s.

The small Band Cottage, constructed of Dade County pine, is the only other building that remains from Paul Ransom's original campus; it resembles the Pagoda in construction. Built in 1909, it was in danger of demolition to make room for a new Arts Building. A movement to save it mounted among faculty and alumni, resulting in its being moved to a slightly less central area of campus. Over the years, the building has had a variety of uses, from housing for faculty members to practice space for the school band. Currently, the building is used for meetings, small receptions, and social events.

Carrollton School of the Sacred Heart, Barat Campus (El Jardin)

B80

3747 Main Highway
El Jardin: Kiehnel and Elliott, 1918
Renovation of El Jardin: Geoffrey Steward, 2002
Science Hall & Library: Martinez & Alvarez Architecture, 2004
Barry Building: Martinez & Alvarez Architecture, 2005

B80

The core of what is now the Carrollton School's Barat Campus was the 10-acre bayfront estate of Pittsburgh steel magnate John Brindley. Brindley commissioned the Pittsburgh firm of Kiehnel and Elliott to design the home, bringing German-born architect Richard Kiehnel to Miami and launching that architect's long and productive career here. The house is patterned on a Renaissance palazzo, and in this regard hews closely to the themes of James Deering's Vizcaya (B47) of 1914. Like Deering's earlier house, it is composed around a central cortile, reflecting the environmentally desirable qualities of the age-old Mediterranean type. However, disregarding stylistic rigor, Kiehnel blurred Mediterranean influences, and deliberately antiqued the house, articulating a hybrid effect that would soon be known in Florida as the Mediterranean Revival. For instance, Kiehnel called the house's southern porch "the Moorish Living Room," referring to its details and materiality. The traditional effects transform what is in many respects a modern home, built of concrete and whose decorative carvings were in fact molded in cast stone. The house opens both physically and metaphorically toward the bay, where it steps down to a grotto that embraces the pool.

The home reopened in 1962 as Carrollton School of the Sacred Heart; many of the students were transplants from the Sacred Heart School in Cuba. Since then the school has grown. The Science Hall and Library addition, which helps frame the approach to El Jardin, is a contemporary take on that building's Mediterranean Revival architecture. The mainly 2-story building's linear form frames an elongated quadrangle aimed at the main façade of the former Brindley House. Loggias carved into the building mass on both floors create pools of shade. At its west end, a colonnaded loggia over three arches makes an explicit play on the façade of its historic neighbor. The opposite, eastern end terminates in the octagonal body of the library. Opposite the library, the Barry addition also frames the central quadrangle, while turning the corner to the old carriage house. Until the early twentieth century, the El Jardin site was a pine rockland landscape, located on the oolitic limestone base known as the Miami Ridge. Today, the richly landscaped campus retains a few pines as well as the exotic materials that were introduced into the lawns and formal gardens.

Carrollton School, Duchesne Campus (Howard Hughes Medical Center)

B81

3645 Main Highway
Taylor Hall: Trelles Cabarrocas, 2004

The Carrollton School's Duchesne Campus occupies part of the original William Matheson Estate, once named Swastika (after the Native American symbol of the four directions) and later renamed Pelican Lodge. The property became the Howard Hughes Medical Center before it was acquired by the Carrollton School in 1991. Taylor Hall, a recent addition, was inspired by the local tradition of Mediterranean Revival architecture, combining a flat-roofed 2-story classroom and science laboratory wing and an assembly space whose gabled front clearly expresses its civic role within the campus. The two structures are tied together by a wrapping porch that faces a spacious green. More than a functional or symbolic element, the porch is a key gathering spot for the campus. Doric columns hold the porch roof, which is elegantly framed in exposed wood rafters and decking. Tile roofs connect to the campus's other buildings, while the fleur-de-lis centered over the gabled front of the assembly hall connects to the French origins of the Sacred Heart order.

Bet-Ovadia Chabad of the Grove (Bryan Memorial Methodist Church)   B82

3713 Main Highway
Kiehnel and Elliott, 1928

B82

Built by William Jennings Bryan adjacent to his home, the Anchorage, this building is an example of Byzantine influence in religious architecture. This is evidenced in the octagonal (rather than a long, rectangular) western nave design. The design included an outdoor pulpit. Unfortunately, Bryan died before its opening and just after the close of the Scopes Monkey Trial, where he led the prosecution.

Kampong   B83

4013 Douglas Road
House: Edward Clarence Dean, 1928
New Educational Pavilion: Max Strang Architects, 2006

B83

The Kampong, meaning "cluster of houses" or "village" in Malay, is the former estate and introduction garden of Dr. David Fairchild, one of America's most distinguished botanists, horticulturalists, and plant collectors. It was because of Fairchild's prominence in these fields that his name was later chosen for Fairchild Tropical Garden. Today, the estate is a branch of the Hawaii-based National Botanical Garden.

The estate's house was designed in 1928 by Edward Clarence Dean, who also designed Fairchild's home near Washington, D.C., and consists of two large wings connected with a large arched stone breezeway. The house's architecture defies any formal stylistic label, but suggests Mediterranean Revival with Southeast Asian details rendered in a Modern manner. While much of the house is obscured by lush vegetation, the elliptical arch in the breezeway terminates the view corridor of the driveway and frames a spectacular view of the bay. The siting of the house at the top of the escarpment allows the view to be fully appreciated only after reaching the breezeway: here, the broad lawn sloping down to a boat basin lined with mangroves becomes apparent. Fortuitously, the boat basin is aligned in such a way that only the undeveloped southern portion of Key Biscayne is visible on the horizon.

A new open-air educational pavilion features oolitic limestone, tropical ipe, quarry keystone, and coffered wood ceilings, as well as a roof that serves to collect water for the gardens.

C

City of Miami: Northeast

This area is bounded by Biscayne Bay on the east, I-95 on the west, I-395 on the south, and the city's northern border. It comprises early settlements, some predating the Florida East Coast Railway. In the 1920s, Biscayne Boulevard/U.S. 1 (the northern approach to the city) would become one of Miami's most important arteries. The area includes formerly independent towns, such as Buena Vista, Little River, and Lemon City, which now constitute a part of the metropolitan core. It also includes once-affluent suburbs like Miramar and Edgewater along the bayfront. Since World War II, the area's characteristic east-west racial divide has shifted. Immigration, gentrification, and prohibitive real estate prices on Miami Beach have all contributed to create one of Miami's more diverse areas.

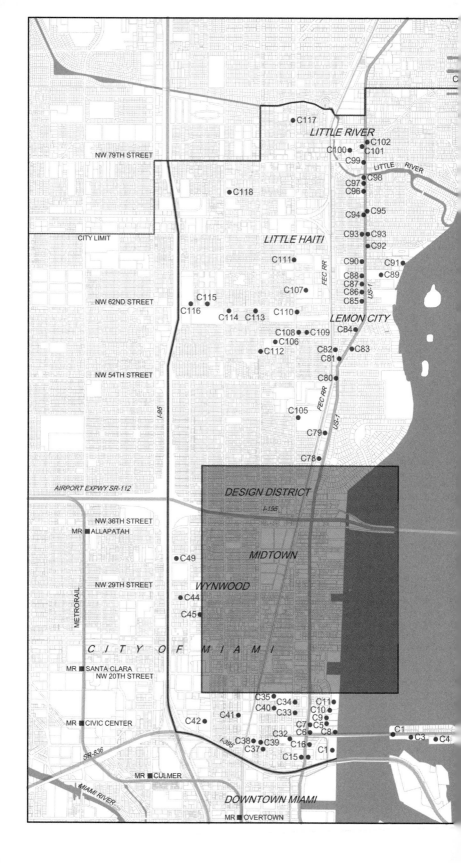

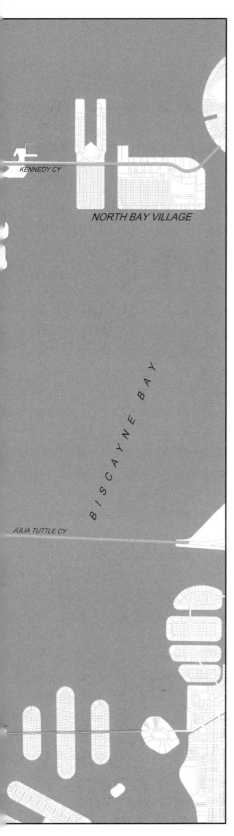

KENNEDY CY

NORTH BAY VILLAGE

B I S C A Y N E   B A Y

JULIA TUTTLE CY

C. City of Miami: Northeast

Miami Herald   C1

Metromover: Omni

1 Herald Plaza
Naess and Murphy, 1960
North wing top-floor addition: Frank Beas, 1984–88

C1   After the secret assemblage of the 10 prime waterfront acres between the
MacArthur and Venetian causeways, a process that took five years, construction began on the Miami Herald Building, the largest building in Florida at
the time. The structure was modeled after the Chicago Sun-Times Building
of 1957, also by Naess and Murphy, on the banks of the Chicago River. Similar
to the Chicago Sun-Times Building, the Herald Building was designed to receive newsprint via barge. While that activity has long since ceased (though
vestiges of the unloading apparatus remain), the building and its ancillary
radio tower maintain an iconic presence on the waterfront between the two
causeways.

With its egg-crate façade screened by sun-protection devices, the Miami
Herald Building exemplifies the regionalist consciousness developing in
mid-twentieth-century corporate architecture. The offices of the newspaper
occupy the southern portion of the building, its windows appointed with
finely crafted metal brise-soleils, originally painted blue to contrast with
spandrel panels covered in gold- and butter-colored mosaic tile. The building's hurricane-proof design was far ahead of its time.

The porte cochere is an essay in Classical proportion and Modern detailing. A colonnade of rectangular piers supports a canopy that tapers, almost
aerodynamically, at the edges and rises three stories to serve doubly as a
low canopy over the parking pedestal, a popular spot for smokers on break.
The canopy is punctured by large, glazed, round openings allowing sunlight
to enter the grand lobby space through an expansive 30-foot-high window
wall divided by a finely crafted grid of metal muntins. Similar to the placement of banking halls within large office buildings, the double-height lobby
features escalators leading to the second-floor business room, a double-
height space with sweeping views of Biscayne Bay. While the business room
is camouflaged during the day behind the window grid, its volume is readily discernable at night from the MacArthur Causeway. Typical of slab-type
construction in Miami, the narrow, south side wall is windowless and clad in
white marble. Below the offices, the parking pedestal is clad in contrasting
brown aggregate over a folded-plate surface pattern. The press room and
printing plant are housed in the windowless north volume of the building
and are separated structurally from the office wing to prevent vibration in
the offices. In response to the need for additional office space, a floor was
added to the north wing in the 1980s, thus the top-floor windows.

Venetian Causeway   C2

Metromover: Omni

Layout of islands: Whitney C. Bliss, 1922–23
Bridge engineer: Harvey Stanley, 1924
Reconstruction: David Volkert & Associates, 1996

The Venetian Causeway follows the alignment of the Collins Bridge, com-
pleted in 1913 as the first roadway connection between Miami and Miami
Beach and, at the time, the longest wooden bridge in the world. The Bay
Biscayne Improvement Company bought the rapidly deteriorating wood

C2

bridge in 1922 and devised a plan to build a new and more permanent causeway of concrete bridges along with a string of planned island communities spanning the bay. The new Venetian Causeway opened in 1926, a few years after the County Causeway (MacArthur Causeway) opened a short distance to the south.

The causeway's rhythmic alternation of land and water features low-slung bridges whose distinctive concrete guardrails allow glimpses of the bay's turquoise waters. In the 1990s, when the Florida Department of Transportation announced the reconstruction of the causeway bridges, community activists led a successful effort against the plan to install taller bridges, and to replace distinctive balustrades with solid concrete barriers, commonly referred to as Jersey barriers. In a compromise, the bridges remain low and the new balustrades are as close in dimensions to the original as current safety codes would allow. Decorative concrete obelisks frame the entrance on the Miami side and identify the causeway as the Venetian "Shortway."

Biscayne Island

While the Venetian Isles were largely planned for single-family houses, Belle Isle on the east end and Biscayne Island on the west end feature clusters of multifamily dwellings. The south side of Biscayne Island offers one such cluster. This portion of Biscayne Island was originally home to Viking Field, a small Downtown waterfront airport that accommodated both land and amphibious aircraft. Constructed in 1928, the airport closed by 1937 and was redeveloped after World War II.

1000 Venetian Way   C3
Tomas L. Lopez-Gottardi, 1980

The condo boom of the 1980s produced sculptural variations on high-rise apartment slab design. Here, a hybrid design strategy was employed to address different scales of urban frontage. One of the few high-rise buildings located in the center of Biscayne Bay, the distinctive L-shaped form and stair-stepping profile of 1000 Venetian Way make it a prominent landmark. Two thin residential towers face south to the bay while the stepped west wing faces west toward Miami. A network of interior streets, lined by 3-story townhouses at the base of the towers, separates the complex from the multistory parking garage located along the causeway. The roof of the parking garage is a landscaped patio, pool, and community room accessed by bridges from the towers. The towers are extraordinarily thin, allowing only two apartments per floor, each with 270-degree views and wrapping balconies.

C3

The Sandpiper   C4
1100, 1110, 1120, 1130, and 1140 Venetian Way
1949

The Sandpiper is a snapshot of the modest scale and pretensions of postwar garden-apartment living in a bayfront setting. A primary impression of the

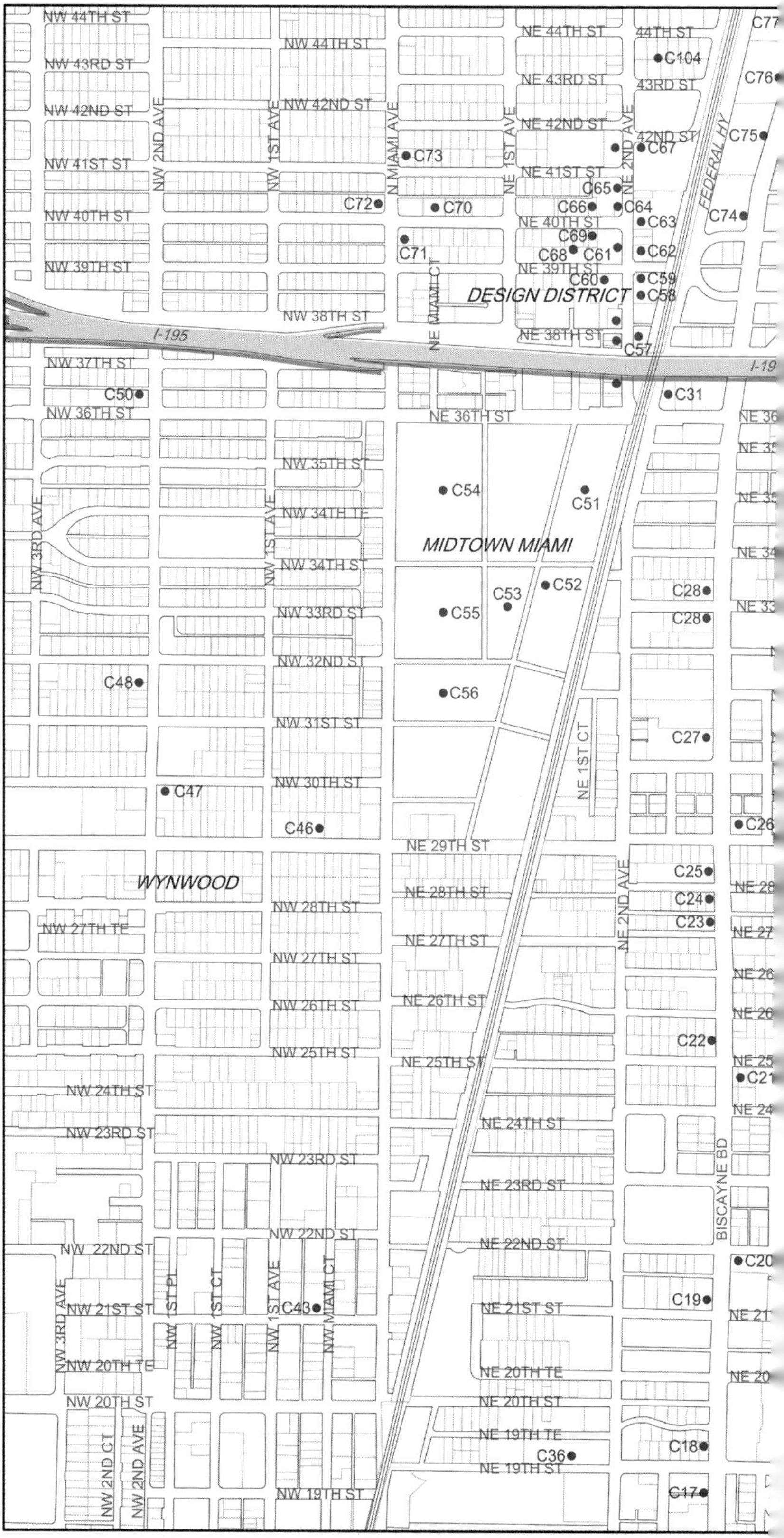

NW 44TH ST
NW 43RD ST
NW 42ND ST
NW 2ND AVE
NW 1ST AVE
NW 44TH ST
NW 42ND ST
NE 44TH ST
44TH ST
• C104
C77
C76•
NE 43RD ST
43RD ST
NW 41ST ST
NE 42ND ST
N MIAMI AVE
NE 1ST AVE
NE 2ND AVE
• C73
42ND ST
• C67
C75•
NW 40TH ST
NW 39TH ST
C72•
• C70
NE 41ST ST
C65•
C66• •C64
NE 40TH ST
C69•
C68• •C61
• C63
C74•
FEDERAL HY
NE 39TH ST
C60•
•C59
•C58
• C62
C71•
NE MIAMI CT
DESIGN DISTRICT
•C57
NW 38TH ST
NE 38TH ST
•C57
I-195
• C31
I-19
NW 37TH ST
C50•
NW 36TH ST
NE 36TH ST
NE 36
NE 35
NW 35TH ST
NW 3RD AVE
NW 1ST AVE
• C54
C51
NE 35
NW 34TH TE
MIDTOWN MIAMI
NE 34
NW 34TH ST
• C52
C28•
NE 33
NW 33RD ST
C53•
• C55
C28•
NW 32ND ST
C48•
• C56
NW 31ST ST
C27•
NW 30TH ST
• C47
C46•
• C26
NE 29TH ST
WYNWOOD
NW 28TH ST
NE 28TH ST
C25•
NE 28
NW 27TH TE
NW 27TH ST
NE 27TH ST
C24•
C23•
NE 27
NW 26TH ST
NE 26TH ST
NE 26
NW 25TH ST
NE 2ND AVE
NE 26
C22•
NE 25
NW 24TH ST
NE 25TH ST
• C21
NE 24
NW 23RD ST
NE 24TH ST
NW 23RD ST
NE 23RD ST
BISCAYNE BD
NW 3RD AVE
NW 22ND ST
NW 22ND ST
NE 22ND ST
• C20
NW 1ST PL
NW 1ST CT
NW 1ST AVE
NW MIAMI CT
NW 21ST ST
C43•
NE 21ST ST
C19•
NE 21
NW 20TH TE
NE 20TH TE
NE 20
NW 20TH ST
NE 20TH ST
NW 2ND CT
NW 2ND AVE
NE 19TH TE
C36•
C18•
NE 19TH ST
NW 19TH ST
C17•

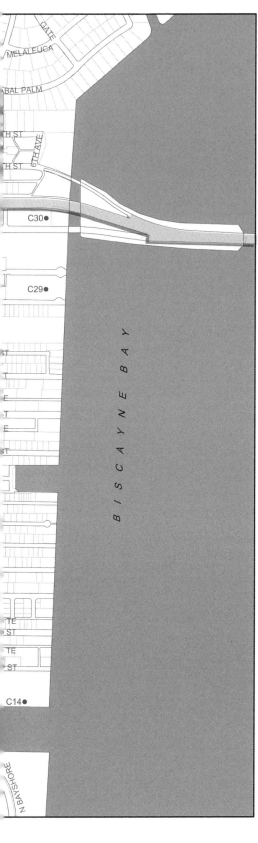

Edgewater, Midtown,
Wynwood, Design District

ensemble contrasts their low-slung volumes with counterposing vertical elements, whose alternating shed roof slopes give a syncopated rhythm to the complex. Overhanging planes, beanpole columns, slump brick, decorative metal railings, and quarry tile floors are the Sandpiper's chief decoration.

The five 2-story apartment buildings are neatly aligned as if along a street, although they are set back a considerable distance from Venetian Way. The buildings are mirrored around patio and service courts, and every unit has a private balcony or stoop/terrace.

Edgewater/Biscayne Boulevard

Informally bounded by Biscayne Bay and the Florida East Coast Railway, from the Arsht Performing Arts Center to NE Thirty-sixth Street, the Edgewater neighborhood comprises one of Miami's first suburban districts. Today, it is a neighborhood in transition, with some of Miami's oldest homes and apartment buildings interspersed among new and larger structures. Edgewater is an assemblage of many small subdivisions (most comprising only one or two streets), offering little coordination and only intermittent waterfront access. This chaos was partly unified by the later construction of Biscayne Boulevard, which cut a grand four-lane thoroughfare through the existing grid. When the developers of Biscayne Boulevard, the Shoreland Company, became casualties of the 1926 bust, the company was purchased by Henry Phipps of the U.S. Steel Corporation and reformed as the Biscayne Boulevard Company. As the Shoreland Company had planned, Phipps completed the boulevard to Miami Shores and purchased most of the property between Thirteenth and Fortieth Streets with the intention of developing an upscale commercial district away from the Downtown bustle, and providing a beautiful and prominent linkage between Miami and Miami Shores. Although the real estate bust of 1926 had dampened the construction of new buildings in Miami, the initiation of Miami's first suburban shopping district along Biscayne Boulevard between 1929 and 1930 spurred commercial development and architectural innovation. This area produced several of Miami's first fully realized Art Deco edifices (including a Sears Roebuck store at Thirteenth Street and Biscayne Boulevard [C15] and the Shrine Building [C16]), as well as new building types designed to complement the character of the boulevard.

The Miramar subdivision, at the south end of Edgewater between NE Seventeenth and NE Nineteenth streets, offers one of Edgewater's most civic-minded plans. Here, North Bayshore Drive forms a waterfront boulevard, or malecón, today fronted by Margaret Pace Park. Eighteenth Street, which bisects the subdivision, terminates in the Miami City Cemetery. Farther north, the struggle to allow Edgewater residents and their Wynwood neighbors access to Biscayne Bay continues with at least one battle over a bayfront street end, and with recent proposals to extend a baywalk along the neighborhood's east flank.

Trinity Cathedral   C5

Metromover: Omni

464 NE 16th Street
Cathedral: Harold Hastings Mundy, 1923
Bell tower: James Deen, 1984

Along with the nearby Miami Woman's Club (C11), Trinity Cathedral is a surviving fragment of the once elegant Biscayne Park subdivision of Edgewater.
Today it is hemmed in by the large concrete towers and parking decks of
the Plaza Venetia complex.

Trinity is a descendant of Miami's first church, supported by city pioneer
Julia Tuttle and organized in 1896 (the year of Miami's incorporation) in a
modest wooden structure. In sync with Miami's explosive growth during
the Great Florida Land Boom, the Episcopal congregation grew rapidly, and
acquired property in the half-platted district surrounding North Bayshore
Drive. There, Trinity built a grand stone church that could house more than
1,100 worshipers.

The church, designed by Harold Hastings Mundy, is said to have been
inspired by the twelfth-century church of St. Gilles du Gard in France,
whose nave was similarly fronted with a three-bay narthex. Romanesque,
Byzantine, and Italianate features mesh here, even before such synergies
became an intrinsic principle of Florida's Mediterranean Revival. Of note are
the stained-glass windows and the 56-rank E. M. Skinner/Æolian Skinner
pipe organ, whose warm tones reverberate in the extraordinary acoustical
space. In 1970, Trinity was elevated to the Cathedral of the Episcopal Diocese
of Southeast Florida.

Trinity Church's bell tower, including hand-cast bells, appears to have
been a peace offering from Tibor Hollo, developer of the surrounding Plaza
Venetia complex, who commissioned James Deen to design it in keeping
with the church's distinctive roofline.

Miami International University of Art   C6
and Design at Omni (Jordan Marsh
Department Store)

Metromover: Omni

1501 Biscayne Boulevard
Weed Russell Johnson Associates, 1955
Renovations: Alfonso Architects, 2004–6
Renovation of former department store: Robin Bosco/Architects & Planners, 2004–8

When it opened in 1956, this former Jordan Marsh department store was an
urban-suburban hybrid; it lined Biscayne Boulevard with generous vitrine
windows, but actually opened toward parking lots on its east side. Almost
two decades later, the store was transformed into an anchor of the Omni
Mall complex (C7).

After the failure of the mall, the store's lower floors were converted
to house the International Fine Arts College (later renamed Miami
International University of Art and Design). Most recently, the upper floors
have been reclad in blue and silver curtain wall, and repackaged as commercial office space.

Plaza Venetia

An alternative "urbia" bounded by Fifteenth and Seventeenth streets between Biscayne Boulevard and Biscayne Bay, Plaza Venetia was the umbrella concept for a vast urban complex of apartment buildings, hotels, offices, shopping centers, and entertainment venues. Developer Tibor Hollo conceived the complex in the late 1960s as an alternative to suburbia whose reassemblage of the basic components of urban life would be a first step in the regeneration of Miami's Downtown. Atlanta architect Joseph Amisano, designer of three structures in the complex, shared Hollo's convictions. At the heart of the project is what Hollo termed a "concept of living," the idea of an urban village. The dream of an urban core was joined by the conviction that size and density would assure its success. The project proudly proclaimed its status as a multiuse megaplex. Yet, its very size, requiring many variances and zoning amendments, combined with the spatial environments it produced, made Venetia the subject of abundant controversy, especially among planners, architects, and environmentalists.

Plaza Venetia occupies a strategic site just north of Downtown, at the midpoint of the automotive trajectory connecting Miami International Airport and Miami Beach. Its location was intended to reinvigorate the surrounding area as a major shopping destination, a status it had enjoyed since the northward extension of Biscayne Boulevard by the Phipps Family in the 1930s. Although conceived as a complex, the buildings developed incrementally with few connections nor much for the pedestrian at street level. Venetia dwarfs North Bayshore Drive, as well as buildings like the Miami Woman's Club and Trinity Episcopal Church (which is surrounded by the project). Sparse on "plazas" or "Venetia," its lack of public open space juxtaposed with very high density defines a mixed legacy. On the other hand, the Biscayne Bay Marina, an integral component of Hollo's master plan for a vibrant urban complex, includes a baywalk that ties together the Biscayne Bay–facing Venetia components.

C7

Omni International   C7

Metromover: Omni

1601 Biscayne Boulevard
Toombs, Amisano & Wells, 1973

Plaza Venetia began with a proposal for two residential towers and a 5-story hotel over a shopping center facing Biscayne Boulevard. The project was sold in development to Atlanta-based International City Corporation, which completed it as an "Omni" complex based on its similar urban projects in Atlanta and Norfolk. For some twenty years, this multiuse megastructure fulfilled its goal of being a "city within a city." In concert with the overall concept of Venetia, its intention was to replace the "inconvenient" and "haphazard" arrangements of older cities with a rationalized structure based on vertical layering of components and amenities.

The Omni exploited the popularity of enclosed urban shopping malls in the 1970s. On the bottom levels, the shopping mall was anchored by an existing Jordan Marsh department store (C6) and a new J. C. Penney. The pedestal also contained 165 shops, six movie theaters, fifteen restaurants, and an indoor entertainment center complete with carousel. At the entertainment center, the mall merges into the hotel lobby, a multistory atrium. Here, glass skylights cascade from the roof decks to the street, stairs zigzag upward, and glass elevators whoosh up and down. The pedestrian bridge across NE Fifteenth Street to the Omni Metromover was added in the 1990s.

Typical of such complexes, the Omni was inward facing, with uninterrupted opaque walls of 30-foot precast-concrete panels along most of its Biscayne Boulevard frontage. The bronze glass-clad hotel tower with 550 rooms rises above. Today, the hotel continues to operate, but much of the center remains empty, awaiting redevelopment.

For a time, the Omni brought much-needed commercial activity to the area, but overall, it is an architecture of massive features, with little to offer the pedestrian. Emblematic of the problems, the center is served by a massive 2,700-car parking garage along the east side, facing North Bayshore Drive. Occupying nearly two blocks with no habitable space on the ground floor, the garage presents a harsh face to the rest of the Venetia complex and Trinity Cathedral.

Plaza Venetia Building   C8

Metromover: Omni

555 15th Street
William Dorsky, 1980

Soon after completion of the Omni, the 35-story Plaza Venetia Building was developed just to the east, on the corner of NE Fifteenth Street and North Bayshore Drive. This apartment-hotel follows a tower-over-pedestal organizational scheme, and although its components are bulky, the bay-facing

C8–C10

portion of the pedestal is concealed behind a liner of living units (a practice common today, but progressive at the time). Unfortunately, the untreated walls of the parking garage loom up behind Trinity Cathedral. Subtle and abstract variations in the balconies, and offset vertical pylons give some play to what is otherwise a plain multiplication of floor trays.

Miami Marriott Biscayne Bay   C9
Metromover: Omni

1633 North Bayshore Drive
Toombs, Amisano & Wells, 1983

The 31-story, L-shaped tower of the Marriott Hotel rises just to the north of Plaza Venetia. Like the Omni hotel tower, its façade presents simple variations on a grid of windows. Its parking structure is well concealed from the bay, but all too evident from North Bayshore Drive. Access to the building is either through the uninviting auto ramps that approach the lobby porte cochere, or via a pedestrian bridge connecting to the Omni parking garage.

The Grand (Venetia)   C10
Metromover: Omni

1717 North Bayshore Drive
Toombs, Amisano & Wells, 1986

The most ambitious Plaza Venetia project was simply called "Venetia." Its massive block rises 365 feet, containing 820 apartments and 152 hotel suites around twin 32-story interior atria (the building was noted to contain more space than the Empire State Building). The merging of apartments and hotel facilities was rare at the time, but predicted the popularity of this scheme in recent times. At its base is a full shopping concourse.

In the manner of architect John Portman, the tower slab incorporates two full-height enclosed atria. Interior galleries surround the atria, which also have windows and skylights to bring in daylight. On the west, these windows face the street, constituting the building's main decoration in that direction. Owing to a desire to exploit bayfront views, the eastern atrium has a narrow window facing south, a poor echo of the breezeways that pierce many Miami buildings, and Arquitectonica's famously perforated Atlantis tower on Brickell Avenue (A120). The building's north façade rises like a steep cliff behind the Miami Woman's Club (C11) and Margaret Pace Park to the north. Like the other Plaza Venetia pieces, it presents an intimidating scale to the street, largely ignoring the pedestrian while interiorizing public spaces and amenities.

Miami Woman's Club   C11
Metromover: Omni

1737 North Bayshore Drive
August Geiger, 1926

The Miami Woman's Club was the largest of many such facilities in Greater Miami, and its location along Biscayne Bay in the once-fashionable Edgewater district was a mark of distinction. Chartered in 1911, the club acquired this site in 1925 through the generosity of Florida East Coast Railway

C11

magnate Henry Flagler. With Flagler's support, the building's lower floors were developed to house the Flagler Memorial Library, forerunner of the Miami-Dade Public Library System. The design also anticipated an expansion, the later construction of Miami's largest auditorium on its west side.

August Geiger was one of the most important architects of boom-time Miami, serving as the architect of the Dade County School Board, in addition to performing many private commissions for Carl Fisher across the bay. Geiger here employed the rich vocabulary of Mediterranean and Renaissance Revival design that he had earlier pioneered in buildings like the Alamo (D2) in Miami and the Golf Club House in Miami Beach: arched windows and doors and a detailed ornamental package that suggested references from the Levant to Gibraltar. Fine-grained metal cresting once enlivened the façade, but has since been removed, a modernization required by rapid deterioration. The U-shaped building was designed with open galleries surrounding a garden courtyard that have since been enclosed. In recent years, the building served as the main campus of International Fine Arts College (today Miami International University of Art and Design [C6]) and as the backdrop for the design and furnishings exposition Casa Décor. The club still operates from the building, and was racially integrated in 2008.

Paramount Bay C12

Metromover: Omni

2066 North Bayshore Drive
Arquitectonica, 2007

Set at the western edge of a bayfront inlet, and at the north end of a segment of North Bayshore Drive, Paramount Bay certainly occupies a prominent position in the city's geography. Exploiting this position, its stepped and curved 46-story residential tower offers a striking sculptural profile to Biscayne Bay and North Bayshore Drive. The sweeping curve is a device with lineage back to Morris Lapidus's arcing design for the Fontainebleau Hotel (G1), but it also connects with Arquitectonica's own preoccupation with sail forms at nearby buildings like Marina Blue (A69) in Downtown and Blue

C12

(C30) in Edgewater. On its eastern frontage, angled balconies alternate 45 degrees, creating a rich "prismatic" pattern that animates the façade.

In order to contextualize the tower, early versions of the project engaged the preservation of the so-called "Mary" house, the 1920s-era waterfront home featured in the movie *There's Something about Mary*. The structure was a survivor of the affluent private homes that once claimed this waterfront area. Instead, the home was demolished, and low wings flank an automotive drop-off and porte cochere. Raised terraces on either side overlook the extension northward of North Bayshore Drive, whose new bayfront promenade is a major achievement of the project. To the west, the pedestal stretches back to Biscayne Boulevard, employing townhouses to partly conceal its parking decks, and offering office and commercial space toward Biscayne Boulevard.

C13

Unity by the Bay   C13

Metromover: Omni

411 NE 21st Street
Parish Hall: 1919
Church: Robert Fitch Smith, 1958

Although technically and formally less radical than some of its contemporaries, this Unitarian Universalist church nevertheless challenged standard ecclesiastic representational norms. The façade presents a gentle bow reflecting the vaulted space in its interior, and the bow is asymmetrically offset by the pylon of the church's belfry, which is partly enclosed with perforated-concrete breeze-block panels. Additional breeze-block screens wrap the entrance and community center on either side.

Behind the postwar structure are the well-preserved remnants of a 1920s estate that, before landfilling created the site of Biscayne 21 (C14), occupied a full block fronting Biscayne Bay. The U-shaped former home frames an internal sunken court. Its front porch, featuring Doric columns, leads to the main suite of rooms, including a beautifully preserved octagonal parlor. When the Unitarian Church purchased the property in 1954, it converted the home into a parish hall.

Biscayne 21   C14

2121 North Bayshore Drive
Melvin Grossman, 1963

Lining the north side of the inlet above Margaret Pace Park, this slab-type apartment tower designed by Melvin Grossman was the harbinger of a wave of high-rise residential development that has largely evaded Edgewater until recently. Grossman, the most prodigious architect of residential towers in Miami Beach in the 1960s, did little to distinguish Biscayne 21 from his many waterfront buildings on the other side of the bay.

Adrienne Arsht Center for the Performing Arts (Carnival Center)

Metromover: Omni

1300 Biscayne Boulevard
Cesar Pelli, 2004
Sears Roebuck building: Nimmons, Carr & Wright, 1929
Renovation of Sears Roebuck tower remnant: R. J. Heisenbottle Architects, 2004

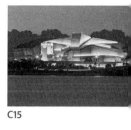

C15

Many in Miami had long harbored the dream of uniting the performing arts in a new state-of-the-art facility at a central location. That dream, begun as early as the mid-1970s, was given a significant boost in the early 1990s, when financing for the public-private partnership fell into place, and the newly formed Performing Arts Center Trust initiated a design competition for the project. The site chosen, while remote from Downtown, is strategically located near the interchange of Biscayne Boulevard and I-395, easily accessible to both Miami Beach and western Miami-Dade County. It falls directly on the site chosen in 1927 by the Shoreland Company as the entrance to its northern extension of Biscayne Boulevard, likewise chosen for its proximity to the MacArthur Causeway (which originally aligned with Thirteenth Street). The Shoreland Company marked this spot with chamfered corners surrounding a traffic island through which the streetcar line to Miami Beach ran. The northwest corner became the site of a Sears Roebuck store designed by the Chicago firm Nimmons, Carr & Wright. Featuring one of Miami's first Art Deco façades, the store had a prominent tower. As part of the performing arts center project, the base of the tower remnant was renovated for use as a restaurant.

Beyond Miami's artistic ambitions, the center was targeted to spur the redevelopment of the city's northeast section. Cesar Pelli's design, chosen at the close of a design competition, is comprised of two prismatic volumes wrapped in variegated granite that embrace a virtual plaza bisected by Biscayne Boulevard. Historic preservation concerns insisted on at least the preservation of the richly decorated tower of the Sears Roebuck building in the overall campus. On the east side of Biscayne Boulevard is the Symphony Hall. On the west side, the center includes major halls for ballet and opera, as well as a smaller black-box studio, a banquet hall, and an education center. Each structure features a multistory entrance hall that opens to city views through expansive glass walls that form billboards, looking up and down the boulevard. The Arsht Center is the home of the Florida Grand Opera and the Miami City Ballet, and features performances by local arts groups like Miami Light Project and Camposition.

Boulevard Shops (Shrine Building)

Metromover: Omni

1401 Biscayne Boulevard
Robert Law Weed, 1930
Renovation: Bouterse, Perez and Fabregas, 1980

In 1930, the Biscayne Boulevard Company hired Robert Law Weed to design this elegant and stylized 2-story commercial building. The Shrine Building is a classic type in which civic meeting facilities are located over a ground-floor market or shops. It derived its name from its initial and longtime second-floor occupant, the Mahi Shrine Temple. The Shrine Building was one of the first buildings to employ a cast imitation of local keystone, and its cast decoration heralded the flourishing of regional motifs in Art Deco. Most notable in this regard are the engaged, sculpted figures of Seminole Indians on the corners of the second-floor wings. The large spandrel panels below the second-floor windows of the wings feature sunburst reliefs. Renamed Boulevard Shops after a renovation in 1980, the building is the last intact structure from the genesis of Biscayne Boulevard as a prestigious suburban shopping address.

First Church of Christ Scientist   C17

Metromover: Omni

1836 Biscayne Boulevard
August Geiger, 1925

A vestige of the suburban affluence that once characterized the Edgewater neighborhood, this elegant church gives emphatic weight to the idea of a grand boulevard. Its sober Neoclassical lines clad in stone contrast with the more scenographic Mediterranean Revival–style buildings of the era. Broad stairs sweep up nearly a full floor to a grand portico of Ionic columns, topped by a tall attic story.

C17

Mead Building   C18

Metromover: Omni

1900 Biscayne Boulevard
Pancoast, Ferendino, Skeels and Burnham, 1959

After its initial development in the 1920s and 1930s as a suburban extension and retail corridor, Biscayne Boulevard was transformed after World War II into an important axis of commercial office building construction. Typical of its generation, this low-slung horizontal slab is distinguished by a layered façade system designed to screen the air-conditioned interior from the sun. Its window wall system, composed of alternating glass and composite green panels, is recessed behind the building's egg-crate concrete frame. Projecting in front of this frame are finely detailed, aluminum grate-type sunscreens. The rest of the building is sheathed in bands of white mosaic tile divided by aluminum strips. Entranceways are subtly announced by cantilevered concrete canopies. Built-in planters along the sidewalk in the layer between the window wall and metal screens blur the line between indoors and out, and emphasize suburban scale and street interface at odds with nearby retail frontages.

C18

Bacardi USA   C19

Metromover: Omni

2100 Biscayne Boulevard
Enrique Gutierrez, 1963
Annex: Ignacio Cabrera-Justiz, 1974

Political upheaval in Cuba and the completion of the Seagram Building in New York set the tone for Bacardi's development in Miami of a new corporate headquarters. As was the case with the Seagram Building, designed by Mies van der Rohe with Philip Johnson (1958), Modern architecture was

C19

employed to expunge the Prohibition-era association of alcohol with a
nebulous underworld, and to put forth a new image as an international con-
glomerate. Bacardi's chief Jose "Pepin" Bosch commissioned Mies to design
Bacardi's new offices in Santiago de Cuba in 1959, but political problems
pressed Bosch to diversify his company throughout the Americas. While
the Santiago project was never built, Mies and protégé Enrique Gutierrez
completed a new Bacardi headquarters in Mexico City in 1962. Gutierrez was
then hired to execute a building in Miami. The Miami building clearly be-
longs to Bosch's modernization campaign; the Classically proportioned slab
of offices is sheathed in an elegant glass curtain wall on its east and west
sides. Thousands of hand-painted blue and white *azulejos*, created by artist
Francisco Brennand of Recife, Brazil, form murals that cover the entire north
and south façades, tempering the building's cool modernity with an Iberian-
tropical flavor. The structure floats over its recessed glass lobby, which rests
on a raised plaza that hovers over the sidewalk. The structural concept,
which relates to seismic design, has floors hung from rooftop trusses, which
in turn were supported on four marble-clad piers.

Behind the main tower yet set on the same plinth, the Bacardi annex
achieves a different floating effect with two floors of offices cantilevered

from a compact recessed core. The upper floors feature translucent glass brick mosaic walls by German artist Johannes Dietz that complement the original building.

2125 Biscayne Boulevard (IBM Building)   C20

Metromover: Omni

Herbert H. Johnson Associates, 1965

C20

For corporate blue-chip IBM, Herbert Johnson created this almost entirely glass building, whose upper floors are shaded by a deep egg crate of unusually thin horizontal and vertical planes.

Gold Coast Pharmacy   C21

2419–2435 Biscayne Boulevard
C. C. Weber and Alexander D. Lewis, 1926

C21

This block-long commercial strip with second-floor apartments was the first structure by the Biscayne Boulevard Company to address the new boulevard and its carefully conceived design standards. Devised by the team that established the character of the road, it was styled Mediterranean Revival (complete with turret and tower), part of the effort to brand Biscayne Boulevard as an upscale, suburban alternative to Downtown. Rather than create a grand effect, the structure simulates the cumulative architecture of a village street. The variety of rooftops and fenestration could imply separate buildings, an artistic deception common in the style.

Wolpert Apartments   C22

2500–2512 Biscayne Boulevard
Apartments: 1924
Commercial addition: C. C. Weber and Alexander D. Lewis, 1927

This hybrid commercial and residential building was developed in two phases, responding to the construction of Biscayne Boulevard just to the east. The original apartment building preceded the boulevard, and was later adapted with a new commercial block facing the new thoroughfare. The Biscayne Boulevard Company, which adapted the building, used the same architects and builders responsible for the Gold Coast Pharmacy (C21) one block south. The residential building, rendered in rusticated stucco ornamented with quoins, is set back from the boulevard behind the new structure, which is faced with smooth stucco; a 3-story tower addresses the corner. The Wolpert Apartments was once part of an ensemble that included the Algonquin and Priscilla Apartments, located several blocks south (since demolished). Now solitary, its discreet intersection of commercial and residential wings, while accidental, could serve as a prototype for mixed-use development along the boulevard.

Granite Transformations (St. Paul Catholic Book and Film Center) C23

2700 Biscayne Boulevard
Murray Blair Wright, 1960

Originally developed as a Catholic film and book center (a product of the new Miami Archdiocese established in 1958), this 2-story commercial block is distinguished by its visible response to Miami's climate. The building featured a recessed ground-floor loggia (now filled in) and inverted U-shaped concrete canopies, originally designed to hold metallic sunscreens over its second-floor windows. A small chapel is still evident on the building's north side.

2742 Biscayne Boulevard (The Physician's Building) C24

Martin Luther Hampton, 1938

From the boulevard's first heyday, this 1-story building once housed the medical offices, operating rooms, and laboratories of physician E. C. Lunsford. It is classic Art Deco, with luxuriant cast-stone relief work depicting tropical vegetation in the panels below the windows and quarry keystone cladding around its recessed entrance. The Classical proportions of this small building lend it an air of dignity.

New Times Building C25

2800 Biscayne Boulevard
Arquitectonica, 1986

Arquitectonica's first office building brought the firm's trademark verve to Biscayne Boulevard in the otherwise dark days of this neighborhood in the 1980s. The firm's playful architectonic strategies animate the rectangular block of this modest tower, with a piano curve wall facing south and two glass cylinders that rise partway along the building's cutaway corner, ironically suggesting a sense of structural support. The cylinders create projecting window bays that frame views up and down the boulevard. The building's collage of façade types, from horizontally banded ribbon windows to punched square ones, reinforces its Postmodern sensibility.

2915 Biscayne Boulevard (National Cash Register Building) C26

T. Trip Russell and Associates, 1965
Renovation: Allan T. Shulman Architect, 2003
Renovation: Kobi Karp Architecture & Interior Design, 2007

C26

A late example of Biscayne Boulevard's midcentury transition toward office uses, this elegant block presents a Modern yet Classically conceived face to the street. The recessed ground floor features a Modernist loggia defined by the abstracted syncopation of cantilevered vaults. Above, the 2-story office block projects, its walls entirely wrapped by decorative precast-concrete screens. The screens define a tight grillage with serpentine bands that run horizontally across the façade. Behind the screens are a limited number of small windows, confirming a suspicion that such screens are often used to create image, and only symbolically "tropicalize" its architecture. The rear block, formerly a windowless computer center, has been opened up with large, new picture windows. Similarly, the ground-floor storefronts are new, reflecting the revival of retail use on the boulevard.

Chesterfield Smith Legal Services of Greater Miami (Ranni Building)   C27

3000 Biscayne Boulevard
Steward & Skinner Associates, 1964

This mid-rise office building along the upper Biscayne Boulevard corridor in Edgewater was described by its architects as an example of modified Italian Renaissance architectural styling, a description that masks its obvious Modernist cast. Gold-anodized aluminum sunscreens and gray-black granite window frames were designed to contrast with the light-colored Italian marble facing of the building's upper walls. The ground floor has since been filled in, and this initially luxurious workplace appears more commonplace today beneath uniform layers of beige paint.

C28

Beverly Terrace Apartments and Beverly Terrace Manor   C28

3224 and 3300 Biscayne Boulevard
Martin Luther Hampton and E. A. Ehmann, 1925

This pair of 3-story Mediterranean Revival residential structures is the remnant of a planned ensemble of four complementary buildings. Together, the four buildings were to frame a plaza and fountain at the intersection of NE Thirty-third Street and NE Third Avenue (now Biscayne Boulevard). The Beverly Terrace master plan preceded the development of Biscayne Boulevard, which fortuitously was aligned to preserve its central axis. One of the eastern buildings was demolished; the other building and the fountain were never built. Each structure is L-shaped, creating ample gardens at the street. At first, the two surviving buildings appear as twins, but there are differences in form and in decorative features. The northern building has an extended parapet with what appears to be a terrace at the fourth floor. Both have faux vigas, or applied rafters, extending out from under the roofline, but with different decorations.

Hamilton on the Bay   C29

555 NE 34th Street
Joseph Farcus Architect, 1981

Carnival Cruise Lines founder Ted Arison developed this fantastic rocket-shaped condominium whose public spaces conjure up thoughts of Tomorrowland at Disney World, or even the set of an Austin Powers movie. Here is the futuristic impulse of the early postwar years realized with 1980s budgets. The 28-story tower is shaped like an elongated polygon, with its piers flaring out at the base, recalling the fins at the base of a rocket. The flared piers allow for voluminous and porous open spaces at the lower levels. The automobile arrival sequence effectively transports the visitor to

C29

a future where the line between indoors and out is erased and lush vegetation and expansive water features flow uninterrupted between the lobby area and the surrounding gardens. A running track rings the top level of the tower as does a neon strip visible from great distances.

Blue   C30
601 NE 36th Street
Arquitectonica, 2005

C30

Blue's sail-like 36-story tower enjoys a prominent site. Rising from a sliver of land formed by the fork of the Julia Tuttle Causeway (I-195) and NE Thirty-sixth Street, it visibly terminates the westward alignment of the causeway. Blue is architecturally legible as a tower formed of two intersecting, curved wedges that rise in opposite directions over an 80-foot parking pedestal. On the north, the convex wall of deep-blue glass faces toward the bay. On the south, a concave façade of open, white-painted galleries screens the units from sunlight.

The south-facing galleries are a device that allows efficient egress from the narrow tower's multiple cores, decreasing the number of stair towers. They illustrate an evolution of Arquitectonica's planning concepts since the development of its first thin towers along Brickell Avenue in the 1980s.

Borinquen Clinic (Buena Vista Tower)   C31
3601 North Federal Highway
Isaac Sklar and Associates, 1985
Renovation: Lee Ramos, 1993

The Borinquen Clinic was founded to meet the needs of Miami's Puerto Rican community, historically centered in nearby Wynwood (sometimes called "Little San Juan"). In 1987, it acquired Buena Vista Tower, an empty office building that had been completed two years earlier during the height of a local construction boom. Renovations were completed in 1993. The building features cutaway volumes and a strongly streamlined façade with ribbon windows wrapping rounded corners. It marks the southern entrance to the Design District and is quite visible from the elevated I-195 Expressway.

Miami-Dade County School Board   C32
Administration Building South Tower
(Lindsey Hopkins Vocational Building)
Metromover: Omni

1450 NE 2nd Avenue
T. Trip Russell and Associates

The 7-story South Tower of the Miami-Dade County School Board campus derives its spirit from the work of Paul Rudolph and others (Roche-Dinkeloo's Ford Foundation Building in New York [1967] comes to mind). The L-shaped building rises and projects out at its upper levels, covering a multistory midblock plaza that faces NE Second Avenue. In contrast to the glazed covered atrium of the Ford Foundation, the South Tower is an open arrangement that protects without enclosing an open plaza and shades its southeast-facing windows. Windows on the projecting upper portion are

C32

further protected by vertical fins for sun control. Entirely cast in concrete, the structure is a monumental presence within the school board campus.

The South Tower is part of the multiblock Miami-Dade County School Board administrative complex, which is tied together with pedestrian bridges above NE Second Avenue and NE Fifteenth Street. Adjacent, just to the west, is the 9-story complex's North Tower. Across NE First Court is the WLRN Public Radio and Television Building. Immediately to the south, a parking lot occupies the site of the Lindsey Hopkins Vocational Center, a 15-story structure converted from the boom-era white elephant Roosevelt Hotel (Louis Kemper, 1926). The Metromover passes just to the north.

Franklin Square   C33
Metromover: Omni

1601 NE 2nd Avenue
Attributed to Alden Freeman, 1924

Mayflower descendent Alden Freeman first came to Miami as consul to the Dominican Republic, and has been credited as the designer of the imposing Franklin Square. Previously known as "Franklin Court," it was named for the Franklin auto dealership that occupied the ground-floor retail space.

C33

The 4-story Franklin Square is distinguished by its veranda rising three
stories over the sidewalk (once a common feature in Downtown Miami.)
The building is U-shaped in plan, with open galleries surrounding a narrow
courtyard that opens toward the east. It was the grandest early mixed-use
building of its time in Miami and could serve as an anchor for the revitalization of the surrounding neighborhood. Note how it terminates the eastward
view corridor of Sixteenth Street. Freeman would return to the Miami area
to build Casa Casuarina (E31) on Ocean Drive in Miami Beach.

S&S Restaurant   C34

Metromover: School Board

1757 NE 2nd Avenue
1938

C34

The S&S Restaurant is known by many Miamians for its home-style cooking
and uniquely charming wait staff; Art Deco enthusiasts know it as a surviving 1930s diner, notable for the colored-glass bands covering the front and
side façades. Its Vitrolite or Carrara glass (depending on the manufacturer)
presents tan upper walls over a black base; red and ivory horizontal and
vertical segments frame a cut corner door at the southwest of the building,
protected by an aluminum-clad eyebrow. While not prefabricated like many
diners produced immediately before and after World War II, the S&S shares
many of the traditional diner's design characteristics: hygienic modernity
elaborated in streamlined decorative (as well as functional) metal and glass
sheathing.

Miami City Cemetery   C35

Metromover: School Board

1800 NE 2nd Avenue
1897

Miami-Dade County's oldest and only municipal cemetery is the resting ground for members of most of the city's important pioneer families.
Located on 10 acres of land donated in 1897 by William and Mary Brickell,

the site includes the grave of Julia Tuttle, "the mother of Miami," as well as members of the Burdine, Seybold, Peacock, and Sewell families. Dr. James Jackson (A117) is also buried here.

While today considered part of the inner city, the site was originally chosen for its location just beyond Miami's original northern limit. The modest design of the long rectangular tract consists of a bisecting thoroughfare with two circles in its eastern quadrant. At the center of the cemetery is a monument memorializing Confederate soldiers, marking one of the many heritages that made up early Miami.

A wide variety of headstones is found in the cemetery, reflecting the development of tombstone design from the late nineteenth century to the present. The cemetery also includes a number of mausoleums designed in a variety of styles. Its vegetation, much of it rare and exotic, was first introduced in the 1920s from a neighboring city nursery, as well as from the U.S. Experimental Station at Cutler. The surrounding fence and gates were added later.

C36

Temple Israel   C36

Metromover: School Board

137 NE 19th Street
Robertson and Patterson, 1927
Gumenick Chapel: Kenneth Treister, 1967

Home of the oldest Reform congregation in South Florida, the main sanctuary of Temple Israel expresses the Moorish Revival style popular in synagogue design of the early twentieth century and parallels the Mediterranean Revival of the 1920s boom in Florida. The façade composition is handsome in its simplicity, deriving visual interest from a single large pointed arch trimmed with a slightly projecting, robust relief band. The current sanctuary was completed five years after the congregation was founded, and later additions reflect the pledge of the congregation to a variety of Jewish spiritual, social, and educational as well as architectural experiences. The synagogue's growth in place also reflects the congregation's long-term and at times difficult commitment to remain in this center-city location that, until recently, had declined severely in the face of suburban flight. Once at the heart of a thriving and affluent neighborhood, Temple Israel was more recently an island surrounded by industrial uses and vacant lots. The turn-of-the-twenty-first-century building boom served to begin to reconnect Temple Israel with its surroundings.

The most significant of the synagogue's several additions is the Gumenick Chapel. Architect Kenneth Treister developed the highly sculptural form of this chapel, seeking to create a bridge between art and architecture. Constructed using ferro-cement—a process in which concrete is sprayed over metal reinforcing and wire mesh—the organic form recalls the Art Nouveau work of Antoni Gaudi in Barcelona. The chapel grew from Treister's early experiments in ferro-cement technology at Elizabeth Virrick Park (B74), further pursued at his Mayfair project in Coconut Grove (B63). Similar to Gaudi's all-encompassing design work, Treister designed the furnishings for the chapel in addition to the building and interiors. Its abstract stained-glass windows, designed by Benoit Gilsoul and Karel Dupre, are made of more than 2,200 thick chunks of colored Belgian glass set in epoxy.

Citizens Bank   C37

Metromover: School Board

1361–1367 North Miami Avenue
H. George Fink, 1925

C37

This bank's Neoclassical façade—including a pilastrade of engaged Corinthian columns, arched openings, and powerfully expressed base and cornice—wraps the southeast corner of North Miami Avenue and Fourteenth Street, a prominent intersection. Its stucco monumentality is reminiscent of that found in Caribbean urbanism.

Ice Palace Film Studios   C38
(Florida Power and Light Ice Plant)

Metromover: School Board

1400 North Miami Avenue
1924
Renovation: Eugene Rodriguez, 1998

Film studios and sound stages are a major industry in Miami, and many exist in recuperated theaters, industrial buildings, warehouses, and commercial buildings. The Ice Palace Film Studios occupy a converted 1920s ice plant, an innovative adaptive use by Big Time Productions, who previously converted the Paris Theater on Washington Avenue in Miami Beach for similar uses. The studio's large open hangars accommodate photo shoots, television, and film and video production. The complex opens into the garden, where hammocks swing from coconut palms in a space cloistered by walls within the 3-acre property. From the garden, the complex's eclectic group of structures, painted white, are related by minimal decoration that includes repetitive pilasters.

Fire Station No. 2   C39

Metromover: School Board

1401 North Miami Avenue
August Geiger, 1926

C39

Product of Miami's breakneck expansion during the 1920s boom, Fire Station No. 2 illustrates the city's contemporary ambition to develop an attractive new infrastructure of prominently located public facilities. This Mediterranean Revival–style fire station presents a suitably imposing frontage toward the small plaza created by the kink in the alignment of North Miami Avenue at Fourteenth Street. At the center of this composition are an arched entrance portal and a small tower, whose flanking 2-story gabled wings address both segments of the avenue. The offset in Miami Avenue conveniently makes a wide-open path for fire trucks to emerge from both wings. Twisted columns and balconies are decidedly nonfunctional for a fire station, but the extravagances of the 1920s boomtime sometimes led designers into irrational exuberance.

C40

Parc Lofts   C40

Metromover: School Board

1749 NE Miami Court
Bermello Ajamil & Partners, 2005

The formula of "loft" residential space varies, but here in this mixed industrial neighborhood, it is taken to an apotheosis. Parc Lofts comprises large
multistory spaces with an industrial flavor and a style that hews closely to
stereotypical loft buildings in older cities. Eighteen-foot ceilings with up-
stairs mezzanines are typical, and the 72 lofts include 2-, 3-, and even 4-story
units. The L-shaped building embraces a multilevel patio, partly topping
covered parking, that includes a ground-level pool and landscaped garden
privatized by a tall hedge. The varied materials include Chicago brick (recuperated from demolished buildings) and stucco, mixed with contemporary
perforated aluminum and glass balcony guardrails. Horizontal window bays
recessed in an exposed structural grid recall early-twentieth-century factories, yet the projecting balconies portray the building's real contemporary
vintage and residential purpose. The Filling Station, located directly across
the street, is a follow-up to Parc Lofts. Using the same "blank canvas" loft formula, its ground floor was designed to offer a basketball gym, theater, and a
small amount of retail space.

Northeast Overtown

*Like Southeast Overtown, the northeast quadrant of the Midtown
Expressway Interchange is a fragment of the once-bustling heart of
Miami's black community. The area contains some of Overtown's
most significant surviving buildings.*

C41

Dorsey Memorial Library   C41

Metromover: School Board

100 NW 17th Street
Paist and Steward, 1941

A simple Masonry Vernacular structure topped by a prominent hipped roof
and with a raised parapet at the doorway, the Dorsey Memorial Library recalls Miami's conflicted past as a segregated city. The "separate but equal"
facility reflected the rigorous separation imposed on Miami's black community. This was the second library building dedicated to serving Overtown's
residents, and the first building constructed by the City of Miami designed to function as a library. The library was named for Dana A. Dorsey,
a prominent African American carpenter, contractor, and businessman
who donated the land. Paist and Steward, among the imaginators of Coral
Gables, were also the architects of Liberty Square (D27), a housing project
for African Americans undertaken in much the same spirit as the Dorsey
Memorial Library.

St. Agnes' Episcopal Church   C42
1750 NW 3rd Avenue
Harold Hastings Mundy, 1930

The 1926 hurricane was a recent memory when architect Harold Hastings Mundy designed the roof of this building with a rounded rather than a wind-vulnerable gabled shape. The interior of the building is also noteworthy, especially the barrel-vaulted ceiling. The Episcopal tradition reflected the religious preference of Miami's numerous black Bahamians, for whom this congregation was organized in 1898.

Wynwood

The boundaries of Wynwood are defined variably, but most consider the area to stretch between Seventeenth Street and Thirty-sixth Street and between NW Seventh Avenue and NE Second Avenue. Wynwood is "El Barrio," home to Miami's substantial Puerto Rican community (overshadowed by Miami's much larger Cuban community, it has been called the "Quiet Community"). The neighborhood has generated numerous Puerto Rican institutions, including Eugenio Maria de Hostos Senior Center, the Dorothy Quintana Community Center, ASPIRA, and the Puerto Rican Chamber of Commerce. Roberto Clemente Park, Eneida M. Hartner Elementary, and Jose de Diego Middle School lie just to the west. Wynwood also includes one of the city's prominent industrial and warehouse areas, recently rescripted as the creative center of a vibrant visual arts community. Another subsection, along NW Fifth Avenue, between Twenty-third and Twenty-ninth streets, is Miami's Fashion District, an area thick with garment manufacturing and wholesaling establishments. At the northeast border is Midtown, a new mixed-use development that replaces the former Buena Vista Railyards. Diverse uses, a varied demographic, and diverse building types make Wynwood a prime urban revitalization opportunity.

2100 NW Miami Court   C43
1940

With its rounded corner, eyebrows, and exuberant, stepped corner feature shooting toward the sky, this industrial warehouse building would look at home on Collins Avenue in the Miami Beach Architectural District. The use of Moderne styling in an out-of-the-way corner of the Wynwood Warehouse District reflected the ambitions of its owner, and of Miami industry in general, to put forward a Modern, progressive, and even civic image.

C43

Margulies Collection at the Warehouse   C44

576 NW 28th Street
1969
Conversion: Cohen Freedman Encinosa, 1998

The Margulies Collection was an important pioneer in the transformation of the Wynwood Warehouse District into the nexus of Greater Miami's art scene. The building's significance is found mostly on the interior.

MOCA at Goldman Warehouse   C45

404 NW 26th Street
1953
Renovation: Beilinson Gomez Architects, 2005

This exhibition and arts space housed in a former warehouse donated by South Beach rehab developers Tony and Joey Goldman serves as a satellite branch of the North Miami Joan Lehman Building of the Museum of Contemporary Art (MOCA).

C46

Rubell Family Collection and Residence   C46

95 NW 29th Street
1972
Additions and adaptive use: Allan T. Shulman Architect, 2005

The Rubell Family Collection (RFC) and Residence is a highly unusual project type, especially notable for programmatic innovations that suggest a new relationship of public and private uses, spaces, and identities. The project involved the transformation of a disused warehouse building (former Drug Enforcement Agency impoundment facility) into a vibrant public/private cultural compound that notably includes a prominent research library and the collectors' own residence. The project has been a closely watched generator, spurring activity as an anchor for the flourishing Wynwood Arts District.

The collection occupies the shell of the existing warehouse that has been transformed into a public venue. From the street, it is spartan in character: the building's original notched precast-concrete, double-tee wall-panel façades offer its chief decorative expression. The new entrance is a cubic block whose Cyclopean window provides a first glimpse of the interior. The entry sequence utilizes the overhang of the second floor (typical in Miami) to create a protected front court. Interior spaces were transformed by opening connecting vertical and horizontal vistas while developing new circuits for exploring more than thirty specialized exhibition rooms. The largest gallery flows into the former loading dock, recalibrated as a garden, sculpture court, and performance area. The tall walls of the research library located in the center of the complex are lined with books.

The new residence bridges the mixed commercial and residential fabric of the block while making its own quiet statement visible behind gardens to the north. Partially impacted into the volume of the warehouse, the house emerges into its own residential garden as a glazed pavilion. Internally, it is organized around a 2-story, skylit atrium. By locating the residence within the block of the collection, residential space is infused with a sense of artistic relevance and civic participation.

Gallerie Emmanuel Perrotin   C47

194 NW 30th Street
1959
Renovation: Oppenheim Architecture+Design, 2006

Even in its original construction as a warehouse/showroom, this building evokes the optimism and gestural clarity inherent in some of the best
postwar commercial architecture. The building's roof, made of precast
concrete tees, floats over tile-clad walls that enclose its main interior space.
Clerestories occupy the voids between the tees and the walls, an efficient
and honest gesture. Additional concrete tees project from the main block to
provide a broad concrete canopy.

    The building marks the pivot point between the heart of Puerto Rican
Wynwood north of Twenty-ninth Street and the Wynwood Arts District to
the south. A 2006 renovation highlighted its native features, while adapting
the building as a gallery for the Parisian art dealer Emmanuel Perrotin. On
the interior, terrazzo floors and a mosaic-tiled staircase were restored. The
spacious rooms are large enough to stage three exhibitions simultaneously,
and to provide room for social activities as well as viewing. Among the additions are loggia facing the garden. Plans for a new residence, following the
model of the nearby Rubell Family Collection (**C46**), are on hold as of this
writing.

San Juan Bautista Mission   C48

3116 NW 2nd Avenue
Duany Plater-Zyberk & Company (DPZ), 1999

C48

The San Juan Bautista Mission works as a small outreach facility for the
Catholic Corpus Christi Parish, which was severed from Wynwood by the
construction of I-95 in the 1960s. The expressway distanced the community's
poorer sectors from the main church on NW Seventh Avenue. The mission
building allows the residents of Wynwood to walk to church. It also acts
as a substantial anchor for the community's main street along NW Second
Avenue north of Twenty-ninth Street, hosting a variety of religious and non-
religious activities, including those of other civic institutions.

    The building's design follows that of traditional neighborhood churches
in Latin America and the Caribbean. It provides a courtyard, an urban strategy that makes good use of the small site by minimizing side and rear setbacks and placing its front building at the edge of the sidewalk. The front
façade is a simple wall with modest decoration framing the entrance opening and two rectangular window portals. The stucco has been convincingly
applied and molded to give the appearance of a much older building. The
cloistered courtyard, a refuge from the comings and goings on NW Second
Avenue, contains a baptismal font and bell tower. Clerestory windows in the
inner nave of the small church flood the interior with light. A ceiling mural
by a local artist provides a strong ornamental feature.

Bakehouse Art Complex (American Bakeries Company)

C49

561 NW 32nd Street
1934
Renovation: Lester Pancoast, 1986

At one time, the American Bakeries Company occupied the site, hence the two flour silos, but the building was long vacant when a group of artists, gentrified out of Coconut Grove in the 1980s, established an artists' collaborative and adaptively reused the structure as an art studio complex. The Bakehouse Art Complex formally opened in 1986.

Renaissance Arts Emporium (Smith Building)

C50

203 NW 36th Street
1946

This quirky standout along the NW Thirty-sixth Street commercial corridor marks the intersection of NW Second Avenue with a chamfered corner. A composite of several distinct structures, its still-visible 2-story core is canted 45 degrees to address the intersection. Later additions include a 2-story block along NW Thirty-sixth Street and a 1-story bull-nose wing. Miami's twentieth-century art of urban accretion is illustrated well here.

Midtown Miami

Developed on the site of the former Buena Vista Railyard just south of the resurgent Miami Design District, Midtown is a notable and large-scale effort at urban infill in a former industrial district. The 56-acre container yard and railroad maintenance area, as old as the city itself, was increasingly considered a blight on surrounding areas, and a hole in the city's urban fabric. Plans for its redevelopment were hastened by the economics of the railroad and the rising values of Miami real estate. The master plan, developed by Zyscovich Architects, extends the grid of adjacent streets into the site, while also resolving the clash of geometries that arises from the diagonal passage of the Florida East Coast Railway line on the site's east side. Three new longitudinal axes, Buena Vista Avenue, Midtown Boulevard, and East Coast Avenue (running along the tracks) trisect the project into zones that transition from east to west. Economic studies established the goals for each zone: high-rise towers rise on the east side, exploiting views of nearby Biscayne Bay; mid-rise buildings including an entertainment complex, hotel, and park in the center; low-rise commercial buildings (including big-box stores) are aligned on Midtown's west side, facing the emerging Wynwood Arts District.

The new urban quarter has been only partly realized, yet it has already hastened the rehabilitation of Miami Avenue as a retail corridor, and joins the general improvement in the surrounding Edgewater, Wynwood, and Design District neighborhoods to offer expanded commercial and lifestyle opportunities in the heart of Miami. Of note are the richly appointed streetscapes, which feature ample sidewalks, a growing tree canopy, buried utilities, and coordinated street furniture, paving, and lighting.

Midtown 2   C51

3470 East Coast Avenue
Zyscovich Architects, 2007

C51

The first completed building of the tower group slated to rise along East Coast Avenue, Midtown 2 is a targeted illustration of the zoning guidelines developed for the district by the same firm, Zyscovich Architects. As planners for the district, Zyscovich established block sizes based on the width necessary to fully wrap an efficient parking garage with habitable spaces. In order to avoid the tower-over-pedestal effect common in Miami, the wrappers are intended to hug the streets and offer each frontage a distinctly different cast to avoid a monolithic impression.

Indeed, Midtown 2 offers an assemblage of distinct architectural pieces that occupy a complete block along Midtown's east flank. The L-shaped tower faces the northeast corner, offering projecting concrete slabs, and glass-rail balconies that wrap the building's glass-façade walls. Facing west, a nearly separate mid-rise slab rising 120 feet features a tic-tac-toe grid of solids and voids that frames the east side of Midtown Park. On the project's south side, a lower volume with a more solid stucco and masonry façade and deeply projecting balconies faces a pedestrian mews.

Midtown 2 is large, yet its stair-stepping profile, especially as seen from the southwest, serves to break up the scale. The massing successfully internalizes the parking garage, which is topped by a south-facing pool and amenity deck. The deck is surrounded on three sides by taller building elements, but its presence is identifiable from the street by a sky-lobby, voids in the tower, and a grand north-facing terrace. Accents in stone and wood add richness to Miami's more standard vocabulary of stucco and glass.

Midtown 4   C52

3301 NE 1st Avenue
Nichols Brosch Sandoval & Associates, 2006

The L-shaped Midtown 4 tower faces northwest, wrapping the corner of NW Thirty-fourth Street and NE First Avenue in a continuous streamlined gesture. In contrast with the more complex motives of Midtown 2, this structure is oriented simply toward Midtown's central park, allowing the amenity deck exposure to the southeast.

Midtown Mid Block East   C53

3250 Buena Vista Boulevard
Peter Spittler–FORUM Architectural Services, 2006

Eleven-story Mid Block East, occupying the center block of Midtown, provides a transition from the high-rise scale on the east side of the development to the low scale on the west. It is a busily articulated horizontal mass that, through fine detailing and use of robust materials, including locally rare brick, manages to pull off its visual complexity in a pleasing manner. The residential structure includes ground-floor retail and internalized parking. Its complex massing results from the outward expression of the three residential unit types. The parking pedestal is wrapped with ground-floor retail space, and double-height lofts on the north, south, and east façades. Above, an apartment tower faces east while townhouses face the crescent of Mid Block West. The townhouses are entered from a linear space on the

C53

pedestal deck, perhaps evoking a mews or an alley formed between them and the tower.

    An inverted and truncated glass cone punctuates the northeast corner of the building to dramatic effect, and the north wall of the apartment tower cants outward as it rises. Together, the "special effects" and long, narrow proportions suggestive of an ocean liner imbue the structure with a dynamism reminiscent of Greater Miami's speed-obsessed commercial architecture of the 1930s and 1950s.

Midtown North Block   C54

3401 North Miami Avenue
Peter Spittler–FORUM Architectural Services, 2006

Covering two city blocks, the North Block contains Midtown's largest concentration of retail, including the heretofore best insertion of big-box retail into Miami's urban fabric. The voluminous big-box retail spaces are placed at the four corners of the block, with the larger of these facing Thirty-sixth Street. Traditionally scaled retail storefronts line the Miami Avenue and Buena Vista Avenue frontages.

    The North Block also includes double-height live/work spaces above the single-story retail base, further breaking down its scale on the more fine-grained south, east, and west frontages. The double-height spaces were provided as loft shell to allow for flexibility of use including office, studio, and showroom. A promenade serving these spaces runs behind the retail parapet and above the storefronts.

At the center of the block, the parking garage is well-camouflaged in every direction except to the north, where tall signage announces Midtown to the nearby I-195. The building's most overt feature is the elevator tower projecting from the northeast corner of the block and housed in a stout cylindrical mass with open lobbies. The elevators reach ground level at the entrances to two of the big-box stores, deftly bringing constant activity to the street corner.

Midtown Mid Block West   C55

3201 North Miami Avenue
Peter Spittler–FORUM Architectural Services, 2006

Mid Block West is a single-story crescent, bisected into two buildings by a pedestrianized portion of Thirty-third Street. In keeping with the grand allusions of the crescent plan, the ornamental program hews toward the Mediterranean Revival style, expressed dramatically by an arched sidewalk arcade encircling the entire crescent. Skylit pedestrian passages connect the arcade to Thirty-second and Thirty-fourth streets. At the center lies a green park space punctuated by a fountain that terminates the view corridor of Thirty-third Street. Retail spaces also face North Miami Avenue as at North Block.

Midtown South Block   C56

3101 North Miami Avenue
Peter Spittler–FORUM Architectural Services, 2007

Anchoring the southwest corner of the current development is South Block, a parking structure that includes retail spaces facing Miami Avenue. Note the parking garage elevator building disguised as a clock tower that terminates the southward view corridor of Buena Vista Avenue.

Design District

The Miami Design District is bounded roughly by NE/NW Thirty-sixth Street, NE/NW Forty-sixth Street, the Florida East Coast Railway, and NW Second Avenue. Its proximity to the Julia Tuttle Causeway and Airport Expressway (S.R. 112), partway between Miami Beach and Miami International Airport, makes the Design District an important node in Miami's northeast side.

The Design District evolved from the business district of the former village of Buena Vista, which predated the Florida East Coast Railway on the site of a former pineapple plantation. The opening of the Dixie Highway in 1915 and the extension of a streetcar line from Downtown Miami in 1918 ignited the village's transformation from an agriculture-based economy to one based on diverse businesses. Buena Vista received its major impetus through the efforts of Davis P. Davis (better known for the development of the Davis Islands in Tampa in the 1920s) beginning in 1919, and the area was incorporated into the City of Miami in 1925. Buena Vista is still used to describe the residential area immediately north of the Design District.

Furniture showrooms serving the resort industry appeared here as early as the 1920s. The center of the district, NE Fortieth Street, became "Decorator's Row," where large showrooms and galleries still abound. The area was renewed beginning in the 1960s with important showrooms servicing the design and building arts. In the 1980s, several large, new buildings were added along NE Second Avenue, shifting the district's center. Competition with the new Design Center of the Americas (DCOTA), opened in 1985 adjacent to I-95 and Fort Lauderdale–Hollywood International Airport, as well as rising crime in the neighborhood, eventually led to its decline as a design center. Its current revival, both as a neighborhood and magnet for design and art, dates from the 1990s and especially the efforts of the Dacra Companies, its most important landowner. The magnet design high school helped to pioneer the area's revival, and many good eateries have broadened its appeal as a neighborhood. The district is particularly vibrant during Miami's perennial Art Basel Miami Beach, when its infrastructure of galleries and showrooms make it an important center for temporary exhibitions including the major Design Miami.

The Design District's coherent and intact street architecture features continuous commercial storefronts lining wide newly tree-lined sidewalks. Nestled within this context are some larger showroom buildings and some more exotic retail structures that explore new types of urban commercial interaction. An urban design charrette by Duany Plater-Zyberk & Company in 1997 set the tone for an urban retrofit that has resulted in a new plaza and street, improved streetscapes, and the still largely unrealized idea of introducing residential development. Creative adaptive use and the weaving of newly commissioned civic art into the structure of everyday commercial buildings transform the district into an experimental canvas.

C57

Buena Vista Commercial Group   C57

Barton G.
3622 NE 2nd Avenue
1924

Power Studios
3701 NE 2nd Avenue
1925
Renovation: Arthur Thomas Posher, 1975
Renovation: Borges + Associates, 2006

3704 NE 2nd Avenue
1926

Ceramic Matrix
3800 NE 2nd Avenue
1926

The arcaded buildings just north and south of the elevated I-195 expressway, along with the Moore Building (C65) and the old Buena Vista Post Office (C64), are vivid reminders of the days when the Design District was known as Downtown Buena Vista. Three of these are among the finest examples of 1920s Mediterranean Revival commercial architecture in the city. Number 3622 displays intricate stucco relief work, casement windows, and a stepped, curved parapet. Number 3704, hard by the north side of the expressway, includes hexagonal columns and double-height pilasters. Number 3800 continues the theme of hexagonal columns but, appropriately for a corner building, in a more elaborate fashion. While this building has undergone some unsympathetic alterations, such as the closing of second-floor window openings, it nevertheless retains a picturesque appearance. Number 3701, with the widest street frontage, is the least elaborate of the group, yet includes the sidewalk arcade typical of the period.

Holly Hunt Showroom   C58

3833 NE 2nd Avenue
1934
Renovation: Bleemer, Levine & Associates
Renovation: Axioma 3 and Allison Spear, 1999

One of the first adaptive-use projects to reinvigorate the Design District, this former quilt factory was creatively transformed into a multistory furniture showroom. The retrofit included a new skylit atrium featuring a grand metal and glass stair to the second floor.

Buick Building (Plaza 1 Building)   C59

3841 NE 2nd Avenue
1926
Renovation: Walter Chatham
Renovation: Keenen/Riley Architects, 2005

One of the district's oldest commercial buildings, it once housed Modernage, for many years a popular chain of South Florida home-furnishing stores. The loft building has a decorative front facing NE Second Avenue, where its stucco lunettes are filled with murals by Jose Bedia, whose large wall murals also soften the impact of the structure's opaque multistory east wall. The building was renovated in 1976 as the Decorating and Design Center, the first of an interlinked quadplex bracing the corner of Thirty-ninth Street and Second Avenue; at that time, it was linked to the Buena Vista Building (C60) by a pedestrian bridge, which has since been removed.

C59

Buena Vista Building (Plaza 2 Building)   C60

180 NE 39th Street
Bleemer, Levine & Associates, 1980
Renovation: Walter Chatham

The Buena Vista Building, along with the renovated Buick Building (C59), were the first components of the Miami Decorating and Design Center. This atrium-type showroom building is typical of the introverted and interiorized character of the Design District in the 1980s. Served by underground parking, it provides internalized connections through the block. Its airy, skylit court features ceramic tile floors and a 12-foot-tall bronze fountain by artist Kenny Scharf. The façade is a porous composition of stuccoed piers, glass window walls, and standing seam metal set on built-in planters.

C60

C61

Melin Building (Plaza 3 Building)   C61

3930 NE 2nd Avenue
Bleemer, Levine & Associates, 1986

Constructed as the final component of the Miami Decorating and Design Center, the Melin Building wraps from NE Thirty-ninth Street to NE Fortieth Street. Its 2-story center atrium features a fountain and winding stair, as well as a domed skylight.

Newton Building (Plaza 4 Building)   C62

3901 NE 2nd Avenue
Bleemer, Levine & Associates, 1983
Renovation: Walter Chatham, 2001

This loft building, also part of the 1980s Miami Decorating and Design Center, was renovated with a new corner rotunda wrapped in perforated metal screens that spiral upward. The rotunda, which dematerializes when backlit at night, emphatically marks the corner of NE Thirty-ninth Street and Second Avenue, the traditional entrance of the district.

C62

C63

Design and Architecture Senior High School   C63
(Decorative Arts Plaza)

4005 NE 2nd Avenue
1938
Retrofit of existing buildings into Decorative Arts Plaza: Arquitectonica, 1981
Retrofit of Decorative Arts Plaza into Design and Architecture Senior High School:
Nazira Abdo-Decoster, 1989
Sculptural group *Kids*: R & R Studios, 2003
Metal fence: Marc Newson, 2006

In 1988, Miami-Dade County Public Schools authorized the establishment of a design and architecture magnet high school in the Design District for the 1989–90 school year. The vacancy of the strategically located Decorative Arts Plaza, victim of the exodus of designer showrooms in the wake of the opening of the Design Center of the Americas (DCOTA) in Fort Lauderdale, provided an ideal location for the school. To its great credit, DASH's reuse of the showrooms brought activity to the Design District during a period of dormancy prior to the area's renaissance in the late 1990s.

The complex of two 1-story buildings, containing 52,000 square feet divided into twenty showrooms, was well-suited for adaptive use as a school facility. Arquitectonica's 1981 retrofit imbued an otherwise unremarkable commercial plaza with striking flair, lending distinction for the building's subsequent role as a facility educating designers. The retrofit from showrooms to school required few alterations, retaining the integrity of Arquitectonica's design. The parking court of brick pavers doubles well as a schoolyard, and its recession from the street allowed the development of a traditional urban forecourt on axis with NE Fortieth Street. The parking court- turned-schoolyard is appointed with scattered and brightly colored platonic sculptural forms. In 1996, the building was connected to the adjacent Miami Inter/Design Center (MID) complex, where the school rents additional space for use as a gallery, gym, and classrooms.

Within the schoolyard, a pair of 35-foot cylinders deliberately terminates the view corridor of NE Fortieth Street like the fragments of a Neoclassical portico. The cylinders, transformed by R&R Studios into a public art project in 2003, are topped by *Kids*, figures of a girl and boy. Securing the schoolyard from NE Second Avenue is another work of civic art. A well-crafted metal barrier features undulating silver aluminum plates that simulate a vertical topography. Bottom-lit at night, the undulations establish a virtual wall of light.

Sra. Martinez Restaurant (Buena Vista Post Office)   C64

4000 NE 2nd Avenue
1921

C64 and 65

As a catalyst for his Buena Vista development, realtor David P. Davis built, at his own expense, a post office building at the corner of NE Second Avenue and Fortieth Street and leased it to the U.S. government. The inscription "Buena Vista Post Office" is still plainly visible above the doorway. For a time, before Buena Vista was incorporated into the City of Miami, the building also served as a village hall. The Classically inspired building, with unassuming Neoclassical references, has been adapted for use as a restaurant.

Moore Furniture Company Building   C65

4040 NE 2nd Avenue
P. J. Davis, 1921–22
Exterior renovation: Architectural Design Consultants, 1992 Renovations and additions: Walter Chatham, 1998
Elastika: Zaha Hadid, 2005

On the L-shaped lot wrapping the post office, Buena Vista pioneer David P. Davis persuaded Theophilus Wilson Moore to build a new showroom for the Moore Furniture Company. The Moore Building, sheathed in brick with large windows and a full-height atrium, celebrates the structural advances of the period and shows the emerging influence of Modern commercial architecture. It certainly must have seemed very modern in early 1920s Miami, compared with its more conservative counterparts in Downtown Miami.

The 4-story atrium facing NE Fortieth Street, which currently serves as an event space, is the building's most remarkable feature. This atrium features mezzanines with ornate metal guardrails supported on metal columns with Corinthian capitals, and a ceiling decorated with plaster relief around a central skylight. Elastika, a site-specific installation by Zaha Hadid, transformed the space in 2005 with organic white steel tentacles that span the atrium, suggesting a "web of new connections." In recent years, the Moore Building has played host to art- and design-related events such as Design Miami, as well as private functions.

C66

Rainforest Garden Lounge C66

NE 2nd Avenue and NE 40th Street (next to Moore Building)
Enea Garden Design, 2005

Designed as an installation and sales booth for Art Basel Miami in 2005, the garden lounge, nestled on the west side of the Moore Building, has since become permanent. The structure is designed like a copper jewel box, where the jewels are a constructed tropical rainforest. This small and cloistered space produces its own botanical Eden, but an urban one. Symbolic of tropical rainforests, and of their destruction, the project mixes natural and man-made elements, like tall stalks of bamboo, lily ponds, and tropicalizing low plantings and concrete furniture. Canvas canopies and steel cables overhead intensify the sense of enclosure. In its evocation of a constructed symbolic nature, the project taps perennial themes of Miami's own identity.

Miami Inter/Design Center (MID) C67

MID 2
4100 NE 2nd Avenue (Vanleigh Building)
1955
Renovation: Patrick Danan, 1983
Renovation: Halberstein/Hurtak & Associates, 1989

MID 1
4141 NE 2nd Avenue
1960
Renovation: 1982
Renovation: Voytek Szczepanski, 1987
Renovation: DZN, 1995
Renovation (Driade Cafe): Studio Marquette, 2007

These two large showroom buildings bracket NE Second Avenue, connected by an pedestrian bridge that forms the northern gateway into the Design District. The conjoined complex was the dream of Canadian developer Jacques Lallouz, who anticipated redeveloping the two buildings into the "Bal Harbour of the Design District" (a reference to the upscale and highly successful Bal Harbour Shops).

Number 4100, the former Vanleigh Building, is a 3-story blockwide building with chamfered corners. It was retrofitted in 1983 with two stories of blue-glass curtain wall (a reference to the "Blue Whale" at the Pacific Design Center in L.A.) above ground-floor storefronts. The building was outfitted at one time with interior glass walls and a large skylight to enhance transparency.

Number 4141, on the east side of NE Second Avenue, was connected by bridge in 1984, and substantially renovated in 1987. Like the earlier Buena Vista and Melin Buildings (C60 and C61), it has showrooms organized around a large central atrium. The lower surrounding wings are covered by a rooftop parking deck, through which the building was formerly entered. Recent renovations improved the building's connection to the street by moving glass window walls forward, enhancing the front entrance, and installing a popular eatery right on the main façade. The interior atrium was reimagined as a hidden piazza; a new look was achieved here by revealing structural systems and by emphasizing transparency between spaces with full walls of glass.

Oak Plaza Complex   C68

KVA Building
150 NE 40th Street
Khoury & Vogt Architects, 2006

Twery Building
160 NE 40th Street
Cure & Penabad, 2006

Loggia Building
163 NE 39th Street
Cure & Penabad, 2007

Collins Building
139 NE 39th Street
1951
Renovation: Keenen/Riley Architects, 2006

C68

The Oak Plaza complex interprets new commercial buildings as urban space-makers, defining a new public plaza and private street within the existing street grid of the Design District. Both elements were first suggested in Duany Plater-Zyberk & Company's Design District Master Plan (1997). The master plan and the buildings were commissioned by Dacra as part that company's targeted civic enhancements that have constructed a new sense of place in the area. The complex notably provides a tangible new center for the Design District.

At its southern end, Oak Plaza incorporates a stand of mature oaks—the site of a former parking lot—into a shaded public space paved with slabs of quarry keystone. The Loggia Building wraps two sides of the plaza, comprising a narrow restaurant space along the street and a shallow dining loggia along the back of the plaza. The two wings are transformed into an abstracted landscape by the application of green and blue glass mosaic tiles in a "leaf and sky" pattern. The third side of the plaza is made by the Collins Building, whose elegant recessed entry, lined by tall, wood-framed windows, is itself another loggia.

A new arcaded street, bracketed by the KVA and Twery buildings, links Oak Plaza to NE Fortieth Street, bisecting the long block and providing pedestrian connections in the guise of urban space (a critique partly of the district's closed atrium buildings, which do a similar task in air-conditioned space). By creating the arcaded street on private property, the arcades are allowed to fully cover the sidewalk and come directly to the street, a return to the pattern of Miami's early development, currently disallowed by zoning. The buildings are lyrical in their articulation, with subtle variations in columnation, roof types, and details like the decorative use of Cuban (cement) tile that play off one another in delightful ways.

Atlas Building (Buena Vista Design Plaza)   C69

130 NE 40th Street
Sarille & Associates, 1969
Renovation: Lawrence Simon, 2001

The Atlas Building uses a commercial arcade arrangement to organize retail
fronts along a narrow open plaza, perhaps the first step in another new
cross-block connection. The plaza is semi-covered but open-air, partly sheltered by an umbrellalike roof. At this writing, it is well used as the outdoor
dining area of a popular restaurant.

Decorator's Showcase   C70

35 NE 40th Street
Thurston Hatcher Associates Architects, ca. 1971

Built during the apex of "Decorator's Row" as a center of Miami's interior
design industry, this elegant brick showroom building is organized around
an open-air patio sheltered from the street. More than a decade before
the district's new showroom buildings featured air-conditioned atria, the
Decorator's Showcase used its open patio to showcase smaller designer
spaces and a dining area. A 3-story tower on the structure's east side is tied
into the overall complex with brick parapets and projecting canopies made
from weathered copper.

C70

    The building is distinguished by the quality of its materials and spaces.
A low brick wall, perforated by three broad arches that spring from concrete
bases, defines the streetfront of the structure. One of the arches opens
through a type of zaguán to the brick paved court, which features a fountain and is wrapped by a loggia supported on columns made of bundled
square wood members. The prominent and decorative use of brick, while
unusual in this area, creates an opportunity for the color, texture, and expressed craftsmanship often lacking in Miami buildings. In combination
with stained cypress, African mahogany, copper, bronze, and clay tile roofs,
the building offers a rich eclectic palette as prized in Miami during the 1970s
as it was during the 1920s and 1930s.

2 NE 40th Street   C71

1980

In contrast with the low-rise patio concept of the Decorator's Showcase
Building (C70) opposite, this 4-story block, rendered in rough-cast stucco,
is carved to create a multilevel covered court open toward the street. The
influence of Brutalist work like Paul Rudolph's Yale Art and Architecture
Building is translated to a commercial vitrine concept, where multilevel
glass showrooms are bracketed by fountains, planters, stepped platforms,
projecting terraces, and ribbons of glass to make a massive yet spatially
complex and flowing composition.

C71

Outdoor Living Room   C72

402 North Miami Avenue
R & R Studios, 2001

Marking the corner of North Miami Avenue and NW Fortieth Street, the
Outdoor Living Room creates a curious public plaza, a fragment of civic
art and urban place-making along an otherwise unremarkable commer-

C72

cial thoroughfare. Rising 40 feet, it models in cutaway form a surreal parlor whose sofa, lamps, framed window, wallpaper, and chandelier are fantastically scaled to the space of the street. Miami's love of ambiguity between indoors and outdoors is here lyrically balanced with commentary about the confrontation of public and private, of civic monumentality and domestic intimacy. Since its construction, the surrounding building into which the Outdoor Living Room was embedded has been demolished, repositioning the piece more as an isolated art object.

International Design Centre   C73

4141 North Miami Avenue
James Deen, 1961

C73

The International Design Centre was one of the first showroom buildings to reflect the 1960s influx of designers and vendors into the Design District. Originally, it housed more than 150 display areas for manufacturers serving Miami, the Caribbean, and Latin America. The complex was developed by English interior designer Henry End with the goal of raising the general level of taste in Miami, and in its heyday, the board of directors comprised Miami's most prominent architects and designers. The opaque showroom building is wrapped in a skin of tiled panels framed by concrete structures that look like giant tuning forks. Its entrance is framed in black and white marble. An atrium just inside the entrance contains a multilevel grand stair screened with bronze dividers. Today, the building is used primarily for offices.

Upper East Side

Miami's Upper East Side runs from NE Thirty-seventh Street to the city's northern boundary at NE Eighty-seventh Street, and from the Florida East Coast Railway tracks near NE Fourth Court eastward to Biscayne Bay. It encompasses some of the oldest settlements in Miami: Buena Vista and Lemon City (comprising the neighborhoods of Nazarene, Knightsville, and Boles Town). Today, the sector's eastern flank follows Biscayne Bay, including the waterfront neighborhoods of Baypoint, Morningside, Bayside, Belle Meade, and Shorecrest. Biscayne Boulevard bisects the Upper East Side, separating Palm Grove from the bayfront neighborhoods. Revitalization efforts have been propelled by the designation of residential historic districts in Morningside, Bayside, and Palm Grove. In 2006, the MiMo/Biscayne Boulevard Historic District became the city's first commercial historic district.

Biscayne Boulevard was developed as an automotive corridor connecting Miami Shores to Downtown Miami, and automobile dominance is in its DNA. The boulevard is a heavily trafficked artery that forms a barrier to east-west pedestrian access, yet newer developments like Fifty-fifth Street Station and the restaurants and shops in the MiMo/Biscayne Boulevard Historic District are reclaiming the thoroughfare as a neighborhood center for pedestrians.

Bay Point Office Group

The 1960s construction boom was well under way when suburban office buildings began to line up along Biscayne Boulevard, including this stretch just opposite the fashionable Bay Point neighborhood. Formerly part of the first Charles Deering Estate, the strip along the west side of Biscayne Boulevard remained unplatted in the Shoreland Company's 1926 Biscayne Boulevard master plan, as well as in their contemporary plans for the surrounding new community of Miami Plaza. The parcel was also left out of the later Bay Point development. Yet it was always conceived as part of a striking new automotive entrance to Miami from the north. Today, a virtual anthology of postwar office building types (square blocks on pilotis, patio buildings, and slabs, for instance) is found here, each in some way also a reflection of Miami and its climate. These office buildings are urban/suburban hybrids, most with landscaped plazas, forecourts, and plenty of parking.

Miami Arts Charter School (Channel 10 Studio Building)   C74

3900 Biscayne Boulevard
Herbert H. Johnson Associates, ca. 1965
Retrofit: Kobi Karp Architecture & Interior Design, 2009

Built for ABC network affiliate WLBW, this structure was designed to reflect its function as a broadcast studio. WLBW had succeeded WPST, the city's second ABC affiliate, and a subsidiary of Miami-based National Airlines. The 3-story structure sandwiched studios on the second floor, largely enclosed with precast concrete panels, between recessed glass volumes on the ground and third floors that opened widely to the surroundings. The ground floor was severely bunkerized after Hurricane Andrew. WPLG, as it is known today, has decamped to a new location closer to the Miami-Dade/Broward County line, joining all but the public television station in seeking to be more geographically centered in the South Florida coverage area. In 2009, the building was adapted as the home of the new Miami Arts Charter School.

Greater Miami Jewish Federation Headquarters (Stanley C. Myers Building)   C75

4200 Biscayne Boulevard
Morris Lapidus, 1968

For this headquarters building, Lapidus contrived a Cubist composition of stepped building volumes with smooth stucco walls and flush ribbon windows. The composition is offset by contrasting volumes that house the building's stair and elevator cores. These are generally bull-nosed, and rendered in a rough, textured concrete. Facing Biscayne Boulevard, a glass entrance wall and concrete canopy form an inviting focal point.

Unika (AAA Building)   C76

4300 Biscayne Boulevard
Ferendino/Grafton/Pancoast, 1970
Renovation: Borges + Associates, 2004

C76

Constructed to house the Miami headquarters of the American Automobile Association (AAA), this low-rise office building on pilotis originally featured a ramped system that allowed cars to rise to the entrance plaza level and circulate around the glass lobby. The solid, bulbous pylon facing Biscayne Boulevard featured the logo of the AAA on its raw cast-in-place concrete face. Today, the pylon is surfaced with an abstract tableau of glass mosaic tiles, and the automobile has been relegated to its traditional Miami role of surrounding the building. A planned 15-story apartment building on the building's south side would infuse a residential character to the commercial strip.

IVAX Building   C77

4400 Biscayne Boulevard
Hellmuth, Obata + Kassabaum, 1983
Renovation: Diez, Mora Architects, 1995

Built as the headquarters of Miami-based Key Pharmaceuticals, this 15-story building sat empty for several years. After selling Key to Schering-Plough in 1986, Dr. Phillip Frost founded pharmaceutical giant IVAX, which occupied the building until its merger with Teva Pharmaceutical Industries. The building features intersecting volumes covered in mirrored-glass curtain wall. The volumes have radiused edges that cascade toward Biscayne Boulevard.

Atrium Building   C78

4500 Biscayne Boulevard
1973
New entrance and rooftop addition: Allan T. Shulman Architect, 2004

This 4-story office building built over a low pedestal that contains most of the building's parking has an open-air atrium at its core. Reversing a classic Modernist formula, it has two stories of curtain wall–clad offices raised over a recessed base of masonry and stucco. Progressive additions have expanded the fourth floor, most prominently by a penthouse whose concave root recenters the building's façade along an axis extending into the entrance of the opposite Bay Point neighborhood.

Bay Point Office Tower   C79

4770 Biscayne Boulevard
Johnson Associates, 1981

The Bay Point Office Tower rises 15 stories to exploit views of Biscayne Bay over the fronting Bay Point subdivision. Indeed, all of the offices face east, housed behind a long wall of artfully contrasting dark glass and white-painted concrete spandrel ribbons. A corollary feature of the building is its circulation system, in which access to the offices is by exterior galleries on the building's west side (a rare solution among office buildings). The galleries are landscaped with continuous planters, transforming the west façade into a hanging garden.

Gas Station (Little's Cities Service Station)   C80
5402 Biscayne Boulevard
M. M. Vaviloff, 1956

Where Biscayne Boulevard, Federal Highway, and NE Fourth Avenue pinch together, the once-voluminous glass lobby, splayed beanpole columns, and floating roof of Little's Cities Service Station formed a fitting counterpoint to the opposing wedge of General Tire at 5600 Biscayne Boulevard (now Andiamo Pizza). Though the glass volume has been largely covered over, the sensitive renovation and adaptive use of the pizzeria begs a similar treatment for the gas station.

55th Street Station   C81
Soyka
5556 NE 4th Court
1938
Renovation: Carl Myers, 1998

5580 NE 4th Court (Food Fair Supermarket)
1948

5582 NE 4th Court
1982

This highly successful complex of restaurants, bars, and retail shops was cobbled from an existing commercial cluster. The group adaptively uses older retail buildings, including a former Food Fair supermarket, and adds new ones to establish a new critical mass. More than just an assemblage of commercial buildings, the group combines with Andiamo Brick Oven Pizza (C82) to make a vibrant neighborhood center, an urban district of patios, raised covered porches, and pedestrian-scaled frontages.

C82

Andiamo Brick Oven Pizza (General Tire)   C82
5600 Biscayne Boulevard
Weed Russell Johnson Associates, 1954

Designed as a prototype showroom and outlet for General Tire, this structure was placed for maximum exposure at a curve in Biscayne Boulevard. Its adaptive use as a pizzeria creates a highly visible Modernist dining loggia and symbol of the renaissance of the Upper East Side of Miami. The building's saucerlike trapezoidal roof with streamlined corners floats over a glass-box showroom cum dining area/pizza oven on thin steel columns. The broad area beneath the canopy proves at least as valuable for outdoor dining as it was for vehicle parking and maintenance.

Flats at Morningside Condo   C83
5701 Biscayne Boulevard
Clayton Danek Architects Associates, 1973
Renovation: Telesco Associates, 2002

After a period of concentrated commercial development in the 1950s and 1960s, new residential apartment buildings were introduced to Biscayne Boulevard in the 1970s. The arcing alignment of Biscayne Boulevard is sensitively traced in the façade of the Flats at Morningside. The glass curtain wall of its upper floors makes a public vitrine of the building's circulation corridors. On the opposite east façade, private balconies overlook a backyard pool and Biscayne Bay beyond.

Cushman School   C84

592 NE 60th Street
Russell T. Pancoast, Architect and Robert Skipton, 1926
Restorations and renovations: Max Wolfe Sturman, 1992, 2005
Additions and new construction: Max Wolfe Sturman, 1992, 2003, 2005

An exception to the general pattern along Biscayne Boulevard, where pre–World War II structures have been adapted for commercial uses, the original Cushman School retains its Mediterranean Revival styling and purpose as a private day school. The V-shaped original building faces away from Biscayne Boulevard, reflecting the fact that it was constructed before the boulevard itself. It also seems designed to capture the southeast breezes. Unlike the grander massing and Neoclassical styling of Miami's public schools in that era, the Cushman School had narrow building wings with open porticos substituting for enclosed hallways, giving all classrooms cross-ventilation. This model of school construction proved popular in the postwar period and is coming into vogue again today after an unfortunate period of uninspiring, windowless structures in the 1960s and 1970s.

An ambitious restoration and renovation of the original building began in 1992 and continued until 2005. Much of the original wood framing and trim remains intact or has been restored. While plate-glass windows have been installed in some spaces, the original mesh mosquito screening of the fenestration has been preserved, recalling a day when South Florida schoolchildren lived as close to the outdoors as possible. New additions to the original structure and a large new 10-classroom building on the west side of the campus are clearly contemporary, but remain compatible with the original Mediterranean Revival–style structure.

Mimo/Biscayne Boulevard Historic District

This segment of Biscayne Boulevard, from Fifty-fifth Street to the city limits at Eighty-third Street, comprises a rich assortment of commercial architecture, a legacy of its one-time role as the Gateway to Miami along U.S. Highway 1. In 2006, the City of Miami designated the stretch a historic district, acknowledging the contribution of its post–World War II structures to the history of design and development in Miami. While there are storefronts, hotels, and even houses dating from the 1920s and 1930s, the dominant building type here is the postwar motel, or motor hotel, collectively recognized as examples of the MiMo, or Miami Modern, style, a local term for midcentury Modern. This is the City of Miami's first historic district comprising a commercial area.

Recently, the district has acquired the character of a neighborhood center for the adjacent communities and has become a regional dining destination. Residences constructed in the 1920s and 1930s have been adapted for retail or commercial use and motels are being creatively adapted for new uses.

Shalimar Motel   C85

6200 Biscayne Boulevard
Edwin T. Reeder Associates, 1951
Addition: 1953

While its name may conjure up an exotic, faraway place, the design of the Shalimar Motel squares more aptly with romantic postwar notions of the American home. Domesticity was expressed through the use of a gabled roof elongated at its ends to reach the sidewalk, and whose broad eaves form an edge to the boulevard. The sloping roof covers the single-story reception booth, which originally functioned as a drive-thru. The motel's trapezoidal signage pylon parallels and accentuates the slope of the roof. A C-shaped front court is screened by a low wall, cloistering the parking area that most motels advertised. In its 1950s heyday, the Shalimar was home to the popular Sammy Walsh's Restaurant.

C86

South Pacific Motel   C86

6300 Biscayne Boulevard
Charles Giller, 1953

The 20-room South Pacific illustrates the extraordinary role that signage, thematic allusion, and even whimsy played in defining the architectural character of the postwar motel. In an attempt to grab the motorist's eye, architect Charles Giller went so far as to make the building look like it was toppling over. Along Biscayne Boulevard, the single-story office lobby and wing forms an alluring head house, whose walls are faced with a stone veneer that steps down to create a zigzag lightning bolt. The motel's distorted façade predicts similarly disorienting effects in the late 1970s work of James Wines for the showrooms of Best Products Co.

6400 Biscayne Boulevard   C87

Theodore Gottfried, 1965
Stained glass: Kay Pancoast, 1965
Renovation: Cynthia Dembrown Junkin, 2006

This modern peristyle commercial building was originally built for a purveyor of liturgical vestments and other church paraphernalia. It was located across the street from the Catholic Church's Miami Archdiocese, established in 1958. The building's extensive glass walls are set beneath a deeply projecting roof supported on rough concrete piers that form a Modernist loggia. Originally, screens suspended between the piers of the loggia provided shade for the interior and enclosed gardenlike spaces. Extant stained-glass panels on the building's south side, designed by ceramicist and artist Kay Pancoast, attest to its original use.

Davis Motel (New Yorker and Audubon House Motels)   C88

6500 Biscayne Boulevard
New Yorker: Norman M. Giller & Associates, 1953
Audubon House: Tony Sherman Associates, 1953

The Davis Motel combines two originally separate entities that illustrate, either by the presence or absence of key features, the architectural strategies

C88

once employed along Miami's Motel Row. On the south side of the block, the New Yorker is an L-shaped complex that frames its parking lot and features a powerfully streamlined head house facing Biscayne Boulevard. Designed to contain the lobby, public rooms, and owner's residence, the head house is bull-nosed on both sides, a gesture to the vehicular artery of Biscayne Boulevard. On the north side, planted in the center of its parking lot, the Audubon House is a simple rectangular block housing back-to-back motel units surrounded by wrapping galleries. Its exotic head house no longer exists: a 2-story glass terrarium lobby is stocked with tree branches and stuffed birds.

Legion Park   C89
Biscayne Boulevard at NE 66th Street

Legion Park, its majestic stands of live oaks, and its community center building are vestiges of the assemblage of oolitic limestone–clad estates that once lined the bayfront in this area. The property once belonged to Baltimore millionaire William B. Ogden, for whom architect George Pfeiffer improved and expanded an old residence on the site. Pfeiffer's 2-story addition, which survives, formed the northeast wing of the house. Completed in 1910 and entirely clad in oolitic rock, the building contained public rooms opening to a bayfront porch, and faced southeast to catch the breezes. Ogden planted citrus and avocado groves, as well as mangoes and sapodillas on the site, and called the estate Tee House Plantations.

With the commercialization of Biscayne Boulevard in the 1920s, the house became a speakeasy and casino. Acquired by the State of Florida in 1934, it was deeded to the American Legion, and later became a kind of local attraction and civic center for veterans who lived and vacationed in the area. The American Legion added an auditorium and terrazzo dance floor at the center of which a flagpole now sits. In 1966, Miami acquired most of the site and converted it to a park. The American Legion later built a new, modern center immediately to the south. The current stand of oaks slowly replaced the plantation groves, reestablishing a native hammock.

Biscayne Inn (Stardust Motel)   C90
6730 Biscayne Boulevard
Maurice S. Weintraub, 1956

This U-shaped, 54-unit motel features 2-story wings that wrap around a 2-level center court (upper-level pool and deck, lower-level parking). Confronting southbound motorists on Biscayne Boulevard, a 20-foot glazed triangular volume (since covered) topped by a shed roof announced the motel's head house. Forsaking a functionalist approach, the large glass volume existed just for the ultramodern sake of it.

Palm Bay Tower   C91
720 NE 69th Street
Lawrence & Belk, Architects with James Deen, 1972

The Palm Bay Club and Marina occupy the well-landscaped bayfront site of the former Charles Torrey Simpson estate, known as the Sentinels. Simpson, a pioneer naturalist, developed the site as a tropical garden that was visited

C91

by thousands (Simpson Park, in the Brickell area, resulted from his efforts to preserve the last stand of native hammock in that area).

The property was purchased in 1963 by Atlanta hotel mogul Cornelia Vandegaer (Connie) Dinkler, who transformed the site into a club and 50-slip marina. The synthesis of club and marina heralded a new concept of development in Miami, serving a jet-setting elite and a new class of megayachts in a swinging club setting. Wanting to create a club only fun people could join, Dinkler solicited like-minded socialites; eventually, the club grew to 1,400 members, some of whom bought condominiums on the grounds. The club's centerpiece was the private marina, designed to accommodate boats up to 145 feet in length. Tennis courts, a pool, and a 65-unit apartment building completed the picture. The 9-story Palm Bay Condo, designed by Eugene Lawrence and Ronald Belk (1964), borders one side of the marina, its zigzagging balconies cantilevered over its waters.

Today, the focal point of the site is the Palm Bay Tower, a trylon-shaped 27-story tower also developed by Dinkler and straddling the shore of Biscayne Bay. The tower is buttressed at its three ends by battered or up-curving pylons that form end caps, two of which swoop directly into the bay. Parabolic balconies project from glass walls framed by the aggregate surface of the building's concave walls. At its base, a glass lobby fronts the circular core, and is wrapped by a faceted plaza that cantilevers over open water. Consistent with the building concept, the plaza was designed to be accessed by boat as well as by land. In addition to the Palm Bay Condo and Tower, a small captain's house and clubhouse and the Palm Bay Yacht Club (1982) occupy the property. The site preserves a large amount of open land, including some tree specimens from the original Simpson estate. The original Palm Bay clubhouse, posh scene of countless parties, has since been demolished. The club-marina-residence concept would be repeated many times along the coast, most notably at the nearby Jockey Club.

Saturn Inn   C92
6999 Biscayne Boulevard
1952

The 16-unit Saturn is the most reductive motel on the strip. Its 1-story block has back-to-back rooms that face parking on both sides (paradoxically a rare condition on this urban motel row). Decoration is provided by the front reception, a secure booth framed by double projecting delta wings and by an ornamental cornice of precast-concrete fins that create an indirect lighting effect at night. A sign shaped like Saturn with its ring of light rounds out the period motifs.

7100 and 7101 Biscayne Boulevard   C93
7100 Biscayne (Sir William Hotel)
Joseph J. DeBrita, 1939
Frontal addition and conversion to offices: A. Herbert Mathes, 1960

7101 Biscayne
1939
Frontal addition and conversion to offices: H. Maxwell Parish, 1961

These two commercial buildings illustrate something fundamental about the character of Biscayne Boulevard: its progressive evolution from residential to resort, then to commercial office corridor, and, finally, to neighborhood center. The intertwined transformation of its use and architectural expressions lends the boulevard a rich, eclectic, and layered appearance.

Number 7100 Biscayne best illustrates the shift from resort Main Street to commercial office corridor. Originally constructed as the Sir William Hotel, one of four 1930s-era hotels built along this stretch, this 3-story structure was converted to offices in 1960. At that time, its street frontage was modernized with a new glass-walled lobby that spilled into a landscaped front yard, and metallic screens around the upper floors. The current aluminum screens, replaced in 1964, feature gold-anodized vertical battens and vertical aggregate panels that literally cocoon the original façade. More recently, the lobby has been converted into a restaurant, and the suburban-style front yard colonized with café seating. The sedimentation of uses and architecture is visible on its side façade, where the prewar-postwar connections are manifest.

Directly opposite, Number 7101 was built as a 2-story apartment building. In 1961, the property was converted to office uses, and a 2-story commercial front was added in front. The metal screens protecting its glass façade play off the frontage of Number 7100. Note the cutaway at the building corner, which exposes a floating staircase that rises in a landscaped open-air atrium.

International Book Building   C94

7300 Biscayne Boulevard
R. William Clayton, Jr., 1964

The skin of this 4-story commercial building was created economically of full lengths of precast concrete double-tees. The heavily ribbed façade features continuous vertical gaps where the windows are located. Of note is that the building's north façade is the new home of "the Coppertone girl," a large illuminated sign advertising the famed tanning product invented in Miami. The iconic metal and plastic sign created by Larry Moore and Moe Bengis of Miami signage company Tropicalites was originally mounted on the north wall of Parkleigh House at 530 Biscayne Boulevard. Entrusted to Dade Heritage Trust when the Parkleigh House was demolished circa 1990, it was moved to the blank side of an office building on Flagler Street. Now passed on to the MiMo-Biscayne Association, the sign was installed here in 2008.

C94

Vagabond Motel   C95

7301 Biscayne Boulevard
Robert Swartburg, 1953

Designed to lure southbound tourists as they entered Miami, the Vagabond Motel beautifully embodies the characteristic elements of motel culture on this one-time resort strip. The U-shaped structure opens toward the boulevard, exposing its parking court and an alluring pool deck elevated on undulating brick retaining walls. At the rear center of the court, a perforated masonry wall draws the eye in and creates a theatric backdrop for the activities at the pool. Eye-catching imagery and graphics were, of course, part of the formula. A fieldstone grotto featuring frolicking bare-chested nymphs who are gazed upon by friendly dolphins greets the motorist at the northwest corner of the building. On the opposite southwest end is the head house, originally containing the lobby, office, restaurant, and bar. Its space-age porte cochere is held on metallic pylons, while the main building signage is hoisted aloft on a pylon of synthetic slump brick. The pylon's angular form was exaggerated by a metallic scaffold that supports stars that sparkle at night. The Vagabond was once an anchor of nightlife on the boulevard, its restaurant and lounge designed to feature the musical group after which the motel was purportedly named.

C95

Church of the Nazarene (Biscayne Boulevard   C96
Lutheran Church/New Mount Pleasant
Baptist Church)

7610 Biscayne Boulevard
Igor Polevitzky, 1951

The first Biscayne Boulevard Lutheran Church occupied this site since at least the 1930s. The church burned in 1951, and was replaced by a new, larger one designed by Igor Polevitzky. In contrast to the earlier structure, which faced Biscayne Boulevard, Polevitzky oriented the new church sideways, forsaking the commercial tangle of the boulevard for the residential character of NE Seventy-sixth Street. A tall pylon carrying a neon cross, certainly an abstraction of a steeple but also a characteristic feature of postwar roadside

C96

architecture, mediates sacred and profane. The pylon and the lower portion
of the church's entrance portico (whose upper walls feature colorful stained-
glass windows) are clad in crab orchard stone inspired by the organic manner of Frank Lloyd Wright.

Florida International Academy Charter School   C97
(Atlas Sewing Machine Building)
7630 Biscayne Boulevard
Norman M. Giller & Associates, 1956

C97

Now a charter school, this office building for the Atlas Sewing Machine
company lined Biscayne Boulevard with two stories marked by strongly cantilevered canopies and a recessed entrance court. The roof of the recessed
court is perforated with square cutouts to let pools of light into landscape
planters, and trees now grow within. The butterfly profile along the canopy
edges, and walls composed of granite panels alternating with plate-glass
windows and clerestories, are particularly handsome.

Boulevard Theater   C98
7778 Biscayne Boulevard
Robert Law Weed and Edwin T. Reeder Associates, 1941

Once a grand cinema, the Boulevard Theater has served a series of strip
clubs in recent times. The pylon that sets off the theater's rounded corner
and marquee entrance is the principal visible element of the original structure. Originally, it featured projecting radiator fins outlining "boulevard"
in neon letters. Weed was also responsible for the Paramount Theater on
Flagler Street in Miami, and the Beach Theater on Lincoln Road in Miami
Beach, among others.

Seventy-ninth and Biscayne

*Before the Interstate Highway System, U.S. Highway 1 (Biscayne
Boulevard) was the way into Miami, and the intersection of NE
Seventy-ninth Street was the city's entrance portal. Here, a small ur-
ban core developed. The importance of this crossroads is significant.
To the north lay growing residential neighborhoods stretching to the
county line. To the south are Motel Row and its striking competition
of commercial signage and architectural stagecraft. To the east, the
John F. Kennedy Causeway (originally completed as the Everglades
Causeway in 1929) connects to the North Beach section of Miami
Beach. The Little River and Florida East Coast Railway pass just to the
west. Farther west, Seventy-ninth Street terminates at Hialeah Park
Racetrack. As a gateway in each direction, the center had to carefully
mediate the diverse commercial, residential, resort, and retail charac-
ters of its surroundings. Its vehicular accessibility and open, modern
planning contrast with the traditional commercial heart of Little
River, centered several blocks west on NE Second Avenue.*

7880 Biscayne Boulevard (Gulf American Corporation Building)   C99
Steward & Skinner Associates, 1964

Conceived to anchor the southwest corner of Biscayne Boulevard and Seventy-ninth Street, this 12-story tower was built to house the headquarters of Gulf American Corporation. More recently, the building housed the Immigration and Naturalization Service (INS). The square tower is a monumental presence, with solid corners and vertical bands of gold-anodized metal screens concealing window bays that rise in the center of each face. The 2-story pedestal was originally clad in glass, with expressed concrete fins that projected along its roof; these were closed, probably for security reasons. The tall fascia crowning the top of the tower once held a moving digital sign that broadcast the news in all directions.

Biscayne Plaza Shopping Center   C100
C99   561 NE 79th Street
Robert Fitch Smith, 1954

The Biscayne Plaza Shopping Center was Miami's first automobile-oriented shopping plaza. Built along the city's northern frontier, it was designed to exploit growing traffic at the important crossroads of Biscayne Boulevard and NE Seventy-ninth Street.

     By mixing uses and forming spaces, like many early shopping centers, this one is more interesting than most of its progeny. The complex comprises three main buildings tied together by overhead bridges that frame entrances from the surrounding streets. The three wings roughly form a C-shape, whose southeast wing extends to meet and partly address the corner of Biscayne Boulevard and NE Seventy-ninth Street. By virtue of its defining walls, the mall's central parking lot seems like a civic space in waiting. Around the mall, deep overhangs shelter walkways and shade plate-glass walls. Offices are on the second floor, accessed by cantilevered stairs that form sculptural features facing parking areas. A semi-attached bank

C100

and separate motel (the Admiral Vee [C101]) complete the complex. More commercial structures surrounded the adjacent intersection, transforming it into a postwar regional center. Towers placed at entrances to the complex, Postmodern follies, are a later addition.

8000 Biscayne Boulevard (Admiral Vee Motel)   C101
Maurice Weintraub, 1957

C101

Real estate was at such a premium in the Seventy-ninth and Biscayne area in the 1950s that a new genre of mixed-use, multistory motel was devised to fit this extraordinary location just east of the Biscayne Plaza Shopping Center. Outside-the-door parking, a standard of motel design, was abandoned for a parking garage tucked beneath the building, behind a fronting wall of retail shops. The motel was elevated above the parking, but beyond that it offered all the amenities expected, including a swimming pool and Googie-style double-height lobby lounge wrapped in canted glass and a great sloping roof. Its vertical fin, or, more precisely, wing, can be seen for blocks to the south on Biscayne Boulevard. The motel has most recently served as a production studio.

Bank Lofts (Miami National Bank)   C102
8101 Biscayne Boulevard
Smith and Korach, 1956
4-story addition: Rene C. Brugnoni, 1964
1-story rooftop addition and adaptive use: Beilinson Gomez Architects, 2008

Originally constructed as a 2-story building to house the Miami National Bank, the structure was expanded in 1964 with four additional floors of offices. The bank closed in 1990, and the building was damaged by Hurricane Andrew in 1992. Most recently, it was expanded with one additional floor and repositioned as 73 live/work lofts. The 7-story building has an egg-crate façade whose irregular alignments betray its construction in phases. Glass window walls, some with expressed guardrails, have replaced the adjustable vertical louvers that once defined the building's principal façades and were designed to track the sun. The change reflects not just its new residential use, but a parallel cultural migration from sun protection to views.

Lake Belmar   C103
NE 89th Street east of 10th Court

This waterfront subdivision in the Shorecrest neighborhood of Northeast Miami offers a civic approach to canalfront living, transforming docks and yachts into public features of neighborhood life. At its center is Lake Belmar, a finger canal from Biscayne Bay that bulges at its west end (at NE Tenth Court) to form a kind of water plaza. Coral rock walls form a small seating area here, with steps and planters that descend to the water (a faint echo of Rome's Porto di Ripetta). Houses front the canal across NE Eighty-ninth Street, which surrounds the canal on both sides. Verges between the road and seawall have been improved with landscaping, umbrellas, concrete tables, and benches. Unfortunately, the configuration of the waterfront as public space is the exception in South Florida, and not the rule.

Buena Vista East

The neighborhood immediately north of the Design District, bounded by NE Second Avenue and Miami Avenue, contains an exceptionally rich collection of houses and apartment buildings, most of it now codified within the Buena Vista East Historic District.

Westminster Presbyterian Church C104

4201 NE 2nd Avenue
Robert Fitch Smith, 1956

Just north of the Design District, this modest church at the border of commercial and residential areas mixes modern and traditional elements. Gabled components like the sanctuary and front porch are rendered in a stripped Classical vocabulary the architect termed a "modified form of Colonial Georgian." The tower is remarkable for its lacy aluminum steeple that supports a Celtic cross and screens an electronic belfry.

C105

Archbishop Curley Notre Dame High School C105 and Brothers' Residence and Chapel

4949 NE 2nd Avenue
School: Gerald A. Barry and Fred D. Kay, 1952
Brothers' Residence and Chapel: Arthur Pochert, 1966

Archbishop Curley High School and Notre Dame Academy were founded in 1953–54 and merged in 1981. The most noteworthy structures on this combined campus lie adjacent to NE Second Avenue south of the entry: the Brothers' Residence and the Chapel. The Residence, a rectangular Modernist block, features wrapping galleries screened by precast concrete panels, adorned by four-pointed, star-shaped cutouts. To the east, the Chapel's narrowly pitched roof evokes hands at prayer. Its stained-glass windows display traditional scenes from Catholic sources, as well as a depiction of the later beatified Kateri Tekakwitha, an indigenous American, whom the American Catholic Church and the Jesuit Order promoted vigorously for canonization during the middle of the twentieth century.

Little Haiti

Through most of the twentieth century, the bayfront areas of Lemon City and Little River stretched from today's NE Fiftieth Street to the city line. To the west of the Florida East Coast Railway tracks lay the black settlements of Nazarene, Knightsville, and Boles Town. Today the area is known as Little Haiti, acknowledging the more than thirty-five thousand Haitian Americans who live there. Much of the commercial activity is along North Miami Avenue and NE Second Avenue. The bright Caribbean colors that adorn many of Little Haiti's buildings clearly demarcate it from the surrounding areas, even if there are no official boundary lines. Recent efforts have focused on developing a civic identity for the community's Main Street along NE Second Avenue between the 5800 and 5900 blocks.

Toussaint L'Ouverture Elementary School   C106

112 NE 58th Terrace
Zyscovich Architects, 1989

Named after Haiti's preeminent patriotic heroic figure, the first urban school
built in Miami in over a decade signaled, along with the construction of the
nearby Haitian Marketplace, the emergence of Greater Miami's significant
Haitian American community.

    While clearly contemporary, the design references the Neoclassical pat-
terns and plan organization of Miami's pre–World War II school buildings, as
well as Caribbean traditions. The school is arranged around four axially oriented courtyards surrounded by classroom wings accessed by shed-roofed
open galleries. Open corridors and operable louvers on all outward-facing
windows reintroduce an environmentally sustainable model, found in earlier local school designs. The main entrance consists of a double-height
breezeway entered through a slightly bowed evocation of a portico. A high-
pitched canopy, recalling the roofs of traditional Haitian architecture, proj-   C106
ects outward to the curb. Once inside, two symmetrical opposing staircases
lead to a second-floor corridor bridging across the breezeway and frame
views of the courtyard beyond.

Little Haiti Community Park   C107
and Soccer Stadium

Park: bounded by NE 64th Terrace to the north, 62nd Street to the south, NE 2nd Avenue
to the west, and NE 4th Avenue to the east
Zyscovich Architects, 2008

Soccer Stadium
6301 NE Second Avenue
Zyscovich Architects, 2008

This community park was originally intended to cover ten city blocks, but
has been only partly realized. The project sprang from the quixotic vision
of the late city and county commissioner Arthur Teele. Carved from the
warehouses and commercial buildings that define Little Haiti, the park
was a long-promised boon for this traditionally underserved area of the
city. Linked in planning vision if not by proximity, the soccer stadium and
Neighborhood Enhancement Team office are some four blocks north of the
Caribbean Marketplace (C108) and the newly completed Cultural Center
(C109). The airy stadium has a graceful barrel-vaulted roof cantilevered from
vertical stanchions that project from the grandstand below.

Caribbean Marketplace   C108

5925–5927 NE 2nd Avenue
Charles Harrison Pawley, 1990
Restoration: Zyscovich Architects, 2007

Created in 1990 as the Haitian Marketplace, this lighthearted folly was inspired by Port-au-Prince's famous Iron Market. The structure was the product of a design competition organized to reinvigorate the center of Little
Haiti with a characteristic Caribbean building type. The winning entry, by
Charles Harrison Pawley, a prominent Miami architect of Haitian descent,
incorporated the high-pitched, corrugated metal roofs typical of Haitian

C108

vernacular architecture. After falling into disuse, the building was renovated and has regained its luster as a landmark in its Little Haiti neighborhood.

C109

Little Haiti Cultural Center   C109

212–216 NE 59th Terrace
Zyscovich Architects, 2008

Immediately to the east of the Caribbean Marketplace, two contemporary structures stand in a relaxed architectural conversation with their western neighbor. The buildings, with angular and triangular features referring both to the rooftop of their neighbor and to typical Haitian architecture, contain a 250-seat black-box theater, an art gallery, a dance studio, visual art studios, and classrooms. The courtyard between the buildings is highlighted by a 2008 mural by Ralph Allen depicting Haitian daily life.

DuPuis Medical Office and Drugstore   C110

6041–6045 NE 2nd Avenue
1902

This fine vestige of the pre-railroad village of Lemon City is distinguished by its sidewalk-covering arcade. Still owned by the DuPuis family, this building is a rare example of early commercial architecture in Miami-Dade County and the earliest-known concrete building constructed north of Downtown. At this writing, the building is in an advanced state of neglect.

MacArthur Dairy Administration Building   C111

6851 NE 2nd Avenue
Robert Fitch Smith, ca. 1952

The MacArthur Dairy Building is a compositional assemblage that blends the imagery of suburban office buildings with the showmanship of 1930s world's fair architecture. The complex features 2-story administration and public relations wings (each with its own entrance) sheathed in blue-green terra-cotta tiles. The main stair is identified on the façade by corner-wrapping glass block; concrete canopies, originally topped with porcelain signage, shelter the glass-walled entrances. The overall composition is balanced by the building's prominent pylon. Unfortunately, the building has lost its central showpiece: a cylindrical pavilion that once housed the dairy's

C111

"Milk Bar." Supported by a circular array of tall concrete fins, each framing and shading 22-foot-high glass jalousie windows, the Milk Bar was an iconic feature on NE Second Avenue.

Villa Paula   C112

5811–5837 North Miami Avenue
C. Freira, 1926

As Miami boomed and the traffic across the Florida Straits expanded in the mid-1920s, the Cuban government commissioned Havana architect C. Freira to design a Cuban consulate along North Miami Avenue. Named for the wife of Miami's first Cuban consul, the structure reflects the Neoclassical style popular in Cuba in the 1920s. Indeed, the consulate, with its fronting porch, balustrade roof, 18-foot ceilings, Tuscan columns, tall, arched windows, and hand-painted cement tiles, seems a fragment of Havana's Vedado district. Even the building materials were imported from Cuba. In its neighborhood context today, the building appears as a magnificent relic of a more opulent prior civilization.

C112

Toussaint L'Ouverture Memorial   C113

Place Toussaint L'Ouverture, SW corner of North Miami Avenue and 62nd Street
Sculptor: James Mastin, 2005

This commanding statue honors Toussaint L'Ouverture, the greatest figure of the Haitian Revolution of 1804. The revolution established the world's first black republic, a title Haiti has held through two centuries of trial and tribulations. William Wordsworth wrote in his poem "To Toussaint L'Ouverture": "Though fallen thyself, never to ride again,/Live and take comfort./Thou has left behind/Powers that will work for thee." In the early days of large-scale Haitian migration to Miami, this spot served as a meeting place for Haitian day laborers seeking work.

Miami Edison Middle School   C114

6101 NW 2nd Avenue
Middle School and Gymnasium: H. H. Mundy, 1928
Auditorium: Pfeiffer and Robertson, 1931
Renovation and addition: R. J. Heisenbottle Architects, 1998

The current complex opened in 1928 as the Miami Dade Agricultural School. The death of Thomas Edison in 1931 inspired the name change to Miami Edison Senior High School in the following year. The building's E-shaped plan with open galleries is typical of local school buildings of the period and was a response to the need for light and ventilation before the introduction of air-conditioning. The classroom building displays a rare melding of Modern Classical and Prairie style influences. The main façade of the classroom building is centered by a 3-story central portico. Its columns and pilasters are embellished by a triangular motif broken by horizontal bands. This element, combined with longer horizontal banding elsewhere, gives the building its Prairie style reference. Decorative tile work appears in the portico's cornice and spandrel panels. The gymnasium is distinguished by a low-pitched "jerkin head" roof. The auditorium building is one of Miami's finest in the high Art Deco style, in large part due to its ornate interior.

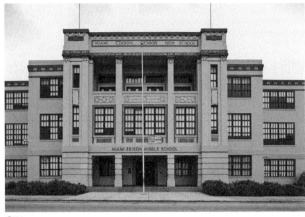

C114

In 1979, the high school moved two blocks west to a windowless new facility at 6161 NW Fifth Court, hard-up against I-95. A well-conceived addition connecting to the rear of the original classroom building and creating a central courtyard between the two was completed in 1998. The work included the full restoration of the Auditorium and the exterior restoration of the original Classroom Building and Gymnasium.

Edison Courts   C115

NW 62nd Street
Paist and Steward with Robert Law Weed, Vladimir Virrick, and E. L. Robertson, 1939

Sponsored by the Miami Housing Authority, this New Deal housing project was intended for white residents; it was sited east of NW Twelfth Avenue and the wall (D28) that separated black Liberty Square (D27) from white areas. The project, a fine example of WPA aesthetic standards, included notable technical innovations such as built-in solar water heaters. Both Edison Courts and Liberty Square were integrated in 1960.

Edison Center Branch Library   C116

531 NW 62nd Street
Weed Johnson Associates, 1958

Soon after the completion of Miami's first central public library in Bayfront Park (1951), the city embarked on a program to develop, consolidate, or replace branch libraries in its constituent neighborhoods. The Edison Center Branch Library, in the predominantly black Liberty City neighborhood, was one such effort and of a set with other branch libraries throughout the city.

C116

Typical of the modest nature of most branch libraries, Edison's low-slung, 1-story structure has a flat roof, crab orchard stone veneer, and extensive glass window areas. Its broad projecting canopy, supported on a pair of V-shaped beanpole columns, was a rare concession to public monumentality. Clerestories flood the interior with light, and glass interior partitions allow plenty of transparency while maintaining quiet. In another concession to suburban iconography, a screened patio behind the library at one time provided an outdoor reading room.

Little River

Miami's second river is the Little River. Early on, it gave its name to the village—later, the Miami neighborhood—that grew up around its intersection with the Florida East Coast Railway. The area has become home for Haitian Americans spilling north from Lemon City, and is now considered part of Little Haiti.

8300 NE Second Avenue (First Federal Savings Office Building)
C117

Robert Fitch Smith, 1951

This substantial commercial block along NE Second Avenue, Little River's historic main street, adapts urban commercial architecture to the age of the automobile. While the building meets the street with a nearly continuous stretch of retail spaces, a spacious midblock breezeway connects the sidewalk to the rear parking lot and provides access to the offices above. The size and ambition of this mixed-use block are indicative of the neighborhood's upper-middle-class cachet in the postwar period.

At the north end of the block was the keystone-clad platonic cube of First Federal Savings Bank, later Amerifirst Savings. Projecting fins, ashlar-set quarry keystone, wrapping glass walls, terrazzo steps, and framing planters mark the entrance to the bank and contrast with an otherwise spare Modernist ornamental program.

Cathedral of Saint Mary
C118

7525 NW 2nd Avenue
Barry and Kay, 1957
Chapel: 1965

Saint Mary's perches majestically on a rise in NW Second Avenue, discernable even by motorists on I-95. Its dignity and unmistakably crisp 1950s interpretation of Mediterranean architecture demonstrate that even historicist buildings can be products of their time, an oft-used excuse for discrediting the desire to evoke the past in architecture. Note the simple, yet powerful façade composition, with its Churrigueresque references and the grid of shadow effects on the expansive stucco field. Its spare ornamentation notwithstanding, it is an architectural descendent of the more ornate Coral Gables Congregational Church. An imposing dome clad in colorful tile rises from the rear of the nave.

C118

D

City of Miami: Northwest

This section covers the part of Miami bounded by the Dolphin Expressway on the south, I-95 on the east, and the city limits on the north and west. The area includes the Civic Center and the neighborhoods of Spring Garden, Allapattah, and Liberty City, as well as industrial sections along the Miami River and Miami Canal. Warehouse districts stretch inland.

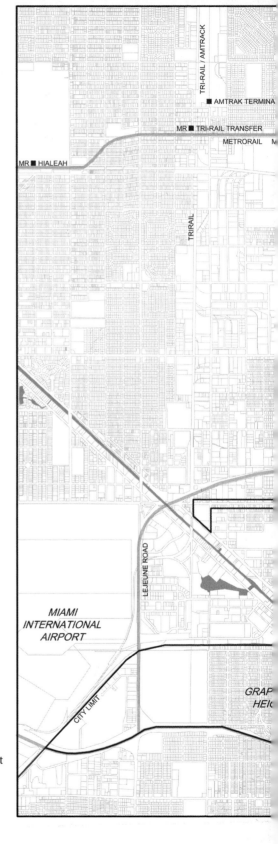

D. City of Miami: Northwest

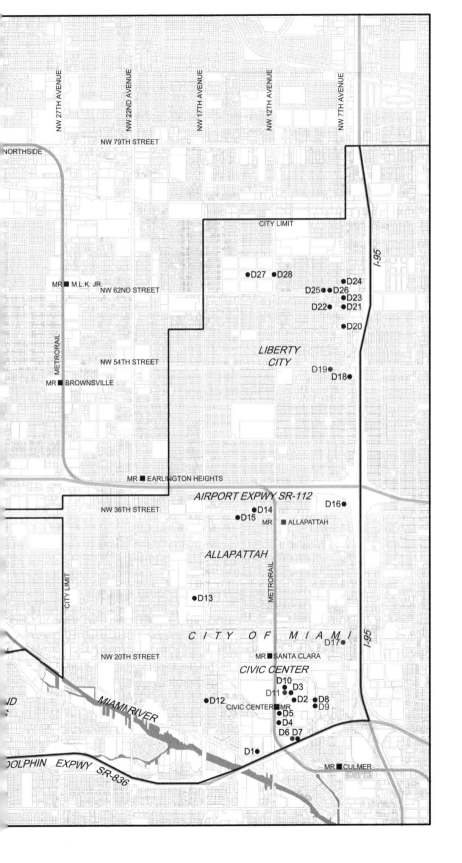

Civic Center

*Miami's Civic Center includes the University of Miami Health
Center and Hospital, Jackson Memorial Hospital, and the Veterans
Administration Hospital, as well as the Richard Gerstein Justice
Building (criminal courthouse) and the county jail. The mix of governmental facilities and medical institutions provides one of Miami-Dade
County's major employment centers. Metrorail runs along the center
of Twelfth Avenue in this area, passing through the center of the district. The Civic Center station straddles the avenue, producing an unusual station type, with stairs and escalators cascading down either
side to spacious covered plazas.*

*Much of the site was formerly the Miami Country Club,
which straddled the Miami River and Seybold Canal just north of
Downtown. In 1950, a Beaux-Arts–inspired design for a county civic
center on the site, endorsed by the Urban Land Institute, drew much
interest. All buildings were to be designed by a board of architects
led by Edwin T. Reeder, and all were to be connected by tunnels or
bridges. Opposition to relocating civic facilities stalled the plan, which
was never realized. From its original campus to the northeast, Jackson
Memorial Hospital and a series of related medical facilities have since
merged with the Civic Center district.*

D1

Richard E. Gerstein Justice Building   D1

Metrorail: Civic Center

1351 NW 12th Street
CODA with Steward & Skinner Associates, 1961

Prominently visible from the Dolphin Expressway bridge over the Miami
River, this 9-story courthouse housing Miami-Dade's Criminal Justice
Building is one of the most heavily trafficked buildings in Miami (more than
fifteen thousand visitors per day). Among its programmatic challenges is
sorting the movement of judges, juries, prisoners, and visitors through a
complex series of interior corridors.

The monumental structure has a rich palette of materials, including
decorative mosaic tile, ornamental metalwork, stone, and precast concrete
with an aggregate finish. Set on a tall podium, its ground-floor glass walls
are recessed behind metal screens. Above, 6 stories of courts and offices rise
behind the panelized concrete walls. The top two floors are set in. New circulation cores have been added on either side and along the back without
severely compromising the original design.

Jackson Memorial Hospital

*Jackson Memorial and the University of Miami's hospitals are
the main teaching hospitals of the University of Miami School of
Medicine. With a research center, trauma center, and more than 1,500
beds, this complex is the most complete and extensive health system
in the region, if not the southeastern United States.*

When Miami outgrew its first hospital at Biscayne Boulevard and NE Eighth Street, a site was chosen far from the city to provide room for future expansion. The hospital was renamed James M. Jackson Memorial Hospital in 1924 after the city's pioneer physician (see Dr. Jackson's House near Brickell [A117]). From modest foundations, it has grown to occupy a sprawling and eclectic campus. The campus lacks a distinct focal point, and an abundance of parking lots and garages negatively impacts a nascent urbanism. Nevertheless, it offers a number of interesting moments, and several buildings merit a look. Maps are located throughout the area to orient the first-time visitor.

Alamo   D2
Metrorail: Civic Center

1611 NW 12th Avenue
August Geiger, 1916

D2

Built as the main facility of the Miami City Hospital, the Alamo was a portent of the Mediterranean Revival style popular in the 1920s. Similar to August Geiger's Miami Beach Municipal Golf Course Building of the same year, it employs a formal façade treatment inspired by the Spanish Colonial architecture popular in America in the wake of the Panama-California Exposition in San Diego (1915). Its octagonal cupola, clay tile roof, fronting porch, and reiteration of a gabled parapet motif illustrate efforts toward creating an appropriate regional style.

As Jackson Memorial Hospital grew, much of the original complex was demolished to make way for today's extensive campus. In 1979, the Alamo was moved 475 feet to create space for the construction of a maternal child-care center and reprogrammed for use as a visitors' center. Today it is the centerpiece of a landscaped plaza at the heart of the campus.

South Wing (White Addition)   D3
Metrorail: Civic Center

Behind the Alamo
Steward & Skinner Associates, ca. 1950

Something of Alvar Aalto's iconic Paimio Sanatorium in Finland (1929–30) is visible here in the elongated massing, pinwheel dynamic, and projecting balconies of this structure, which once served as an addition to an earlier (now defunct) Neoclassical building. Long attenuated fins surround the window bays, and the main block blends two offset volumes with a bull-nosed balcony. The entrance block pivots to hinge the intersection of several diverse buildings at this point.

Halissee Hall   D4
Metrorail: Civic Center

1475 NW 12th Avenue
George Pfeiffer, 1912–18

John Sewell, a prominent early merchant and Miami's third mayor, built this 2½-story house on the highest point in the city. He named the house

D5

Halissee Hall after the Seminole word for "new moon." Rough-cut, native oolitic limestone forms the primary building material, offset by a formal portico, which is supported by 2-story, fluted Ionic columns. Sewell came to Miami to supervise the construction of Henry Flagler's Royal Palm Hotel, excavating the foundations in Miami's native oolitic limestone bedrock. Later, Sewell promoted the use of oolite as a building material (as did architect George Pfeiffer), for which Halissee served as a fine showcase. The home was restored in 1977 for use by the medical center. Its interior, though compartmentalized into offices, is largely intact. At one time, the house overlooked an extensive garden and an allée of royal palms. Today, Halissee Hall is unceremoniously embedded in the Jackson Memorial Campus. The size of the original Halissee Hall estate can be gauged by the location of its entry gates, still found on NW Tenth Avenue just south of the Dolphin Expressway.

Mailman Center for Child Development   D5
Metrorail: Civic Center

1601 NW 12th Avenue
Pancoast, Ferendino, Grafton, 1969

The sweeping bell-bottom profile of the Mailman Center departs from the more boxlike architecture found throughout the Jackson campus. This heroic Brutalist building is entirely cast in concrete with solid end walls and a fine-grained egg crate along the broad north and south faces. Stair and service towers at each end form boldly polygonal volumes articulated in ribbed cast concrete. The expanding profile of the building at the lower levels allows larger public rooms fed from a generous multistory lobby that opens to sunken walled courts. Three rectangular concrete scoops facing NW Sixteenth Street feed the building's air-conditioning system. On the south side, a raised concrete plaza with built-in ledges is flanked by the complementary concrete structures of the Debbie Institute. While the addition of hurricane protective screening in all the openings has diminished the clarity of the building's exterior grid of crisp concrete planes, the structure remains a powerful marker at the entrance to the Jackson Memorial campus, plainly visible from the Metrorail and along NW Twelfth Avenue.

Professional Arts Center   D6

Metrorail: Civic Center

1150 NW 14th Street
Johnson Associates, 1969

This medical office building is a monumental block, powerfully solid in its middle, with a recessed glass base and an abstract full-story cornice. It would be undistinguished, however, were it not for its skin of multistory precast-concrete wall panels, each of which bears a unique carved image. The ensemble, titled *Procession* and sculpted by Al Vrana, includes two hundred panels in which humans offer themselves to the knowledge of medical professionals. The panels were made from styrofoam molds, carved and then cast by Vrana in his studio. The technique was an improvement over the sculptor's earlier sand-casting process, employed during the 1950s to clad the community room of the A. Herbert Mathes's Miami Beach Public Library in Collins Park.

D6

Clinical Research Building and Wellness Center   D7

Metrorail: Civic Center

1120 NW 14th Street
Perkins + Will, 2006

Built at the southern end of the medical campus, against the Dolphin Expressway and Wagner Creek, the project links a 15-story research facility with an open 2-story Wellness Center perched on the roof of the almost 1,500-car garage. The tower's finely filigreed skin of glass and aluminum curtain wall with projecting vertical and horizontal battens recalls the Cartesian cladding of postwar office buildings. The Wellness Center, hoisted high above the neighboring traffic arteries, glows like a lantern at night. The Clinical Research Building and Wellness Center is considered one of Miami's first "green" projects and is located in close proximity to Metrorail; the large parking garage, a less sustainable feature, serves the medical campus.

D7

Bascom Palmer Eye Institute   D8

Metrorail: Civic Center

900 NW 17th Street
Pancoast, Ferendino, Grafton, 1976

The Bascom Palmer complex is an L-shaped block framing a substantial courtyard. These days, the court is a popular outdoor dining terrace. The building's cast concrete façade is molded to produce flush, as well as re-cessed, bays of ribbonlike windows. A notable detail is the molding of the building name in its concrete skin. A sunken court, accessible through the building's 3-story entrance lobby and grand stair, wraps the outside corner.

Louis Calder Memorial Library   D9

Metrorail: Civic Center

D8

1601 NW 10th Avenue
Steward & Skinner Associates and Little, Lair and Pilkington, 1971

This modest yet distinguished medical library is clothed in ribbed cast-concrete walls whose frequent indentations and gently radiused corners suggest discrete cubic volumes. Gaps between the volumes allow light to penetrate through bronzed glass windows. The structure is raised on a low concrete plinth that forms a wrapping plaza. Ceramic murals are cast into the upper façade along NW Tenth Avenue. On the interior, a 2-story atrium reiterates the ribbed skin of the building in its wrapping second-level con-crete parapets.

Institute (Tuberculosis Building)   D10

Metrorail: Civic Center

Steward & Skinner Associates, 1954–55

This severe Modern Classical design is one exemplar of the midcentury ar-chitectural character Steward & Skinner set for the hospital. Monumental and functional, it suggests a distant echo of Paul Philippe Cret's Federal Reserve Bank in Washington, D.C. (1935–37).

Rehabilitation Hospital (Psychiatric Ward)   D11
Metrorail: Civic Center

1611 NW 12th Avenue
Steward & Skinner Associates, 1954–55

Originally the psychiatric ward of Jackson Memorial Hospital, this building once contained segregated facilities for hydrotherapy, electrotherapy, and shock treatment as well as occupational and recreational therapy. The building is a fine illustration of postwar institutional architecture. Together with the Institute, the Rehabilitation Hospital forms a small quadrangle facing Twelfth Avenue.

Allapattah

While the young city of Miami boomed in the 1920s, much of Allapattah (Seminole for "alligator") remained seasonal wetlands (or slough) and rich farmland. The Allapattah Prairie did not become primed for development until after Everglades drainage canals were constructed in the mid-1920s. By the mid-1930s, the entire district was being urbanized. After World War II, it experienced rapid growth.

The Seaboard Railroad opened an Allapattah station in 1927. A spur of what is now CSX Railroad bisects Allapattah between Twenty-second and Twenty-third streets, serving a number of warehouses on either side; these warehouses comprise the Twentieth Street Merchants' Corridor between Twentieth and Seventeenth avenues, now famous for its numerous garment and notion manufacturing and wholesale outlets. Its proximity to Miami International Airport attracts buyers and exporters from Latin America and the Caribbean. To the northeast, the warehouses of the produce market form the largest food distribution center in Greater Miami.

Today, Allapattah is the center of Miami's Dominican American community, which has breathed life into the quaintly scaled Seventeenth Avenue commercial corridor. Numerous Art Deco and postwar Modern buildings line the neighborhood's arterial streets.

International Brotherhood of Electrical   D12
Workers Local 349
1657 NW 17th Avenue
Walter DeGarmo, 1948

Walter DeGarmo, one of Miami's most talented architects working in the 1920s Mediterranean Revival, designed this powerfully streamlined structure for the International Brotherhood of Electrical Workers. It is perhaps his only known work in the Modern Classical style. For years, the project was known primarily through a rendering in the collection of the Bass Museum of Art, and was thought to have remained unrealized.

D12

Juan Pablo Duarte Park (Comstock Park)   D13
2800 NW 17th Avenue

One of the last agricultural parcels in Allapattah was the Exotic Gardens Nursery, which later became Comstock Park. When Allapattah became the center of Miami's Dominican population in the 1980s, it was renamed after Dominican patriot Juan Pablo Duarte. Taking up a large city block, the park is notable for its enormous mature trees and as the source of Wagner Creek. The creek begins in the park and then goes underground at Seventeenth Avenue until it reappears near Jackson Memorial Hospital and eventually flows into the Miami River via the Seybold Canal at Spring Garden.

D14

Bank of America (Central Bank &   D14
Trust Company)
Metrorail: Allapattah

1313 NW 36th Street
Weed Johnson Associates, 1962

This prominent postwar Modern office building, originally Miami Central Bank, announces Allapattah from the Airport Expressway. The building's window walls are lent interest by perforated concrete sunshades that throw patterns of light and shadow. The end walls are nearly opaque and clad in aggregate. Like many Modern buildings in the area, changing fortunes have led its tall, glassy ground floor to be boarded up, although the structure still functions as a bank and office building.

1400 NW 36th Street (Dade Federal   D15
Savings and Loan Association)
Metrorail: Allapattah

Edwin T. Reeder Associates, 1952

This midcentury bank building had offices raised on pilotis over its glass banking lobby. Notably, and with respect toward its context, the complex was set back to create a corner garden, across from which a canopy connected the building to the street. Unfortunately, the yard has now been fenced, and the building substantially altered.

Fire Training Tower   D16
3700 NW 7th Avenue
Federal Emergency Relief Administration (FERA), 1934

This 5-story tower was conceived to improve the training of Miami's firefighters. It stands like a mysterious sentinel near the interchange of I-195, I-95, and the Airport Expressway. Partially financed by the Works Progress Administration (WPA), the building features geometric Art Deco ornamentation and finials at the roofline.

Seaboard Airline Station Entrance Arch   D17
2200 NW 7th Avenue
ca. 1926

The grand arched entrance, a remnant of the demolished Seaboard Airline
Railroad's Miami terminal, stands divorced from place, time, and function in
the front yard of the South Florida Evaluation and Treatment Center (1981,
now vacant). The complex does a good job of staying clear of the arch,
though not of engaging it.

Masjid Al-Ansar   D18
5245 NW 7th Avenue
1937

South Florida's oldest and largest orthodox Muslim mosque, Masjid Al-Ansar
is located in the Edison Center neighborhood. Both Muhammad Ali and
Malcolm X are said to have worshipped here.

Miami Times Building   D19
900 NW 54th Street
Alfred Browning Parker, 1959

Built for General Capital Corporation and now the home of the *Miami Times*,
Miami's leading African American daily newspaper, this is one of Alfred
Browning Parker's last remaining nonresidential works in South Florida.
The influence of Frank Lloyd Wright, which runs through Parker's work, is
abundantly clear here. The rectangular building is anchored to the land on
a stepped base and incorporates integrated planters. Battered concrete
walls set off a ribbon of clerestory windows. Parker's sensitivity to the warm

D19

climate and flat topography of South Florida are reflected in the double-pitched roof structure, whose deep overhangs and creased ribbed fascia seem reminiscent of Polynesian architecture.

Chase Bank (Dade Federal Savings & Loan)   D20
5800 NW 7th Avenue
Edwin T. Reeder Associates, 1957

This well-maintained 2-story bank building is representative of many fine postwar Modern commercial structures in Liberty City. The ground-floor window wall fronting the banking lobby and entrance hall is matched on the second floor with a grille-block screening system that sheathes the upper windows in an unusual geometric pattern. A semi-engaged signage pylon rises at the center of the building, signaling the location of the bank and the office floor above.

Carver Theater (Center Theater)   D21
6040 NW 7th Avenue
Robert E. Collins, 1939

D21

Originally named the Center Theater (after the area's former name of Edison Center), this venue provided a local alternative to the entertainment hubs of Downtown Miami and Miami Beach. Like many urban cinemas in prewar Miami, the Carver was lined with ground-floor retail on NW Seventh Avenue. The prominent concave corner entrance features a fluted parapet and projecting marquee that is little more than a metal frame today.

Church of the Open Door   D22
6001 NW 8th Avenue
T. Trip Russell and Associates, 1964

This United Church of Christ congregation was formed in 1958, and the present church constructed six years later. The founding impetus came from Marie Faulkner Brown, spouse of Dr. John Brown, a leading participant in

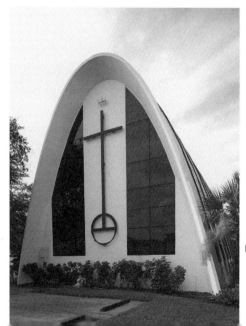

D22

the 1959 Burdines sit-in (**A44**). From the beginning, the congregation has aspired to Dr. Martin Luther King Jr.'s idea of "the beloved community," joining
whites and blacks in pursuit of racial equality and social justice.

The parabolic arches of the church's nave give a soaring, open feeling to
the relatively small interior, enhanced by the generous provision of natural
light. Of special interest on the church grounds is the Aubrey Watkins Simms
Memorial Garden designed in 2006 by Reginald Whitehead, then chair of
the Horticulture Committee on the board of trustees at the Fairchild Tropical
Botanical Garden.

Dr. Martin Luther King Jr. Mural   D23

SW corner of Dr. Martin Luther King Jr. Boulevard (NW 62nd Street) and 7th Avenue
Oscar Thomas, painter, 1994

This photorealistic mural of Dr. Martin Luther King Jr. is an icon of the local
African American community and has been used to portray black Miami
around the world in brochures, books, and films. In 2001, it became the
subject of controversy when it was mishandled as part of a remodeling of
the building to which it is affixed. The painting was removed in order to
create the entrance for a check-cashing store. Public outcry, led by activist
and artist Marvin Weeks, prompted restoration of the artwork in its original
location.

Carrie P. Meek Entrepreneurial Education Center   D24

6300 NW 7th Avenue
Ronald E. Frazier & Associates with Spillis Candela & Partners, 1989

D23

As a result of the Miami Street Uprising of 1980 (ignited by the acquittal of
police officers connected with the death of black insurance salesman Arthur
McDuffie), Miami-Dade College chose to invest in the future of Liberty City
through the erection of this satellite facility. The building uses a vocabulary
of open-air spaces that marks the college's other campuses and is so well
suited to Miami's subtropical environment.

Number 1 Pallbearers Association Building   D25

801 NW 62nd Street
1947

The true significance of this Streamline Moderne building lies not in its
architecture, but in its use by the Pallbearers Association to support the
African American community during a time when exclusionary policies prevented blacks from taking burial insurance.

Laborers' International Union Local 478 Building   D26

799 NW 62nd Street
1953

Like the Pallbearers Association Building (**D25**), this postwar Modern structure is significant primarily for its role in the social history of Miami's African
American community.

Founded in 1903, the Laborers' International Union sought to combat dangerous working conditions and poor wages for workers of all races. In 1920, the union supported efforts by African Americans to achieve equal treatment in all unions and denied requests to create segregated local chapters. Local 478 occupied this building in 1967, and as the area's population changed from white to black, has acted on behalf of the local African American community and its residents employed in the construction industry.

Liberty Square   D27

NW 62nd–67th streets and NW 12th–15th avenues
Phineas E. Paist, Harold Steward, and E. L. Robertson with Associate Architects Walter DeGarmo, Vladimir Virrick, and C. Sheldon Tucker, 1937
Expansion: 1939

Liberty Square is a 20-acre low-cost housing project designed in the 1930s to serve Miami's black community. It was the first of its kind in the United States. As a New Deal statement of architectural and urban ideals, Liberty Square's progressive design cannot be separated from Miami's intricate social matrices.

The housing, underwritten by the Reconstruction Finance Corporation, was intended for working-class African Americans who could afford the rent. Self-interest, racism, a "racial uplift" ideology, traditions of segregation, and national urban design goals all factored into its planning and construction. Miami's white elite supported the project's use of federal money to relocate blacks from Overtown, which was in the path of Downtown's projected expansion. Notwithstanding the boldly self-interested motives of its sponsors, Liberty Square also represented an opportunity for Miami's blacks to leave crowded Overtown behind.

Federal housing policies determined the campuslike layout of its low-scaled structures, as well as the basic layout and size of the apartments. The local Miami architects Paist and Steward and their collaborators were assigned to design the exterior elevations and did little to alter either the site plan or the interiors of the apartments. The basic design plan of Liberty

D27

D28

Square is still in place, though significant additions were added to the east of the original project in 1939. The additions kept the scale but not the density of the original, and more than tripled the number of inhabitants without offering more public amenities.

The area's contemporary air of neglect reflects civic disengagement, but early residents remember that Liberty Square was "beautiful then, with plenty of coconut palms and no litter" (George and Petersen, "Liberty Square"). This project can be compared with Edison Courts (C115), its "white" counterpart nearby, in today's Little Haiti.

Liberty Square Wall Fragment   D28
West side of NW 12th Avenue between 62nd & 67th streets

When the federal government proposed the expansion eastward of Liberty Square in 1939, the white residents of the adjacent Seventh Avenue Park neighborhood protested. Liberty Square architect Harold Steward suggested the construction of a concrete wall along NW Twelfth Avenue, separating black and white areas. A fragment of this "social rampart" still stands.

The City of
Miami Beach

Randall C. Robinson Jr.

The first successful pioneer of European descent in what is now Miami Beach was John Collins, a farmer from New Jersey. Collins settled on the barrier peninsula in 1907, planting mangos and avocados in the high land that is now the west Mid-Beach section of Miami Beach. Unlike a previous coconut plantation, Collins's venture succeeded. The oldest landmark in the city, the Australian pines (*Casuarina equistifolia*) in the median of Pine Tree Drive were planted as a windbreak to protect Collins's orchards.

The initial planning of Miami Beach can be attributed to banker brothers J. N. and J. E. Lummus. The brothers had been the first investors in the cross-bay bridge scheme of Collins's son-in-law Thomas Pancoast and saw the development potential of what was then known as Ocean Beach. Through their Ocean Beach Realty Company, they bought 500 acres at the southern tip of the barrier peninsula in 1912, even before work had begun on the bridge. (The barrier peninsula would become a barrier island in 1924 with the creation of Baker's Haulover Cut.)

The brothers progressively platted their land, starting in 1912, laying an "engineer's grid" over land mainly created by dredge from bay bottom and mangrove forests. The division between natural and man-made Miami Beach is most evident in the South Beach plats of the Lummus Brothers, where Washington Avenue demarcates natural upland to the east and reclaimed mangrove forests to the west.

Another investor in the bridge scheme was Carl Fisher, an Indiana tycoon. In contrast to Fisher and Pancoast's vision of Miami Beach as a playground for the rich, the Lummus Brothers planned for a modest community of vacation homes. The high density and compact scale of South Beach compared to suburban Mid-Beach and sprawling North Beach is a testament to the competing visions of Miami Beach's pioneers.

Miami Beach was incorporated in 1915 by the Lummus Brothers; Fisher; and Collins and Pancoast, the three major development interests that shaped South Beach and Mid-Beach. The city gained its current size in 1924, when the northern boundary was moved from Forty-sixth Street to Eighty-seventh Terrace, bringing today's North Beach and much of Mid-Beach into the fold. In 2000, its 7.1 square miles were home to nearly eighty-eight thousand residents. The city is divided into South Beach, which stretches from Government Cut to Twenty-third Street and the Collins Canal; Mid-Beach, which extends from Twenty-third Street to Sixty-third Street; and North Beach, which runs from Sixty-third Street to Eighty-seventh Terrace.

The interwar building booms—the Great Florida Land Boom of the 1920s and the Depression-era boom of the late 1930s—were responsible for the build-out of half the city. By the eve of World War II, the urbanized area stretched uninterrupted from Government Cut to Forty-fourth Street. After the unbuilt land did wartime duty as a training station for the military, nearly all of it was filled in during the postwar boom, which tapered off in the late 1960s.

After a decade-long dormancy, an Art Deco preservation movement, led by preservation legend Barbara Baer Capitman, soon focused efforts to preserve the intimate urbanity and lyrical architecture of South Beach. In the 1980s, Miami Beach reemerged as an international tourist destination and a cultural nexus of South Florida.

Miami Beach's economic renaissance is written indelibly across its impressive, some might say offensive, new skyline of big and tall residential towers. In the 1980s, in a desperate attempt to stimulate redevelopment, zoning restrictions were essentially lifted across the city's urbanized areas. Ironically, it was the success of the preservation movement that stimulated redevelopment, making the massive towers an attractive development proposition. Though appropriate zoning restrictions have since been reinstated, the boom of the 1990s deposited an additional, if overscaled, layer on this small city of wide contrasts.

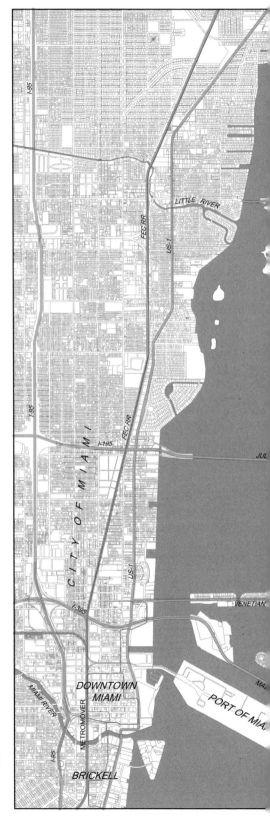

City of Miami Beach map: Sections E–H

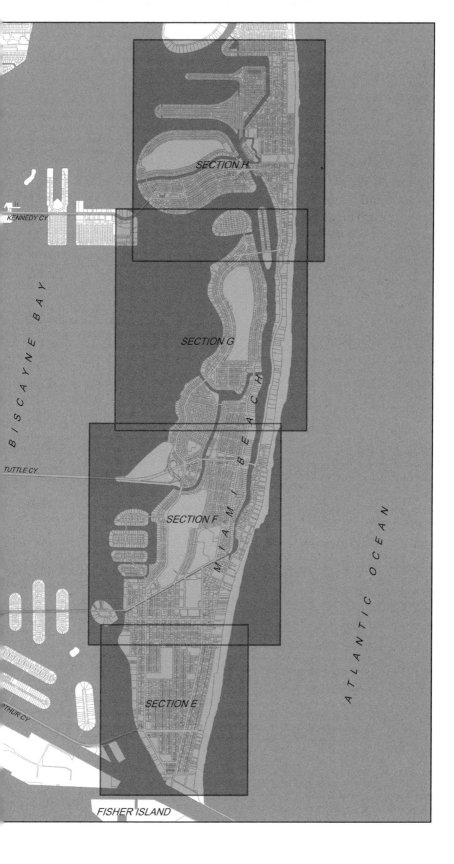

E

City of Miami Beach:
Lower South Beach

This section comprises the southernmost part of Miami Beach, bounded by Government Cut on the south and Fifteenth Street on the north. Beginning at Terminal and Causeway islands, the area covers a portion of South Beach, including the South of Fifth neighborhood, the South Beach Commercial and Resort Area, Flamingo Park, and the West Avenue high-rise corridor. The area is most famous for containing the greater part of the Miami Beach Architectural District, popularly known as the Art Deco District.

The evolution of this area is readily visible in the two grids that meet along Washington Avenue. To the east are the first subdivisions, built along the dune of the barrier island. To the west were mangrove wetlands that have been landfilled to provide the basis for residential neighborhoods facing the bay. The meeting of these two grids animates Washington Avenue, which continues to play a role as one of the area's main streets. Alton Road, Washington Avenue's counterpart on the west side, is emerging as a major commercial corridor. Fifth Street, the continuation of the MacArthur Causeway, is the most prominent gateway to the beach from Miami.

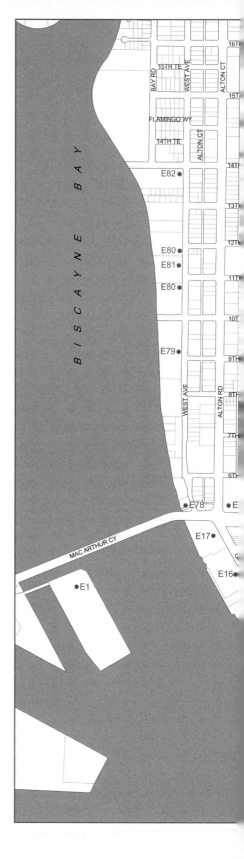

E. City of Miami Beach: Lower South Beach

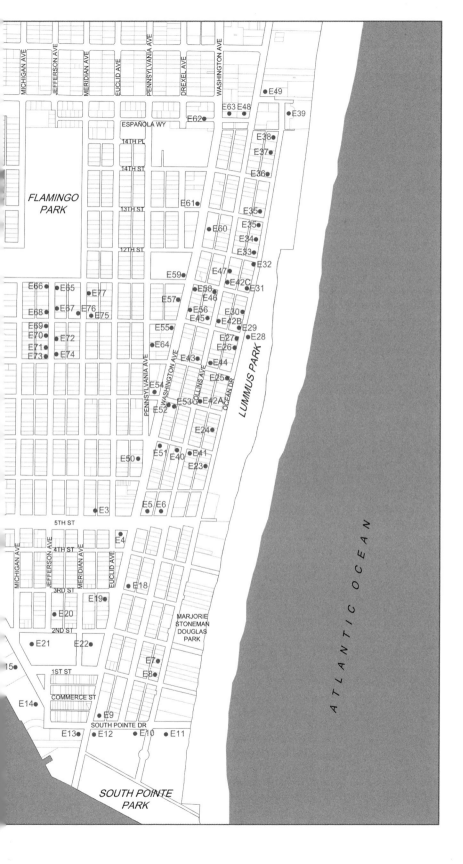

U.S. Coast Guard Housing (Personnel Support   E1 and Unaccompanied Personnel Housing Building)

100 MacArthur Causeway, Causeway Island
Harper Carreno Mateu

Visible from the east end of the MacArthur Causeway, this straightforward block of housing sits on Causeway Island, a base of the U.S. Coast Guard. The structure stands 4 stories, commanding views across the causeway and over the otherwise low-rise island, whose quays are ordinarily ringed with sleek clippers and cutters. The residential portion of the building is clearly legible, occupying the top two floors, which are wrapped with continuous exterior galleries. This section is cantilevered over the pedestal containing service facilities for the guardsmen and -women.

Causeway Island sits opposite Terminal Island, a small container facility and ferryboat terminal for Fisher Island. With direct access to the Port of Miami and Government Cut, the islands occupy a key position in the overall port complex. Both were developed with the MacArthur Causeway, and originally housed a power plant and the maintenance shops for the Miami Beach Railway.

Fifth Street Corridor

When the County Causeway (renamed MacArthur Causeway in 1942) opened in 1918, Fifth Street became one of Miami Beach's most important thoroughfares, with a streetcar line and the city's first post office and chamber of commerce office at Alton and Fifth. As development moved northward through the mid-twentieth century, Fifth Street's fortunes fell along with the rest of South Beach. In an attempt at revitalization and to handle increasing traffic volume, the street was doubled in width and a median added in the 1960s. This was done by demolishing the buildings on the south side of the street, explaining why the ragged sides of once-midblock buildings cover much of the south side today. By the time the Art Deco renaissance started in the late 1970s, the once-bustling intersection of Fifth and Alton had become a no-man's-land of parking lots and little else. At the time of this writing, new commercial buildings are rising along both sides of this landscaped boulevard, exploiting the traffic on this important gateway to the beach.

Fifth and Alton South Beach   E2

Robin Bosco/Architects & Planners with STA Architectural Group, 2007

It was not without some difficulty that the City of Miami Beach approved this 185,000-square-foot "vertical retail center," which establishes a new scale for this key regional intersection. Along with fears that the complex would be overwhelmingly large came alarm, in some quarters, at something so mundane as a shopping center with chain stores marking the entrance to South Beach. To the credit of the architects and the city planning department, Fifth and Alton transcends its building type. Its 3 tall stories make a grand scale seem quite appropriate at this entry point, and its rich interplay of stucco and glass forms and surfaces makes a fitting first image for Miami Beach. Parking is well handled in vertical garages. Extensive use of glass and terraces allows transparency, and ground-floor storefronts bring pedestrian life back to the intersection where streetcars arriving from Miami once made their first stop in Miami Beach.

Aviator (Lindbergh Hotel)   E3

701 5th Street
T. Hunter Henderson, 1930, 1936
Renovation: Jaime Salles, 1983

One of the few prewar buildings extant on Fifth Street, this mixed-use 3-story structure built in three phases spans an entire city block, connected via a bridge that spans the intervening alley. Originally a hotel occupied the upper floors; the units were later converted to apartments, and are now live/work spaces.

404 Washington Avenue   E4

Bermello Ajamil & Partners, 1996

Number 404 Washington is a marker in both time and space. The 8-story structure marks the entrance to the oceanfront, sitting like a pivot between areas to the north and south. It was the first major office building completed in Miami Beach in more than two decades, a signal of the transformation of Fifth Street to commercial uses, and one of the first new projects in the South of Fifth neighborhood.

The structure was built as the headquarters of Portofino, the company that during the early 1990s acquired large areas south of Fifth Street for redevelopment. Portofino's master plans devolved into a series of individual projects by other developers, and this office building was the only structure built by the company.

The scheme of the building essentially places three stories of offices above five levels of parking and ground-floor retail space. The building dissimulates its enormous bulk and the enormity of its parking garage

E4

through offsets in massing, architectonics, and color variations that include pastel tones of blue, red, green, and yellow. Loggias wrap the retail fronts, responding to the juncture of street grids at Washington Avenue. The nearly 125-foot-tall cylindrical glass-block shaft—a virtual campanile or light-house offset from the building mass on the corner of Washington and Fifth Street—is the building's most remarkable feature. The tower comes alive at night when it cycles through patterns of colored illumination (a contemporary take on Miami Beach's obsession with the play of colored light).

As the building neared completion, scandal erupted when it was discovered that it was built taller and larger than permitted. The oversight was written off as a "scrivener's error," and the issue was subsequently negotiated with the city.

Warner Music Latina Building   E5
555 Washington Avenue
Arquitectonica, 2002

The mixed-use Warner Building reinforces the emerging commercial character of Fifth Street while creating a bold new marker at its intersection with Washington Avenue. In a well-scaled response to its context, the structure appears as a series of discrete urban pieces. The main piece is the 4-story office building with ground-floor retail spaces. An elliptical rotunda, sheathed in blue and black glass and wrapped by a radiator grille of aluminum fins, addresses the site's prominent corner position. North of the office block is the 5-story garage structure, also with ground-floor retail. The strategy of segregating parking in plan, rather than section, avoids the sandwich effect and gives clear urban delineation to each piece.

The façade of the office block and garage are differently articulated. The former reduces the structure's apparent scale, with upper windows grouped every two floors and joined with recessed spandrels tiled blue. The latter's shading eyebrows and streamlined appearance tie into the city's prewar design traditions. The overall impression is of multiplicity, avoiding the bulky effect such large buildings often have in the tight-knit urban fabric of South Beach.

500 Block of Collins Building   E6
500 Collins Avenue
Zyscovich Architects, 2004

The 500 Block of Collins Building does a fine job of transitioning from the increasingly commercial Fifth Street corridor to the more intimate scale of old South Beach. The building provides three levels of much-needed parking over 2 stories of retail space. Along Fifth Street, its garage levels are clad in freeform folded-metal screens that are colorfully backlit at night (a distant echo of Frank Gehry's chain-link covered house in Santa Monica). As the design moves north, the metal screens give way to retail spaces individually articulated to give the appearance of a row of separate storefronts. At the north end, the garage recesses beyond the retail parapets, its stucco walls and eyebrowed openings dissolving quietly into the visual feast around it.

South of Fifth

The South of Fifth neighborhood of Miami Beach, the first area to be colonized and also the first to decline, has been the object of large-scale redevelopment efforts since the 1970s. It was here that the settlement that would become known as Miami Beach began, as this was where a ferry service arrived before the barrier island was connected to the mainland by bridges and causeways. Originally referred to as Ocean Beach, to distinguish it from the bay beaches on the mainland, the barrier island's first business district developed here along Biscayne Street, today's South Pointe Drive. Joe's Stone Crab (E9) is one of the last vestiges of this early Downtown. In the 1970s, as Miami Beach's center of gravity moved northward, the neighborhood was renamed South Shore, declared blighted, and designated a redevelopment area. The resultant South Shore project would have wiped clean the neighborhood south of Fifth Street, with a few notable exceptions like Joe's, and carved a series of canals and lagoons through a completely reformulated area of mid- and high-rise buildings and resort amenities. Meanwhile, new building permits in the area were prohibited and code enforcement was suspended, causing the neighborhood to sharply decline.

The South of Fifth neighborhood has been the chosen locale for large-scale redevelopment projects. In 1979, when the Miami Beach Architectural District—commonly referred to as the Art Deco District—was placed on the National Register, preservationists reluctantly left the neighborhood out of the district boundaries. The City of Miami Beach was determined to expedite redevelopment plans for the area. However, as the area north of Sixth Street began to thrive through preservation, intrepid pioneers began renovating buildings in what had become known officially as South Pointe. By the 1990s, redevelopment plans were shelved in favor of the creation of the Ocean Beach Historic District. More recently, with the development of luxury high-rises along the waterfront of Government Cut and Biscayne Bay, and new urban infill inland, the resurgent area has become known as the South of Fifth neighborhood.

Century Hotel
E7

140 Ocean Drive
Henry Hohauser, 1939
Renovation: Beilinson Architect, 1988

The Century Hotel's crisp white shell, building-length eyebrows, symmetrical, stepped parapet and finial typify the regional adaptation of Modern architecture and the stylistic melding of Art Deco and Nautical Moderne at work in prewar Miami Beach.

E7

The Century figures prominently in the recognition of the Ocean Beach Historic District. Bucking prohibitions against renovation in the South Shore Redevelopment Area, the Century's owners discreetly improved this small property one step at a time. After completing the renovation of the main structure, these intrepid urban pioneers annexed the adjacent hotel, retrofitting it to provide a ground-floor restaurant beneath its colonnaded portico, the skeletal remains of the hotel's front porch. The rehabilitation of the Century paved the way for the creation of the Ocean Beach Historic District, finally bringing protection to the oldest part of Miami Beach.

E8

Browns Hotel/Prime 112 E8

112 Ocean Drive
1915
Restoration and additions: Allan T. Shulman Architect, 2004

Miami Beach was originally the bucolic setting for small homes and larger villas, a residential island destined to privacy and tranquility. In 1915, however, the character of its southernmost section—Ocean Beach—shifted with the completion of Browns Hotel, the first hotel ever conceived for this now-famous resort city. Browns, a modest hostelry for middle-class tourists, was a harbinger of the area's urbanization, and the archetype for the small urban hotels that would soon define the character of South Beach.

The 2-story structure, which is wood-framed and clad and supported on concrete piers, was completed before the development of Ocean Drive, and faced the wood boardwalk that originally traversed the beachfront in this area. Designed with 30 rooms on the second floor, it had changing rooms with kitchenettes for day visitors below. Browns was restored and expanded in 2004 as a multiuse building including the adaptive use of the ground floor as a restaurant. A modest rear addition complements the original structure.

An enduring legend says that Browns Hotel was built upon the ruin of an early shipwreck that included 10-inch oak timbers and large iron belts. However, evidence of the shipwreck was not found during archaeological explorations undertaken before the hotel's restoration. More enduring was the basic plan type of the hotel—a deep rectangular structure, bisected by a corridor along its entire length, with apartments arrayed into the depth of the lot and facing sideways. Its pattern of freestanding building, front yard, and frontal progression from the avenue persist today as the basic urban unit of South Beach's resort hotels and apartment buildings.

Joe's Stone Crab E9

11 Washington Avenue
1920
Renovation and expansion: Peter Blitstein, 1995

Joe's Stone Crab restaurant is a Miami Beach institution. The first Joe's, at 213 Biscayne Avenue (now South Pointe Drive), dated to 1912. That building served both as restaurant and home to the family of Joe and Jennie Weiss, its first owners. A second, 2-story building at 227 Biscayne Avenue was built shortly thereafter. The second building still exists, though enveloped by expansions in the 1930s and 1990s. Today, its much-expanded facilities extend north from the corner of South Pointe Drive and Washington Avenue.

South Pointe Tower E10

400 South Pointe Drive
Y. H. Lee Associates, 1986

South Pointe Tower is the most prominent result of yet another redevelopment scheme. It was planned to be the first of several identical towers; the rest are unrealized. Although its raised pedestal, accessible mainly by car, reflects the anti-urban, pedestrian-unfriendly tenor of its times, the tower portion fits well enough within the masonry fantasy architecture of Miami Beach and has come to appear quaint in its contrast to the towers of the Portofino development that surround it.

Portofino Tower Group

Continuum   E11
100 South Pointe Drive
Skidmore, Owings & Merrill, 2002

Portofino Tower   E12
300 South Pointe Drive
Sieger Architectural Partnership, 1994

Apogee   E13
800 South Pointe Drive
Sieger-Suarez Architectural Partnership, 2008

E10–E12

E14–E17

Murano   E14

1000 South Pointe Drive
Fullerton Diaz Architects, 2002

Yacht Club   E15

90 Alton Road
Cohen Freedman Encinosa, 1999

Murano Grande   E16

400 Alton Road
Sieger-Suarez Architectural Partnership, 2003

Icon   E17

450 Alton Road
Sieger-Suarez Architectural Partnership with Philippe Starck, 2005

After the failure of the 1970s South Shore and South Pointe redevelopment efforts, the area south of Fifth Street lingered in a state of disinvestment and dilapidation. In the 1980s, in a desperate attempt to spur new development, the City of Miami Beach relaxed zoning regulations and removed height limits throughout the city. Meanwhile, the little hotels of the newly created Miami Beach Architectural District, just to the north, were turning the city's fortunes around. On New Year's Eve 1992, German multimillionaire Thomas Kramer came to local prominence by purchasing 45 waterfront acres along Government Cut and the shore of Biscayne Bay. Kramer formed Portofino Properties to develop the land that had gone from worthless to priceless in a mere decade.

Like the failed South Shore project, early visions called for an exclusive resort village, this time based on the Italian port of Portofino. A charrette organized by Duany Plater-Zyberk & Company (DPZ) drew leading architects, including Robert A. M. Stern, Michael Graves, Arquitectonica, Bermello Ajamil & Partners, Sieger Architectural Partnership, Sandy Babcock, Abdel Wahed El-Wakil Associates, and others to create innovative plans. Few of the ideas generated by the charrette withstood the magnanimous development rights that had been granted to stimulate development, nor the market forces that seemed to demand high-rise construction. When it came time to sell real estate, the romantic and idealistic visions dissolved into the row of massive high-rises that began with the construction of Portofino Tower (E12) in 1994.

The tower's sprawling, segmented, three-pointed floor plates create a massive silhouette, although voids placed midway up its shaft allow some transparency. Its eclectic crown blends traditional and futuristic motifs, including hipped roof turrets that recall those found on Old City Hall (E59) and a circular fanlike feature that suggests a landing pad for aircraft. In spite of its size, the changing attitudes of tall buildings toward street life are reflected in Portofino Tower's more pedestrian-friendly 2-story mixed-use base. Unfortunately, this habitable space wraps only the north side of the parking pedestal, forsaking the extensive frontage on South Pointe Park.

Rather than develop the area according to its underlying zoning (already relaxed in the previous decades), the developer negotiated a master development agreement with the City of Miami Beach, which was opposed by a broad spectrum of citizens. The resulting towers, each some 30 stories tall with large floor plates, provide dramatic silhouettes against the sky yet are grossly out of step with the intimate scale of the South of Fifth neighborhood. In a compromise between the idealism of the initial charrette and unbridled market forces, DPZ were consulted on design guidelines for the tower pedestals in order to make them more pedestrian-friendly. County guidelines that require a generously wide baywalk were included in the plan, initiating a continuous pedestrian promenade from the MacArthur Causeway to the tip of the barrier island. This public waterfront esplanade, with sweeping views of the ocean, bay, port, and the Miami skyline, was carved from private bayfront properties.

It is unfortunate that DPZ's guidelines were not adhered to as closely in the later towers. To wit, Yacht Club, Murano, and Continuum are skirted by habitable space in the form of townhouses, health clubs, and apartments. By the time Icon was approved, a much larger parking garage, with no habitable space facing the street on the ground floor, was permitted by the City of Miami Beach Commission. In the most curious devolution of the DPZ vision, the last tower, Apogee, located on the crucial pivot between Biscayne Bay and Government Cut, was built without habitable space facing South Pointe Park.

Temple Beth Jacob and Jewish Museum of Florida
E18

Temple Beth Jacob
311 Washington Avenue
H. Frasser Rose, 1928
Schoolroom addition: Robert Swartburg, 1946

Jewish Museum of Florida
301 Washington Avenue
Henry Hohauser, 1936
Renovation and adaptive use: Giller and Giller, 1993

E18

Thirteen years after Miami Beach became a municipality, the permanent Jewish population was large enough to sponsor a congregation and erect its own building. The members of Orthodox congregation Beth Jacob constructed their first house of worship in Miami Beach in 1928 (the original sanctuary is the second building from the northeast corner of Third Street and Washington Avenue). Later, two of Miami Beach's most significant architects, Henry Hohauser and Robert Swartburg, would expand the synagogue with additional structures. Hohauser's new second sanctuary, built in 1936, reflects locally popular themes of late 1930s Modernism while expressing Jewish iconography in an Art Deco framework. Most notable is the superimposition of the Star of David on the building's spandrel panels.

The two synagogue structures point not only to the early presence of Jews among the pioneers of Miami Beach, but to the unique role of the city as a "second promised land" for the Jewish community. The 1928 building, handsome in its vernacular simplicity, still serves the religious needs of a now-diminishing congregation, while Hohauser's 1936 sanctuary has become the home of the Jewish Museum of Florida, a fine example of adaptive use.

El Cyclon E19

248 Washington Avenue
STA Architectural Group, 1997
Ceramic artwork: Carlos Alves

El Cyclon updates the classic Miami Beach single-lot apartment building type through innovations in its planning and the styling of its façade. The building comprises 4 units; in contrast to the traditional pattern, which arrays apartment units transversely, the building is bisected longitudinally, with a ground-floor flat and a 2-story upper-level loft on each side of a center wall. The upper units, which feature 24-foot ceilings, were designed to house live/work spaces for photographers.

E19

El Cyclon's Washington Avenue façade could be described as "Jules Verne Modern." The inverse conical stair at its center suggests the form of a cyclone. Its walls are embedded with ceramic fish created by ceramic artist Carlos Alves. A trapezoidal entrance portal framed in keystone opens into the center of the cyclone through a steel gate ornamented with the likeness of an octopus. Double-height windows on the upper façade reveal the spacious interiors of the upper units. In spite of (or perhaps because of) its distinct architectural syntax, this 3-story building nestles comfortably into the surrounding context.

Ilona E20

221 Jefferson Avenue
Oppenheim Architecture+Design, 2003

The Ilona is a notable example of the urban infill projects that are proliferating in the Ocean Beach Historic District in the wake of its stasis as a redevelopment area. Rising 5 stories, its white volumes, glass planes, and expansive terraces derive from Miami Beach's own synthesis of modernity and climate-consciousness. The Ilona is distinguished, however, by its elongated hexagonal body, which breaks from South Beach's orthogonal form

E20

and space traditions. Tapered like a ship's hull, partly detached from the surrounding fabric, and raised off the ground by means of a recessed base, it exhibits something of the nautical imagery popular here in the 1930s and 1940s. Generous patio spaces on either side are screened with perforated aluminum bands on the lower floors, extending the reach of the façade and integrating with the street wall of the surrounding district. The focal point of the street façade is a multistory window framed with a wide stucco band. Underneath the building, entry gates sculpted of sinuous metal strands screen an open-air entrance area and small pond.

The Courts E21

Block bounded by First Street, Alton Road, Second Street, and Meridian Avenue
Phase I: Schapiro Associates, 1998

The Courts is perhaps the only major product of the city's 1990s-era efforts to redevelop the inland portion of Ocean Beach. Sponsored by the Miami Beach Redevelopment Agency, the 8.5-acre project was designed to sweep several blocks of the district into a vast megablock spanning from Washington Avenue to Alton Road and transforming thru-avenues into interior streets for parking access. It took an aggressive approach that required broad use of eminent domain and required the demolition of all existing

E21

buildings. The last component of the project was developed separately as the Cosmopolitan (**E22**).

The project name describes its principal feature: a system of internal courts with amenities. The courts were designed to be interconnecting, creating a semi-private and intimate community of village patios on a raised deck over grade-level parking. These patios included gardens, terraces, and a pool. A library, health club, day-care center, and retail spaces wrap the ground-floor parking. The various components were joined by the use of Mediterranean Revival styling.

The urban strategy evolved as the project progressed from west to east. In the first phase, it comprised a series of smaller buildings, intimate courts, ground-level terraces, and, especially toward the plazas that front Alton Road, mixed uses. Its 100 units, some multistory, featured idiosyncratic lay-outs, each facing both the street and courtyard. In the second phase, prin-cipally between Jefferson and Meridian avenues, larger apartment blocks simply framed a large central pool deck.

In spite of its sprawling size and its interconnectivity, the project defines a well-integrated mid-rise urban frontage along surrounding streets, and retail frontages along Alton Road. It is distinct from other large-scale efforts, which ordinarily result in towers. Habitable bridges span Jefferson Avenue, connecting the two phases.

Cosmopolitan   E22

110 Washington Avenue
Mouriz Salazar & Associates, 2004

The last planned phase of the Courts project (**E21**), the Cosmopolitan was designed and built as a separate entity. Rising 8 floors, it is taller and denser than the earlier Courts buildings yet similarly lifted over a podium that con-ceals lower-level parking areas. It comprises two nearly separate buildings, each with its own courtyard.

The Cosmopolitan departs from the Mediterranean Revival styling of the Courts. Rather, it is Moderne in appearance, with smooth white walls and streamlined corners of wrapping glass and balconies. Its mass is broken by frequent shifts in building wall and materials. Corners are marked with a raised crown of outward-leaning pylons. The pedestal, in contrast, is marked by a continuous projecting loggia housing retail uses that face Washington Avenue. A grand stair symbolically connects the raised courts to the avenue.

Miami Beach Architectural District

The Miami Beach Architectural District—commonly known as the Art Deco District—was placed on the National Register of Historic Places in 1979 though the efforts of the Miami Design Preservation League, founded in 1976 by Barbara Baer Capitman, Leonard Horowitz, and other collaborators. From 1976 through 1979, the members of the league catalogued the buildings of the district, whose boundaries run roughly from Sixth Street north to Twenty-third Street, from the Atlantic Ocean to Alton Road. It was the first district on the National Register to consist of twentieth-century buildings and the largest at the time. After designation, the Miami Design Preservation League commissioned a study to guide the district's preservation and development. The Boston firm Anderson Notter Finegold produced the Art Deco District Preservation and Development Plan in 1981. Though never formally adopted by the City of Miami Beach, the Anderson Notter Finegold Plan is arguably the most successfully implemented redevelopment plan in American urban history.

From the mid-1980s through 1992, the City of Miami Beach gradually recognized ever-larger portions of the National Register district, thereby bringing them under the protection of local historic preservation ordinances. There are more than 1,200 buildings in the district, of which the City of Miami Beach today recognizes 1,000 as contributing to the significance of the area as a record of the development of design during the first half of the twentieth century.

South Beach Resort and Commercial Area

Park Central Hotel   E23

640 Ocean Drive
Henry Hohauser, 1937
Interior Renovation: Françoise Schoen and Ingrid Hundsvedt, 1987
Renovation: Beilinson Architect, 1988

Although larger than many of its neighbors, the 7-story Park Central joins miniature skyscrapers like the Tides, Victor, Winterhaven, and Netherland, animating the city's façade to Lummus Park. The Park Central contributes to that façade with characteristic features of Miami Beach architecture, like an inset porch, corner windows, and a tripartite front whose central bay has a projecting canopy topped by octagonal windows. The hotel is distinguished by its telescoping lobby that begins in the double-height, mezzanined reception area. The ground-floor rooms step up incrementally from the street, allowing better views of the ocean from the back of the lot. The sequence ends with an intimately scaled dining room that opens to a glassed-in terrace. Beach replenishment and dune creation circa 1980 now obscure views of the sand and water.

E23

Colony Hotel   E24

736 Ocean Drive
Henry Hohauser, 1935
Renovation: Moshe Cosicher, 1989

Designed shortly after Hohauser's more eclectic Edison (E27), the Colony
Hotel was the first new hotel on Miami Beach to reflect the Modern styling
and forms of representation that would soon become the norm across the
city. The building's cubic white façade is dematerialized by corner windows
and strongly horizontal projecting eyebrows. Incised racing strips and polished metal tubing provide most of the decoration. The façade's abundant
horizontality is balanced by the vertical pylon of a theatrical marquee that
carries the hotel's name in neon and metallic channel letters. The lobby is
notably sheathed in mint green Vitrolite panels, one of the last intact examples in Miami Beach of this popular substitute for marble. The focal point is
the fireplace, which features an original inset mural by Paul Simone depicting tequila agave cultivation in northern Mexico.

Waldorf Towers   E25

860 Ocean Drive
Albert Anis, 1937
Renovation: Sender Tragash, 1986

The locally habitual combination of a symmetrical Art Deco front, wrapping
eyebrows, and streamlined corners are offset here by a lyrical faux light-
house, which tops the parapet and marks the beginning of Ninth Street. A
large raised terrace provides plenty of room for the hotel's restaurant/café.

Breakwater Hotel   E26

940 Ocean Drive
Anton Skislewicz, 1939

This Streamline Moderne building has the largest porch on Ocean Drive, reflecting the particular urban style of this beachfront resort. Above, the body
of the hotel floats, a broad nautical façade centered on a marqueelike prow
that bears the hotel's name. The finial was used by photographer Bruce
Weber as the backdrop for his 1984 fashion photo shoot for Calvin Klein's fra-
grance "Obsession." Although European photographers had been working
in the area for some time, Weber's work established South Beach as a mecca
for fashion photography.

Edison Hotel   E27

960 Ocean Drive
Henry Hohauser, 1935

Completed during the early years of Miami Beach's Depression-era boom,
the Edison exhibits a latent Mediterranean Revival spirit, but it also shows
traces of Modern styling. Arched openings wrap the ground level from
Ocean Drive to Tenth Street, as well as the upper façade on Ocean Drive, yet
the building also displays the crisp planarity of modern structures. Note the
twisted column in the center that appears to be part of a machine lifting the
building upward.

Beach Patrol Headquarters and Ocean Front Auditorium

E28

1001 Ocean Drive
Headquarters building: Robert Taylor, 1939
Auditorium: Leonard Glasser, 1954
Renovation: STA Architectural Group, 2008

The Beach Patrol Headquarters is one of Miami Beach's most refined structures in the Streamline Moderne style. It appears like a stranded ferry on a sandbar: rounded corners, portholes on the lower decks, and a "captain's bridge" above allow the building to slice through the prevailing easterly breezes. It is sited at the center of Lummus Park, terminating the axis of Tenth Street. This nautical folly was set back from Ocean Drive beyond a palm-shaded plaza until the Ocean Front Auditorium was attached on the west in 1954. Originally planned to serve as a community center for the elderly residents of the neighborhood, by the 1990s the building had been repurposed to house the Miami Design Preservation League (MDPL). The facility has since been reconstructed to better serve MDPL and the Beach Patrol. The improved facility maintains the austere postwar façade of the auditorium, although the larger mass of the new building exacerbates its imposition on Lummus Park. Fortunately, the project also disconnected the Beach Patrol Headquarters, resulting in the restoration of its west facade.

Clevelander Hotel

E29

1020 Ocean Drive
Albert Anis, 1938
Additions: Robert Swartburg, 1951, 1953; Beilinson Architect, 1986, 1991; STA Architectural Group, 2007

The 5-story Clevelander was a moderate-sized hotel by the standards of interwar Miami Beach. Tracking changes in the character of Ocean Drive, it has grown since then into a larger, more entertainment-oriented complex. Built in 1938 by Charles Ratner, founder of Cleveland-based Forest City Enterprises, the main body of the hotel was set perpendicular to Ocean Drive, the better to provide a garden along its sunny south side. The postwar redevelopment of this garden, in stages, transformed the Clevelander and its context by adding new facilities and recreational amenities.

The transformation began in 1951, when a canopy was added to connect the front porch with a parking area that had developed in the garden. Set at an angle to the street, the long concrete canopy is supported by metal "beanpoles," and topped by a neon-backed aluminum letter sign spelling "Clevelander." An undulating fish and duck pond stretches along one side. At the end of the canopy, a roguish concrete disk supported on curving limbs conveys the imagery of a flying saucer, a mushroom, or perhaps even a lily as seen from the bottom of the pond. Just behind the canopy, the swimming pool added in 1953 takes an amorphous form, comprising compound amoebae and a serpentine wall that creates "aqua pockets," tiled alcoves in the side of the pool. The pool's built-in seating transforms it from a recreational facility into a relaxation space.

As part of the mid-1980s revival of Ocean Drive, food and beverage service were dramatically increased. In 1986, the porte cochere was redeveloped as a bar with the installation of a glass-block and marble counter beneath the canopy. In 2000, planning began for a project to further develop the south lot, comprising a new wing at the rear of the pool area with a separate entrance on Tenth Street. The addition expands the hotel and its hugely successful ground-level bar area, and restores the hotel lobby fronting Ocean Drive to its original guest check-in function.

Strand (includes Ben-Stan, Congress, Waves, Bon Air)   E30

1052 Ocean Drive
Renovations, additions, and new structure: Kobi Karp Architecture & Interior Design, 2005

The 2005 Strand project comprises five buildings, four from the twentieth century and one from the twenty-first century. It is illustrative of the recent trend of grouping diverse structures into a new and more economically sustainable model of boutique hotel.

Ben-Stan, 1024 Ocean Drive: J. Meyer, 1964
Congress, 1036 Ocean Drive: Henry Hohauser, 1936
Strand, circa 1040 Ocean Drive: Kobi Karp Architecture & Interior Design, 2005
Waves Apartments (remnant), 1052 Ocean Drive: M. Tony Sherman, 1950
Bon Air, 1060 Ocean Drive: Henry J. Moloney, 1934

Four existing buildings were retained and joined together toward the rear by new construction that also meets the sidewalk by filling an unbuilt lot in the center of the block.

The oldest component of the project is the Bon Air, a late Mediterranean Revival building by Henry Moloney, a prolific architect of the 1920s. It is said to be the last home of Kid Gavilan, famous boxer of the post–World War II period.

The Congress came early in architect Henry Hohauser's turn to Modernism. Similar to the Colony Hotel (**E24**), it balances horizontal features (eyebrows and racing stripes) with the vertical thrust of a marquee pylon. Elemental twin frozen fountains, the symbol of the 1925 Paris Exposition of Modern Decorative and Industrial Arts, frame the doorway.

While postwar motel-type accommodations were abundant in Miami Beach, the front portion remnant of the Waves is a rare example located

E30

directly on Ocean Drive. The functionality of the type is leavened here with a lyrical play of porthole windows, a projecting bay window, and a cutaway corner that highlights the front stairway.

The balconies of the 1964 structure at 1024 Ocean Drive are that building's only decoration, and balance privacy and breezes with perforated-concrete balustrades.

The new infill portion of the project (between the Congress and Waves Apartments) draws on the stucco Modernism of its surroundings; its curved façade quietly complements the rich vocabulary of its neighbors.

Casa Casuarina   E31
1116 Ocean Drive
Henry LaPointe with Alden Freeman, 1930
Adaptive use, renovation and south wing and pool additions: Hawrylewicz and Robertson, 1993

Named for a W. Somerset Maugham story titled *The Casuarina Tree*, the exotic structure is a terminal vestige of Miami Beach's Roaring Twenties, when Mediterranean Revival styling was employed as the essential backdrop for a winter vacation. Its outward appearance simulates an urban palace whose eclectic elements were built in stages over several centuries. It was originally an apartment building, built to house the friends of New York socialist and Standard Oil heir Alden Freeman. A grand Moorish arch and great wood door frame entrance into its inner world. In sync with the fiction of a Mediterranean house offered up in so many other Miami confections of the period, Casa Casuarina is built around a private interior patio. Surrounded by continuous wrapping galleries, the courtyard is centered on a fountain that brings to mind those found at the Alhambra Palace in Granada, Spain.

When Italian designer Gianni Versace announced his plans to renovate and expand Casa Casuarina into a private residence for himself, the project elicited tremendous controversy. In addition to the privatization of a very public section of Ocean Drive, Versace's plans called for a new swimming pool and garden on the southern edge of the property, requiring the demolition of the Revere Hotel (A. Herbert Mathes, 1950). Preservationists lost the battle to save the Revere, but used the ensuing uproar to expand protection against demolition to contributing postwar buildings. Casa Casuarina acquired international fame as the site of Gianni Versace's murder in 1997.

Versace's renovation and expansion included the restoration of many original features such as the copper observatory dome, which originally housed an astronomical telescope. Unfortunately, it also closed off this once-accessible landmark, transforming a rich element of Miami Beach's public and semi-public urban fabric into a gated mansion. At this writing, it has recently reopened as a hotel after operating as a private club.

Victor Hotel   E32
1144 Ocean Drive
Lawrence Murray Dixon, 1937
Addition: Lawrence Murray Dixon, 1938
Renovations and additions: Perkins + Will, 2003

When completed in 1937, the Victor was one of the largest new hotels on Ocean Drive, and a striking reflection of the improving outlook of Depression-era Miami Beach. Like the nearby Tides, its size (8 stories with more than 100 rooms) provided amenities like a grand lobby, full restau-

E32

rant, and extensive public terrace, and generated a skyscraper silhouette among the lower residential structures on Ocean Drive. Strikingly modern in appearance, the Victor presents a tall and narrow façade to Ocean Drive. Its composition of banded windows, counterbalanced by a thrusting vertical pylon and porthole windows, was probably influenced by Howe and Lescaze's PSFS tower in Philadelphia. The Victor's 2-story lobby, long and narrow, is surrounded by ancillary functions on both the ground floor and mezzanine. Its walls are clad in Georgia marble, and view lines from the entrance lead directly to a pastoral mural by Earl LaPan. Originally located at the west end of the lobby, the hotel's signature Buccaneer Dining Room was relocated in 1938 to a streamlined salon built on the tower's north side, where it opened to a small garden. The hotel and restaurant, managed by the Adler Hotel of Sharon Springs in the northern Catskill Mountains, advertised its adherence to Jewish dietary laws.

First renovated in the early 1980s by Art Deco Hotels (founded by preservationist Andrew Capitman, the son of preservation leader Barbara Baer Capitman), the hotel became a famous destination for lectures, theater, and comedy. Closed in 1984, it did not reopen until 2003. At that time, the tower, with the adjacent dining pavilion, front porch, exterior fountain, terrazzo floors, and historic signage were all refurbished. Art conservator James Swope chemically embalmed LaPan's mural during construction and then restored it to its original luster. Additions transformed the original tower into one element of a U-shaped courtyard with a pool at its center. The additions mesh well with the tower, as well as with the streetfront along Ocean Drive.

1200 Ocean Drive   E33
Gilbert Fein, 1958
Renovation: Beilinson Architect, 1992-2000

This modest postwar apartment building, ornamented with a crab orchard stone pylon and rakish, metal-louvered balcony parapets, illustrates the nearly seamless integration of midcentury Modern architecture with the strip's more characteristic Mediterranean Revival and Art Deco structures. The protection of postwar structures was not a priority in Miami Beach until 1993.

Tides Hotel   E34

1220 Ocean Drive
Lawrence Murray Dixon, 1936
Renovation: Mosscrop Associates, 1997

One of Lawrence Murray Dixon's "little skyscrapers" (like the Victor, Raleigh, and Ritz hotels), the 10-story Tides exhibits Modern Classical styling and the stepped profile of a 1920s-era New York City tower. Set back 50 feet from the sidewalk behind a stepped plaza, the façade is centered on an imposing pilastrade nearly 3 stories high with deep stone portals. Above, a vertical integration of window bays and spandrels between the intervening pilasters emphasizes the formality and vertical surge of the building. The overall symmetry is subtly agitated by the offset mass of the elevator tower, and the asymmetrical articulation of bow windows on the lower façade. The mix balances public prominence with a visible response to local contingencies of context, structure, and program.

The sequence of public spaces at the Tides leads from the streetfront dining terrace to the 2-story lobby at the center of the plan. Its original features—mezzanine balconies (now closed in), circular columns, decorative metalwork, and wall murals—were details employed at Rockefeller Center's Radio City Music Hall, which was the model for many public spaces in Miami Beach. The ancillary dining room, cocktail bar, and card room were distributed from here.

After many years of closure, the Tides reopened in 1997 with a series of improvements orchestrated by its new operator, Island Outpost. The hotel's 115 rooms were reduced to 45 by realigning the central corridor to the tower's west wall, providing deeper and more luxurious units that all look toward the ocean. The Tides' colorful terrazzo floors are a reminder of the polychromatic character of early Miami Beach lobbies.

Leslie, Carlyle, Cardozo, and Cavalier Hotels   E35

Leslie Hotel
1244 Ocean Drive
Albert Anis, 1937
Renovation: Mosscrop Associates, 1996

Carlyle Hotel
1250 Ocean Drive
Kiehnel and Elliott, 1941
Restoration and rooftop addition: Blake Thorson, 2002

Cardozo Hotel
1300 Ocean Drive
Henry Hohauser, 1939
Renovation: STA Architectural Group, 2000

Cavalier Hotel
1320 Ocean Drive
Roy France, 1936

While these four hotels may appear to have been designed by the same hand at the same time, the opposite is true. Much of the coherence of the Miami Beach Architectural District is suggested in the balance of uniformity and variety displayed here (a balance multiplied by hundreds across

South Beach). The Cavalier and Leslie, with tall tripartite fronts and square-cut corners, belie a more classical inspiration, amplified at the Cavalier with copious Art Deco ornamentation in the surface of its façade. In contrast, the rounded corners of the Cardozo and Carlyle, built a few years later, reflect the more modern, horizontalizing spirit of streamlining popular through the eve of World War II. Coincidentally, the two pairs also represent typical solutions to standard South Beach lot sizes. The Cavalier and Leslie each occupy a single midblock lot with a simple rectangular bar-shaped block. The Carlyle and Cardozo, meanwhile, each occupy a double corner lot, and employ more sophisticated "letter forms," explicitly J- or C-shaped plans. Both buildings feature a courtyard space beyond the lobby, opening to the south to make the most of the winter sun.

In 1979, Andrew Capitman purchased these four buildings (and several others) with the intent of making them the vanguard of socially responsible renovation and restoration. Capitman's investment company, Art Deco Hotels, flamboyantly publicized the notion of a tropicalized Art Deco—lush, exotic, and unabashedly ornamental. Capitman's efforts were instrumental in updating Miami Beach's image as a paradisiacal warm-weather city. The later bankruptcy of Art Deco Hotels led to the commercial transformation of this area and a somewhat less idealistic outcome.

Winterhaven Hotel   E36

1400 Ocean Drive
Albert Anis, 1939
Renovation: Perkins + Will, 2001

When the Winterhaven Hotel was completed, its state-of-the-art commercial styling was described by contemporary sources as "Swedish modern." While the precise meaning of the term is not known, the hotel was certainly a well-crafted specimen of Moderne architecture. Its tall façade was abundantly textured with projecting eyebrows, stepped walls of stucco, and spandrels featuring a folded-plate motif rendered in glass and quarry keystone.

Facing Ocean Drive, the building presents a generous raised porch with broad windows that open to a multistory lobby. Within, fanciful terrazzo with a checkerboard motif, fluted columns, ornate Chinese mirrored panels, and etched-glass wall panels set off a sculptural stair that winds up to the mezzanine and beyond. The stair is a handsome piece, with terrazzo steps, metallic bar railings with glass-ball inserts, and scalloped plasterwork on its underside. The multilevel mezzanine seems like an extension of the stair. The hotel was recently renovated with new replicas of the original chandeliers, and maple and mirror registration desk.

E36

Crescent, McAlpin, and Ocean Plaza (Clyde) Hotels

E37

Crescent Hotel
1420 Ocean Drive
Henry Hohauser, 1938
Renovation: Beilinson Architect, 1988
Renovation and rooftop addition: James Silvers with Allan T. Shulman Architect, 1999

McAlpin Hotel
1424 Ocean Drive
Lawrence Murray Dixon, 1940
Renovation: Beilinson Architect, 1990
Renovation: Nichols Brosch Sandoval & Associates, 1999

Ocean Plaza (Clyde) Hotel
Lawrence Murray Dixon, 1941
Renovation: Beilinson Architect, 1990
Renovation: Nichols Brosch Sandoval & Associates, 1999

These three buildings, almost identical in plan, feature original façades that provide subtle variations on a simple theme. The Crescent's asymmetrical façade arrangement was a break from the Classical symmetry of Miami Beach's earlier Art Deco buildings. Its innovative expression includes a zipperlike focal element that divides the surface of the façade, and lunar themes, which are cast into the concrete railings of the front porch and into the terrazzo floors. Next door, L. Murray Dixon's McAlpin echoes the Crescent's eyebrows and circular boss motif, but draws the eye upward to the nautically inspired bridge at the roof. The later Ocean Plaza, also by Dixon, employed a more taut composition of projecting horizontal window bands juxtaposed by a central vertical block faced in green dyed keystone and topped with a glass-block panel.

The three buildings, with their raised porches, 3-story building walls, and articulate parapets, reinforce the careful relationship between building and street that gives Ocean Drive its particular urban quality. Rooftop additions to the Crescent and McAlpin are sufficiently set back from the parapet to be visible only from across the street. The addition over the Ocean Plaza unfortunately compromised its crowning three-dimensional cube of glass block. All three, however, are in contrast to the heavy-handed additions in the 900 block of Ocean Drive.

E37

Betsy Ross Hotel   E38

1440 Ocean Drive
Lawrence Murray Dixon, 1941
Renovation: Diamante Pedersoli Design with Beilinson Gomez Architects, 2008

The 2-story, 5-bay porch of the Betsy Ross, an outstanding feature that
might go unremarked in other settings, seems out of place and time amid
the Mediterranean and Modernist structures along Ocean Drive. In the late
1930s, there is evidence of a patriotic revival of iconic American architectural
styles, as well as names, in Miami Beach. The White House and Jefferson
hotels (both lost to fire) stood nearby. Besides the impending war, the 1930s
reconstruction of Colonial Williamsburg and movies like *Gone with the Wind*
probably had something to do with this revival. Like a movie set, Dixon's
conjuring of a southern antebellum estate, or a classic American grand hotel, is merely a skillful application of style to a flat-roofed building with a cor-
niced parapet. Dixon, a Florida native, was especially adept at handling traditional features, sometimes combining Neoclassical, Regency, and Colonial
Vernacular elements within otherwise Modern façade arrangements.

Il Villaggio   E39

1455 Ocean Drive
Fullerton Diaz Revuelta, 1996

The success of Ocean Drive, touched off by the Art Deco preservation movement and the designation of the Miami Beach Architectural District, greatly
increased the value of the large waterfront parcels north of Lummus Park.
The wide, deep site of the former White House Hotel on the northern border
of the park saw two attempts at redevelopment, including a more appropriately scaled and contextual design by Japanese architect Arata Isozaki,
before construction of Il Villaggio in the mid-1990s. Attempts were made to
mitigate the large mass of the building to varying degrees of success, the
most prominent and least successful being the cluttered roofscape. In fair-
ness, there is probably little the architect could have done to allay the combination of lot dimensions and zoning allowances that permitted a building
of this size. More successful is the retail pedestal on Ocean Drive, which
emulates the pedestrian-friendly frontage of adjacent structures. Although
hampered by a parking garage that lifted the first floor a half level above
the sidewalk, the pedestal continues the scale and animating rhythmic
cadence of Ocean Drive through its division into discrete storefronts, while
providing a buffer for the tower mass beyond. A break in the pedestal leads
to a raised entrance court formed by the J-shaped plan of the tower.

Ballet Valet Parking Garage   E40

210 7th Street
Arquitectonica, 1996

An inventive yet controversial solution to the confrontation in Miami Beach
between historic building fabric, vibrant street culture, and the attendant
insatiable need for parking, the Ballet Valet Garage combines historic façades and ground-floor retail into a new, larger structure with upper-level
parking decks. The project required the demolition of most of the existing
structures. Yet, the façades of the modest commercial buildings on-site—
including a former Greyhound bus station at 638 Collins Avenue (Russell T.

E40

Pancoast, 1947) and two Mediterranean Revival buildings at 660-666 Collins Avenue (Robert Taylor, 1925)—were preserved and infilled to create a continuous retail base. Rising behind is the garage, completely covered in shrubbery growing from planters attached to a metal framework enveloping the parking decks. While not an ideal preservation strategy, the garage works successfully at several scales. From a distance, the building floats over the surrounding low-scaled neighborhood like a shaggy box, effectively camouflaging the impact of the more than one thousand cars housed within.

E41

Gap E41

673 Collins Avenue
Beilinson Gomez Architects, 1996

This playful bauble, characteristic of commercial development during the boom from the 1990s to the early years of the twenty-first century, marries the disorienting plasticity of Deconstructivism with Miami Beach's colorful stucco vernacular.

The Hotel (The Tiffany) and Essex House E42

The Hotel (The Tiffany)
801 Collins Avenue
Lawrence Murray Dixon, 1939
Renovations, rooftop addition, and pool: Todd Oldham with Beilinson Gomez Architects, 1998

Essex House
1001 Collins Avenue
Henry Hohauser, 1938

The Essex House and Tiffany hotels, along with the Tudor (**E47**), form a remarkable ensemble and identifiable specialty building type anchoring northeast corners on Collins Avenue. These L-shaped buildings on double corner lots are sited for their specific urban condition, cleverly configured to maximize ocean views from their porches and hotel guest rooms. They resolve multiple design challenges by presenting a continuous street-fronting mass along Collins Avenue and the corner, and are stepped back to create a southeast-facing courtyard that opens views toward the ocean. Each had a prominent rounded corner crowned by a signage finial, a generous ter-

E42

race carved from the mass of the building, and an articulate lobby entrance fronting the porch.

The Essex House, designed by Henry Hohauser, is the founding example of the type. Its severe streamlining and illuminated signage gave it the appearance of a world's fair pavilion. Although never explicitly coordinated, its distinct echo is found in the competing work of Lawrence Murray Dixon and Albert Anis at buildings like the Tudor House, Tiffany, Senator (demolished 1988), and Bancroft hotels (**E49**), which mark similar corners along Collins Avenue. The echo is further amplified by complementary structures like the Beach Plaza, Kent, and Palmer House hotels (**E47**).

The Essex House is notable for its well-restored and -maintained interior, which offers a glimpse of the voluptuous splendor and Art Deco flourish of prewar Miami Beach. The mural and fireplace form the focal point of the lobby, anchoring a seating area just inside the porch. The mural, by Earl LaPan, features a Seminole rowing a canoe, and explores romantic notions of flora and fauna in the Florida Everglades. The ziggurat-shaped fireplace is clad in deep-chocolate scagliola, a composite that, like tinted keystone, was a cheap substitute for marble. A rare original etched-glass panel can be found adjacent to the east lobby doors over a stairway banister that references the Egyptian influence on 1920s Art Deco. The intricate plaster filigree pattern at the top of the walls is repeated in wood above the mail slots, and a vibrant terrazzo floor pattern begins on the porch and leads into the lobby mirroring the tray ceiling above. Finally, chandeliers in the shape of polished metal half spheres adorn the alcove along Collins Avenue, which is itself punctuated by octagonal windows.

At the Tiffany, a rooftop pool and exercise room were added in the late 1990s. The pool deck offers views to the ocean, while the building's signage spire, overlooking Collins Avenue, looms over a patio lounge beneath.

Coral Rock House (Avery Smith House)   E43
900–904 Collins
1918

At this writing, a remnant of probably the oldest private home on Miami Beach stands tenuously at the corner of Collins Avenue and Ninth Street. Smith's Casino at the southern tip ten blocks south was perhaps the first tourist attraction in this area, and its owner lived here. Avery Smith also ran a ferry from Miami to Miami Beach, a good business in the days before the County Causeway and streetcar lines were constructed. The structure was built of wood frame clad with oolitic rock walls, once a common construction technique that reflects the search for an appropriate residential architecture for this subtropical region.

In 2007, a redevelopment plan for the site was approved that called for construction of a new building incorporating the front and side walls of the house. While partial demolition has proceeded, the completion of the new project and the fate of the remnant remain in doubt.

Sherbrooke Coop   E44

901 Collins Avenue
MacKay & Gibbs, 1947

A nautical fantasy a block from the ocean, with portholes on the lower deck and openings at the parapet from which to drop an anchor. Its entrance and rooftop signage address the corner, while the strongly streamlined façade sweeps toward the ocean.

Fairwind Hotel (Fairmont Hotel,   E45
Fairmont Apartments)

1000 Collins Avenue (Fairmont Hotel)
Lawrence Murray Dixon, 1936
New covered porch: Lawrence Murray Dixon, 1945

1020 Collins Avenue (Fairmont Apartments)
Lawrence Murray Dixon, 1945

1030 Collins Avenue
Leonard Glasser, 1952

The Fairmont Hotel (1936—the name was tweaked after brand litigation in the 1990s) and Fairmont Apartments (1945) were both designed by Lawrence Murray Dixon, one of Miami Beach's most prolific architects of the 1930s.

The 3-story corner hotel illustrates the transition to Modern styling underway in the mid-1930s. The building retains a symmetrical and classically ordered façade, but its smooth finish articulated with glass-block panels and geometric patterns exhibited a completely new aesthetic. The other street-facing buildings exemplify the changing priorities and design idioms of the postwar period. The 1020 Collins Avenue building has an asymmetric façade that joins clay tile, slump brick, and corrugated glass with projecting concrete canopies and fins.

The plan for expansion by Allan T. Shulman Architect comprises three 5-story buildings constructed at the rear of the lot, with a new hospitality deck and suite on top of the old Fairmont Hotel. The planned addition is segmented into pieces that respect the district's 50-foot lot structure without altering the appearance of the historic structures from the street, and creates new semi-private garden courtyards between the old and new buildings, shared by facing hotel units. Ivy screen-walls transform each patio into an outdoor room. Its moderate-scaled, fine-grained structures will reflect their context while introducing a new, contemporary layer to the site. The new semi-private and restored open patio expands Miami Beach's network of public and semi-private spaces.

David's Café and Market   E46

1058 Collins Avenue
House structure: William Burbridge, ca. 1915
Service station: DeBruyn Kops, ca. 1925
Adaptive use: Allan T. Shulman Architect, 2006 (market) and 2009 (café and restaurant)

E46

This assemblage of small structures, today one of Miami Beach's favorite
Cuban eateries, exemplifies the eclectic and compact construction of South
Beach. Built and rebuilt over many years, the site is a virtual palimpsest trac-
ing the area's development. The masonry and wood home at the rear of the
lot was constructed prior to the city's incorporation in 1915. A decade later,
as Collins Avenue became more commercial, a service station was added
on the corner of Eleventh Street. The station featured a Mission-style porte
cochere over the gas pumps.

    The recent renovation and expansion has revealed and restored these
historic pieces and tied them together. The house was converted into a marketplace, while the single-story corner service station was converted into a
café. The arched openings of the former porte cochere were uncovered and
glazed to create an airy seating area. New additions in back and on top, as
well as a paved patio, complete the complex with new indoor and outdoor
dining facilities.

Tudor, Palmer House, and Kent Hotels   E47

Tudor Hotel
1111 Collins Avenue
Lawrence Murray Dixon, 1939
Rooftop addition: Max Wolfe Sturman, 2007

Palmer House Hotel
1121 Collins Avenue
Lawrence Murray Dixon, 1939
Renovation and addition: Max Wolfe Sturman, 2007

Kent Hotel
1131 Collins Avenue
Lawrence Murray Dixon, 1939
Renovations and addition: Giller and Giller, 2005

E47

The east side of Collins Avenue in the 1100 block is a particularly well-coordinated ensemble. Florida-born architect Lawrence Murray Dixon was responsible for the three buildings, all constructed in 1939. The Tudor does double-duty, forming a separate ensemble with the Tiffany and Essex House hotels (**E42**).

Dixon's ability to adeptly combine Historicist and Modernist elements is evident in all three structures. At the Palmer House, the dynamic composition of the façade, a vertical pylon and signage finial counterbalance the horizontal stretch of the ground-floor loggia porch as well as bands of ribbon windows and continuous eyebrows. The base is clad in quarry keystone framing a more traditional elliptical window and pedimented door that are scaled to the pedestrian. Such combinations would become a common feature of the city's resort architecture after World War II. Still surviving on the Tudor are the original wooden doors with superimposed metallic elements and an outstanding design in the terrazzo floor of the front porch.

Jerry's Famous Deli (Hoffman's Cafeteria)　 　E48

1450 Collins Avenue
Henry Hohauser, 1940
Renovation: Charles Benson & Associates, 2001

Built as Hoffman's Cafeteria, this expressive interpretation of a ferryboat chugging its way down Collins Avenue is an exuberant and lyrical structure even by the standards of Miami Beach's resort architecture. Along the parapet, diminishing circular forms suggest a wake or plume of smoke billowing from one of its stacks, trailing off beyond the corner feature to create a false perspective and a sense of motion along the east and south façades. Etched-glass panels above the main entrance, depicting heroic figures in the act of harvest, bestow a touch of Depression-era glamour to the proceedings inside.

E48

After World War II, the building became a social hall for retirees of Polish descent and was renamed the Warsaw Ballroom. For much of the late twentieth century, a gay-oriented nightclub—or "dance hall," in the somewhat dated terminology of Miami Beach's zoning code—operated at this corner under various names, the most famous of which was the Warsaw. In 2002, the space was converted back into a twenty-four-hour cafeteria to serve the needs of South Beach's sleepless population. The 2002 rehabilitation highlights the grandeur of the 1940 original, removing added partitions and restoring the impressive double-height dining room to its full volume.

Ocean Steps (includes Bancroft Hotel)   E49
Bancroft Hotel, 1501 Collins Avenue: Albert Anis, 1939
Adaptive use and additions: Michael Graves, 1995

The loss of the Jefferson Hotel at the east end of Fifteenth Street due to a fire circa 1990, and the joining of its lot with the adjacent Bancroft Hotel property, provided the opening for a multiuse development combining new construction with historic preservation. The site occupies a strategic location at the northern terminus of Ocean Drive, providing a bridge in scale and use to the convention hotels to the north. In the early 1990s, the Constructa Corporation, the developer of the CocoWalk shopping complex in Coconut Grove (**B64**), hired architect Michael Graves to add a tower and shopping arcade to the narrow lot perpendicular to the shoreline. Graves's Postmodern tower complements the whimsy of the prewar Art Deco–style buildings that surround it. Conversely, the shopping arcade, sited between the new tower and the Bancroft Hotel, and configured to terminate the view corridor of Ocean Drive, hews closely to Constructa's earlier CocoWalk development. The complex has the Disney-esque flavor, as well as the U-shape organization, of its predecessor. It was designed to connect with the adjacent Royal Palm Crowne Plaza, but the connection was not built, and the multilevel arcade has suffered.

The old Bancroft has suffered the most. It was substantially gutted, partly to allow the installation of underground parking, and partly to realign floor plates to obtain commercially marketable ceiling heights in its new retail spaces. While the street façades and lobby have been well-renovated, its windows are opaque, hiding the misalignment of floors and windows.

Anglers Boutique Hotel and Spa   E50
(Anglers Hotel and Anglers Villa)
660 Washington Avenue
Henry J. Moloney, 1930
Additions and renovation: Allan T. Shulman Architect with Ralph Choeff Architect, 2006

E50

The original Anglers Hotel and adjacent Anglers Villa, both designed by Henry Moloney, offer a rare snapshot of Washington Avenue in its prewar life as a hotel corridor, and illustrate two complementary scales of resort accommodations during the 1920s-era boom in Miami Beach. The buildings' Mediterranean Revival styling includes arched windows, decorative iron railings, and parapets with a Mission-style profile. The Anglers Villa has applied masonry porches with arched openings and clay-tile parapets.

In 2006, the abandoned structures were renovated and expanded with two new wings inserted at the margins of the property. The new wings create a unified complex that is both introspective and extroverted, and that respects the surrounding district's fine-grained texture. On the south side is a new 5-story structure, a "miniature tower" whose slender mass accommodates the narrow available space. Its tripartite façade is a contemporary reference to the front of the old Anglers Hotel. Two-story townhouse hotel suites are accessed either from the courtyard or from exterior catwalks on the upper floor. Behind the villa structure is the other new addition, a 2-story wing of cabana suites that frames a new pool deck. Semipublic and private gardens fill the remaining spaces between the structures, linking them functionally and aesthetically.

665–685 Washington Avenue   E51
E. L. Robertson, 1932–33

Among the first modern commercial structures in Miami Beach, this row of storefronts was built in the period of near-dormancy between the Hurricane of 1926 and the boom of a decade later. Its Art Deco monumentality and careful attention to detail are rare for a modest single-story commercial block. The prominent polygonal corner pavilion, a translation in modern styling of the city's Mediterranean Revival corner towers, illustrates a local tradition of urban continuity in the face of stylistic change.

The architectural significance of the row is overshadowed by the role it played in the renaissance of the Art Deco District. In 1984, the richly painted corner feature appeared on the cover of *Progressive Architecture*, headlining a piece about the district's preservation and revival. Early preservationists look back to that moment as a turning point in the fortunes of the district, bringing its architecture, newly added to the National Register of Historic Places, and designer Leonard Horowitz's pastel palette, to national attention.

In late 1986, three entrepreneurs from New York's Downtown "scene" opened the Strand Restaurant at 671 Washington Avenue, formerly a popular delicatessen called the Famous. The restaurant quickly became the social center of the preservation movement in Miami Beach. For some years, the Miami Design Preservation League had its headquarters next door at 661 Washington. During the late 1980s and early 1990s, the Miami Beach Development Corporation (MBDC; now Miami Beach Community Development Corporation) held its monthly networking dinners for South Beach pioneers in the Strand's private dining room. The MBDC dinners shared space and schedule with the forums of the South Beach New Democrats and with the Acme Stage Company, an artistic and cultural pioneer of a revived entertainment scene. Later in the 1990s, this block of Washington Avenue almost entirely succumbed to nightclubs and bars, rendering its storefronts dark and empty during the day.

Fin Fed (Miami Beach Federal Savings &   E52
Loan South Shore Branch)
743 Washington Avenue
Edwin T. Reeder Associates, 1957
Renovation: Markus Frankel & Associates, 1992
Sculpture: Antoni Miralda, 1992
Washington Avenue storefront: Chad Oppenheim, 2004

This complex—anchored by a 1965 former Financial Federal bank branch (hence the current name) at the corner of Washington Avenue and Eighth

Street and two storefronts from the early renaissance of South Beach
(E53)—embodies the expressive form of rehabilitation done by pioneering
South Beach developer Dacra, who eventually went on to reposition the
Miami Design District for its turn-of-the-twenty-first-century revival.

The former bank has been embellished by a metallic octopuslike sculpture by Catalan artist Antoni Miralda, reaching from behind the disengaged
cylindrical piers along Washington Avenue. The southern portion of the
bank building was transformed into a new double-height storefront whose
giant concrete S-shaped façade screen draws on the shape and material of
the bank's soaring tripod signage pylon for inspiration.

Eighth Street Storefronts E53

224 8th Street: Trelles Architects and Teofilo Victoria, 1992
226 8th Street: Markus Frankel & Associates, 1992

E53

The addition of new commercial storefronts along side streets reflected
the intensification of this area as a fashion retail center in the early 1990s.
Dacra, owner of the parcel, commissioned separate architects to expand
the Fin Fed building (E52) eastward toward Collins Avenue. The whimsical,
idiosyncratic storefronts enliven the street as a public space. The tall, narrow building at the east end explores Ovian geometries as cut-outs from
a deep masonry façade wall. Next door, geometric bay windows project
from the recessed plane of the façade, framing the keystone-shaped entry.
It has taken time, but the neighborhood has caught up to their surrealist
expression.

Blackstone E54

800 Washington Avenue
B. Kingston Hall, 1929
Renovation: Santos & Raimundez, 1990

The tallest contributing building in the Miami Beach Architectural District,
the Blackstone's size reminds the viewer of the pretensions of the 1920s
boom era in Miami Beach. The relatively austere façade treatment has a
limited number of Mediterranean Revival details, including hipped clay-tile
roofs at its tallest portion. Its tallest feature is the clock tower that conceals
the hotel's elevator machinery. The lobby, not readily accessible, is far more
decorative. The Blackstone is reputed to be the first Miami Beach hotel to
solicit Jewish guests, and also the first to give accommodation to African
Americans.

Astor Hotel E55

956 Washington Avenue
T. Hunter Henderson, 1936
Renovations and addition: Kobi Karp Architecture & Interior Design, 1993

The Astor embodies well the ambivalent modernity of Miami Beach's 1930s-
era development boom. The building's cubic massing and flush rectangular windows manifest a functional spirit. Yet, projecting eyebrows—a
characteristic feature of the city's modern architecture—are used only to
mark the building's corners. Decorative grilles play across the parapet. The
upper floors are clad in the rough stucco texture typical of Mediterranean

Revival buildings, while the corners are rounded almost imperceptibly. The formal gesture of a pair of stripped Classical pilasters bracketing the entry is countered by the horizontal thrust of stone cladding that wraps the first floor. Here, pink-tinted keystone is striated with thin, contrasting black-dyed bands of the same material, creating speed stripes that continue across the windows in the form of horizontal muntins.

The 1993 renovation brought a level of hotel investment to Washington Avenue that had previously been seen only on Ocean Drive and Collins Avenue. It was the first renovation to reintroduce casement windows to the Architectural District and was the subject of much controversy for the handling of the lobby. Coupled with Phillipe Starck's contemporary radical alteration of the public interiors of the Delano Hotel (**F6**), the renovation of the Astor's lobby precipitated the revision of Miami Beach's Historic Preservation Ordinance to include language protecting public interiors.

Controversy notwithstanding, the interior alterations are, for the most part, successful in maintaining period character while introducing contemporary features. Fluted plaster columns, geometric terrazzos, decorative metalwork, and Vitrolite glass wainscots (some original and the rest replicated) make this one of the city's best lobby spaces. Reconfigured subtly, the space flows around the vestige of the original reception desk and down into an expansive double-height glass-enclosed restaurant space carved from the basement level. Its undulating glass enclosure is effectively hidden from the street. In order to achieve the double-height space, the hotel rooms on south side of the first-floor corridor were removed. Their doors were kept along the hallway to maintain its appearance from the lobby.

E56

Wolfsonian–Florida International University   E56

1001 Washington Avenue
Robertson and Patterson, 1927
Two-story addition: R. M. Little, 1936
Conversion to museum: Hampton & Kearns, 1992
Dynamo Café: Mark Hampton with Richard Miltner, 2006

Built the year after the devastating hurricane and local bust of 1926, this monumental pile is evidence of Miami Beach's economic resiliency even as the region entered the Great Depression four years earlier than the rest of the country. The original 3-story structure, lavishly ornamented in the Spanish Baroque style, served as an off-season storage facility for Miami Beach's winter residents, who banked furs, furniture, and even automobiles here. A major addition in 1936 reflected the building boom taking shape here in the late 1930s. This addition, in a plainer, less ornate style, extended the building two stories. Another major addition, in the 1990s, accompanied the building's conversion to use as the Wolfsonian Museum of Decorative and Propaganda Arts.

In 1987, philanthropist and collector Mitchell Wolfson Jr., owner of the world's largest private collection of decorative and propaganda arts, began storing parts of his collection here. By 1993, he had retrofitted and expanded the building an additional two stories and one bay to the east. The additions reflect a minimalist/conservative approach to differentiating new and old. It is respectful and complementary, yet displays subtle and clever variations on the original architecture. The window of the rooftop addition recalls the outline of the ornate entry carving, while projections on the parapet recall similar projections on the 1927 parapet. The extensions of the friezes onto the new rear bay along Tenth Street are made of the same materials as the original work but are simplified. Instead of employing decorative shields, the frieze extensions are punctuated with the carved faces of figures instrumental in the conversion to a museum, among them Mitchell Wolfson Jr., the collector; Mark Hampton, the architect; Billy Kearns, the interior designer; and Peggy Loar, the first director of the Wolfsonian. Although the building is fortresslike from most perspectives, the glass entry wall allows two key pieces of the collection to be seen from the street. The focal point of the entry hall is a 20-foot-high glazed terra-cotta marquee salvaged from the Norris Theater (1929) in Norristown, Pennsylvania. Set on the rear wall beyond a pool of water, the marquee is silhouetted against a frosted window, making it visible from the sidewalk. At night, from across Washington Avenue, one can peer into the top-floor gallery whose decorative wood ceiling was salvaged from a 1920s automobile showroom in Downtown Miami.

1000–1050 Washington Avenue　　　E57

The Best Western organization sponsors a hotel that occupies an entire block of Washington Avenue, comprising five historic buildings of diverse character. The ensemble is unified by the late-1980s walled garden patio that stretches the full block along Washington Avenue. Located at the intersection of Miami Beach's two major street grids, the closing of Drexel Avenue allowed for the opening of open space. While the wall is attractive, it gives the impression that the space is private; in fact, it is public.

Davis Hotel (Adelphia Hotel)
1020 Washington Avenue
Henry Hohauser, 1941

The hotel's Cubist façade suggests multiple stucco planes with deep recessed voids for windows. Notable are the tinted keystone skirt along the first floor, and glass-block panels on the upper façade that angle like a ship's prow.

Coral Rock Cottage
1024 Washington
1921
Renovation: Martin J. Hyman & Associate, 2001

Locally quarried oolitic limestone cottages are common in some older sections of Miami, but rare in Miami Beach. This was the home of one of Miami Beach's most important developers, Henri Levy, who planned and executed much of what is now North Beach.

Bel Air
1036 Washington Avenue
Gerard Pitt, 1953

This building's trapezoidal signage pylon, with its neon script, adds a postwar Modern touch to the block.

Taft Hotel
1046 Washington Avenue
Henry Hohauser, 1936

The Taft presents classic Art Deco geometry and tropically inspired ornamentation in a formal synthesis.

Kenmore Hotel
1050 Washington Avenue
Anton Skislewicz, 1936

The Streamline Moderne Kenmore sits at the head of the group. Its tall frontal façade dissolves into powerfully horizontal bands at the building ends, while the concrete canopy sheltering its entrance swings around to embrace a nautically inspired glass and glass-block salon that projects into the south-facing court. This was one of the first hotels to be repainted and refurbished with public funds in the 1980s. The interior features spectacular original neon lighting that highlights its modern stair.

11th Street Diner   E58

1065 Washington Avenue
Originally constructed in Haledon, N.J., and moved to Wilkes Barre, Pa., 1949
Moved to current site, 1992

Although Miami Beach can boast a plethora of prewar commercial architecture, it has never had a metallic diner. During the phase of the city's redevelopment when "Deco-ization" was in vogue, this diner was imported from Pennsylvania to help complete the picture. It certainly fits quite well among its masonry and concrete neighbors. Stainless steel makes a suitable building material for this epitome of Streamline Moderne styling.

Miami Beach Police and Court Facility   E59

Police Headquarters
1100 Washington Avenue
Jaime Borelli, Markus Frankel, Peter Blitstein, 1987

Old City Hall
1130 Washington Avenue
Martin Luther Hampton, 1927
Renovations: City of Miami Beach, 1993, 1999, 2006

The Miami Beach Police and Court Facility comprises the city's police headquarters and the old Miami Beach City Hall, which originally sat prominently on its own wedge-shaped block at the confluence of Washington and Drexel avenues. A symbol of the city's resurrection after the disastrous Hurricane of 1926, the 9-story city hall tower included a fire station in its north wing. Vestiges of the arched garage door openings are still apparent from Twelfth Street. Disused when city hall was moved to the nascent City Center area in 1975 (F34), it regained civic importance as an element of the new complex, serving as the home of the Miami Beach branch of the county court system.

The development of the police station engendered much controversy, in part as a symbol of governmental largesse, but mainly because it required the clearing of an entire city block of small hotels and apartment buildings contributing to the Miami Beach Architectural District. Further, the large multistory parking structure occupying the west end of the block and serving both the police and the public, although stepped to reduce its visual impact, is foreign to the character of the neighborhood. Still, at least along Washington Avenue, the police station adeptly manages its prominent urban siting and reflects its environmental and architectural contexts.

E59

Highlights include the multistory lobby and the east façade, whose massing and volumes derive inspiration from the city's abundant streamlining, as well as from the manner of Richard Meier. The closing of the southernmost block of Drexel Avenue created a suitable forecourt for the police station, giving it a civic presence on Washington Avenue and creating one of the area's few real plaza spaces.

Commercial Block, 1201–1255 Washington Avenue

E60

1201 Washington Avenue
Lawrence Murray Dixon, 1941

1225–1255 Washington Avenue (Cinema Theater)
T. Hunter Henderson and Thomas White Lamb, 1935

The use of keystone as a decorative cladding material distinguishes this block-long mixed-use structure built in two stages. The first phase, 1225–1255 Washington Avenue, was home to the Cinema Theater. One of the district's most lavish Art Deco interiors, its design is attributed to a collaboration between T. Hunter Henderson and New York architect and theater designer Thomas White Lamb, who also collaborated on the design of the Lincoln Theatre (F14). The theater featured a towering carved keystone marquee that has long since been removed, leaving a noticeable void. For a time, the theater space was called the French Casino Supper Club and reputed to be controlled by Al Capone. Since the mid-1980s, the space has served as a nightclub under various ownerships, and with various levels of attention to historic authenticity. (In the 1990s, the musical artist Prince used the space as a nightclub called Glam Slam.)

A second phase completed the block by filling in the two southernmost lots. The change in the sill height of the second-floor windows indicates where the two phases come together. The building is one of the few on Miami Beach to preserve its original casement windows, which have been well maintained.

E61

U.S. Post Office   E61

1300 Washington Avenue
Howard L. Cheney, 1937
Renovation: General Services Administration, 1977

Miami Beach was building rapidly by the late 1930s, yet the city was still
the beneficiary of Depression-era New Deal programs that financed new
construction in the hope of stimulating a moribund economy. The U.S.
Post Office was a project of the U.S. Department of Treasury, and notably
featured an artistic program commissioned by the department's Section of
Painting and Sculpture. The government's resources allowed for civic gravitas and a level of detail, craftsmanship, and materials unheard of in the surrounding privately built structures of the period.

The Post Office presents a vocabulary of Modern Classical features, recalling institutional European, particularly Italian, architecture of the late
1930s. The imposing drum-shaped rotunda on an elevated base of rose marble is an important yet modestly scaled civic gesture toward Washington
Avenue, the popular commercial main street of the city. The marble steps,
under constant threat from skateboarders, hint at the quality of materials
within. In the rotunda, a central fountain masquerading as a village well,
mailboxes in gold-painted metal, and a large mural by Charles Hardman
depicting scenes from Florida history animate the marble-clad main space.
Although Hardman proposed a mural depicting activities associated with
Florida, such as golf and agriculture, Ed Rowan, of the Section of Painting
and Sculpture, preferred historical scenes depicting Native Americans and
Spanish conquistadores. The first two panels achieve this, but the third,

showing a peaceful communion of U.S. troops and Native Americans, is a product of New Deal hopes rather than history. Crowning this space, the painted ceiling suggests the dome of heaven; in the center, a sunburst radiates from the skylight through which artificial and natural light from the lantern cupola enter the rotunda. References to Classical Roman iconography, in particular the fasces, are found in the adjacent vestibule. The iconography was likely used by the U.S. government for its symbolism, imparting a sense of unity, as well as permanence and stability. The U.S. Postal Service renovated the building in 1977; the renovation represented the first victory of the newborn Miami Design Preservation League.

Spanish Village E62

1434–1440 Washington Avenue and 400–517 Española Way
Robert Taylor, 1925
Renovation of south side: Randy Sender, Stuart Grant, Dixon Alvarino, and Todd Tragash, 1984
Renovation of north side: Sender Tragash, 1986
Plaza de España: Savino & Miller Design Studio, 2002

E62

Richard Carney, foreman of the failed 1882 coconut plantation that predated Miami Beach, purchased a long, narrow tract of land on the border between the holdings of John Collins and the Lummus Brothers, between today's Fourteenth and Fifteenth streets. This tract was platted as Española Villas in 1922 by William Whitman, a Chicago industrialist. Whitman envisioned detached houses on a narrow street he named Española Way. Only a few of Whitman's villas were built, and in 1924 the development was purchased by N.B.T. Roney, an important real estate developer in both Miami and Miami Beach. Roney, who was building the palatial Roney Plaza Hotel at Twenty-third Street and the Atlantic Ocean at the time, hired Robert Taylor to design a mixed-use Spanish Village that could serve as a bohemian entertainment destination for his hotel guests. Legend has it that Whitman's villas were relocated to the west end of Española Way, where they survive.

Although only a portion of his design was built, Taylor nevertheless produced one of South Florida's most fully realized examples of the scenographic potential of the Mediterranean Revival style. The Spanish Village comes complete with a network of picturesquely planned and appointed streets and alleyways and provides a primer on the architectural history of the European Mediterranean region from the Medieval through the late Renaissance periods. Miami Beach preservationist and historian Barbara Baer Capitman cited the Spanish Village as the likely inspiration for Addison Mizner's later development of Worth Avenue and the adjacent shopping passages of Via Parigi and Via Mizner in Palm Beach. Roney's public-relations machine pitched the village as an artists' colony in the tradition of the Left Bank in Paris and Greenwich Village in New York.

The hype finally turned to reality in the 1980s with the opening of the International Youth Hostel and the Española Way Art Center, in the Clay and Cameo Hotels respectively. A vivid, though not historically accurate, paint scheme turned the village into a magazine-cover confection. The pastel colors have since become part of the character of the village. The Plaza de España streetscape project, inaugurated in 2002 and inspired by the checkerboard patterned plazas of the Iberian Peninsula, transformed the intersection of Española Way and Drexel Avenue into the living room centerpiece for the village.

Crobar and Osteria del Teatro (Cameo Theater) E63

1445 Washington Avenue
Robert E. Collins, 1938
Renovation of the theater: Telesco Associates, 1999

Originally the Cameo Theater, this Streamline Moderne building has been adaptively used several times and now houses a nightclub and restaurant. Over the entrance marquee, a large, framed glass-block panel centers the façade. Atop this panel, carved into the keystone, is a small "cameo," a romantically styled face amid a gathering of Art Nouveau flowers and ferns.

E63

Flamingo Park Neighborhood

The true charm of the Flamingo Park neighborhood lies not in the architectural value of its individual buildings (although these are quite often extraordinary), but rather in the aggregation of many related buildings. Nearly any block comprises a rich mixture of the city's constituent layers. Each is a "Noah's Ark" of style, building type, and living arrangements.

The Flamingo Historic District (FHD) was first created by the City of Miami Beach in 1990, and the district has expanded a few times since then. FHD surrounds Flamingo Park, and includes most of the area recognized as the National Register Art Deco District. The FHD now extends roughly from Washington Avenue on the east to Alton Road on the west; from Fifth Street on the south to Lincoln Road on the north. Less well-known than its neighbors to the east on Collins Avenue and Ocean Drive, the FHD is where Barbara Baer Capitman's vision—"using these lovely buildings to save the people who live in them," has been most faithfully realized.

The north-south streets on the west side of the district—Meridian, Jefferson, Michigan, and Lenox—have relatively good shade trees, making even summertime walking possible and pleasant. The FHD includes hundreds of Mediterranean Revival, Art Deco, and postwar structures as well as a few bulky 1970s-era condominiums whose main virtue is the view of the district you can get from their balconies.

Seymour E64

945 Pennsylvania Avenue
B. Kingston Hall, 1936
Renovation and adaptive use: STA Architectural Group, 2001

The Seymour was designed by architect B. Kingston Hall and built in 1936 as a 36-room winter hotel. Hall was better known for work in the Mediterranean Revival style, but his work here is a fine example of the Modern residential architecture produced in Miami Beach in the 1930s. The façade and lobby, which retain their original features, are distinguished by bold horizontal and vertical elements and extensive use of the ziggurat motif.

The building was converted to one-bedroom rental apartments in 1955 and remained in continuous use through 1990. After years of neglect

E64

followed by an extensive restoration, the building reopened as a multi-use facility in 2001, and currently functions as a community center, the Art Deco District Building Museum, and the headquarters of the Miami Beach Community Development Corporation.

A Walk through the Flamingo Historic District (see entries E66–E78)

Free daytime, off-street parking is available, for three hours, during the week and on weekends, in the Flamingo Park lot west of the junction of Eleventh Street and Jefferson Avenue.

Standing at the southern end of Flamingo Park at Jefferson Avenue and Eleventh Street, you can immediately see the buildings of five of Miami Beach's most significant architects: William F. Brown, Lawrence Murray Dixon, Henry Hohauser, Morris Lapidus, and Norman Giller.

Fire Station No. 1   E65
1051 Jefferson Avenue
Morris Lapidus, 1966
Addition: Giller and Giller, 1989

E65

Morris Lapidus designed the original Fire Station building, a laconic but richly textured building by the standards of the author of "architecture of joy." Notable are the precast roof forms that recall bull's horns, and roof and walls clad in a locally popular brown aggregate stone. Giller's discreet and restrained addition complements the original. The two structures are sensitively connected by a bridge. The 2-story parking deck next door is an unfortunate legacy of the tall apartment block behind at 1020 Meridian Avenue.

Helen Marie   E66
1050 Jefferson Avenue
Lawrence Murray Dixon, 1948

The Helen Marie is an impressive example of the small apartment-hotel
buildings that clustered in this area in the 1930s–1940s. After World War II,
Lawrence Murray Dixon and the other architects of prewar Miami Beach
continued their experiments with multifamily housing, evolving the area's
characteristic blend of privacy, urbanity, and tropical landscaping. This
J-shaped building is reminiscent of Dixon's 1941 delight on the southwest
corner of Thirteenth Street and Pennsylvania Avenue and Lincoln Terrace
(F32), as well as Roy France's 1945 Decolux at 826 Euclid Avenue.

Brompton Manor   E67
1017 Jefferson Avenue
William F. Brown, 1925

During the 1920s boom, Mediterranean Revival buildings like the Brompton
were built to house the professionals and skilled employees of Carl Fisher's
hotels and other resorts. The historicist decorative details and the Brompton
Manor name were intended to convey luxury and lineage. The asymmetrical façade is an artifice suggesting a kind of mature, accretive growth that
Miami Beach would only acquire later in its life. It is instructive to compare
and contrast this building with the Depression-era Jade Apartments across
Jefferson Avenue (E68).

Jade Apartments   E68
1008 Jefferson Avenue
Henry Hohauser, 1935

This is one of Henry Hohauser's earliest buildings on Miami Beach, and an
early product of the 1930s boom that transformed South Beach. Hohauser's
drift from revivalism toward Modernism is evident in the more abstract
nature of the building's decorative features. The archway over the entry employs a widened, Modernist interpretation of the historic arch. Fluted end
pilasters straddle the stylistic divide, while speed stripes in the center bay
hint at the spirit of the new era.

960 Jefferson Avenue   E69
Henry Hohauser, 1936

The Jefferson Avenue façade illustrates how the austere planar volumes
of Depression-era Modernism can appear richly decorated through subtle
means: planar offsets, project concrete eyebrows, and incised racing stripes.
The poor side frontage illustrates how poorly this building type functions
on a corner lot, in comparison with walk-ups. Contrast with 901 Tenth Street,
the postwar gallery access building directly to the north.

950 Jefferson Avenue   E70
Henry Hohauser, 1940

Set at the back of its lots, undoubtedly behind an older structure since
removed, Number 950 is a continuation of Henry Hohauser's experiments

with the decorative Modernism we call Art Deco today. The asymmetric façade suggests a dynamic assemblage of components drawn together by projecting stucco bands. Eyebrows over the window are radiused to reflect streamlining.

940 Jefferson Avenue E71
Lawrence Murray Dixon, 1940

This modest but meticulously renovated Art Deco building was one of a series of similar buildings Lawrence Murray Dixon designed on Miami Beach. Each combines a "rule of three," or tripartite, façade organization and a miniature cupola centered atop the parapet. The front stairway is prominently featured through vertical strips of corrugated and clear glass above the front door, which is framed in a reasonable approximation of original black Vitrolite. Its dignified, gently stepping façade should be contrasted with the rougher and less street-friendly front of 945 Jefferson Avenue, the more contemporary structure directly across the street. The effect of streamlining is visible in radiused eyebrows and the cylindrical drums that frame the stair-hall windows.

Nola Apartments E72
927 Jefferson Avenue
1920

The Nola Apartments, though much modified, are a reminder of humbler times on South Beach, before the 1920s boom, when Miami Beach was planned as a leisure suburb and Miami residents were enticed across the bay by the hope of catching a sea breeze. It most likely began as a 1½-story masonry and wood bungalow, either simply framed or built from one of the ready-made bungalow plans available in the era.

Coronet E73
900 Jefferson Avenue
Lawrence Murray Dixon, 1940

Famously the canvas for a Victor Farinas 1980s Memphis Style coloring fantasy published in Barbara Baer Capitman's book *Deco Delights*, the symmetrical Coronet now illustrates a delicate color balance set off by the green quarry keystone framing its entrance portal, and is more in keeping with 1930s Miami Beach.

901 Jefferson Avenue E74
Henry J. Moloney, 1929

Several versions of this duplex apartment building, designed by Henry J. Moloney, were built in 1920s South Beach. In a vivid illustration of the area's evolution, this modest structure has been converted into a quadriplex, while the former garage and chauffeur's apartment at the rear have been transformed into a triplex.

1007–1009 Meridian Avenue   E75
Gene Bayliss, 1939

This L-shaped, 2-story structure is an example of the trend toward "walk-up" apartments common in 1930s Miami Beach.

Ambassador Court   E76
1008 Meridian Avenue
Lawrence Murray Dixon, 1945

This U-shaped building, like the nearby Helen Marie (E66) is a notable variation on Miami Beach's prewar Modern tradition of using residential building blocks to frame semi-public patios and landscaped gardens. Compared to the oblong box shapes of Brompton Manor (E67) and the Jade Apartments (E68), its community-oriented open spaces afford a generous advance in urban living.

Flamingo Plaza   E77
1051 Meridian Avenue
Lawrence Murray Dixon, 1937

A classic 1930s Miami Beach hotel inspired by Art Deco flourish, the Flamingo Plaza has a symmetrical and tripartite façade, with both vertical and horizontal design elements. Nearly all of the elements defining local character of the 1930s are here: eyebrows, glass block, tinted keystone, bas-relief of stylized tropical vegetation, neon, terrazzo, and a lobby mural of frolicking flamingos by Miami muralist Earl LaPan. (LaPan also painted the murals in the Essex House [E42] and Victor [E32] hotels.) The Flamingo Plaza is probably the most decorated hotel outside the environs of the oceanfront and Lincoln Road, an indication of the attraction of nearby Flamingo Park. Around are many similar buildings, few as fully developed as this, but all worth a moment to absorb and compare.

E77

West Avenue

Miami Beach pioneer developer Carl Fisher chose the city's bay front-age as the location for his grand hotels—the better to sell oceanfront land as valuable private estates. Between 1921 and 1925, the Flamingo, Floridian, and Fleetwood hotels were planted on large tracts of land. In the 1950s and 1960s, these were transformed into the high-rise Biscayne Bay frontage of South Beach.

Bentley Bay   E78
520 West Avenue
Arquitectonica, 2005

Bentley Bay occupies a prominent position on the approach to Miami Beach, framing (with Icon [E17]) the Miami Beach end of the MacArthur Causeway. It comprises two undulating towers (23 and 25 stories) that occupy a broad but shallow frontage between West Avenue and Biscayne Bay. A combination of projecting floor plates and eyebrows wraps each building, dissipating its mass and projecting a strong horizontality. The subtle distortion of building form is achieved by sculpting the projecting planes, producing concave and convex edges that suggest billowing sails. The floor-through apartments produce thin towers, but here one by-product is that the cores are located on the east frontage, turning a mainly windowless face toward the city (an effect mitigated by the projecting eyebrows).

The two buildings are connected by a partly covered plaza that forms a portal to the water and baywalk along Biscayne Bay. Extensive restaurant and retail space lines the pedestal on either side. To one side, the pedestal is shifted toward the causeway, allowing the walls of the north tower to come down to the ground. The parking garage is inventively screened with white metal poles in abstraction of bamboo, over which natural vines play. Rich landscaping is clearly evident on the amenity deck over the parking garage.

Bentley Bay occupies the site of Igor Polevitzky's iconic 1930s-era Gulf Station and Hotel, demolished in the 1960s during reconstruction and re-alignment of the MacArthur Causeway Bridge. This colorful landmark at the entrance to Miami Beach wrapped a hotel, restaurant, gas and service station, bait and tackle shop, and radio station around a symbolic lighthouse.

Southgate Towers   E79
900 West Avenue
Melvin Grossman, 1957

Among the first in the postwar trend toward large apartment buildings in Miami Beach, Southgate Towers offered facilities comparable to the city's resort hotels (at lower cost). Southgate was also the first major new building in South Beach during a period of decline.

The campus of two 14-story chevron-shaped tower slabs comprises 550 units of housing on 5 acres of land. The buildings are tied together by a central lobby on the ground floor, and share facilities like swimming pool, cabana club, restaurant, lounge, and garden. The project was developed by the Equitable Life Insurance Company, and most of its units were destined for the retired "snowbirds" who were beginning to dominate the area.

The towers employ a single-loaded design, with wide open-air galleries along their west frontage opening up on the water. The galleries are unusual in that they double as both access and terrace.

Mirador and Mondrian (Forte Towers)   E80

1000, 1100, and 1200 West Avenue
Melvin Grossman, 1964–66
Renovations: Zyscovich Architects, 2001

This integrated group of three 15-story towers originally comprised 1,100 units on a 10-acre residential campus. These were the Forte Towers, and replaced the grand Fleetwood Hotel. Melvin Grossman, preeminent Miami architect of tower apartment houses by the 1960s, designed the ensemble, as well as Southgate Towers, across Tenth Street to the south, and Morton Towers (now the Grand Flamingo) at Bay Road and Fifteenth Street. By distributing the complex's large number of apartments into three structures, Grossman produced his own context and environment for 930 linear feet of bay-facing amenities. The large bayfront deck, including three swimming pools, is bracketed by the L-shaped north and south towers, with the trylon-shaped center tower in the center. The deck tops a ground-level parking garage that stretches the entire breadth of the site. Second-level porte cocheres lend West Avenue a Modern monumentality. In 2001, the overall site was renovated into the Mirador. The most recent renovation has been the creation of the Mondrian Hotel (**E81**) out of the central tower.

E80

Mondrian   E81

1100 West Avenue
Marcel Wanders, designer, with Ralph Choeff Architect, 2006

Beginning in 2006, Morgans Hotel Group converted the center tower of
the Mirador (Forte Towers, E80) into the Mondrian Hotel. The conversion
marked a significant phenomenon: the return of luxury hotels to the bayfront at West Avenue, early center for some of the city's grandest hotels. In
contrast with the oceanfront, the city's bayfront offers views across Biscayne
Bay to Downtown Miami. The Mondrian was designed by Marcel Wanders,
whose branded touch set a radically new tone for the functional structure. The theatrical design, an interpretation, according to the designer, of
Sleeping Beauty's castle, included Surrealist furnishings, supersized architectural motifs, strong contrasts, and abundant use of patterning. A new
15-story mosaic mural faces West Avenue and features stylized floral designs.
So does the new grand stair, a dark, winding feature in an otherwise white
lobby. Here, floral designs were laser-cut into the guardrails.

Waverly at South Beach   E82

1330 West Avenue
Arquitectonica, 2001

Sited perpendicular to the shoreline, the 35-story Waverly is best appreciated from the west, where it appears to rise from the water's edge. Large
floor plates were truncated to make the tower appear as two separate but
overlapping slabs. The simple and inexpensive curving of the parapets
provides whimsy for the skyline. At street level, the design is less effective.
The multistory parking garage is directly visible and not well screened. Yet
the lobby entrance adroitly terminates the southward view corridor of Bay
Road, and a recessed arcade connects this entrance to West Avenue.

Flagler Memorial   E83

Monument Island
Ettore Pellegatta, H. P. Peterson, 1920
Restoration: STA Architectural Group, 2006

E82

Originally a spoil bank resulting from the dredging of a channel on the west
side of Miami Beach as early as 1913 (the channel created a motorboat race
course in Biscayne Bay), the spot became an island with permission from
the State of Florida in 1919. The rampant creation of islands for waterfront
homesites had transformed Biscayne Bay into an almost suburban lagoon
by the late 1920s. The Flagler Memorial was unusual, in this context, for a
city not given to grand civic gestures. Miami Beach developer Carl Fisher
named the island for Henry Flagler, the railroad tycoon whose Florida East
Coast Railway opened Florida's east coast to development and spurred
the incorporation of the City of Miami in 1896. Fisher, an admirer of Flagler,
believed himself to be following in Flagler's footsteps. To honor the latter,
Fisher erected a monument in the form of an obelisk surrounded by four allegorical figures. The figures represent prosperity, industry, education, and
the pioneer.

F

City of Miami Beach: Upper South Beach and Lower Mid-Beach

This section comprises Miami Beach between Fifteenth and Forty-fourth streets. It notably includes Lincoln Road, Collins Park, and the City Center area in South Beach. The area is bisected by the Collins Canal. To the north, lower Mid-Beach includes the commercial service zone west of Alton Road, the Pine Tree Drive corridor, and the beachfront districts extending up Collins Avenue. The Forty-first Street business district at the north end of this area forms a crucial east-west link between the beach and the Julia Tuttle Causeway (I-195).

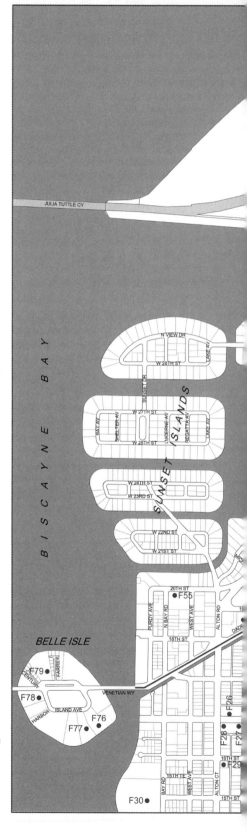

F. City of Miami Beach: Upper South Beach
and Lower Mid-Beach

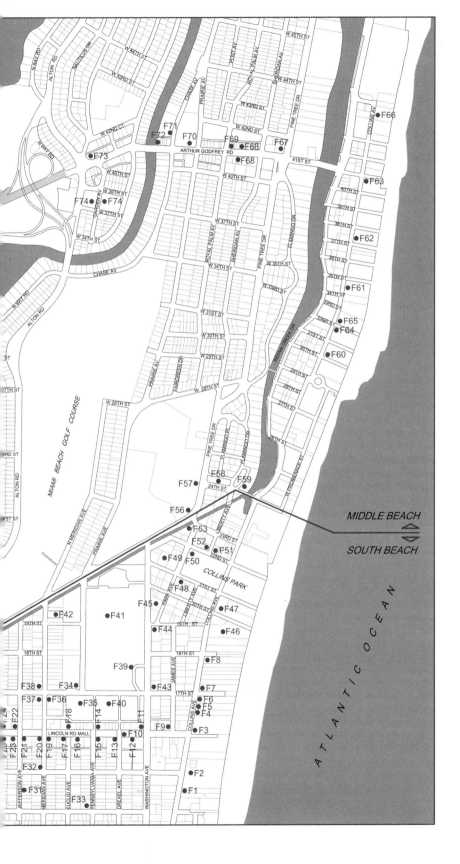

F1

Royal Palm Resort (Royal Palm and Shorecrest Hotels)

F1

1545 Collins Avenue
Arquitectonica, 1998
Shorecrest façade: Kiehnel and Elliott, 1940

Like the adjacent Loews Miami Beach Hotel (F2), the Royal Palm Resort was the result of a city-issued request for proposals for a convention hotel. Likewise, the request stipulated the retention of at least portions of architecturally significant hotels on-site. Unlike the Loews, however, no single proposal met both the city's financial requirements and the favor of an architectural selection committee. The impasse was broken by the Miami Design Preservation League, which championed a design by Arquitectonica. The Preservation League's support was based largely on the concept of dispersing the hotel into two separate towers replacing the rear portions of the 1939 Royal Palm and 1940 Shorecrest Hotels. Although the strategy of retaining only small portions of the significant buildings was questioned by some, the towers, oriented perpendicularly to the ocean, notably allowed views to the ocean and sky from Collins Avenue. In contrast to the historicist vocabulary of the Loews Hotel, this contemporary version of Miami Beach's stucco-Modern-fantasy architectural idiom is bold and refreshing. During construction, the existing Royal Palm was deemed structurally unsound and subsequently demolished. The front portion, as required by Arquitectonica's winning scheme, was successfully reconstructed.

Loews Miami Beach Hotel (including St. Moritz Hotel)

F2

Loews Miami Beach Hotel
1601 Collins Avenue
Nichols Brosch Sandoval & Associates, 1996

St. Moritz Hotel
1565 Collins Avenue
Roy France, 1939
Renovation: Zyscovich Architects, 1996

The expansion of the Miami Beach Convention Center in the mid-1980s (doubling its size) had to be matched, according to the prevailing political wisdom, with the construction of an oceanfront convention hotel in close proximity. A large open parcel along Collins Avenue, in the vicinity of Sixteenth Street, provided a central location with access to the beach that easily met the city's size and proximity criteria. The site had been created by the demolition of the New Yorker in 1981, the Poinciana in 1988, and the Sands in 1992 (all significant Art Deco hotels, the Sands demolished on the eve of its incorporation into the extended Collins Avenue Historic District). Generous public subsidy attracted sufficient responses to the city's request for proposals, which required the retention of Roy France's 1939 St. Moritz Hotel and the development of a parking garage. The winning entry, by Nichols Brosch Sandoval and Zyscovich Architects, called for the extension of Sixteenth Street from Washington Avenue to Collins Avenue in order to improve traffic flow and provide access to a new garage. The street extension required the demolition and relocation of all but the front portions of two architecturally significant hotels on Washington Avenue. The remnants of the Anchor and Pittsburgher hotels were eventually relocated and incorporated into the Washington Avenue façade of the parking garage. A neon sign from the Anchor Hotel now graces the glass-wrapped stairwell of the garage.

To its credit, the connection between the new Loews and the historic St. Moritz is handled well and allows the period piece to maintain its integrity. The historicist architectural vocabulary of the Loews ranges from the grand to the clumsy. The telescoping rotunda feature at the juncture of the two wings memorably fills the eastward view corridor of Sixteenth Street, creating a rare example in Miami of a terminated vista. Attempts at recalling 1930s Art Deco, however, did little to disguise its inescapable mass and bulk. In the old Miami Beach tradition of satisfying mass-market expectations, the interiors interpret luxury in an eclectic if incongruent confection of patterns, real and faux materials, and historical references.

DiLido Ritz-Carlton (includes One Lincoln Road Building and DiLido Hotel)   F3

DiLido Hotel
Melvin Grossman with Morris Lapidus and Associates, 1953
Additions and adaptive use: Nichols Brosch Sandoval & Associates, 2000

One Lincoln Road Building
1 Lincoln Road
Igor Polevitzky, 1949
Upper-floor addition: Igor Polevitzky, 1950
Renovations and adaptive use: Nichols Brosch Sandoval & Associates and Allan T. Shulman Architect, 2000

Formerly, along with the neighboring Sagamore Hotel (F4), part of Goodyear Tire magnate Frank A. Seiberling's estate, the DiLido Hotel was developed in the 1940s to 1950s, following the transformation of the east end of Lincoln Road into a thriving and increasingly commercial area. Igor Polevitzky's initial architectural proposal for the site, tentatively called the Center Building, would have established the kind of mixed-use, all-inclusive resort that Morris Lapidus later perfected at hotels farther up the beach. As it happens, the outline of the center was realized over the next ten years in three parts: the One Lincoln Road Building (offices and retail); the DiLido (hotel); and the Town and Beach Club (cabanas). All three elements figure prominently in the current DiLido Ritz-Carlton.

Polevitzky's design for a multistory commercial building lining the intersection of Collins Avenue and Lincoln Road was completed in two phases. It is distinguished by the wrapping cast-concrete brise-soleils that sheath its upper floors, a solution later reiterated by Polevitzky at the Downtown Miami Plaza Building (A30). Polevitzky later added a beach club and cabana colony at the eastern terminus of Lincoln Road. Finally, in the early 1950s, construction began on the DiLido Hotel. The commission went not to Polevitzky, but to Melvin Grossman with associate architect Morris Lapidus, the latter a rising star in resort hotel design at the time. Lapidus used the hotel commission as a laboratory, testing themes he would later use in solo productions like the Fontainebleau (G1) and Eden Roc (G2) hotels.

The lines of the DiLido respond to its unique siting, wrapping the One Lincoln Road Building and offering a unique double lobby that bent from Collins Avenue to Lincoln Road. Egg-crate façades on the hotel's narrow end walls are set off by lyrical features from Lapidus's "bag of architectural tricks": a serpentine canopy, cylindrical lounge, and thematically stylized signage. Its 2-story lobby had hanging mezzanines, bridges, and an open stair that wrapped the cylindrical entrance to the nightclub. A bowed feature wall set off the main lounge, which fed patrons to convention facilities, a banquet room, a nightclub, and a restaurant. When completed, the DiLido was briefly the largest and most complex hotel on Miami Beach.

In 2000, the hotel and accessory structures were joined, reconfigured, and substantially expanded to create the DiLido Ritz-Carlton. The main hotel structure was topped with 3-story additions rendered in dark glass. An expansive new ballroom was carved out of the office space of the One Lincoln Road building, whose service yard was transformed into a function court. On the ocean side, the Town and Beach Club was the template for two new cabana wings. The cabanas frame a grand pool deck that sits atop the complex's 2-story parking garage and stretches to the beach. The L-shaped lobby has been restored and adaptively used, in part for a restaurant.

Sagamore Hotel   F4

1671 Collins Avenue
Albert Anis, 1948
Additions and renovations: James Silvers, 1998
Lobby, public spaces, and rooftop penthouse: Allan T. Shulman Architect, 1998

The Sagamore Hotel's expansion and transformation into an "art hotel" have blurred the lines between hospitality and art patronage, a synthesis now nearly institutionalized by Miami Beach's yearly Art Basel festival.

Formerly (along with the adjacent DiLido Hotel [F3]) part of Stafford House, Goodyear Tire magnate Frank A. Seiberling's estate, the Sagamore's creation followed the 1930s commercial transformation of the east end of Lincoln Road. This postwar resort hotel hewed closely to prewar architectural conventions. It rose only 5 stories, had modest amenities including a generous front porch and a façade that mixed concrete eyebrows, quarry keystone cladding, and colored terrazzo. Yet the Sagamore also illustrates the evolution of hotel architecture immediately after the war. The building's asymmetrically composed, angled façade planes and projecting corner windows create a boldly dynamic play whose graphic effects include sky signage on the parapet. A thin concrete porte cochere projects from the façade to welcome cars. In the lobby, smooth, coved ceilings and wall planes highlighted with indirect tube lighting, and round columns enhance an austerely Modern space.

When the building was redeveloped in 1998, the former dining room was converted to a lounge, and the card room to a bar. The public interiors were extended eastward to create a gallery joining the streetfront lobby with the beach. Beyond the lobby, the sequence continued in a new video garden and pool area, framed by a new 5-story cabana wing. The hotel's extensive suite of public rooms provides a backdrop for the Sagamore Collection, whose rotating contemporary artwork includes paintings, works on paper, photography, mixed media, sculpture, and video art by emerging and recognized artists. Massimo Vitali's four-part series *Pic Nic Poker* (2001) lines one wall of the lobby, next to Roxy Paine's *Amanita Virosa Wall #4* (2001), which transforms the historic lobby desk with thermoset plastic and stainless-steel mushrooms that climb its upper surfaces. Spencer Tunick's photographic installation, just behind the lobby, features the Sagamore itself as the setting for an installation (curated by Kimberly Marrero). The abundant artwork amplifies the character of this hotel as a stagey, theatric space that celebrates modern transience.

National Hotel   F5
1677 Collins Avenue
Roy France, 1940
Renovation: Gail Baldwin, 1996

The most architecturally conservative of the "skyscraper" hotels that rise north of Lincoln Road, the National reflects a familiar and comfortable Modernism amalgamated with traditional details, like the rooftop lantern and cupola. The increasing importance of cars, even in prewar resort culture, is revealed in the circular drive and set-back porte cochere. On the inside, however, an impressive sequence of restored public spaces leads through the lobby and lounge to the rear porch. On axis is the hotel's signature feature, an elongated lap pool.

Delano Hotel   F6
1685 Collins Avenue
Robert Swartburg, 1947
Renovation: Philippe Starck, 1994

This postwar "skyscraper" hotel captures a moment in the evolution of tower forms in Miami Beach, halfway between the sculpted, tapered masses of prewar Art Deco towers and the bulkier, plastic volumetry of postwar resorts. The Delano's symmetrical, frontal composition, centered on a projecting front porch and crowned by winged finials, makes a striking ensemble with its flanking prewar neighbors. The body of the tower erupts in angular jaunts that reflect a dynamic spirit, but the stepping is also a practical device: it provides more rooms with ocean views and corner windows, and lightens the composition as well as the interiors. Befitting the formality of the Collins Avenue façade, the tall, relatively shallow, entry portico is in the prewar vein (that is, not designed to cover cars) and led to a succession of grand public spaces that flowed eastward toward the ocean.

Reformulated by French architect Philippe Starck in 1994, the hotel was for a time the paragon of South Beach chic. Starck radically transformed the interiors of the old hotel. Reinforcing its theatrical subtext, he opened the ground-floor spaces into a continuous axial hall sectioned by layers of sheer curtains—each section elaborating a separate function or identity. Out back, grand stairs lead through a garden to the hotel's innovative pool that thrusts from the ground and has a shallow zone furnished with a table and chairs. The Delano's cabana residences, a transformation of Miami Beach's habitual oceanfront bathing cabins into exotic pool-front luxury suites, set yet another standard and trend that would become common in this area of the city.

F5–F7

Ritz Plaza Hotel (Grossinger Beach Hotel)   F7

1701 Collins Avenue
Lawrence Murray Dixon, 1940
Renovation: Beilinson Architect, 1990

The Ritz Plaza is Lawrence Murray Dixon's most fully realized interpretation of the skyscraper aesthetic. The stepped massing of the Collins Avenue façade culminates in the two piers of the central window bay, which shoot up from the parapet. Its vertical thrust is offset by the taller elevator shaft behind, whose telescoping form, convincingly camouflaged in a composition of rectangular and cylindrical volumes, meshes the traditional imagery of a rooftop lantern with the modern suggestion of a smokestack. The narrow south façade produces a different effect, with a pair of monumental striped Classical pilasters rising full height from above the side entrance to an attic story formed by extending the two top corner windows an extra bay. The vertical proportions of the double-height lobby suggest the formality and pretension of public life in this otherwise modest middle-class resort. The vestige of an original mural map linking Florida and the Caribbean can be seen on the south wall.

The Ritz was built as the Grossinger Beach, the southern outpost of the famed mountain resort in Upstate New York, and evidence remains of the historic and sociocultural ties between the Miami Beach and Catskills hospitality industries. Although it was the first of the "skyscraper" Art Deco hotels north of Fifteenth Street to be renovated in recent years, it now sits an empty shell, its redevelopment interrupted by recent crises. It forms, along with the Delano (F6) and the National (F5), an extraordinarily rich and characteristically Art Deco skyline when viewed from the west on Seventeenth Street.

Raleigh Hotel   F8

1773 Collins Avenue
Lawrence Murray Dixon, 1940
Renovation: STA Architectural Group, 2007

The same year that Lawrence Murray Dixon explored Art Deco skyscraper iconography at the Ritz Plaza (F7), he exercised a more streamlined vocabulary at the Raleigh Hotel, at the opposite end of the same block. Where the Ritz exhibits a powerfully vertical, tapered massing, the Raleigh has a horizontal emphasis, with banded ribbon windows amplified at the streamlining of the building's prominent rounded corner. The effect is balanced by competing vertical features and a large glass window wall that centers the façade. The interweaving leads the eye upward to the squared-off elevator shaft and its monogrammed insignia.

In keeping with the Sir Walter Raleigh theme, Dixon introduced a Neobaroque decorative layer over the building's broader modern framework. First apparent to the visitor in the wood-paneled dining room beyond the lobby, the theme reaches a spectacular crescendo in the design of the swimming pool, whose configuration is based on Sir Walter's coat of arms. Done as seamlessly as a movie set, the hotel's theming presages the liberally ornamented resort hotel interiors of the postwar period.

The Raleigh's public interiors are among the richest and best-preserved in the Miami Beach Architectural District. Of note is the two-level lobby, whose central pillars are topped by florid Art Deco capitals. The pocket "American" bar is a tiny jewel box, a space once adorned with mirrors and frescoes of Sherwood Forest, and whose still-intact terrazzo floor features representations of martini glasses.

Albion Hotel   F9

1650 James Avenue
Polevitzky and Russell, 1939
Renovation: Studio Carlos Zapata, 1997

Rich in allegory and maritime allure, the Albion demonstrates the ability of local vernacular to generate sophisticated urbanism and a powerful iconography. Architects Igor Polevitzky and T. Trip Russell created a mixed-use resort complex whose smooth, streamlined skin blends hotel, retail, and office uses into a seamless whole. Ground-floor retail spaces and two levels of offices face Lincoln Road, while the hotel's 7-story tower block flanks the ocean. Smaller wings along the back and side of the property house a raised pool and restaurant with a rooftop "beach." The various components "pinwheel" about the interior courtyard whose streamlined intersection of building forms was once likened to the General Motors Pavilion at New York's 1939–40 World of Tomorrow exposition. In fact, contemporary newspapers advertised the Albion as the "Hotel of Tomorrow," a reference to the exhibition, because of its futuristic amenities and styling.

The Albion is a complex visual narrative layered with references to nautical, aquatic, and celestial themes, as well as to the ancient kingdom for which it is named. Porthole windows, a smokestack finial, streamlined corners, and open galleries at the roofline all work to create the illusion of an ocean liner in motion. The transparency of the double-height lobby's glass wall transformed the lobby into an allegorical aquarium set into the wall of the James Avenue façade. A three-dimensional celestial mural, cylindrical aquaria, and an armillary sphere that once graced a fountain in the center of the lobby have been stripped away over the years. However, a gold-painted relief of Neptune still graces the Lincoln Road entry to the building's interior court; columns in the lobby suggest strands of seaweed reaching to the water's surface. One can still see swimmers, like fish in an aquarium, through portholes in the courtyard at the end of the Lincoln Road entry passage.

The Albion's restoration in 1997 maintained most of the building's extant features, while introducing a floor-to-ceiling water wall in the lobby (at the location of the former mural) and a dynamic rework of the hotel's pocket bar.

F10

Lincoln Road Mall   F10

Lincoln Road between Washington Avenue and Alton Road
Morris Lapidus and Associates, 1960
Renovation: Benjamin Thompson & Associates, 1997
Renovation of 1100 Block: Herzog & de Meuron Architekten with Raymond Jungles, 2006

Lincoln Road is the civic-commercial urban centerpiece of Miami Beach. Initially developed by Carl Fisher as the commercial main street of his Alton Beach development, he named it (as he named his idea for a transcontinental highway) after his hero Abraham Lincoln.

Fisher was not a man of small visions. He cut a path through mangrove swamp to create a 100-foot-wide four-lane avenue connecting his hotels on the bay side to estates along the ocean. The avenue was lined with 20-foot-wide double sidewalks and palm trees. Completed in the late teens, Lincoln Road became the prestigious address for fashion and shopping that Fisher envisioned. By the early 1950s, the center of chic in Miami Beach had moved northward to hotels like the Fontainebleau, many with their own shopping, causing a decline in Lincoln Road's fortunes. In the late 1950s, merchants along the road enlisted Morris Lapidus, architect of the Fontainebleau Hotel, to revive Lincoln Road's glamour and commercial appeal. After all, it was the Fontainebleau, with its shopping arcade, that had dealt the first major blow to the primacy of Lincoln Road as an upscale shopping destination. Under his slogan "A Car Never Bought Anything," Lapidus proposed closing the road to create a landscaped "shopping park," or pedestrian mall. Lapidus's renovation, though compromised by budgetary constraints, endowed the road with a rich array of tropical landscaping, fountains, miniature yet audacious concrete canopies, and a new theatrical lighting scheme. The mall produced a brief upsurge in business, but by the late 1970s, it had fallen back into decline.

The nadir provided an opening for new cultural uses of this once-grand thoroughfare. A community of artists, under the leadership of Ellie Schneiderman, established the cooperative South Florida Art Center (now ArtCenter South Florida) in 1984. The cultural renaissance initiated by the Art Center, and followed by the New World Symphony at the Lincoln Theatre (**F14**), the Concert Association at the Colony Theater, and the Miami City Ballet at its former headquarters at 901 Lincoln Road (**F52**), reinvigorated the road as a public gathering place and as a center for culture and commerce. By the early 1990s, as Lincoln Road rebounded economically, planning began for its renovation. A majority of the property owners wanted to reopen it to traffic, but community pressure and the undeniable realization that revival had already been set in motion prevailed to save the pedestrian mall. The renovation by Ben Wood of Benjamin Thompson Associates variously incorporated and jettisoned aspects of Lapidus's original mall, yet retained and strengthened the street's pedestrian-friendly and civic character.

407 Lincoln Road (Miami Beach Federal Savings and Loan)

F11

Edwin T. Reeder Associates, 1955

This tall, dark slab is a conspicuous landmark at the eastern end of Lincoln Road Mall. When completed, the Miami Beach Federal Savings and Loan tower was a striking expression of postwar business culture in the heart of Miami Beach's resort/retail main street. It demonstrated functionality and progressive imagery, but also luxurious materiality, with its sheer walls, mixed black granite pilasters, and a graphically expressive curtain wall of alternating tones of blue and gray glass set between stepped aluminum mullions. Glazed black brick comprises the building's west façade, and a digital clock and thermometer that faces the four cardinal directions tops the building.

The ground-floor public areas are marked by a recessed pedestal with broad glass walls offset from the tower mass. Following urban tradition in this area, the lobby forms an arcade connecting Lincoln Road with the lane behind. Here, dark tones of black granite and marble are mixed with variegated blue and green mosaic tiles, wood panels, and mosaic tile artwork by Kay Pancoast, which adorns both the building lobby and the adjacent bank lobby.

F12

420 Lincoln Road (Mercantile National Bank Building)   F12

Albert Anis, 1940
Beach Theater: Robert Law Weed and William Pereira, 1946
Washington Avenue annex: Albert Anis, 1946
Drexel Avenue annex: Edwin T. Reeder Associates, 1956
Drexel Avenue mosaic: Dodson, 1956

The large office block as a viable building type for Miami Beach debuted here, at the strategic intersection of the city's two principal commercial axes, Lincoln Road and Washington Avenue. Originally the site of the 1916 Lincoln Hotel, Miami Beach's first full-service resort built by developer Carl Fisher, the Mercantile Bank Building marked the city's evolution from seasonal resort to full-service city. The all-business block required tenants to remain open year-round. A sober Modern Classicism, wrought in polished black granite, quarry keystone, and bright metal spandrels, wraps the building. The Lincoln Road frontage, a full block in length, is arranged about a shallow forecourt at the main entrance. Here the façade steps up to its tallest projection, establishing monumentality in step with its commercial and cultural ambition. In the double-height lobby, murals added by Russian cartoonist and artist Leo Birchansky in 1947 celebrate America's rise to prominence through industry, power, opportunity, and agriculture. The work is directly referential to the themes of the Depression-era WPA, although painted in the postwar era. Small retail spaces line the arcade that bisects the building, and an escalator ascends to the grand banking lobby on the second floor. The now defunct Beach Theater was located behind the offices and stores facing Lincoln Road. Its once-beautiful marquee has been lost, and the hall is now used as a television production facility. The penthouse office suite was linked to the S&G gambling syndicate that collected all horse-race wagers on Miami Beach from the late 1930s until the coming of the Kefauver Committee and its organized crime hearings in 1951.

The building received two major additions. The first, completed in 1946, extended southward along Washington Avenue and employed the Mercantile National Bank Building's original Modern Classical vocabulary. The second addition faces Drexel Avenue and was designed to extend the space of the bank. Mirroring the postwar role of the automobile, it also provided Modern drive-in teller facilities. Crowning the Drexel Avenue façade is the 2-story multicolored aggregate stone mosaic, which appears to depict the role of banking in support of the commerce and cultural life of the city.

Miami Beach Community Church   F13

Church: 500 Lincoln Road, Walter DeGarmo, 1920
Parish Hall: 1620 Drexel Avenue, Russell T. Pancoast, 1949

The story goes that Carl Fisher's wife, Jane, insisted that Fisher's planned community on Miami Beach would be incomplete without a church. Fisher was not a noted churchgoer, though he befriended many clergymen. When the church was finished, Fisher is supposed to have said to Jane, "Here's your goddamn church." The irreverent have kept the name alive. Anecdotes aside, Fisher had every reason to endow his new city with the trappings of culture, spirituality, and history.

Employing an otherwise rustic vocabulary, Walter DeGarmo created, in the entrance surround, one of Miami's finest expressions of the Spanish

Churrigueresque style. The ornate nature of the entry gives way to sparely appointed interior. While there is a place for a bell in the cupola, the Community Church relies upon an electronic carillon.

The Moderne-style parish hall behind the church was designed by Russell T. Pancoast and constructed in 1949. Perhaps the influx of soldiers and airmen from across the country during World War II had raised expectations that the Beach's traditional hedonism might be converted to more pious pursuits. The churchyard on the corner of Lincoln and Drexel is a singular opening in the otherwise continuous wall of storefronts that line Lincoln Road. Beyond the yard is the smaller parish hall entry court facing Drexel Avenue.

Lincoln Theatre   F14

541 Lincoln Road
Robert E. Collins and Thomas White Lamb, 1936
Adaptive use and renovation: Gerald F. DeMarco Architect, 1989

The collaboration of Robert Collins and Thomas White Lamb, a leader of American theater architecture, produced this remarkable urban hybrid of street-level retail space, upper-level offices, and full-service cinema theater. The building is also notable for the decorative flourish of its bas-relief panels, and for the deeply cantilevered marquee that projects into Lincoln Road.

The theater itself is concealed behind a block of commercial space but, through the monumental composition of the vertical and horizontal marquees, loses none of its identity on the street. The frontal marquee, flanked

F14

by narrow blade signs and topped by a floral tableau, counters the stream-lined thrust of the building's rounded corner, matched a year later by the Lincoln Road Office Building across Pennsylvania Avenue. The Lincoln along with the Beach, Colony, and Carib theaters made Lincoln Road an important venue for entertainment.

The Lincoln's monumental urban frontage on Lincoln Road, its large theater hall, and sufficient ancillary spaces made it an attractive home for the New World Symphony (NWS), founded in 1987 by the Arison family and Michael Tilson Thomas, who also serves as artistic director. The NWS acquired the building and converted it into a 750-seat orchestra hall. Along with the South Florida Art Center and the Miami City Ballet, the symphony was instrumental in the arts- and culture-based renaissance of Lincoln Road. Although the theater and lobby have been partly altered, the intact ellipti-cal lobby and vaulted theater retain something of the glamour of the earlier cinema. As of this writing, NWS is completing its new facility (**F40**) in the former parking lot behind the Lincoln.

Cadillac and Quittner Buildings   F15

546–560 Lincoln Road
Carlos Schoeppl, 1929
Additions: Giller and Giller, 2001

F15

The renovation of the Cadillac Building and addition of the 4-story Quittner Office Building behind it helped reactivate the corner of Lincoln Road and Pennsylvania Avenue. During the renovation, important bas-reliefs includ-ing emblems of two biplanes, a lightning bolt, and four halves of a 1920s Cadillac were revealed directly over the corner entrance. Other original cornice moldings were replaced with new castings that encircle the top outer edge of the first floor. The new office building has its entrance on the Pennsylvania side, and was set back to respect the scale of the original building.

Lincoln Center Building   F16

1637 Euclid Avenue and 630 Lincoln Road
Igor Polevitzky, 1937
Adaptive use: Mark Campbell, 2005

The Lincoln Center Building couples an ordinary streetfront commercial block containing ground-floor shops with a mixed retail and office building (formerly a hotel) that wraps the other three sides of the property, forming a shared patio court. The commercial block faces Lincoln Road, while the entrance of the former hotel fronts Euclid Avenue, a residential street. A projecting canopy over the hotel entry is topped by a cast-concrete sky-sign that announces the name of the building. The synthesis of the two building types pays homage to Miami's legacy of patio buildings while spawning a new mixed-use building type. The patio plays multiple roles, serving not only as an amenity for the building, but also as an extension of the public space of the street, inviting the shopper and passerby. A narrow commer-cial arcade from Lincoln Road and a small passageway from Euclid Avenue amplify the city's fine-grained circulation network. The transparency of the glass-enclosed lobby exposes the full width of the patio to Euclid Avenue.

In the patio court, the mass of the former hotel is lifted on pilotis, providing an arcade around the continuous shop spaces below. The relative austerity of the architecture was leavened by landscaping, and by an azul- and gold-tiled fountain in the center of the patio. The Lincoln Road mixed-use patio building type reached maturity only three years later at Polevitsky and Russell's Albion Hotel (F9).

In 2005, an adaptive-use project converted the Euclid Avenue hotel into offices.

Nexxt Cafe (Goldwassers)   F17
700 Lincoln Road
Lawrence Murray Dixon, 1937

This building's corner rotunda and spectacular curved-glass window-walls frame its corner doorway. The composition is a standout illustration of streamlining applied to a commercial structure. Number 1646 Euclid Avenue was once architect Lawrence Murray Dixon's office and, later, a headquarters for the Miami Design Preservation League.

701 Lincoln Building   F18
(Saks Fifth Avenue Building)
Igor Polevitzky, 1939
Addition: Polevitzky and Johnson, 1956

Built to replace the earlier Saks Fifth Avenue store located in the Mediterranean Revival–style Dowling Building at 826 Lincoln Road, this structure expressed asceticism and Modern Classical sophistication. The original building presented one tall story entirely clad in quarry keystone panels and stainless-steel vertical battens. A recessed entry defined by scalloped radius corners, as well as a cornice frieze topped by a projecting eyebrow, are the building's main decoration. The largely solid stone façade formed a backdrop for pin-mounted stainless-steel letters that spelled the store's name.

In 1956, two additional floors were added by Polevitzky; the superimposed addition continues the syncopation of keystone panels and vertical battens that marks the original design. The additions were also notable for the highly articulated rear façade on Lincoln Lane. With the departure of Saks in the 1980s, the building was reconfigured with a bisecting commercial arcade on the ground floor and offices above. In combination with a vaulted glass canopy over the entry, a large fan-window was later cut into the Lincoln Road façade, an insensitive concession to the fact that the building's upper floors have no windows.

BCBG Max Azria/Apple/En Avance   F19
(Chrysler Building)
734 Lincoln Road
Robert Law Weed, 1930
Restorations: Allan T. Shulman Architect, 2004, 2008

F19

Originally delineated in 1929 as a flamboyant Mediterranean Revival structure, the Chrysler Building was redesigned on the eve of its construction, and on the cusp of the aesthetic revolution wrought by the Modern movement in Florida. The result is one of Miami's earliest Modern retail buildings, whose styling can perhaps be described as "High Art Deco." It housed two specialty fashion shops as well as a Chrysler showroom on its corner (one of several automobile showrooms on Lincoln Road—see the Cadillac Building [F15] and the Packard showroom in the Sterling Building [F24]). On both the Lincoln Road and Meridian Avenue fronts, monumental entrance porticos were framed by stepped pylons connected by flared arches. Windows were hooded with decorative friezes and fluting, executed in precast concrete, or "cast stone." The interior of the corner store employs decorative terrazzo floors, stepped ceiling coffers, and a skylight to create a lofty retail space. The building shares a familial resemblance with Miami Shores Elementary School, a collaboration between Weed and Robertson & Patterson of the previous year.

The distinctive architectural features of the façade were largely stripped or concealed until 2007, when they were exposed and restored or reconstructed.

ArtCenter South Florida (Burdines Department Store)   F20

800 Lincoln Road
Robert Law Weed, 1935
Gallery and renovations: Allan T. Shulman Architect, 2005

This streamlined commercial block was built as Miami Beach's first Burdines department store. It was also intended to serve as the pedestal for at least five additional office floors that would be added as the economy improved (part of an incremental strategy by Miami Beach's Depression-era developers). The additions never materialized, and the building largely retains its original appearance. Its exterior is cleanly streamlined, with a broadly sweeping corner, metallic speed stripes, and a strongly projecting eyebrow cornice that exaggerate the horizontality of the building.

In the 1950s, Burdines moved to new and larger quarters on the corner of Meridian Avenue and Seventeenth Street. As Lincoln Road lost favor as a shopping center, the original building was chopped up to create multiple offices, and later found new life as a facility for the nascent South Florida Art Center as part of its arts campus on Lincoln Road. Initiated in 1984 by Ellie Schneiderman as an "an access point for artists, curators, and visitors alike," the ArtCenter transformed the building into artists' studios, galleries, and workshops. By the late 1980s, the ArtCenter occupied all or part of five separate buildings on then low-rent Lincoln Road. Consolidated today to two major locations (the other is at 924 Lincoln Road [F25]), ArtCenter South Florida continues to thrive as a center for art production, exhibition, and education.

The interior is now divided in two, but it retains Burdines' original double-height atrium space and wrapping mezzanine, the first of its kind in the city. The broad terrazzo steps that lead to the mezzanine are at the back. Tile work by Carlos Alves adorns the west entrance, and a new gallery is sited on the building's corner.

Van Dyke (Fisher Properties)   F21

840 Lincoln Road
August Geiger, 1925
Renovation: Carl Myers, 1993

The Van Dyke Building originally housed the offices of the Carl G. Fisher Company, the creator of Lincoln Road and a major generator of develop-

ment in Miami Beach. The building featured prominently as the logo for Fisher Properties in numerous
advertisements. Fisher was a publicity man turned
tycoon, and his energy infused every part of the
city—nowhere more than on Lincoln Road, which
was the centerpiece of his development vision.
With Lincoln Road, Fisher hoped to create an elegant shopping boulevard to match Worth Avenue
in Palm Beach or Fifth Avenue in New York. It was
on this boulevard that Fisher constructed a 7-story
tower for his own offices (his first house was at the
road's eastern terminus). The top-floor penthouse
has a balcony with views to the north, east, and
west, where the bulk of Fisher's lands lay. Here, in
view of the entire domain, prospective land buyers were given the final pitch. The building was
renovated in the 1990s and renamed Van Dyke, also
the name of the popular restaurant on the ground
floor.

F21

Victoria's Secret (Mead Building)   F22

901 Lincoln Road
Russell T. Pancoast, 1928
Restoration: Allan T. Shulman Architect, 2006, 2008

Originally called the Mead Building, this four-bay commercial structure featured two grand Moorish arched portals that sheltered the entrances to its
retail spaces. The portals, along with the tall windows topped with leaded-
glass lites, made this Mediterranean Revival structure a landmark on Lincoln
Road. When completed, it was home to New York–based Bonwit Teller.

Renovations in the 1950s removed the Moorish portals and the large
windows. The building functioned for some years as office space and then
as the headquarters and studios of the Miami City Ballet. Dancers famously
practiced behind the plate-glass windows along Lincoln Road. When the
ballet relocated to its new building in Collins Park (F52), the structure was
restored to its 1920s appearance.

Antique Dome Building   F23

910 Lincoln Road
Walter DeGarmo, 1929
East side addition: Russell T. Pancoast, 1940
Renovations: Ramon Pacheco with Puenta + Pila, 1995

Designed by Walter DeGarmo, important pioneer and practitioner of the
Mediterranean Revival style in Miami, the Antique Dome has something of
the character of a church. It was originally conceived to showcase an international collection of antiques, fine art, and jewels. Its noble façade was so
highly considered that it remained largely intact, even in the postwar era
of modernization and replacement. The interior, however, was reconfigured many times, in consideration of a series of adaptive uses. It served as
a stock brokerage in the 1950s, and later as a synagogue, a meeting hall for
Jehovah's Witnesses, and a restaurant/lounge.

F24

Sterling Building

F24

921–939 Lincoln Road
Original buildings: Alexander D. Lewis, 1928
Courtyard patio building: Alexander D. Lewis, 1929
Renovation and additions: Victor H. Nellenbogen, 1941
Rear office addition: Melvin Grossman, 1956
Restoration: Fabregas & Mann, 1985

While outwardly seamless, the Sterling Building is really a composite of independent structures and a microcosm of the process of accretion, renovation, and modernization typical of Lincoln Road from the 1920s to the 1950s. First built in 1928 by William Taradash, retired Chicago manufacturer of women's dresses, the structure was named the Taradash Building. Designed by architect Alexander Lewis, it comprised two independent Mediterranean Revival–style structures (one of which was the showroom of Packard Motors) with a 20-foot gap between. Within a year, Lewis added a retail patio court behind the original structures, creating a sheltered space entered through the gap between the two original structures.

In 1941, Victor H. Nellenbogen renovated the appearance of the buildings by joining them at the second floor, creating a recessed central block and covered breezeway to the patio. More dramatically, he created a new Moderne façade that restyled the structure according to the prevailing trend of streamlining. The chamfered corners that led toward the patio were replaced by smooth curves, and the previously asymmetrical façades were regularized. The storefronts were faced in tinted keystone, and curving plate-glass windows; above was a continuous frieze of glass block that, illuminated from behind, formed a colored backdrop for the tenants' neon signs. The frieze was capped by continuous planters, fluted keystone pilasters, carved stone coping, and textured banding of precast-concrete panels with inset black ceramic tiles. Since the 1941 renovation, the structure has been known as the Sterling Building.

In the postwar era, the patio was incrementally filled in with office space, although one fragment of the original Mediterranean Revival façade exists on its east side. The Wolfson Initiative Corporation restored the structure in 1985, and used part of the second floor as a private club for women called the Foundlings Club.

Nunally Building

F25

924 Lincoln Road
Kiehnel and Elliott, 1936
Renovations, alterations, and additions: Polevitzky and Johnson, 1950s
Linear gallery and western storefront restoration: Allan T. Shulman Architect, 2006

Originally home to Nunally's, a restaurant and candy purveyor, the Nunally Building reflects the Modern Classical style that was an intrinsic characteristic of the commercial/civic architectural mix of 1930s Lincoln Road. Bracketed by lower commercial storefronts on either side, its gabled central hall was one of the few buildings on Lincoln Road to step back from the road. The resulting forecourt, or "Cour d'honneur," allowed streetfront dining even before Miami Beach legalized it on the sidewalks. Nunally's recessed central bay once had a projecting stainless-steel marquee, mixed marbles, geometric-patterned terrazzo, and carved Florida quarry keystone walls with elaborate scrollwork that were a masterpiece of Art Deco styling. Behind the central bay was the restaurant's 2-story dining room, which opened to a private courtyard behind.

Following postwar trends, the building was carved up for less glamorous office uses, and its stone façades were modernized with corrugated aluminum panels and channel glass. Today, it is the administrative center for ArtCenter South Florida, which maintains studios and educational and exhibition spaces there. The original storefront partly survives in the two side wings, the western one of which was recently uncovered and restored. The linear glass gallery in the current entrance hall was installed in 2006.

1111 Building (Pioneer Bank)   F26
1111 Lincoln Road
Ferendino/Grafton/Pancoast, 1971
Addition/Garage: Herzog & de Meuron Architekten with Raymond Jungles, Landscape Architect, 2010

The combination of this commanding 1970s bank building and the ultralight tectonics of its new and famous addition make a compelling cap to the west end of Lincoln Road Mall (and a counterpart to the 407 Building on the east end). The bank building was decidedly set back from the corner of Alton and Lincoln roads, originally offering a plaza in the location of its demolished predecessor headquarters. The plaza capped the mall and set off the building's apparent height and weight, although the plaza was later converted to parking. The building has rather solid lower floors with projecting volumes and a second-floor balcony. The four upper floors form a permeable block bracketed by the pylons. The sculpted block features cast concrete with a ribbed finish at the rounded corner pylons, contrasting with the grid of lightly textured precast concrete window frames that surround its upper floors. Projecting balcony rails, also made of precast concrete, wrap the second floor. In the interior was a multistory banking lobby with six floors of offices and boardrooms above. Work by Florida artists Kay Pancoast, Dick Hartman, and Peg and Otto Holbein adorn the walls.

The multiuse addition on the site of the former plaza has been termed a "parking sculpture" by its developer, Robert Wennett. Designed by Swiss architects Herzog & de Meuron Architekten, it reworks the western gateway to Lincoln Road and tweaks architectural and urban assumptions of building type in new ways. The dynamically stacked plates of the structure (floor heights vary and are as large as 30 feet in areas) mix parking for 300 cars, ground-floor retail, five residences, and a rooftop dining complex. The irregular stacking of slabs is supported by an elegant grillage of angular piers, prismatic concrete shards that form a backdrop for the building's variety of sandwiched spaces. Glass boxes encapsulate enclosed areas like the residences, which are organized around landscaped courtyards. The most conventional aspect of the project is the ground-floor retail, which wraps the corner and opens up the partly opaque base of the original 1111 Building.

The 1111 Building redevelopment includes the remalling of the last block of Lincoln Road, originally included in Morris Lapidus's 1960 mall plan—transformed into a paved plaza in the 1980s and ultimately returned to a street when the road was renovated in the 1990s. Jungles's plan is a striking and more organic reworking of Lapidus's original formula that includes amoebalike islands of water set against a patterned landscape.

Banana Republic (Chase Federal Bank)   F27

1100 Lincoln Road
August Geiger, 1937
Renovation: Banana Republic and Allan T. Shulman Architect, 2005

The exquisite façades and interior spaces of August Geiger's Chase Federal
Bank mark a civic presence at the west end of Lincoln Road. The Modern
Classical box mixes black granite and limestone, and features a carved eagle
above its main entrance. A central portal of glass and aluminum window
wall frame the entry doors, which feature an applied metallic motif suggesting a money belt. Adaptive use for retail purposes retained the building's
sober monumentality, and creatively celebrated the overlap of old and new
uses.

F27   The restored historic interior includes extensive marble fittings, an
extraordinary marble stair, terrazzo with diamond-patterned accents, and
decorative metal fittings. The main elements of the banking lobby were
put to new uses: teller windows became cash/wrap counters, check-writing
tables became display platforms, and even the vault is the entrance to the
dressing rooms.

Regal Cinema   F28

1100 Lincoln Road
Zyscovich Architects, 1998

During its heyday in the years immediately before and after World War II,
Lincoln Road was home to several movie theaters; by the 1970s, all but the
Lincoln Theatre (F14) had been converted to other uses. In the early 1990s,
community discussions about Lincoln Road's revitalization emphasized the
generative role of a new movie theater. However, these discussions also

F28   raised issues about the impact of a multiscreen movie theater on the cul-
ture- and community-based renaissance of Lincoln Road under way since
the 1980s. After an attempt by the city to attract a movie theater to one of
the public parking lots north of Lincoln Road, a private developer moved
forward with this project consisting of 18 movie screens, a 287-car parking
garage, and 35,000 square feet of retail space. The project also included the
retrofitting of the adjacent Chase Federal Bank building into retail (F27).
Besides returning moviegoing to Lincoln Road's array of activities, the construction of the theater reanchored the important intersection of Lincoln
and Alton, which had lost its prominence with the demolition of the flanking Mediterranean Revival buildings that once framed the roads' eastern
gateway.

The cinema building is intended to be a theater "turned inside out." A
42-foot-high glass wall, compositionally divided into multicolored panels,
makes the theater lobby a participant in the life of the street. The glazed
circulation space mitigates the effects of a large windowless box in an urban
context, a strategy that works equally well at the nearby Publix on the Bay
(F55). The Regal Cinema's rounded corner, with prominent vertical and horizontal marquees, and the expressed metal banding of the façade, recall local traditions of streamlining. At night, the glazed lobby walls dematerialize
into patterns of color with varying degrees of transparency. Colored lighting
effects are also used to camouflage the large wall expanses facing Alton
Road.

Firestone Auto Center   F29

1569 Alton Road
John L. Lewis, 1939

In the land of eyebrows and cantilevered projections, this folly grabs the
eyes of passing motorists with a daring cantilevered canopy, presaging the
roadside Googie architecture of the postwar era. Restorative work has allowed this magnificent composition to continue defying gravity.

Grand Flamingo   F30

1504 Bay Road
Melvin Grossman, 1960
Renovation and expansion: Zyscovich Architects, 1998

This site, the western terminus of Fifteenth Street, was formerly the location
of the Flamingo Hotel. Its demolition and redevelopment in 1960 produced
two three-pronged 15-story towers embracing a central plaza.
    In 1998, the gargantuan high-rise apartment complex was redeveloped
with several new wings that infilled the parking lots along the site's open
margins. A new tower bridges the two existing buildings at the center entrance, supported on concrete piers of Corbusian inspiration and creating a
monumental portal to an inner garden. Townhouses line a Bay Road parking
garage, as well as the opposite bayfront parking garage, which is topped by
a health club.

Luna Mar (Temple Beth Raphael)   F31

1545 Jefferson Avenue
Gerard Pitt, 1965
Mackenzie Architecture, 2001

Luna Mar is an adaptive-use project that transformed a synagogue into
eight 2-story condominiums. The transformation from sacred to profane
largely preserved the original structure, including its projecting barrel-
vaulted entrance; its once-extensive symbolic mural art was sadly sacrificed
in the bargain.

Lincoln Terrace   F32

1600 Meridian Avenue
Lawrence Murray Dixon, 1940

Designed for urbanites in a tropical setting, the sophisticated plan organization of Lincoln Terrace shows Lawrence Murray Dixon at the top of his

F32

place-making form. Based on the narrow massing and walk-up–type unit organization initiated with the architect's earlier Harriet Court Apartments (F33), residential buildings evolved according to a series of formal experiments. The Lincoln's J-shaped plan creates an alluring and semi-sheltered courtyard space articulated with richly textured façades of tinted keystone, inset glass block, decorative metalwork, and ornate screen doors. Its balance of privacy, semi-public intimacy, and urbanity places it at the top of the evolutionary chain of prewar residential architecture.

Harriet Court Apartments   F33

1500 Pennsylvania Avenue
Lawrence Murray Dixon, 1935

According to contemporary accounts, Lawrence Murray Dixon's Harriet Court set the style of cross-ventilated apartments in Miami Beach. Although still reasonably tethered to the Mediterranean Revival style that dominated Miami Beach during the 1920s and early 1930s, Harriet Court evidences a new logic, where smooth wall surfaces, restrained use of ornament, and especially a functional plan organization veer toward the Modern. The building's plan arrangements are based on floor-through apartments, which abandon the traditional corridor organization typical in early Miami Beach residential building. Instead, it employs multiple walk-up stairwells, each of which provided access to a limited number of units. The stair halls connected the units to the garden, where they were marked with stoops, built-in planters, and decorative door surrounds that resemble turrets. By avoiding corridors, the building was narrower, and provided better-quality open space in the interior courtyard. Here, on a double lot, the narrowness of the buildings allowed them to be mirrored around a central court.

The Harriet Court complex was converted to condominiums in the 1990s. At that time, its patio court was privatized with fencing, and a pool and deck were added in an adjacent side yard.

Miami Beach City Center

The City Center area replaced the southern half of Carl Fisher's Municipal Golf Course, originally stretching from Lincoln Road across the Collins Canal to Twenty-eighth Street. Fisher sold the golf course to the city in 1930. In 1948, Seventeenth Street was extended from Washington Avenue to Meridian Avenue. After World War II, the City of Miami Beach followed a policy of locating cultural, civic, and administrative facilities in this area.

Miami Beach City Hall   F34

1700 Convention Center Drive
Grove-Haack and Bouterse, 1975
Renovation of ground-floor public areas: City of Miami Beach Property Management Division, ca. 1996

F34

Miami Beach's current city hall is one of the relatively few buildings built in the city during the 1970s. When the city administration outgrew its existing quarters at Eleventh and Washington (E59), a site for a new city hall was chosen on Seventeenth Street in the newly designated City Center area, adjacent to the Convention Center and the Theater of the Performing Arts. Notwithstanding its bermed ground floor and apparent mass, the new building was intended as a direct expression of accessibility and open government.

The completion of Boston's critically acclaimed new city hall in 1969 and concern for energy conservation in the early 1970s were influential in the structure's design. The offices of the city commission and city manager occupy the top and largest floor, with each successive lower floor smaller in size to reflect the hierarchy of the city administration, thereby also providing sun protection for the floor below. The ground floor is surrounded by earth berms for insulation. Interior functions are clearly articulated on the façade, including the 2-story pie-shaped commission chamber on the third floor, which breaks out from the building's volumetric potpourri.

A skylit, landscaped atrium serves as the central organizing space of the building, its dynamic play of curved spaces a signature element of the architect's built work. The atrium opens to the city along different orientations at the first, second, and third levels. Glass cabins run up and down the elevator core at its center, and bridges and hanging patios crisscross the open space to connect different areas of the building. While the arrangement of secondary spaces around a central atrium is revealed through glass walls, a means to make government feel open and accessible, the scheme lacks a sufficient sense of civic weight and of welcome. A reorganization of the ground floor and the addition of a colorful floor-tile mosaic by local artist Carlos Alves circa 2000 have addressed the latter shortcoming in a complementary manner.

The city hall was conceived as part of a larger civic center complex, of which the facing parking garage (F35) is another element. Bridges and raised walkways designed to connect the various elements of the civic center and activate every level of the city hall were never built.

Lincoln Road Parking Garage F35

Block bounded by 17th Street, North Lincoln Lane, Meridian Court, and Pennsylvania Avenue
Norman M. Giller & Associates, 1975

The Lincoln Road Parking Garage, with its Brutalist-inspired concrete expression, was designed to complement the opposite City Hall and emerging City Center district, while providing much-needed parking for Lincoln Road. Visual relief from the rectilinear envelope is provided by gaps housing the domed elevator towers wrapped by stairs with rounded parapets. Though now painted, its corrugated surfaces provide a rich texture that renders well in Miami's sunlight. The garage presents its most interesting aspect when viewed from Meridian Avenue, its floating parapets paralleling a kink in North Lincoln Lane.

Macy's (Burdines) F36

1675 Meridian Avenue
Robert Law Weed with Raymond Loewy, 1953
Renovation: Macy's, 2006

Like many postwar buildings in Miami Beach, Burdines manages to be both Modern and urbane. In 1953, this quintessentially Miami department store moved from its streamlined block at the southwest corner of Lincoln and Meridian to this new site a block north. Robert Law Weed's austere design created a machine for shopping. Eye-catching neon script signage beckoned drivers on busy Seventeenth Street and Meridian Avenue. Nevertheless, the store also retained a human scale with its cantilevered, wraparound canopy, a modern version of the arcades fronting Miami's prewar commercial buildings. The canopies, customary in Burdines stores of the period, also stored roll-down hurricane shutters. A 2006 renovation has restored much of Raymond Loewy's original interior design, including a soaring and undulating cove ceiling that stretches the length of the store from between the Meridian Avenue and Meridian Court entrances.

1688 Meridian Building   F37

Morris Lapidus, 1961
Martin J. Hyman & Associate, 2001

This 9-story office building just off Lincoln Road offers finely grained and detailed window walls that vary according to orientation, reflecting the exigencies of Miami's climate. Clear glass and gold-anodized window mullions form the basic skin of the building. On the north side, the glass walls are set flush with the structure, while on the east and west façades, they are set back behind projecting concrete slabs. On the east side, gold-anodized aluminum sunscreens, formed of a corrugated pattern of angled metal plates, hang from the projecting slabs. On the west side, the screens once covered the whole façade; they have since been taken down, and some have found new use just below, screening garbage and other services on the building's west façade.

The lobby entrance reflects Lapidus's original design verve; a bent canopy extends from the sidewalk into the lobby interior, and is partly suspended from above. The canopy was relocated southward in the 2001 project, providing a more substantial lobby entrance. The adjacent 2-story base impresses pedestrians with a rich palette of materials, including plate-glass windows, black granite column faces, Carrera marble, and mosaic tile. Interiors have been sensitively renovated with a complementary but contemporary blend of new mosaic tiles, copper, and wood wall panels.

Montclair Lofts   F38

1700 Meridian Avenue
Oppenheim Architecture+Design, 2005
Montclair Apartments (remnant)
Gerard Pitt, 1954

As an example of the sort of synthesis inspired by Miami Beach's historic preservation ordinances, this 41-unit residential building has distinctly contemporary elements that integrate a fragment of an older structure. The postwar Montclair Apartments form the nucleus. New 5-story buildings straddle either side and offer a nonfigurative assortment of slot windows that frame the older building, whose roof is reused as an open patio and pool deck overlooking the street. The masonry and glass walls of the new housing blocks are wrapped in perforated aluminum screens, an admirable response to the busy intersection, but also a reference to the abundant metal sunscreening found in this area of Meridian Avenue. The abstract treatment of wall surfaces in the new buildings contrasts with the traditional composition of the historic centerpiece.

Fillmore East at the Jackie Gleason Theater   F39
of the Performing Arts (TOPA)

1700 Washington Avenue
Henry Hohauser, Lawrence Murray Dixon, and Russell T. Pancoast and Associates, 1948
Renovation: Morris Lapidus and Associates, 1974
Mermaid sculpture: Roy Lichtenstein, 1979
Renovation: Borelli, Frankel, Blitstein; Sasaki Associates, 1988

The first component of Miami Beach's City Center area, as it is now officially
known, was the 3,500-seat Miami Beach Auditorium built in 1948. Mirroring
the direction of the city's economy in the postwar era, the auditorium
was designed for convention use in the off-season and entertainment
in the winter. It was originally quite close in design to the Dade County
Auditorium, built years later along Flagler Street. Though little remains of
its original exterior, the theater is notable for the collaboration of three of
Miami Beach's most prolific architects of the prewar era: Henry Hohauser,
Lawrence Murray Dixon, and Russell T. Pancoast.

    In the mid-1970s, Morris Lapidus transformed the auditorium into a
performing arts theater, a project that fits with his parallel work at the
Gusman Auditorium at the University of Miami and the restoration of the
Olympia Theater (A21) in Downtown Miami. Some fifteen years later, in
concert with the contemporary expansion of the adjacent Convention
Center (F41), the building underwent an extensive renovation, giving it its
current Postmodern appearance. In 1987, upon his death, the facility was
named after Jackie Gleason, who had taped his popular television show at
the auditorium in the 1960s. The theater has been renovated many times
over the years. On the theater's southside lawn, Lichtenstein's steel reclining
nude *Mermaid* (1979)—a lyrical piece that incorporates a real palm tree and
pool—is an ode to the city's resort image.

New World Symphony Campus Expansion   F40

Lincoln Road at 17th Street
Gehry Partners, 2008

The changing mission of the New World Symphony left its long-standing
facilities at the Lincoln Theatre (F14) inadequate. In 2007, Frank Gehry was
hired to design a campus expansion, including a new 700-seat performance
hall, practice and rehearsal rooms, and "technology suites," as well as a
600-car parking garage. The site is located behind the Lincoln Theatre, over
surface parking lots originally designated to facilitate Lincoln Road's transformation from boulevard to regional mall.

    The symphony hall, Gehry's first commission in Florida, is relatively
restrained on the outside. Contained in a sober yet subtly inflected white
box, it seems designed to reinforce rather than overwhelm its immediate
context. The architect's characteristic energy is mainly visible on the east
side, where the façade forms a virtual proscenium framed by a large metal
truss, and walls that inflect toward a grand window, effectively exposing the
internal atrium. The glass reveals a stacked series of 26 individual rehearsal
rooms and 6 ensemble rehearsal rooms that conceals the performance
space beyond. Cutting-edge electronic and media support are also part
of the plan. The new facility is designed to allow live video-conferencing,
Webcast, and panoramic projection for long-distance learning. The east

façade features a projection wall on which live concerts, master classes, large-scale images, and films may be viewed.

The symphony hall is part of Miami Beach's ambitious City Center Redevelopment Plan. The building will be a backdrop and stage to the new 2-acre City Center Park along its eastern flank. This park (originally slated to be designed by Gehry and as of this writing being designed by Dutch firm West 8) will create a vast public living room for the theater, and a viewing area for outdoor projection. It will also draw the nearby Theater of Performing Arts, Temple Emanu-el, Convention Center, and City Hall, into a new civic focus with Lincoln Road.

Miami Beach Convention Center   F41

1901 Convention Center Drive
South hall: Robert Swartburg, 1958
North hall: Gilbert Fein, 1968
Wraparound meeting rooms: Watson, Deutschman and Kruse, 1974
East expansion: Borelli, Frankel, Blitstein with Thompson Ventulett Stainback, 1987

As Miami Beach's already formidable hotel room count grew steadily during the 1950s, and as air-conditioning extended the tourist season, new ways of getting "heads in beds" became critical. In order to support the enormous hotel infrastructure that had developed, the hotels would need a constant stream of patrons in the off-season as well as the winter. While the promise of casino gambling—which figured into the design of such hotels as the Fontainebleau (G1), Deauville (H5), and Carillon (H6) hotels—was never realized, many hoteliers attracted convention business in the off-season. To this end, the Miami Beach Convention Hall opened in 1958, adjacent to the Miami Beach Auditorium (F39) in what was becoming the City Center district. Ten years later, in preparation for the Republican National Convention of 1968, the facility's size was doubled with the addition of a north hall. A "wraparound" of auxiliary meeting rooms was completed in 1974. In 1990, a renovation was completed that added two new halls facing Washington Avenue and increased the number of meeting rooms to 74, for a total of just over 1 million square feet.

The design of the 1990 expansion reflected and celebrated a new appreciation for the thematic Modern design of the Architectural District, while responding appropriately to the disparate environments of Convention Center Drive and Washington Avenue. The building faces Convention Center Drive and the parking lots to the west in a monolithic manner, while its Washington Avenue frontage places interior circulation spaces behind generous walls of glass. The massiveness of the structure is further mitigated by a complex layering of stepped parapets, glass-block clerestories, engaged flagpoles, and outsized porthole windows that evoke local Art Deco themes at a large scale. Successful integration of vegetation into the multilayered façade, in concert with an exemplary street tree scheme combining royal palms with canopy trees, further softens the building's large bulk. In an urbanistic near-miss, the interior circulation plan dictated that the imposing main entrance be placed slightly to the south of the center line of Nineteenth Street. However, a subtle gesture effectively terminates the westward view corridor of Eighteenth Street.

F42

Miami Beach Holocaust Memorial   F42

1930–1945 Meridian Avenue
Kenneth Treister, 1990

Conceived as an open plaza and reflection pool, and sculpted in stone and
bronze, this powerful memorial engages the intersection of the Collins
Canal and Meridian Avenue. Entering across a plaza of Jerusalem stone,
the visitor is invited to enter a loggia lined with etchings of historic photographs on the south and east sides of the memorial. At the center, there is
an invitation to understand the despair and horrors of the Holocaust and
confront the hand seeking aid where there was none. Exiting to the north,
the visitor passes a list of Holocaust victims, here remembered by their
family and friends since there is no possibility of a place of burial. At the
northwest corner of the memorial, a sculpted family lies dead. The memorial
invites reflection. In the words of the architect/sculptor:

> The totality of the Holocaust can not be created in stone and
> bronze . . . but I had to try. The rich diversity of the European culture,
> now lost, cannot be expressed . . . but I had to try. The murder of
> one and one half million children show joys turned to sorrow sud-
> denly on September 1, 1939, when World War II broke out, cannot be
> sculpted . . . but I had to try. . . . Six million moments of death cannot
> be understood . . . but we must all try.

Temple Emanu-El   F43

1701 Washington Avenue
Charles Greco and Albert Anis, 1947
Addition: Morris Lapidus, 1967

Until the completion of the kosher Blackstone Hotel at Eighth Street and
Washington Avenue in 1930, Miami Beach's Jewish community was not
welcome north of Fifth Street and was restricted from purchasing property
in most of Miami Beach. During the 1930s, however, the city's Jewish community grew and thrived, though it was still concentrated in the area south
of Lincoln Road. In 1938, several members of the Beth Jacob congregation
at Third Street and Washington Avenue (E18) formed a new congregation
and purchased a house at 1415 Euclid Avenue for use as their synagogue.

F43

By 1944, the swelling Jewish population broke the Lincoln Road barrier when the Miami Beach Jewish Center, as the synagogue at 1415 Euclid was then known, acquired land for a new facility at Seventeenth Street and Washington Avenue.

The site for the new synagogue was significant both for its prominence and for its proximity to what would become the city's civic center in the decades after World War II. When the synagogue was dedicated in 1948, it faced the recently completed Miami Beach Auditorium (F39) across Washington Avenue, and the parallel extension of Seventeenth Street westward. The temple's monumental architecture and rare civic prominence reflected the rising prominence of the city's Jewish community, but also a more self-confident and assertive population.

Architecturally, the synagogue is notable for its blending of Moorish and Modern Classical influences. The main entry features four fluted columns faced in burgundy-dyed keystone. The three transom panels above the doors display intricately detailed concrete grillwork that is repeated in vertical courses in the domed turrets to either side. The stucco facing is scored to give the appearance of large stone blocks.

In 1967, Morris Lapidus added the social hall on the north, facing Washington Avenue. Its façade emulates that of the original building in materials typical of the 1960s. The dyed keystone entry columns are reinterpreted in two-toned burgundy and white mosaic tile. The grillwork from 1947 is recalled through the use of screen block. The second-floor hall is accessed through a double-height foyer and nearly Baroque staircase ornamented with a subdued version of the gilded balustrades found in Miami Beach resort hotels and condominiums of the period.

Octagon Tower Apartments   F44

1881 Washington Avenue
Gene Bayliss, 1967

Facing the Miami Beach Convention Center, this 14-story tower derives its name from its unusual shape. A repeated square bas-relief panel depicting a stylized seagull decorates the exterior walls, which otherwise rise in a smooth, polygonal shaft. A small open-air atrium pierces the interior of the tower, providing catwalk entrances to the units from the elevator core.

Barclay Plaza Hotel   F45

1949 Washington Avenue
Kiehnel and Elliott, 1935

F45

Along with the nearby Governor Hotel, the Barclay Plaza was one of the grander resorts built to serve the golf trade along the east side of the Miami Beach Golf Course (now the Miami Beach City Center). It was also one of the first buildings in the Modern style by Kiehnel and Elliott, prolific throughout Greater Miami in the revivalist styles of the 1920s. The Barclay Plaza is unique in the Miami Beach Architectural District in several respects. Its L-shaped plan organization, massing, and ornamental program respond to its location on a midblock lot with frontage on two parallel streets. The prominence of the Washington Avenue frontage relates to the Miami Beach Golf Course across Washington Avenue. Facing the golf course in the westernmost façade is one of the finest Art Deco compositions in Miami Beach. The tripartite composition is crowned by a crisply articulated stepped parapet, which is countered in the concave by a ziggurat-shaped incision over the upper-most of the stairwell windows. Narrower window bays to either side of the stairwell bay reinforce its verticality. The spandrel panels display reliefs of the frozen fountain motif, symbol of the 1925 Paris Exposition of Modern Industrial and Decorative Arts. The doorway at the base of the stairwell is bracketed by a pair of Modern Classical pilasters supporting a rounded, projecting ziggurat crown. Thin, cantilevered balconies with exquisitely detailed horizontal railings flare outward from the central bay to engage the two recessed bays to either side. Contrasting with these delicate formal gestures are the cantilevered balconies on the building's south side, which are generous in size and supported by bold, mushroom-shaped columns. The Park Avenue façade is subdued in contrast to the showy compositions along Washington Avenue. Once entered, however, the lobby is a complete anomaly with its wall and ceiling surfaces faced entirely in intricate dark-toned woodwork.

Collins Park

The Collins Park neighborhood stretches from Nineteenth Street to Twenty-third Street, and from Washington Avenue to the Atlantic Ocean. It represented the southern end of the Collins and Pancoast holdings and, as demarcated by the change in grid pattern, was developed as a discrete subdivision by their Miami Beach Improvement Company. The defining feature of the neighborhood is a park on land that was donated by the Collins Pancoast interests before the founding of Miami Beach.

The developers donated a swath of beachfront land between today's Twenty-first and Twenty-second streets to the City of Miami for use as a park. In 1920, ownership of the park passed to the five-year-old City of Miami Beach, and, upon Collins's death in 1928, a library named in his honor was proposed for its west end. The siting of the library reinforced the park's symmetrical plan, providing the city a grand, axial public open space with rows of trees and garden parterres that led to the Atlantic Ocean. Two parking lots were carved out of the eastern end of the park but maintained the central axis. In 1962, the park was further diminished when A. Herbert Mathes's new library was built. The postwar building, sited between the Russell Pancoast building and Collins Avenue, turned its back on the old Collins Library, destroying the axial vista and unceremoniously isolating the older building behind the blank service wall of the new.

After deciding to demolish the 1962 library and construct a new regional library in this neighborhood (alternative sites in less well-endowed North Beach were briefly considered), attention turned to the urban strategy of rehabilitating the park and its surrounding urban fabric. In 2003, upon completion of the new Miami Beach Regional Library (**F51**) at Twenty-first Street and Liberty Avenue, the 1962 library was largely demolished and improvements to the park are under way.

The opening of the park reestablished the historic relationship of the Bass Museum building (original library) to Collins Park and the ocean beyond. Around the park, former gaps in the urban fabric have *been plugged with both civic and private development. The Miami City Ballet and Miami Beach Regional Library form the northern edge of the park. Arte City, a residential development, reinforces the park's western edge, while the Plymouth Hotel across from the park's southwest corner has become the residence of the New World Symphony musicians. A mixed-use residential block amplifies a commercial stretch that included famed restaurant Wolfies and the nightclubs Déjà Vu and La Escuela. The W Hotel marks the park's terminus at the Ocean Drive.*

Shore Club   F46
1901 Collins Avenue
Renovations, additions, and new structures: David Chipperfield, 1998

Sharalton Hotel
110 20th Street
Robert Taylor, 1939

F46 Shore Club Hotel
Albert Anis, 1949

The Shore Club combines the postwar Shore Club Hotel and the prewar Sharalton Hotel, with a slender new 21-story tower on the ocean side. The synthesis, by British architect David Chipperfield, maintained public features of the original hotels while instilling a new minimalist aesthetic marked at points with lavish materials and visual effects. The pivot of the new complex is the white cubic shaft of the tower, which literally joins the two older structures. Cut away at the penthouse level, the tower contrasts with the heavier bulk of the nearby Setai, which was built under earlier and more generous zoning allowances. The base of the tower has its suite of dining and lounge facilities (including a Nobu restaurant) notable for their use of stone, metal, and wood.

    The hotel's sequence of public spaces starts from the Shore Club's historic lobby, an austere space whose broad expanse of unpatterned terrazzo is accentuated by amorphous draped seating islands. A backlit wall sculpture is the lobby's only decoration. Behind, a rear court leads to the dining terraces, and a suite of pools, cabanas, and outdoor pavilions.

Setai Hotel (Dempsey-Vanderbilt)   F47
2001 Collins Avenue
New tower and replication: Schapiro Associates, 2006

The 1940 Dempsey-Vanderbilt, designed by Henry Hohauser, was one of the largest and grandest hotels of its era in Miami Beach and the only building in the city to be honored by the Royal Institutes of British Architects (RIBA) by inclusion in the London Collection. Comprising an entire block of Collins Avenue, the hotel tower stepped away from Collins Park, instead wrapping the corner of Twentieth Street. A single-story commercial base, originally Miami Beach's outlet of the famed Jack Dempsey Restaurant and Bar, breaks away from the tower, defining the sidewalk with chamfered corner pavilions. The building's base and tower are elegantly articulated, balancing an overall horizontality with discreet moments of vertical monumentality. Geometric carvings in cast stone adorn the hotel's precise stucco work, rising to a crescendo over the central block on Collins Avenue.

A plan to redevelop the property as a Setai Hotel included the renovation of the Dempsey-Vanderbilt, as well as the addition of an oceanfront tower on Twentieth Street. During construction, the structure of the old hotel was found severely deteriorated, and subsequently demolished. Like the Royal Palm (F1), the strategy evolved toward replication of the Dempsey-Vanderbilt with a new structure.

Of note are the reworked public interiors, which are spacious and richly appointed. A formal court was created at the rear of the hotel, and almost contemplative space centered on shallow pools. A series of oceanfront pools multiplies opportunities to see and be seen. Less successful is the new tower, whose tremendous glassy bulk seems to hover precariously.

Plymouth Hotel   F48
326 21st Street
Anton Skislewicz, 1940

F48

Typical of the work of Anton Skislewicz, the powerful façade of the Plymouth derives its aesthetic appeal from the articulation of its volume and mass rather than ornamental flourish. Here Skislewicz evoked the dynamic imagery and futuristic spirit of the 1939–40 World of Tomorrow exposition in New York. The dramatic corner pylon, which houses the elevator, appears as a prow, crashing through the prismatic and elliptical volume that is the volumetric extension of the space of the lobby. The areas closest to the central drum seem machine-cut from the volume of the structure. Within, an extraordinary mural by Ramon Chatov depicts escapist themes of life on an island off the coast of Miami Beach. The bacchanalia of enchanted dancers, a guitar-playing musician, sublime plant life, and a ravaged lifeboat set the tone for life in the hotel, and bring to mind the idealist paintings of Claude Lorrain and Nicolas Poussin. A second mural, hidden in a room adjacent to the library, adds a Latin subtext. Since 1988, the Plymouth has been a dormitory for the musicians of the New World Symphony (see Lincoln Theater [F14] and New World Symphony Campus Expansion [F40]).

Arte City   F49
2140 Park Avenue
Arquitectonica, 2007

Governor Hotel
435 21st Street
Henry Hohauser, 1939

This residential complex, inspired by the rebranding of Collins Park as an arts district, includes the redevelopment of most of a block between Park and Washington avenues, and between Twenty-first and Twenty-second streets. Anchoring the project is the Governor Hotel, a grand yet low-slung Streamline Moderne hotel created to serve the golf trade using the nearby Municipal Golf Course, originally located just across Washington Avenue. The Arte City project essentially weaves through the block, filling open and interior spaces to create a unified complex. One portion faces the Bass Museum across the prominent intersection of Park Avenue and Twenty-first

Street, while another faces the Collins Canal at the end of Twenty-second Street. The complex features walls set off by undulating parapets that function partly as balconies.

Bass Museum of Art (John Collins   F50 Memorial Library and Art Center)

2121 Park Avenue
Russell T. Pancoast, 1930
South wing addition: 1937
North and south wing additions: Russell T. Pancoast & Associates, 1950
Conversion to museum: Robert Swartburg, 1962
Addition and rehabilitation: Arata Isozaki and Associates with Spillis Candela DMJM, 2000

Completed in 1930, the John Collins Memorial Library and Art Center was designed by Collins's grandson, Russell Pancoast, a prolific local architect most famous at the time for commercial buildings on Lincoln Road and luxurious private villas. One of the first Art Deco structures in Miami Beach, the Library and Art Center drew inspiration from Paul Philippe Cret's Folger Shakespeare Library, a critical source of America's Modern Classicism built one year earlier within the monumental core of Washington, D.C. The Collins Library is clad entirely in keystone with a monumental loggia and carved bas-relief ornament by Gustav Bohland presenting a triptych of symbols of nature and progress in Greater Miami. The center panel featured a stylized pelican and mangroves, while the other two depicted the ships of the first European visitors to South Florida and the wonders of modern Miami: an ocean liner, Pan Am flying clippers, Henry Flagler's railroad to Key West, radio transmission antennas, and the Miami skyline. Bohland also sculpted the stylized seagulls that adorn the building's corners. The center section, fronted with a monumental entry loggia, opened in 1934. In 1937, the south wing and second-floor art gallery were completed. South, north, and west wings were added incrementally. All of the additions through 1950 were designed by Pancoast. In 1962, when the library was moved to the new building by Herbert A. Mathes just to the east, Robert Swartburg was hired to design the conversion to the Bass Museum of Art.

F50

A major expansion of the Bass Museum by Arata Isozaki with Spillis Candela DMJM was completed in 2002. The expansion, the first of two planned phases, maintained the prominence of the monumental east façade, but reoriented the building toward Park Avenue, with a new entrance and second-level wing projecting above a ground-level pool and sculpture garden. In the park, only the exhibit hall and meeting room of Mathes's midcentury survive. The drumlike hall is sheathed in a three-dimensional sand-cast mural by sculptor Al Vrana. (Vrana used the library commission to experiment with sand-casting techniques, molding concrete into narrative murals that were integrated into the skin of the façade.) The mural artwork, described by Vrana as "non-objective symbolism," was meant to add gravitas to Miami Beach's Collins Avenue, where kitsch resort architecture is more common. The panels interpret the role of books in human growth from man's origins to the future. The drum form of the hall sits in a circular pool, designed both to cool the condenser water of the building's air-conditioning system and to throw playful accents of light on the concrete relief at night.

Coupled with the construction of the home of the Miami City Ballet and the new regional library, the improvements, referred to as the "cultural campus," have energized a once moribund quarter of South Beach.

Miami Beach Regional Library   F51

227 22nd Street
Robert A. M. Stern Associates, 2004

F51

Once the site for Miami Beach's new regional public library was decided, Robert A. M. Stern was selected to design the structure. Stern interpreted Collins Park as a town square, and his design for the city's regional library indeed functions as a civic building. Like many buildings in Miami Beach, the volumetrics of the library are a simple interplay of rectangular boxes. The building is at turns Classical and relaxed, communicating just enough civic presence without overwhelming its neighbors. Its focal point is a Modernist portico supported on a single column. The portico responds to the opposite corner entryway of the Miami City Ballet (MCB) in what the MCB's Artistic Director Edward Villela called "a strong reciprocal gesture, our Fred to their Ginger." The move frames Collins Park's main cross-axis: Liberty Avenue.

The library taps into Miami Beach's particular Modernist traditions. Glazed ceramic and terra-cotta details are used in the wainscot, spandrels, and cornice fascia of the building, and cast-stone bases, decorative friezes, and earth-toned concrete panels decorate the façade. These details reflect the colors and textures of the city without literally repeating its most common features. Of special note is the band of blue tile that carries a wave motif across the length of the façade. A nearly 3-story-high central atrium, projecting on the outside of the building, is lit by corner windows in the clerestory. Behind, the courtyard includes a more intimate plaza, whose fountains are cloistered from surrounding streets by perforated masonry walls, and wrapping benches and trellises.

Miami City Ballet   F52

2200 Liberty Avenue
Arquitectonica, 2000

From its founding studios in the former Bonwit Teller space at 901 Lincoln Road (F22), where it grew out of the 1980s arts revival there, the Miami City

Ballet (MCB) relocated to new, larger facilities facing Collins Park, bolstering Miami's plans to develop a cultural campus in that area. Along with the library, the building's siting reinforced the objectives of the city, which were to open the park and complete the urban walls that define it. The 3-story structure houses the ballet's studios, school, administrative offices, and the Lynn and Louis Wolfson II Theatre. It also houses production offices, a costume shop, and storage. The basic block of the building is relieved by a subtle corrugation in the southeast façade—a freehand gesture forming a curved corner on its southeast façade that orients the entrance and fronting plaza toward the corner of Twenty-second Street and Liberty Avenue.

When the ballet studios were on Lincoln Road, a memorable feature was the plate-glass window wall that allowed passersby to follow practice sessions. That feature was preserved in the ballet's new quarters, which have broad ground-floor windows facing Collins Park.

2228 Park Avenue   F53
Oppenheim Architecture+Design, 2006

Comprising two 4-story townhouses on a narrow lot between the Collins Canal and Park Avenue, 2228 Park illustrates a comparatively recent phenomenon in urban infill: luxurious vertical residences. The well-conditioned skin features abundant glass facing north, and a perforated metal cladding system etched with tiny figures of trees, butterflies, and flowers. The delicate effect of these screens mitigates the initial impression of sheer boxiness. The upper half of the façade incorporates a deeply recessed loggia.

Mid-Beach

Mid-Beach, also known as Middle Beach, encompasses the area of Miami Beach between Twenty-third and Sixty-third streets, as well as several residential islands in Biscayne Bay and Indian Creek. It comprises three basic development patterns: high-rise hotels and residential condominiums along the Atlantic Ocean; single-family detached homes west of Indian Creek; and the east-west commercial corridor at Forty-first Street anchored on its west side by Mount Sinai Medical Center, a major hospital complex. Mid-Beach, with its combination of high- and low-density areas, is the political fulcrum of Miami Beach. Mid-Beach can be divided into two areas: Lower Mid-Beach and Upper Mid-Beach. Lower Mid-Beach stretches from Twenty-third Street to Forty-fourth Street.

Publix on the Golf Course   F54
1045 Dade Boulevard
Charles N. Johnson, 1962

America's mid-twentieth-century fascination with speed found inspiration in the swept- and delta-winged military jets of the air force and navy. One of the most vivid architectural evocations of jet wings was the "bat-wing" design of Publix Supermarkets of the 1950s and 1960s. The bat wings are an almost literal representation of a jet, its wings spreading above the supermarket entrance. The stylish design package included glass-block and

F54

F55

black-marble facing on the ground level, as well as extensive neon to grab the attention of passing motorists at night as well as during the day. The vast majority of the bat-wing Publix stores have been updated over the intervening years to reflect changing tastes. While the building has not been officially protected, Miami Beach's preservation ethos and acceptance of its role as a steward of twentieth-century architecture suggests that this Publix will ever remain ready for takeoff.

Publix on the Bay   F55

1920 West Avenue
Studio Carlos Zapata, 1997

As developable land in Miami Beach becomes scarce, urban solutions to typically suburban building types are called for. Here, two levels of parking have been placed on the roof of a Publix supermarket, allowing an otherwise sprawling building and parking lot to occupy a relatively small lot. Designer Carlos Zapata wrapped the building envelope with circulation, both vehicular and pedestrian. Sculptural, cantilevered automobile ramps face east and south, while a fire escape marks the west façade. Most notable is the north face, consisting of a billowing open-air glass and metal volume recalling a ship's hull, topped by a cantilevered roof that resembles an airplane wing. The volume shelters, yet exposes, the moving rampway carrying shoppers with filled shopping carts to the parking levels, turning their activity into public theater. Along with the surrounding Sunset Harbour condominiums and townhouses, Publix on the Bay is part of the transformation of this former service district into a mixed-use neighborhood.

Fire Station No. 2   F56

2300 Pine Tree Drive
Robert Law Weed, 1938

When this building was completed in 1938, the *Miami Herald* ran a piece about it titled, "Yes, Sir, It Is a Fire Station." This small, residentially scaled structure, built with PWA assistance, comprises a hybrid of monumental civic features and quietly discreet residential ones. The center block originally accommodated fire trucks on either side of a semicircular colonnaded portico. Smaller side wings are attached on either side, maintaining a sense of symmetry. Above soars the drill tower, a streamlined pylon that features lines of glass block and a wraparound balcony. The complex is aligned with the bridge crossing the Collins Canal at Twenty-third Street, creating a terminated vista.

Hebrew Academy   F57

2400 Pine Tree Drive
Morris Lapidus, Harle, Liebman with Connell, Pierce, Garland & Friedman, 1961

This private day school is part of a group of facilities including Miami Beach Senior High and Fire Station No. 2 (F56) located north of Dade Boulevard on the former grounds of the Miami Beach Golf Course. Its 23 classrooms, auditorium, library, chapel, and cafeteria are clustered around patios and joined by covered walkways. The building is notable for the repetitive use of concrete channel roof forms, whose corrugations provided a stylish and low-cost canopy for the activities of the school.

Miami Beach Woman's Club   F58

2401 Pine Tree Drive
Russell T. Pancoast Architect, 1933

Fashionable women's social clubs were a fixture of Greater Miami (see B61 and C11) in the early part of the twentieth century. Like other clubhouses built around the same time, the Miami Beach Woman's Club emulates early 1930s high-end residential architecture, mixing Mediterranean Revival styling with hints of modern detailing. The club is a vestige of the Mid-Beach section's first incarnation as an exclusive enclave of wealthy gentiles. Across Pine Tree Drive, where the Hebrew Academy stands today, originally lay the northern reach of the Municipal Golf Course. The lands to the east were filled with apartment buildings beginning in the boom of the late 1930s. The building was ceded to the Wolfsonian-FIU (E56) in the 1990s. At this writing, the building is in ruins as a result of a fire.

Helen Mar   F59

2421 Lake Pancoast Drive
Robert E. Collins, 1936

Dominating the west bank of Lake Pancoast, the Helen Mar is one of the best examples of Art Deco architecture in Miami Beach. This stubby tower recalls the proportions of Deco residential buildings along Central Park West in New York and the Argyle on Sunset Boulevard in Los Angeles. Facing west, the building displays a relatively simple massing. Facing Lake Pancoast and Collins Avenue, the rectangular volume sets off the bay window of the penthouse, which rises to form an elaborate headdresslike parapet. The effect is enhanced by the individual balconets projecting from each window. The penthouse contains one of the most lavish apartments on the entire island, with 15-foot-high, coffered ceilings in the genuine Parisian Art Deco manner. At the ground level, the stucco facing is incised with horizontal bands of black Vitrolite.

F59

Mid-Beach Art Deco Tower Hotels

Palms Hotel (Sea Isle Hotel)   F60
3025 Collins Avenue
Roy France, 1940
South wing addition: Roy France, 1950
Renovations: Mark Campbell, 1991

Versailles Hotel   F61
3425 Collins Avenue
Roy France, 1941
Addition: Roy France & Sons, 1955

Cadillac Hotel   F62
3700 Collins Avenue
Roy France, 1940
Addition: Melvin Grossman, 1956
Renovation: Kobi Karp Architecture & Interior Design, 2001

Crown Hotel (Lord Tarleton Hotel)   F63
4041 Collins Avenue
Victor H. Nellenbogen, 1940
Addition: ca. 1958
Addition and partial reconstruction of original: STA Architectural Group, 2003

While the charm of Ocean Drive is indisputable, Miami Beach's grandest Art Deco grouping may have been along the stretch of Collins Avenue between Thirtieth and Forty-first streets on the ocean side. Four hotel towers the size and shape of the Ritz Plaza occupy full block-size properties with gardens and pool decks surrounding them to the east and south. The homage to the

F61

New York skyline that South Beach hoteliers of the 1930s tried to sell with Art Deco trinkets on 2- and 3-story buildings pales in comparison with the syncopation of carefully formed mini-skyscrapers in this district. Unfortunately, in the 1950s, the towers received additions that obliterated their gardens and transformed them from simple vertical towers to lot-filling behemoths, covering over or erasing completely their distinctive street presence.

After the area became part of the John S. Collins Waterfront Historic District in the late 1990s, two of the four hotels underwent interesting rehabilitations, and one of them received yet another addition. At the Cadillac, the original tower was freed of the screen-block wall that masked its original grand entrance. At the Crown, the lower portion of the tower was completely reconstructed, to breathtaking effect. A new addition respects the original tower.

Sans Souci Hotel   F64

3101 Collins Avenue
Roy France with Morris Lapidus, 1949
Renovation: Martin J. Hyman & Associate, 1996

The Sans Souci opened a year after its neighbor the Saxony (F65). Its clean, rectilinear design was even more Modern than the earlier hotel. Morris Lapidus made his debut in Miami Beach here when the hotel developers brought him in midway through design to improve upon what Roy France had proposed. The unprecedented popularity of both the Sans Souci and the Saxony set the tone for future hotel design in Miami Beach as well as Las Vegas.

F64

Saxony Hotel   F65

3201 Collins Avenue
Roy France, 1948
Rear addition: Roy France, 1958
Renovation and addition (permitted): Revuelta Vega Leon, 2005

Though eclipsed by the larger resort hotels of the 1950s, the enormous success of the Saxony represented a milestone in the evolution of the American
resort hotel. Although impressive new hotels like the Delano (F6) and the
Sherry Frontenac (H4) had opened since the end of World War II, the Saxony
eschewed the tapered Art Deco massing and representation that had been
ubiquitous before World War II in favor of a vocabulary more in keeping with
the functionalist tenets of the International style. Ben Novack, a partner
in the Sans Souci (F64), purportedly planned and built the Fontainebleau
(G1) with the express intent of outshining the Saxony. In the design of the
Flamingo Hotel, Las Vegas's first major resort hotel and gambling casino,
gangster Bugsy Siegel similarly was said to have looked to Miami Beach and
the Saxony as his model.

Soho Beach House (Sovereign Hotel)   F66

4385 Collins Avenue
Roy France, 1941
Renovations and additions: Allan T. Shulman Architect, 2005

The modest Sovereign Hotel was one of a series that Roy France would construct in the prewar and postwar period on this stretch of Collins Avenue.
Constructed at Forty-third Street as the northernmost hotel on Miami
Beach's hotel row, it was also the last Miami Beach hotel to be completed
before the Pearl Harbor attack. This late version of the city's prewar architectural scale and character was given new vitality with its redevelopment as
the Soho Beach House.

The façade of the old Sovereign tower centers on a Modern Classical
composition, with flattened pilasters ordering the tripartite division that
identifies the entrance and climbs all the way to the roof. Projecting eyebrows define a base, middle, and top, and the elevator penthouse deploys
projecting slabs in emulation of a radiator grille. If the existing Sovereign
tower addresses the street, the new 15-story tower behind it addresses
a larger series of concerns. Its slender shaft punctuates the beachfront
of the hotel row, and creates a transition to the scale and expanse of the
Fontainebleau, directly to the north. The modest tower comprises only two
hotel suites per floor, topped by a single 3-story penthouse that opens to
an expansive covered belvedere. Here, staggered outdoor patios are tucked
beneath a protecting concrete canopy or visor, creating a multilevel outdoor living room that defines the pinnacle of the structure. Deep balconies
and metallic brise-soleils—the building's primary decoration—screen the
tower's full glass walls, an adaptation and expression of the subtropical
context.

The ground-floor suites of public areas span in a linear progression from
the street to the dune, topographically merging the hotel into the beachfront and raised boardwalk with a series of sandy or landscaped platforms.
A suite of outdoor public spaces on the second floor similarly projects
toward the ocean, emerging from a terrace beneath the volume of the
new tower that cantilevers over the north end of the site. The Sovereign's
restored 2-story lobby frames the entrance to the hotel. Terrazzo floors and

plaster moldings were restored, and the hotel's original wood wainscot was reconstructed. The multilevel interior scheme is part of a vast makeover that accommodates traditional public functions as well as the club facilities of Soho House.

301 Arthur Godfrey Road   F67
Charles Giller, 1963

By the 1960s, the reductivism of Miesian Modernism was giving way to a multitude of alternative expressions, monumental variants popularized by such works as Edward Durell Stone's U.S. embassy in New Delhi, India, and those of Philip Johnson and others at Lincoln Center in New York. In this vein, the 6-story façade of the 301 Arthur Godfrey Road building is a formal composition crowned by the fiction of an umbrella roof structure. The roof has been rendered in precast structural elements that flare out from piers that climb the full height of the façade. The arrangement seemingly disengages structure and shelter from the building's skin, which comprises ribbon windows and precast spandrel panels that draw the window grid into elongated arches. The arch theme continues in the barreled canopies that project over the entrances; until recently the canopies featured matching globe light fixtures nestled in each arch.

400 Block of West Forty-first Street   F68
433 41st Street
Martin Luther Hampton, 1934

439–441 41st Street
Martin Luther Hampton, 1935

459–469 41st Street
Martin Luther Hampton, 1935

451–455 41st Street
Paist and Steward, 1930s

446–450 41st Street
Lawrence Murray Dixon, 1934

456 41st Street
Victor H. Nellenbogen, 1938

It is ironic that while the designation, alteration, or demolition of lesser buildings can be the subject of pitched battles in South Beach historic districts, the greatest concentration of high-style Art Deco commercial façades in Miami Beach can be found on the 400 block of Forty-first Street. Forty-first Street was a quieter and more genteel street when these were constructed, as the Julia Tuttle Causeway, extending Forty-first Street across the bay and to I-95, did not open until 1960. At the southwest corner of Forty-first and Sheridan was the Sheridan Theater, also by Martin Luther Hampton. The inability to stop its demolition was one of the greatest losses in the Miami Beach Art Deco preservation movement. The site today is occupied by the Sheridan Center Office Building.

At Number 461, note the compressed arch supported by round, fluted pilasters and the griffins supporting a shield above the doorway. Also note the intricate vertical relief work and the chevron incisions across Number 441. Numbers 443 and 439 are variations on a theme. Number 433 is the more ornamented of the two, its fluted columns of frozen waterfalls reminiscent of the fountain motif of the 1925 Paris Exposition. Number 439 sports a shield over the doorway supported also by griffins. The use of griffins in the decoration may relate to the double row of griffin statues at the entrance to the 1933 Chicago Century of Progress Exposition. Number 446 stands out for its sizable band of original casement windows across the second floor. Beyond that, the façade is a feast of three-dimensional and sculptural effects reminiscent of an early Duchamp painting.

City National Bank F69

475 West 41st Street
Arquitectonica, 1998

This City National Bank branch addresses the difficult challenge of respecting its urban corner location while inserting a drive-through teller accessed through the ground floor. The results are mixed, but successfully hold the corner on Forty-first Street. By raising the building on pilotis, the drive-through appears like the shaded plazas found beneath many Miami buildings.

North Beach Elementary School F70

4100 Prairie Avenue
August Geiger and Russell T. Pancoast Architect, 1936
Addition: Giller and Giller with Spillis Candela DMJM, 2003

Not as elaborate as other New Deal–sponsored schools in this area like Coral Way Elementary School (B37), North Beach Elementary perhaps reflects the more utilitarian objectives of its creator, the Federal Emergency Administration of Public Works.

What was once a lawn and pathway to a grand entry has been converted into a playground as the building turned functionally away from Forty-first Street and toward the parking spaces in the rear. The main entry is wrought from keystone as are the two side entries, all facing the corner of Forty-first Street and Prairie Avenue. The building features a substantial pediment, quoins, and a tile roof. From the southeast corner, this is a well-balanced structure, but extensions west and north have robbed it of its symmetry.

Temple Beth Sholom F71

4144 Chase Avenue
Percival Goodman, 1956
Welcome center and school addition: Zyscovich Architects, 2002

Miami's midcentury renaissance of religious architecture produced daring and never-before-seen structures, and symbolism that ranged from domestic forms to space-age iconography. Percival Goodman was a master of synagogue design who believed that history and precedent were no guides for Jewish houses of worship. The concrete shell of Temple Beth Sholom was, accordingly, an original interpretation of the meaning of the Jewish service, the needs of the congregation and contemporary building art.

F71

The shell emerges from the ground, embracing the bema and bathing it with colored light from an array of parabolic vaults. Behind the congregation, the roof shell rises to create a parabolic clerestory, mainly visible from the Forty-first Street Bridge over the Biscayne Bay waterway. Later additions, including a new welcome center and school, have produced a campus in which the sculptural mass of Goodman's original sanctuary forms the core.

Senator Law Center (Arthur Murray Dance Studio)   F72

767 Arthur Godfrey Road
Igor Polevitzky, 1948

Designed for Arthur Murray Dance Studios, this modest single-story structure reflects the architect's interest in adapting small commercial buildings to Miami's subtropical climate. The main south-facing façade wall, with large plate-glass panels that allow passersby a view of the activity within, is screened by a wall of adjustable aluminum louvers. Most curious, however, was the rear ballroom, whose convertible roof could be retracted, exposing its dance floor to the stars. The automobile-scale signage pylon provides a dramatic vertical foil to the functionalist, low-slung character of the building itself.

Giller Building   F73

975 Arthur Godfrey Road
Norman M. Giller & Associates, 1956
Addition: Norman M. Giller & Associates, 1962

The Miami Beach Improvement Company, which developed most of Miami Beach between Nineteenth and Forty-forth streets, foresaw the west end of Forty-first Street as a district for architects' and interior designers' offices. The

F73

intersection of Forty-first and Alton, therefore, became an appropriate location for the headquarters of Norman M. Giller & Associates, at the time one of the ten largest architectural firms in the United States. The Giller Building predated the Julia Tuttle Causeway, subsequently becoming a fitting entry feature for Mid-Beach upon the causeway's completion in 1960. The building's most prominent feature, a 5-story-high, glass-tile mosaic wall, is a subtle expression of the stair tower it camouflages. Clerestory ribbon windows reflected the need for energy conservation between the introduction of air-conditioning and the arrival of reflective glass. The trapezoidal shape of the building responds to the rounded southwest corner of the lot. The prime offices, within the acute-angled corner, featured floor-to-ceiling glass and balconies. The taller east wing floats on pilotis over the parking lot and accommodates a residential penthouse complete with a lap pool.

St. Patrick's Church & School   F74

3700–3712 Garden Avenue
Gerald A. Barry, 1928
Renovations: 1999

Enrollment at St. Patrick's School mimicked tourism as it flourished in Miami Beach after World War II. After the original church structure was decimated by a major hurricane in 1926, a new church and school were built in 1928. The original school building had eight classrooms, a clinic, a library and office suites. In 1934, the school expanded to contain a patio within the grounds. In 1936, an auditorium was erected, and the gymnasium was constructed in 1937.

Mount Sinai Medical Center   F75

Warner Pavilion
Morris Lapidus, 1966

Medical Office Building
Markus Frankel & Associates, 1990

Visitor Parking Garage
Markus Frankel & Associates, 1987

De Hirsch Meyer Tower
Smith and Korach, 1960

Blum Pavilion
Smith and Korach, 1973

Comprehensive Cancer Care Center
Rochlin, Baran and Balabona, 1995

Donald Golden Family Medical Building
Engberg, Anderson Design Partnership, 2007

F75

Mount Sinai Medical Center, Miami Beach's single-largest employer, stands on the site of the early 1920s Nautilus Hotel, the northernmost of Carl Fisher's bayfront resorts. After the United States' entry into World War II, the Nautilus became a military hospital. In 1949, the formerly restricted hotel was purchased by a group of Jewish doctors, who turned it into Mount Sinai Hospital of Greater Miami.

Today's Mount Sinai Medical Center Campus comprises buildings ranging from bland to elegant. The finest is Morris Lapidus's 1966 Warner Pavilion, which bears a familial resemblance to that architect's late, great Algiers Hotel. The exterior is a panoply of thin horizontal planes acting as sun-protection devices, with contrasting vertical planes breaking the horizontality in a rhythmic pattern that is especially eye-catching at the corners of the low-slung pavilion. The upper stories cantilever over the mostly glass ground floor while the rectilinearity is foiled by an arced canopy suspended over the entrance from the second floor. In typical fashion, Lapidus crowned the composition with a recessed penthouse covered by a folded-plate roof canopy.

The Warner Pavilion backs up to and forms a courtyard with the whimsically Postmodern Medical Office Building, whose robust tripartite arrangement looks as if it were constructed of toy building blocks. The Medical Office Building, in turn, is complemented by the sculptural, stair-stepped Visitor Parking Garage fronting Alton Road. When its planters are filled with greenery, the garage is at its best and provides a fine image for the hospital.

The largest building on the campus is the handsome De Hirsch Meyer Tower, distinguished by its trapezoidal volumes and strong horizontality. Unfortunately, the bland, stark Blum Pavilion was added to its south end, compromising its visual integrity.

Facing the Julia Tuttle Causeway is the Comprehensive Cancer Care Center, its glass-enveloped platonic forms reminiscent of Cesar Pelli's Pacific Design Center in West Hollywood, California.

The newest building, the Donald Golden Family Medical Building, is most remarkable for providing the campus its first acknowledgment of its spectacular bayside location. Until its landscaped bayfront walkway with benches was completed, the campus addressed the beauty of Biscayne Bay with its parking lots.

Belle Isle

The only natural island along the Venetian Causeway, Belle Isle (former Bulls Island) was once home to estates like that of J. C. Penney. In the postwar era, paralleling the process under way on Millionaires Row and even on nearby West Avenue, the island's southern flank was transformed from estates to an eclectic palisade of apartment towers. The north side, in contrast, retains older residential streets, low-rise apartments, and a hotel. In the center lies a recently renovated park.

F76

Belle Plaza   F76

20 Island Avenue
T. Trip Russell and Associates, 1962

The chevron massing of this apartment tower is reiterated in exquisite boomerang-themed balcony rails of precast concrete. Other Modernist forms are arranged in front: A convex concrete shell forms the entrance porte cochere, and a separate but equally futuristic-looking structure is the parking garage. The tower façade exhibits strong horizontal banding accentuated by partly recessed balcony areas and awning windows. The horizontality is interrupted by the solid building core, which is sheathed in mosaic tiles that lighten as they rise.

Belle Towers   F77

16 Island Avenue
Robert Swartburg, 1958

F77

The first apartment tower on Island Avenue, Belle Towers was an avatar of the midcentury apartment-tower boom that would transform coastal Miami. The shamrock-shaped apartment block offers multiple fronts and view-multiplying potential. An open-air lobby punches through the building and functions as a grand breezeway, offering spectacular views from the drop-off to Biscayne Bay. The indoor-outdoor space of the breezeway is a subtropical wonderland of landscaped islands and amorphous pools (well stocked with fish, turtles, and, anecdotally, at one time an alligator). The brick walls on either side are adorned with bas-relief panels and hanging planters. Visitors rise over the pools on elegant serpentine ramps that penetrate to the building cores on either side. Robert Swartburg went on to use the shamrock form at his Executive House (G6).

Terrace Towers Apartments   F78

3 Island Avenue
Morris Lapidus, 1960

This straightforward Modern apartment building of banded glass, solid stucco spandrels, and projecting balconies sits prominently on the east end of the Venetian Causeway, to which it turns an unfriendly back. Lapidus's touch is visible in the cantilevered folded-plate concrete canopy at the automotive drop-off as well as in the 2-story lobby. Lapidus occupied a 2-story unit in the building in his later years.

Standard (Lido Spa)   F79

40 Island Avenue
Norman M. Giller & Associates, 1953
Renovation: A. Herbert Mathes, 1960
Renovation: Allison Spear, 2005

Originally constructed as the Lido Spa, a modest seasonal resort, this complex has more recently been redeveloped as the Standard, with stylish updates and amenities that challenge the city's better-known oceanfront hotels. The frontal head house comprises the restaurant, lounge, and spa, while the rooms extend in 1- and 2-story wings toward the water's edge, embracing the garden and pool.

　　One remarkable facet of the redevelopment was its minimalism, which maintained and adaptively used the building's native features. Of note are the main façade and lobby, as well as the motel-like room wings, which have been creatively reworked as patio units. The interiors were designed by Shawn Hausman, and the gardens by Madison Cox.

G

City of Miami Beach: Upper Mid-Beach

Upper Mid-Beach stretches from Forty-fourth Street to Sixty-third Street. Upon the death of John Collins in 1928, the oceanfront mansions that lined Collins Avenue from Fourteenth Street on the south to the Bath Club (**G11**) became known as "Millionaires Row." Between 1928 and 1941, nearly all of the mansions between Fourteenth Street and Forty-fourth Street were replaced by Moderne hotels. The remaining mansions above Forty-fourth Street retained the moniker Millionaires Row for at least another generation. The jog in Collins Avenue at Forty-fourth Street was necessary to accommodate the wide and generous lots, stretching from the ocean to Indian Creek, of Carl Fisher's Indian Beach Subdivision.

The area was rezoned for higher-density uses in the 1950s, with the intention of expanding Miami Beach's resort districts. Instead, following changes in the city's hospitality industry, it was mainly redeveloped with apartment towers. West of Indian Creek, the homes are generally more lavish than those south of Arthur Godfrey Road, and are arranged around the golf course of the La Gorce Country Club (**G16**) and Surprise Lake, with its three radiating waterways: the Flamingo, the Biscayne, and the Surprise. On the bay shore, the waterfront estates along North Bay Road are among the most exclusive in Greater Miami.

G. City of Miami Beach: Upper Mid-Beach

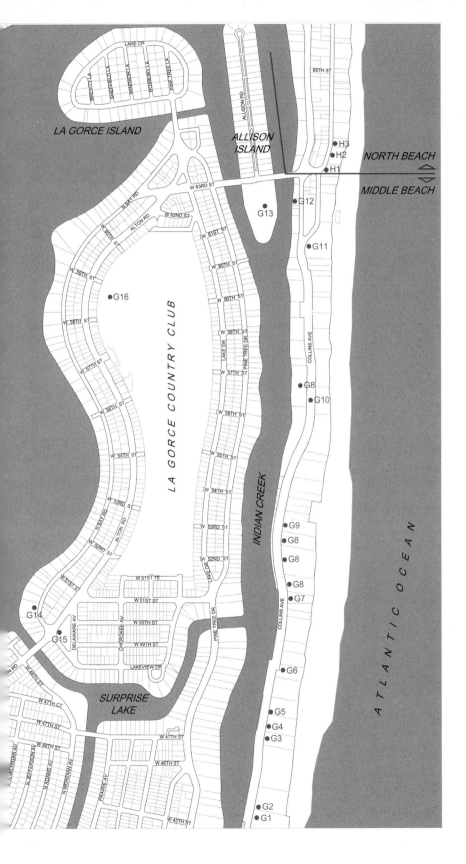

Palisade and Canyon Group (Millionaires Row)

The rezoning of Harvey Firestone's estate in the early 1950s to resort use laid the groundwork for the development of the Fontainebleau and Eden Roc hotels, and ignited the conversion of the rest of Millionaires Row by the mid-1950s. The new scale of these resort hotels required much more property than was conveniently available, even on the estate lots. The Upper Mid-Beach oceanfront soon attracted the development of high-rise apartments, many of which provided grandeur and amenities on a par with the resort hotels. Within fifteen years, Millionaires Row was developed into a palisade of high-rise structures, set elbow-to-elbow. Above Fifty-fifth Street, buildings frame both sides of the street to create a canyon effect. Much-criticized for its automobile-oriented street frontage, lack of public access to the beach, and as a symbol of overdevelopment, the area is nevertheless a formidable architectural ensemble.

Fontainebleau Hotel   G1

4441 Collins Avenue
Morris Lapidus, 1953
North wing additions: A. Herbert Mathes, 1959
Fontainebleau 2: Nichols Brosch Sandoval & Associates, 1998
Fontainebleau 3: Nichols Brosch Wurst & Wolfe, 2003

The Fontainebleau occupies the former estate of Harvey Firestone. In 1952, after a long battle to have the estate rezoned for hotel use, the Firestone heirs sold the property to Ben Novack, codeveloper of the Sans Souci Hotel (**F64**). Opposing the conventional wisdom that Miami Beach could not support more hotels, Novack announced the construction of the largest one ever built here, the more than 500-room Fontainebleau Hotel. He named Morris Lapidus as architect only after being pressed by reporters, leaving the New York architect to find out while reading the newspaper on the subway on his way to work. Lapidus's anonymity was short-lived.

With the Fontainebleau Hotel, his first major solo work, Lapidus was catapulted to fame as a hotel designer. From the bold sweep of its tower to the Baroque curves of its idiosyncratic pedestal base, the Fontainebleau broke the mold of the Miami Beach hotel. The main level, comprising theatrically conceived public spaces and entertainment facilities, was built over a ground-level shopping concourse that fused hotel design with new retailing trends. The complex program and open-plan space configuration reflect postwar trends in hospitality design, but are also reminiscent of casinos found in Havana and some South American cities, perhaps anticipating a nightlife and gaming culture that ultimately eluded Miami.

The Fontainebleau has undergone constant renovation and expansion almost since its opening. Most notable in this respect was the addition of the 14-story north wing and the Convention Hall that is fronted by the building's famous cheese-hole wall. The north wing was built partially to express Ben Novack's distaste for his former partner Harry Mufson's competing Eden Roc. Its windowless back became known locally as the "Spite Wall"; Novack made sure that it was built as close as possible to the Eden Roc in order to cast a shadow over its pool during high season. Ten years later, a south wing was built, connecting the Fontainebleau property to the neighbor-

G1 and G2

ing Sorrento Hotel (Robert Swartburg, 1948). The south wing obstructed the view of Lapidus's curved slab from lower Collins Avenue, and when its open corridors were enclosed, it created a windowless wall similar to its counterpart at the opposite end of the property. In order to mitigate this indignity inflicted on the public, artist Richard Haas was commissioned in 1985 to paint a trompe l'oeil mural (now destroyed) illustrating the original view.

To make way for Fontainebleau 2—yet another major expansion—featuring a 36-story residential tower, the western portion of the south wing was demolished in 2002, restoring the view from the south. In 2003, the façade of the Sorrento was re-created in a slightly different location as part of the Fontainebleau 3 tower. A serpentine glass walkway now connects the new additions with the original complex, commonly known as the chateau. A major renovation in 2008 has restored the chateau, and updated its interiors for a new age of bling. Interiors by Jeffery Beers, lobby chandeliers by Ai Weiwei, and a striking light wall, *Third Eye*, by artist James Turrell, complement Lapidus's original interior concept. The Eden Roc, meanwhile, has undergone a similarly ambitious renovation and expansion. Notably, a new tower addition on the north side of the property resolved the "Spite Wall" issue, masking its enormous blank expanse.

Eden Roc Hotel   G2

Morris Lapidus, 1955
Restoration: Spillis Candela & Partners, Inc., 1997
Addition: Nichols Brosch Wurst & Wolfe, 2006

Next door to the Fontainebleau (G1), and only one year later, Lapidus completed his second major hotel, the Eden Roc. The Eden Roc presents a more formal, Classical façade, reminiscent of earlier Miami Beach hotels like the Sherry Frontenac (H4) and the Saxony (F65). The rear is more dynamic, facing the ocean with rows of cantilevered balconies, and public rooms that billow outward from the hotel's pedestal. The Eden Roc's interior spatial organization honed the ideas introduced at the Fontainebleau. Upon entering the latter, the sweep of its lobby is immediately apparent; at the former, the lobby reveals itself in a nuanced sequence.

Mimosa   G3

4747 Collins Avenue
Melvin Grossman, 1962

By the early 1960s, large amounts of glass had become de rigueur on highrises like the Crystal House (G7) and the Doral(G5). At the luxurious Mimosa, however, architect Melvin Grossman used the very same block, stucco, punched opening, and eyebrow elements that characterized the modest 2-story Miami Beach apartment buildings from the 1930s through the 1950s.

Blue and Green Diamonds   G4

4775 and 4779 Collins Avenue
Robert Swedroe & Associates, 2000

Vilified by many for its size- and scale-shattering height, the Blue and Green Diamonds' biggest transgression is rather in the design of its twin parking garages, which turn multistory slabs of car storage toward Collins Avenue and Indian Creek. Further, reflecting a spirit foreign to Miami Beach, a grand central axis acts as an esplanade, bisecting the symmetrical composition. Dominating the head of the axis, and positioned between the towers, is the clubhouse, a selective reiteration of the mansion that once stood on the site. The project's "gem" theme is carried through the corner beveling of the towers, and the illuminated rooftop finials evoke precious stones in their settings. The glowing "diamonds" recall the illuminated glass dome that once crowned the Flamingo Hotel (Price and McLanahan, 1920), Carl Fisher's first grand hotel on the bayfront.

Miami Beach Resort and Spa (Doral Hotel)   G5

4833 Collins Avenue
Melvin Grossman, 1962

The glass-walled Miami Beach Resort and Spa is an exception to the masonry, concrete, and stucco Modernism that characterizes most of Miami Beach. The 17-story Doral Beach Hotel was one of the last new hotels built on Miami Beach before the resort's dormancy between the late 1960s and the 1980s. Its dark skin emulated the Crystal House's interplay of concrete frame and glass curtain wall in a similarly disciplined tower, although both buildings were probably influenced by the flat-slab construction and balcony-less curtain-wall façades of Norman Giller's Carillon Hotel (H6), constructed farther north. Above all, the Classically inspired Doral is reminiscent of the New Formalism of architects like Philip Johnson and Edward Durell Stone.

G5

Executive House   G6

4925 Collins Avenue
Robert Swartburg, 1959

The Executive House was the first apartment building constructed along this strip. Its shamrock-shaped tower, already used by Swartburg at Belle Towers (F77), distinguishes it among the slab towers of its later neighbors. Its midcentury architectural vocabulary includes a number of works in concrete, including an inverted-V entrance canopy, precast decorative grilles, and Regency details.

G6

G7

Crystal House Apartments G7

5055 Collins Avenue
Morris Lapidus, 1960

The Crystal House can be interpreted as an homage by iconoclast Morris Lapidus to his long dialogue and struggle with the implacable forces of International style Miesian Modernism. By his own account, the homage was in response to the desires of the condominium developer, who admired the German émigré architect. Whatever the case, Crystal House appears as a rather sober and elegant slab-type residential tower on Collins Avenue. Similar to Mies's Seagram Building, it is not a simple slab, but actually a *T* in plan. Its exterior walls are curtain-wall glass interlaced with a concrete structural frame. The austere lobby was originally composed of marble floors and walls, and glass walls, and colonized with Mies's iconic Barcelona chairs and benches. If the main structure was conservative by Lapidus standards, the pool deck was the architect's own. It was a hybrid space that mixed French gardens of the type Lapidus originally designed for the Fontainebleau with a curvilinear pool surrounded with cabanas. The gardens, while formal in the temperate European manner, were composed of tropical plant materials chosen to weather the harsh beach environment. An interesting feature is the circular restaurant structure that commands views of the pool and ocean. It is almost entirely glassed and sheltered by a conical folded-plate concrete roof.

Seacoast Tower Group G8

The largest complex on upper Collins Avenue was the Seacoast Towers group developed by Alexander Muss & Sons, who had already pioneered a similar complex with the same name at the oceanside community of Brighton Beach in Brooklyn.

Seacoast Towers South
5101 Collins Avenue
Morris Lapidus, 1964

Seacoast Towers East
5151–5167 Collins Avenue
Morris Lapidus, 1966

G8

The Alexander (Seacoast Towers North)
5225 Collins Avenue
Charles McKirahan, 1962

Seacoast Towers West
5600 Collins Avenue
Melvin Grossman, 1967

The T-shaped Seacoast Towers South, designed by Morris Lapidus, has a decorative cornice of precast concrete panels and a coffered entrance canopy supported on obelisk columns. The broad tower mass of Morris Lapidus's 17-story Seacoast Towers East (1966) is configured as a shamrock. The design recalls Robert Swartburg's earlier Executive House (**G6**), albeit at a more monumental scale. Its sweeping corner balconies produce a powerfully streamlined effect. Note the graphic device that transforms the

Alexander's blank end-wall into an abstract relief. The relief injects some exotica, suggestive perhaps of Polynesian motifs, a theme that architect Charles McKirahan explored fully in his later (and now demolished) Castaways complex in Sunny Isles.

Imperial House   G9

5255 Collins Avenue
Melvin Grossman, 1961

The tower slab of the Imperial House seems to have been influenced by Morris Lapidus's nearby work; it echoes the Fontainebleau's curved form and southeast orientation, and the Eden Roc's full-height, tile-mosaic panels. Otherwise, the building is notable for its decorative front entrance, approached by a bridge over a small pool of water. The bridge features gold-anodized railings with double rows of beanpoles pitched in opposite directions. On either side of the main doors, water cascades over walls of blue ceramic tile cast in an unusual undulating form, yielding a shimmering effect. Sunlight coming through round openings in the porte cochere dapples the water.

Condo Canyon Buildings   G10

The following buildings, stretching from 5400 to 5800 block of Collins Avenue, are representative of the buildings lining this area of Collins, which has come to be known as the "condo canyon."

Carriage House
5401 Collins Avenue
Melvin Grossman, 1968

Castle Beach Club (Statler Hilton Plaza, Playboy Plaza)
5445 Collins Avenue
Melvin Grossman, 1966

G10

Tower House
5500 Collins Avenue
Reiff-Fellman and Associates, 1972

Oceanside Plaza
5555 Collins Avenue
Morris Lapidus, 1967

Pavilion
5601 Collins Avenue
Melvin Grossman, 1968

Ashley
5640 Collins Avenue
Don Reiff, 1967

5660 Collins Avenue
Reiff-Fellman and Associates, 1970

Grossman's Castle Club hotel closely followed the International style syntax established for the hotel chain the year before with the completion of Skidmore, Owings & Merrill's Istanbul Hilton (1955). Oceanside Plaza featured continuous balconies stretched across the building's entire façade.

Bath Club   G11
5959 Collins Avenue
Robert Taylor, 1927
Condominium additions: Revuelta Vega Leon, 2001
Restoration of Bath Club: Allan T. Shulman Architect, 2002

Early Miami Beach had numerous bathing casinos, oceanfront bathhouses that offered access to the beach and ocean-fed swimming pools, as well as food, entertainment, and social programming. These clubs also provided cabanas, small private changing and living spaces that served as a convenient base of operations for a day at the beach or pool. The Bath Club (and later Surf Club in Surfside), developed during the 1920s boom, provided the same facilities in the context of a private club. Its main structure, styled by architect Robert Taylor according to the Mediterranean Revival, includes reception spaces and ballrooms for a variety of occasions, a wonderful patio, and diverse dining facilities crisscrossed by open-air loggias and terraces. The Governor's Lounge, at the heart of the complex, has great wood beams that span between a series of Moorish arches.

In 1996, R. Donahue Peebles, the Bath Club's first African American member, purchased the property and announced its redevelopment. In an agreement with the City of Miami Beach, the site was designated historic and its main clubhouse structure was retained, while the remainder of the property, including the cabana colony, was redeveloped with new residential condominiums and associated amenities.

The clubhouse retains its physical independence, and its restoration makes apparent the delicate balance of rusticity and sophistication at the heart of its identity as a bath club. Its original plan has been largely recuperated, and terrazzo and clay-tile floors, wrought-iron metalworks and fittings, grand fireplaces, and cypress ceilings have been revealed and restored. To the north of the clubhouse, the new tower, ground-level townhouses, and cabana suites are by Revuelta Vega Leon Architects. The tower's curvilinear volume, articulated principally in projecting balconies, plays off the curves of Collins Avenue in this area.

6000 Indian Creek   G12
Sieger-Suarez Architectural Partnership, 2006

While most towers in the canyon form broad slabs, this slender point tower clad in green glass and projecting balconies features small floor plates that derive from compound elliptical shapes. The limited size of each floor produces only one or two apartments per level, a "floor-through/see-through" plan emphasizing cross-ventilation and multiple views. The tower plunges on its ground level into the waterfront deck, its form mirrored in the curve of the swimming pool facing Indian Creek. A swooping canopy delineates a sort of parking court/porte cochere on the north side. One of the interesting aspects of this tower is that it expands slightly from bottom to top, creating a more interesting profile.

Aqua (Allison Hospital)   G13
South side of Allison Island
Master plan by Duany Plater-Zyberk & Company, 2003

The 8.5-acre site on the southern tip of Allison Island was formerly home to the Allison (later Saint Francis) Hospital (est. 1920s). It sits in the middle of Indian Creek, bracketed by the high-rise towers of upper Collins Avenue on one side and single-family homes of Pine Tree Drive on the other. As an alternative to both environments, the project employs a town-making strategy that urbanizes the property while bridging the scale difference. On the east side of the island rise three mid-rise towers (10–11 stories each) with about 100 units. On the west side are about 50 townhouses. The overall building rights were spread over the site, creating the density necessary to support urban spaces.

G12

Chatham Tower: Walter Chatham, 2004
Spear Tower: Allison Spear, 2004
Gorlin Tower: Alexander Gorlin Architects, 2002
Hariri & Hariri Houses: Hariri & Hariri, 2004
Suzanne Martinson Houses: Suzanne Martinson Architects, 2004
Brown Demandt Houses: Brown Demandt Architects, 2004
Albaisa Musumano Houses: Albaisa Musumano Architects, 2004
Allan T. Shulman Houses: Allan T. Shulman Architect, 2004
Emanuela Frattini Magnusson Houses: EFM Design, 2004
DPZ Houses: Duany Plater-Zyberk & Company, 2004

Aqua is one of the largest urban infill projects ever developed in Miami Beach. In the best Florida tradition, Dacra Company developed the site not simply as a real estate venture but as an integrated concept of community living. Aqua takes cues from such diverse sources as the New Urbanism movement, nearby South Beach, and the private residential islands in Biscayne Bay (like Star Island).

At the heart of the planning strategy are the principles of the New Urbanism, here applied for the first time to a Modernist community in an

G13

existing urban context. The emphasis was on a walkable community of tree-lined streets, squares, and plazas, waterfront promenades and greens. The civic nature of these public spaces is amplified by a creative thrust that integrates architecture, public art, and urban design. The design also allows each home views of the surrounding creek through public spaces that open to the water. The style does not hew to the traditional or romantic, but to Miami Beach's vernacular Modern.

Aqua's concept centers on luxury living, though not in standard building types. Although the site was gated (a controversial decision, especially among New Urbanists), its main development strategies have turned standard local assumptions upside down. First, this secure, private, and high-quality residential district was developed on a compact urban site as a low- to mid-rise community centered on "urban spaces." Second, the imagery of this exclusive complex is founded on Modernist architecture, challenging the supremacy of the city's more august Mediterranean Revival style as the style of wealth.

In lieu of urban conformity, Aqua offers an architecture of multiplicity: urban blocks comprise several types of townhouses, and the complex features the work of ten different architects.

The Chatham Tower notably incorporates the former hospital's parking garage, which was salvaged and converted into the pedestal of a new block of residences. Along the tower's south façade is a multistory tile mural, *Splash*, by artist Richard Tuttle.

Carl Fisher House   G14

5020 North Bay Road
August Geiger, 1925

Miami Beach developer Carl Fisher had used his own home at the foot of Lincoln Road, Shadows, to set the tone for his development. Yet, by 1925, Shadows was neither up-to-date stylistically nor centrally located within his Miami Beach domain. His dredging and development efforts had so enlarged and transformed the barrier island that a more suitable homesite became necessary. He asked August Geiger, his architect of choice, to design a mansion on the bay shore near the mouth of the Surprise Waterway. Typical of the waterfront estates in the area, this new home presented its primary façade to the water and its back to North Bay Road. A 1925 article described the house: reminiscent of an "Italian villa of the Renaissance period. Landscaped sunken garden. Famous Florentine villas provided the inspiration for the main rooms, with their carved, hand-painted wood ceilings, walls hand-plastered in blue and gold, and teak floors." The house's most distinctive feature is an observation tower providing views to prospective buyers of Fisher's surrounding development. He and Geiger had employed a similar observation deck at his office building on Lincoln Road (F21).

Carl Fisher Memorial   G15
NE corner of Alton Road and Lakeview Drive
Russell T. Pancoast Architect, 1941

Carl Fisher, the developer whose creative energies and deep pockets decisively shaped Miami Beach (both literally and figuratively) in its formative years, is memorialized here on Alton Road, not far from his estate on the bay. The memorial, clad in quarry keystone, employs a classic Art Deco composition stylized with suggestions of a griffin's wings. A bronze bust of the storied developer by Gustav Bohland is the centerpiece of the composition. Behind, a map carved in the keystone by Edgar Sutton shows Miami Beach and Biscayne Bay crisscrossed by the causeways that existed at the time of Fisher's death in 1939. Modernistic lettering engraved in the keystone spells out the following words: "He Carved a Great City from a Jungle."

La Gorce Country Club   G16
5685 Alton Road
Allan T. Shulman Architect, 2004

Following the demolition of its original clubhouse, designed by August Geiger, La Gorce Country Club embarked on the development of an entirely new clubhouse and ancillary facilities. Located in a neighborhood of older homes and confronted with the challenge or recalling but not copying the first clubhouse, the new structures hew a fine line between Mediterranean Revival and contemporary architectural traditions. The H-shaped center block of the new clubhouse sits partly on the footprint of Geiger's original structure and presents a formal face to Alton Road; the focal point is an elliptical volume that houses the entrance on the ground floor and a lounge above. Ancillary wings, including the pool house, cart building, and various loggias and service structures, ramble across the side from north to south, creating an extensive but varied frontage along the golf links. This frontage features generous outdoor terraces and loggias, theatrical exterior stairways, and a variety of building forms. The building makes abundant use of traditional materials, like ceramic tile, cypress timbers, and copper.

G16

H

City of Miami Beach:
North Beach

North Beach includes three distinct areas: the Normandy Isles (Isle of Normandy and Normandy Shores), North Shore (from Seventy-third Street to the city limit at Eighty-seventh Terrace), and the area south of Seventy-second Street. Roughly occupying the northern third of Miami Beach, this neighborhood embraced the name North Beach as South Beach solidified its grip on the popular imagination in the 1980s.

Archaeology has revealed that Native Americans were established in this area for centuries, yet the modern history of North Beach begins in 1876 with the federal government's construction of the Biscayne House of Refuge on the beach at today's Seventy-first Street. As early as 1919, new residential subdivisions marched northward along the barrier island, exploiting the opening of new beachfront made possible by the relocation inland of Collins Avenue. The most prominent development efforts were undertaken by Frenchman Henri Levy. Levy's first subdivision in this area, Normandy Beach South, ran east-west, establishing the nucleus for the Everglades (today John F. Kennedy) Causeway, an important cross-bay link. Along the causeway's westward track, Levy further developed the Isle of Normandy, a product of the City Beautiful movement, which extends eastward into Biscayne Bay.

The multifamily areas of North Shore and the Normandy Isles are predominantly filled with garden apartment residences, similar in urban character to the Flamingo Park neighborhood in South Beach, though mainly lower in height and of postwar vintage. Pylon forms, flat roofs, projecting concrete fins, perforated concrete screens, fieldstone, slumped brick, patterned stucco, and decorative metalworks form an architectural language that, repeated throughout North Beach, gives the area its singular coherence as a Modern cityscape.

The area includes the locally designated North Beach Resort Historic District, Harding Town Site Historic District, and Altos del Mar Historic District, and the nationally designated North Shore Historic District and Normandy Isle Historic District.

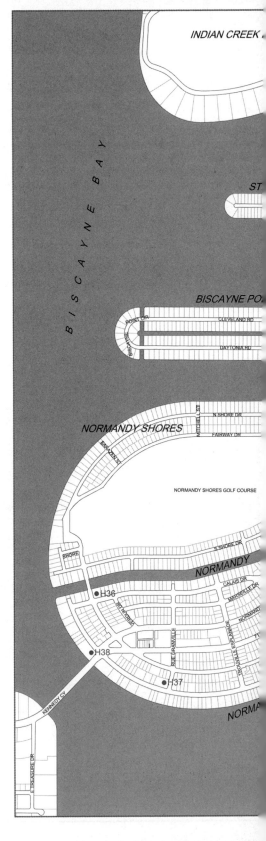

H. City of Miami Beach: North Beach

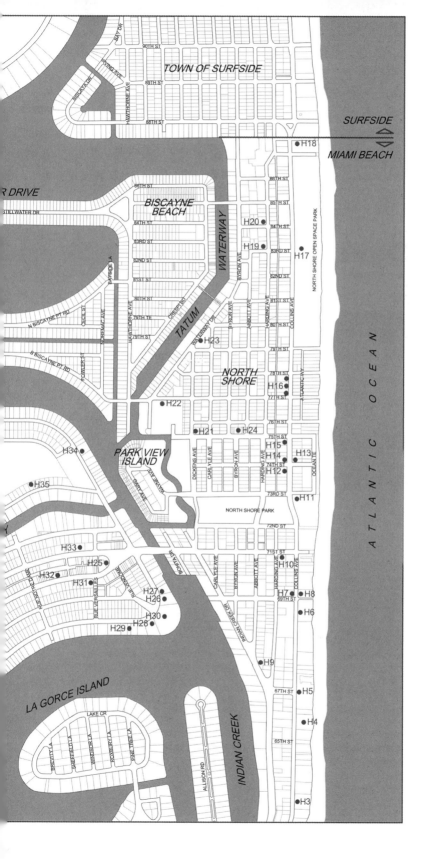

LaGorce Palace   H1

6301 Collins Avenue
Schapiro Associates, 1995

The sculptural mass of LaGorce Palace, accentuated by the integration of
the parking garage into the tower, terminates the vista eastward from Sixty-
third Street, across Indian Creek. The tower is articulated through the simple
use of solid-rounded and trapezoidal-clear balcony types. In addition to the
vertical elements formed by the balconies, floor-to-ceiling glass in the living rooms of the end units form full-height cylindrical elements. These are
crowned by winglike projections, like those on the roof of the Delano (F6),
that are reminiscent of local 1930s architecture.

Casablanca Hotel   H2

6345 Collins Avenue
Roy France, 1949

H2

When gangster Bugsy Siegel was dreaming up gambling resorts in the
Nevada desert in the late 1940s, he was undoubtedly influenced by Miami
Beach hotels like the Casablanca. The lineage between the two is suggested
in the rakish script neon sign atop the tower, and in the exotic turbaned
caryatids holding up the wave-edged porte cochere. The telamones (male
caryatids) were originally nude, but soon after the hotel opened were covered up so as not to offend contemporary mores. The Casablanca also came
near the end of France's successful career and bears some resemblance to
its contemporary, the Sans Souci Hotel (F64).

Akoya   H3

6365 Collins Avenue
Brito, Cohan & Associates, 2004

H3

Originally conceived as the White Diamond (a North Beach counterpart
to the Blue and Green Diamonds in Mid-Beach [G4]), this tower's size and
height make the other diamonds seem restrained in size. On the beach side,
Akoya reveals large, rectangular floor plates, and, with 48 habitable floors,
it is the tallest building in Miami Beach. This white enormity is a sight to be-
hold from the beach against a clear blue sky. Akoya's pyramidal, vegetation-
festooned parking garage would have had habitable space on the ground
floor if city planners could have prevailed. Note how the parking extends
into the lower floors of the tower.

     While the Akoya's zigzag finial may remind some of a midcentury
Modern motif, it is said to represent an *M* or a *W*, depending on whether
one is speaking to the current owner or the developer. The zigzag element
is repeated at the auto drop-off, complementing the porte cocheres of the
Casablanca and LaGorce Palace next door.

Sherry Frontenac Hotel   H4

6565 Collins Avenue
Henry Hohauser, 1947

The Sherry Frontenac was one of the first hotels built in Miami Beach after
World War II and, at the time, the most advanced in design. Unlike the transitional Art Deco styling of the Delano (F6), which opened the same year, this

H4

hotel's low-slung porte cochere and full-height neon signage presaged the car culture of the 1950s. In a departure from the romantic, tapered masses of the 1930s, the Sherry Frontenac's double-tower design evokes twin ocean liners with their smokestack finials. Here, as in the Delano, the architect employed sawtooth floor plans, providing ocean views to rooms facing north and south. The public interiors follow the bilateral symmetry of the massing with a dramatic procession from the front door to a terrace overlooking the pool and ocean. Originally, a bridge, or "gangplank," connected the two towers at the top level. The Sherry Frontenac was the largest, and one of the last, of Henry Hohauser's commissions in Miami Beach.

Deauville Hotel H5

6701 Collins Avenue
Melvin Grossman, 1957

The Deauville site was originally the location of the famous Deauville Casino (later the McFadden Deauville). The old Deauville was a grand hotel notably equipped with an ocean-fed swimming pool surrounded by a gigantic pool deck and cabanas—a space that could fit more than two thousand spectators for shows choreographed in and around the pool. Of special interest here was the diving tower, an almost cinematic construction by architect Igor Polevitzky that arced over the pool and included multiple platforms. Operated as a "health resort," amenities at the old hotel included a grand hall that served as both a gym and lecture hall. With its emphasis on spectacle, the old Deauville was a model for Miami Beach's postwar hotels.

The new Deauville replaced the old in 1957, introducing an even larger and grander structure on one of Miami Beach's largest oceanfront parcels. Designed by Melvin Grossman, it followed the resort hotel template laid out by Morris Lapidus four years earlier at the Fontainebleau, and replicated with fierce abandon by Lapidus, Grossman, and others along the length of the strand. Upon a large pedestal that comprises the lobby, dining rooms, bars, and a ballroom is a 12-story tower with 552 rooms, the second-highest count in Miami Beach. The main focus of the entry is the canopy, with its telescoping vaults supported by a parabolic concrete arch. A pedestrian walkway climbs from the street to the canopy beneath stepped concrete slabs. On the main level is the grand double-height lobby, luxuriously appointed in terrazzo and marble floors and marble and wood-paneled walls and columns. Below is a shopping concourse (originally showcasing an ice-skating rink); its activities are oriented toward both the street and an interior arcade that runs the full length of the building. The main stairs are especially eye-catching, with elegantly shaped metal balustrades, polished wood banisters, and surrounding walls clad in gold mosaic tile.

The Deauville is most famous for a single event: the Beatles' February 16, 1964, appearance on the *Ed Sullivan Show*, broadcast live from the hotel's Napoleon Room. The Fab Four were lodged on the eleventh floor.

Canyon Ranch Living Miami Beach   H6

6801 Collins Avenue
Arquitectonica, 2005
Carillon Hotel (fragment): Norman M. Giller & Associates

The tower of Norman Giller's Carillon Hotel forms the nucleus of the present Canyon Ranch Living complex. The older hotel followed the expansive model of resort hotel design established by Morris Lapidus, joining a substantial room tower to a sprawling and eye-catching pedestal chock full of amenities. The Carillon's tower employed flat-slab construction and slab-to-slab glass window-walls to frame façades of unprecedented transparency. Its delicate weave of recessed balconies and flush window-wall was disciplined by a tartan grid of mullions. Four holes were cut in the projecting concrete canopy atop the tower to accommodate bells (never installed), and an area of blank wall at the end of the building forms a foil for the old hotel's restored cursive reverse channel neon sign. Unfortunately the Carillon's remarkable pedestal is gone, but the tower survives.

H6

Today, the old tower is embedded in a new composition that fully exploits the 6-acre site. The vast complex has two new towers, one on either side of the Carillon tower. The façades take their cue from the original Carillon. Abstract white frame elements appear to float over the façades of the new towers, echoing the grid of the Carillon tower. The enormous cylindrical metal cage that surrounded the grand staircase of the Carillon has been incorporated as a decorative element. The reception desk of the Carillon has also been retained as part of the new hotel, replete with original clock above the counters.

The Carillon's original tower was renovated, although the substitution of glass railing for the hotel's original grille block ones is unfortunate. Conversely, the folded-plate motif animating the Collins Avenue façade reconstructs the original defining feature of the hotel front.

Besides the replacement of the screen block balconies, the Carillon tower has been embellished by arced parapets and has been improved upon by the insertion of an open-air restaurant space in what had been an unfortunate sheer wall at the base of the tower facing the beach. The wavy slits running around the garage pedestal of the tall north tower provide a foil to the re-created folded-plate accordion wall.

6900 Collins Avenue (Sambo's)   H7

William Merriam, 1966

Originally built as a Sambo's Restaurant, this specimen of coffee-shop Googie followed the company's eye-catching formula of colorful interiors and plenty of glass beneath a bent roof. The corrugated roof, which cantilevers over the glass walls, creates an interesting crimped profile along Collins Avenue. Note the compressed arch canopy that hangs over what once served as a drive-up window, a rectilinear foil to the curvaceous roof.

Bombay Hotel Remnant   H8

6901 Collins Avenue
Norman M. Giller & Associates, 1951
Permitted renovation and addition: Revuelta Vega Leon

Originally called the Bombay Hotel, this postwar structure was one of the first in Miami Beach to accommodate parking on-site in a garage. The garage was concealed behind the L-shaped body of the building, and the coming and going of cars past the glass corner lobby was raised to high theater. The lobby, automotive pass-through, and landscaping are joined by a projecting concrete canopy. Notwithstanding the rising importance of the car, meeting the sidewalk was still important in 1951, and a row of retail spaces lines Collins Avenue. Note the prominent signage pylon and the vertical louvers that protect the street façade from Miami's intense western sun. The building rises to more than an illustration of midcentury architectural concerns to become a rather sophisticated urban type. At this writing, the rear portion of the hotel has been demolished to make way for a tower addition.

6727, 6753, and 6767 Indian Creek Drive   H9

Hampshire House
6727 Indian Creek Drive
Leonard Glasser, 1950

6753 Indian Creek Drive
R. M. Little, 1937

6767 Indian Creek Drive
Robert Law Weed, 1948

A trio of modern apartment buildings forms a cohesive ensemble in this prominent wedge between Harding Avenue and Indian Creek Drive. The three distinct buildings by separate architects span more than a decade of stylistic development. In spite of their peculiarities, each is L-shaped, and

H9

they step up as a group toward the north. The tip of the wedge is Glasser's 2-story catwalk-style apartment building, displaying a multitude of angles and wedges. Little's Nautical Moderne 6753 Indian Creek, occupying the middle, has porthole windows, an apse-shaped prow, metal railing, and stepped massing that creates habitable decks. At the northern end is the deepest and tallest structure, Weed's 6767 Indian Creek apartments. Its austere evocation of a tropical Modernism included two sheltered patios, cutaway corner balconies, and projecting eyebrows. Weed and Little were better known for their work at the University of Miami campus.

Seventy-first Street–Henri Levy Boulevard

Although impossible to discern today, Seventy-first Street in Miami Beach, the Kennedy Causeway, and Seventy-ninth Street on the Miami side formed a single axis of early 1960s high life in Miami. On one end of this axis were swanky resorts like the Deauville and Carillon; on the other was the club and nightlife action along Seventy-ninth Street and Biscayne Boulevard.

Seventy-first Street joins the beachfront with the Isle of Normandy. On the island, the street splits into a one-way pair whose westbound lanes are known as Normandy Drive. In the middle of the bay, the area along the causeway (now North Bay Village) was unincorporated; much like the unincorporated area in Los Angeles that became West Hollywood, it was a mecca for South Florida's legendary nightlife. The west end of the Isle of Normandy, close to the glittering waterholes along the causeway, became an especially swinging place for a pad.

A product of the postwar period, the commercial sections of Seventy-first Street never fully developed the traditional continuous street walls that characterize Miami Beach's other main thoroughfares. Seventy-first Street is enlivened today by working-class immigrants, mainly from Latin America, who live in the surrounding small apartment buildings.

Gidney and Co. (North Shore Bank Building)   H10
326 71st Street
Henry Hohauser, 1948
Second-floor addition: Edwin T. Reeder Associates, 1954

Built after World War II, this keystone-clad structure balances Modern Classicism with streamlined elements, like the prominent rounded corner. The keystone provides a formality appropriate to its former use as a bank building.

North Shore

The North Shore neighborhood is defined by gridded residential streets bordered by the Seventy-first Street and Collins Avenue commercial corridors. It is Miami Beach's most modest area; many single-story buildings imbue it with a quaint seaside character. The area's fine-grained grid serves the neighborhood well with a few exceptions. Two of North Shore's most important corridors, Collins and Harding avenues, were made one-way in the 1960s. Various plans have been floated to return them to two-way neighborhood streets. As one of Miami Beach's most architecturally rich corridors, Harding Avenue in North Shore deserves better than to stand in for half an arterial highway.

Harding Townsite, the southern end of North Shore, between present-day Seventy-third and Seventy-fifth streets, is the only part of Miami Beach platted by governmental initiative. In 1921, under executive order of President Warren G. Harding, the federal government released for development a portion of the government tract associated with the former Biscayne House of Refuge. The release followed Harding's January 1921 visit to Miami Beach, a visit made famous by photos of Harding playing golf with Carl Fisher's pet elephant, Rosie, who served as the president's caddy. By 1922, the tract's roughly 40 acres had been surveyed and platted into 133 lots with broad streets, an oceanfront park on its east end, and a bayfront park on its west end. Its planning called for a hotel district along a fragment of the now-defunct Ocean Boulevard, a commercial district along Collins Avenue and a residential district on the balance of the land. This stratified planning assembled the essential features and amenities of a resort community into a compact ten blocks. The plat was renamed the Harding Townsite in 1923, after the president's death in August of that year.

Today, beachfront hotels are organized along the two-block frontage of Ocean Terrace, whose open-to-the-beach public character recalls the character of Ocean Drive in the city's South Beach district. To the west, most of the Collins Avenue retail corridor's rich assortment of shops, restaurants, and movie theaters awaits revitalization. Farther west still, a neighborhood of apartment buildings set along generously sized blocks and wide streets stretches to the Park View Waterway. Interspersed among the apartment buildings are small wood-frame and masonry homes, remnants of the lower density envisioned in the area's early development. The establishment of North Shore Park in 1941 on the remaining grounds of the old House of Refuge provides the neighborhood with a park for active recreation.

H11

North Beach Band Shell   H11

7251–7275 Collins Avenue
Norman M. Giller & Associates, 1957

The North Shore Band Shell in North Shore Park is a fitting counterpart to the Vendome fountain as a public symbol of North Beach. While the fountain is a classic civic monument, the band shell is an active space with a Futurist image that registers well with the high speed of traffic on Collins Avenue. Its most remarkable features are the disc-shaped entry canopies that cantilever a great distance from their supporting vertical pylons and recall flying saucers or the rings of Saturn. As explained by architect Norman Giller, the low-slung discs were meant to go beyond aesthetic concerns to impart a sense of entry into the roofless facility.

Stretching to the west, North Shore Park is an active recreational tract that originally stretched from the Park View Canal to the Atlantic Ocean. It was carved in the 1940s from a remnant of the federal land on which sat the Biscayne House of Refuge. Unfortunately, one of the park's original four blocks has served as a parking lot for many years.

Walgreens (Woolworth's)   H12

7332 Collins Avenue
Maurice S. Weintraub, 1963
Renovation: Brown Demandt Architects with Allan T. Shulman Architect, 2003

Originally a Woolworth's store, a battle ensued when successor Walgreens sought to close its full-glass streetfront façade. As the property is located within the Harding Townsite Historic District, however, the original 1960s façade had to be respected. The resulting adaptive use illustrates the often difficult interplay between historic preservation and modern retailing, and the need for creative approaches on all sides. Walgreens was paired with ArtCenter/South Florida, which now uses the original Woolworth windows as a curated remote exhibition space, or "art windows." The generous amount of glass brings more life to the street than the drugstore chain's typical design. The drugstore also agreed to reuse the building's remarkable glass-tiled upper wall, which served the Woolworth's store as a background canvas for its full building-length signage. Walgreens retained the Woolworth's style of lettering, and in a compromise, "Walgreens" is spelled out in the same font but in metal letters projecting from the tile parapet instead of the fluted, red, plastic letters displayed by the previous occupant.

Venevision Studios (RKO Movie Theater)   H13

7401 Collins Avenue
Albert Anis, 1947

The old RKO Theater was built shortly after World War II. Like most contemporary movie theaters on corner sites, it carved out and leased the valuable corner space to restaurants or retailers. On the tall parapet, reliefs of squares superimposed on double horizontal bars are said to represent the flickering of the moving image as they seem to speed around the prominent rounded corner. Today, the theater serves as production studios for one of Latin America's largest producers of television content, drawing Spanish-language celebrities to this off-the-beaten path corner of Miami Beach. Shows produced here are watched by millions of Spanish-speakers throughout the United States, Latin America, and Spain.

CVS (Food Fair Supermarket)   H14

7410 Collins Avenue
F. J. Tarlowski, 1950

This former Food Fair supermarket once advertised its presence with a recessed square pylon connected to the main façade with projecting flat planes; today, only the base of the pylon remains. Stucco banding connects to Moderne decorative themes, while the more Structuralist handling of the pylon element and flat planes heralds postwar Modern commercial architecture.

Chase Federal Savings and Loan   H15

7474 Collins Avenue
August Geiger, 1950

A monumentalizing Modern Classical composition, this building's formal entrance is framed in an ornamental quarry keystone surround, and the balance of the façade comprises raised stucco medallions and contrasting glazed tile.

Vilasol, Vilazul, and Vilamur   H16

Vilasol
7744 Collins Avenue
HVC Architects, 2006

Vilazul
7728 Collins Avenue
HVC Architects, 2006

Vilamur
7700 Collins Avenue
HVC Architects, 2005

This fine trio of 6-story white stucco condominiums updates Miami Beach's Fantasy Modern architecture to contemporary programmatic requirements of unit sizes and on-site parking, among others. Taking cues from the modest 2-story postwar apartments around them, the three buildings are

H16

wrapped in white stucco and sport vertical fins and horizontal fins, interplay of tripartite and horizontal façade arrangements, eyebrows, some doubling small balconies. Of equal interest is how the façades of the 6-story buildings were deftly made to give the appearance of 3-story buildings to further respond to the context.

North Shore Open Space Park   H17

Originally part of a platted subdivision called Altos del Mar, this 40-acre swath of oceanfront land was converted to an open space in 1972. Owned by the State of Florida, it is currently leased to the City of Miami Beach, which operates it as a public park. In contrast to nearby North Shore Park, this open space is used for passive recreation, offering a naturalistic setting, barbecue areas, and bicycle and walking paths. Along the west side of Collins Avenue (A1A), nearly eight blocks of surface parking lots reserved for the park await redevelopment. North Shore's unfortunate lack of urban frontage on the park compares unfavorably with nearby Ocean Terrace, and with Ocean Drive in South Beach.

Howard Johnson's Dezerland Beach Resort (Biltmore Terrace Hotel)   H18

8700 Collins Avenue
Albert Anis with Morris Lapidus, 1951

At the northern end of Miami Beach, the Dezerland is sited overlooking Open Space Park (once a single-family neighborhood). This building can be regarded as a rehearsal of techniques associate architect Morris Lapidus would go on to perfect at his later, grander hotels. For instance, the building is raised on a podium, employing smooth, white surfaces and sinuous curves on a monumental scale, and alternating these with large expanses of plate glass, like the Fontainebleau (G1). Although most of the lush interior features have been lost or concealed, the unusual lobby choreography of the Dezerland presages that of the later Eden Roc (G2).

H18

Duane Motel   H19

315–321 83rd Street
Robert M. Nordin, 1955

H19

Along with the popular parabola and delta wings, the boomerang expressed the futuristic spirit postwar hoteliers wished to transmit to tourists cruising the streets in their automobiles. The Duane Motel is best approached from the south (on foot, since traffic along Harding Avenue now flows in the opposite direction), where its projecting boomerang sails over the building's eaves. The balance of the building exudes a more functional articulation. The stucco field is scored in a grid pattern to add ornamental shadow to the composition.

Dolphin Hotel Apartments   H20

8400 Harding Avenue
Henry Hohauser, 1949

H20

One distinction between North Shore and Flamingo Park, its South Beach counterpart, is that the average building height is lower in North Shore, due to the preponderance of single-story apartment hotels such as the Dolphin. The Dolphin is rare in that it has a U-shaped plan with a generously sized court facing Harding Avenue. Note the modulation of outdoor space through the use of characteristic postwar design features like beanpoles and slump brick; and the suggestion of Wrightian motifs like shed roofs and built-in planters.

Temple Menorah (North Shore Jewish Center)   H21

620 75th Street
Gilbert Fein, 1951
Additions: Morris Lapidus, 1963

H21

Originally constructed as the North Shore Jewish Center, the structure was expanded by Morris Lapidus in 1963, who employed concrete vaults and a domed shell to give both an ancient and contemporary complexion to this synagogue. The forms are assembled to face a broad plaza on Dickens Avenue, a generous civic gesture. The corner of Dickens Avenue and Seventy-fifth Street is marked by the belvedere, which features walls perforated with circular openings topped with a parabolic shell.

Biscayne Elementary School   H22

800 77th Street
August Geiger, 1941

Completed by the Public Works Administration (PWA) on the eve of World War II, Biscayne Elementary exhibits the more traditional styling reserved for civic structures in this resort city (compare with Geiger's previous Ida M. Fisher Junior High and North Beach Elementary [F70]). Located at the geographic center of the North Beach area, the school's deferential façades are defined by open-air galleries that provide access to the classrooms. The entrance is at the center, marked by a pedimented front portico.

Yeshiva Elementary School and Premier Glatt (Temple Ner Tamid)   H23

7902 Carlyle Avenue
J. Richard Ogden, 1957

This former synagogue now functions as a religious school. The building features fieldstone walls, a prominent pylon made of interlocking fins, a low-slung Modernist loggia, and boxed windows.

Block of World War II–Era Housing   H24

7500 Block of Byron Avenue
Gerard Pitt, 1944

Completed during World War II, this modest group illustrates the urban capacity of small, 2-story walk-up apartment buildings. Each structure displays a synthesis of Neoclassical Revival and Modern themes. The functional structures are fronted with Mount Vernon–type 2-story porticos supported on paired pipe columns with ornamental filigree. Entranceways are crowned with broken pediments. Yet, side and rear façades feature partly cantilevered exterior stairs, stepped parapets, and metal railings. The setting of these six buildings creates a variety of comfortable courtyards.

Normandy Isles

H24   *The Normandy Isles (Isle of Normandy and Normandy Shores) were created from two mangrove islands, just west of the North Shore neighborhood. These are some of Miami Beach's most progressively planned areas, laid out in the 1920s with a civic infrastructure of picturesque parkways, plazas, monuments, and other amenities. If the planning reflects City Beautiful objectives popular in the 1920s, the architecture is emphatically postwar, with colonies of garden apartment buildings that reflect midcentury themes.*

Henri Levy initiated the development of the Normandy Isles in the 1920s. Discouraged from an earlier partnership with Carl Fisher (purportedly because Levy was Jewish) but undeterred, he went on to develop much of North Beach and the neighboring town of Surfside. Isle of Normandy, launched in 1924, continued the alignment of Seventy-first Street. Normandy Shores island, with the Normandy Shores Golf Course as its centerpiece, was created in 1939.

Like its counterparts on the west side of the bay (Coral Gables, Miami Springs, Opa-locka, and Miami Shores), the lozenge-shaped Normandy Isle (Isle of Normandy) is divided into planned zones, including a single-family house area in the center and multifamily apartments surrounding commercial areas at either end. Its neighborhoods feature picturesquely curving streets, some with tree-lined medians. Indicative of changing priorities before and after World War II, the east (prewar) commercial area is centered on the Vendome Fountain, while the west (postwar) commercial area, with a gas station at its center, remains largely undeveloped.

Only a few buildings were built before the hurricane and bust of 1926 effectively halted construction. After World War II, development resumed.

The more civic-minded planning of the Normandy Isles and its large number of waterfront lots inspired the development of numerous showcase buildings by local architects.

Even after the setbacks of 1926, Levy went on the develop the Everglades Causeway (now more commonly known as the Seventy-ninth Street or John F. Kennedy Causeway), the logical westward extension of the spine he had created with Normandy Beach South and Normandy Isle. The causeway was a critical investment in the future of Levy's developments because, besides connecting the barrier island to the mainland, it created a straight shot westward from the resorts of Miami Beach, along with Seventy-ninth Street, to Hialeah Park Race Track and Miami's burgeoning northern suburbs. Levy's developments would be enormously influential in shaping the lucrative Seventy-ninth and Biscayne area in the 1950s.

Vendome Plaza and Fountain   H25
W. H. Phillips, 1925

On the east side of the Isle of Normandy, at the heart of a sizable multifamily area, Vendome Plaza forms a triangular (or funnel-shaped) public space. The plaza is surrounded by a nearly continuous frontage of Moderne and postwar commercial buildings. The area houses a mix of restaurants, neighborhood services, and professional offices. The most recent streetscape improvements, while well-intentioned, render the plaza less accessible. Around the plaza, some recent gentrification mixes with a highly visible influx of working-class immigrants, bringing new energy to the area.

The Vendome Fountain occupies the center of the plaza. Completed in 1925, it is one of Miami Beach's most important and early works of civic art, and a conspicuous remnant of the district's original intended style and planning. Designed by W. H. Phillips, it was built of cast stone, rose to a height of 47 feet, and was finished with tile from Valencia, Spain. The *Miami Herald* attributed some of its artistic adornments to I. G. Black, an architect educated at Harvard and the American Academy in Rome, assisted by Raphael Bollard of the American Institute of Art, Paris. From Vendome Plaza, the Rue Vendome angles out to meet the Brest Esplanade, itself centered on the King Cole (**H30**), the area's foremost property.

H25

H26

Wohl Studios

H26

6865 Bay Drive
Igor Polevitzky, 1948

As an alternative to Miami Beach's more glamorous oceanfront hotels, studio apartments provided tourists with homelike accommodations in garden apartment–type buildings. These studios, however, were glamorous in their own way. Most were 2-story "maisonettes" with double-height living rooms; they were located on desirable waterfront lots, and were sited in lush gardens with pools, shuffleboard, and access to waterways. Igor Polevitzky's Wohl Studios is an excellent example. The spare modern façade (compare Polevitzky's reductive, structural expression with the more stylized group by Robert Swartburg just to the west) is principally articulated by a mix of plate-glass and ventilating jalousie windows. Its five buildings are grouped around a generous court and saltwater swimming pool. Nearby on Bonita Drive are the La Salle Studios, also by Polevitzky, reflecting a later version of the same studio model.

H28

Waterfront Garden Apartment Group

6881 Bay Drive
Robert Swartburg, 1948

H27

Bayside Apartments
910 Bay Drive
Robert Swartburg, 1951

H28

960 Bay Drive
Robert Swartburg, 1951

H29

This trio of separately constructed apartment buildings makes a coherent set that illustrates the stylistic pretentions of North Beach's larger waterfront residences at midcentury. Swartburg employed a compositional approach, mixing prewar and postwar stylistic motifs, varied materials, and graphically textured stucco surfaces. The festooning creates a complex and well-crafted fiction across the otherwise mundane repetition of residential windows. Large portals open to spacious and well-landscaped interior courtyards wrapped by open galleries and equipped with recreational amenities like swimming pools and shuffleboard courts.

Number 6881 has a broad street frontage that features eyebrows and a porthole as well as a stair-step cantilever rising from below second-floor windows to the crown of the parapet. Crab orchard stone, angled walls, cantilevers, and contrasting asymmetry contrive an especially exuberant expression. The Bayside Apartments building presents freeform volumes that create their own language of balance and hierarchy. The front staircase, notably, is camouflaged by a folded-plate motif with a grid of rectangular punched openings and discs pinned to its surface for shadow effect. As a foil to the discs, the center pylon is adorned with cubes applied to a diamond checkerboard score pattern. Number 960 has full-height crab orchard stone pylon, peculiar screen block and corrugated panels. The ensemble presents common elements of Miami's Vernacular Modern architecture.

H30

King Cole Apartments   H30

900 Bay Drive
Melvin Grossman with Fridstein and Fitch, 1961

The King Cole sits prominently on the southeast corner of the Isle of
Normandy. Formerly the site of the North Shore Hotel, its position terminates the axis of Brest Esplanade, one of Miami Beach's rare expressions of
City Beautiful urban planning. The current 1960s apartment block honors
the axis with a symmetrical convex façade, and an entrance framed with
rubble stone walls and concrete umbrellas. On the other side, the boomer-
ang-shaped structure wraps a spacious pool deck at the intersection of
Indian Creek and Biscayne Bay. The building's wrapping glass walls, visible
concrete floor edges, and projecting balconies embody characteristic elements of the high-rise residential architecture that transformed waterfront
districts of Miami Beach in the 1960s.

Deco Palms Apartments   H31

6930 Rue Versailles
Gilbert Fein, 1958

Not Deco at all, the Deco Palms Apartments illustrates well the stylistic and
urban hybridity that characterizes garden-apartment districts in Miami
Beach. This U-shaped building wraps a sheltered central courtyard, open to
Rue Versailles through a gabled breezeway. Note how Fein has adapted the

H31

popular chalet-style façade for a corner location. Perhaps to give the building a presence on Normandy Plaza, a short block away, a prominent brick
corner element with a flared fin-brow were melded into the gabled façade.
The balance of the building represents a functional response to the reductive program of modest garden-apartment building, although everyday
features like the cantilevered catwalk galleries and exterior stairs are used to
decorative effect. The building merges into the dense urban fabric of Miami
Beach, with its tradition of prominently addressed corners.

1191–1197 71st Street   H32

Victor H. Nellenbogen, 1946

Postwar commercial buildings frequently achieved rich visual effects with
an economy of means. This building's 2-story façade frames angled bay
storefront windows between continuous eyebrows. Its central, fluted pylon
rises to a stepped skyscraper parapet and circular vents enhance a sense
of symmetry. Broad projecting concrete canopies shade its upper-floor
residential windows. As was common in the period, an open stairway rises
along the south side of the building toward a broad side terrace serving the
residential spaces above.

Regions Bank (Washington Federal Savings)   H33

1133 Normandy Drive
Francis R. Hoffman, 1958

Edward Durell Stone's seminal U.S. embassy in New Delhi, India, of 1957 did
much to popularize both a monumental formal Modernism and the use of
masonry screen block. The 2-story glass bank features a visible structure
of concrete columns wrapped at the second story in an ethereal half-tone
envelope of circular concrete brise-soleils. Below the projecting upper floor,
stair treads cantilever from the west façade and the graceful, compressed
arch entrance canopy seems to float. Much of the upper floor is taken up by
a delightful, yet small Art Deco–style auditorium space that begs for greater
use.

H33

Avanti   H34

155 North Shore Drive
Beilinson Gomez Architects, 2004

The clearing of several contiguous lots (North Beach has none of the local historic district status that protects similar buildings in South Beach)
allowed for the construction of a new townhouse complex that reflects
contemporary market forces, building typology, and styling. In contrast to
the characteristic Miami Beach condition where multifamily buildings fill
long, narrow lots perpendicular to the street, Avanti is constructed of broad
blocks that layer from the street to the waterway on the back side of the lot.
The structures feature a bold interplay of stucco and glass, a handsome interpretation of Miami Beach's Modern architectural traditions.

275–301 South Shore Drive   H35

Gilbert Fein, 1953

The postwar craze for the swept-wing motif reached critical speed in the
North Beach district of Miami Beach. Delta-winged façades adorn many of
the area's structures, including a substantial number of single-story apartment houses. The feature was a trademark design for architect Gilbert Fein,
who used it to add excitement to an otherwise functional block of modest
H35   apartments.

2131 Calais Drive   H36
Victor H. Nellenbogen, 1947

Prewar and postwar apartment buildings line the streets of the Isle of
Normandy. Here is an example that spans stylistic divides. The basic housing modules are streamlined blocks with prewar features like projecting eyebrows and glass block. On the courtyard side, these are appended
with uncommonly generous porches. The entrance portal to the building's
handsome open court features a concrete slab supported on crab orchard
stone and glass-block piers, framing a breezeway leading to the Normandy
Waterway.

Vernon Arms   H37
1919 Bay Drive
Jos. Vladeck, Abraben, 1958

This mid-rise apartment building is distinguished by a spirited commitment
to Modernist principles of transparency and the structural expression of the
cantilever. The 6-story block floats on pilotis, and its units face southwest to
Biscayne Bay and the Miami skyline. The building presents a crystalline wall
broken only by projecting concrete balconies whose swept-back parapets
lend dynamism to the broad façade. The glass wall is patterned with alternating panels of fixed plate-glass and awning windows, achieving a subtle
graphic effect. On the opposite north side, perforated masonry blocks
screen the open walkways, a decorative feature in the guise of a sun-shading device. Expressed stair and elevator towers punctuate the rear façade
while the pool faces the street (a necessity dictated by solar orientation), occupying a deck that stretches beneath the supporting pilotis that carry the
structure. Actually, the building defies environmental conventions: the un-
protected glass wall faces southwest toward the harsh afternoon sun, while
the screened walkways face northeast.

H37

H38

International Inn   H38

2100 Bay Drive
Melvin Grossman, 1956

The International Inn's double-height glass lobby, sheltered by a mono-pitched roof, makes a striking impression when viewed from the John F. Kennedy Causeway on the approach to Miami Beach. The conspicuous lobby is a theatrical space whose grand staircase, sweeping mezzanine balcony, and walls faced in zebra-striped mosaic tile are a billboard for the kind of glamorous interior arrangements more typically found in oceanfront hotels. The Inn serves as a fitting entry feature into the mainly postwar urban fabric of North Beach.

Acknowledgments

The authors thank the many individuals—among them the residents who attended early community discussion meetings, city officials, historians, and private citizens—who have donated their time, energy, and expertise during the long process of developing this project.

Lydia Aguiar
Shannon Anderton
Judith Arango (+)
Maritza Arceo
Phil Azan
Robin Bachin
Richard & Valerie Beaubien
Judith Berson-Levinson
Dena Bianchino
Warren Bittner
Matti Bower
Seth Bramson
Hector Burga
Gregory Bush
Burr Camp
Mark Cantor
Jane Caporelli
Antolin Carbonell
William Cary
Jose Casanova
Omar Castellanos
Rocco Ceo
Simone Chin
John Claiste
Eureca Coulanges
Marlo Courtney

Elizabeth Cox
Donald W. Curl
Roberto Datorre
Zoila Datorre
John Davies
Manny Diaz
Andrea Dougherty
Beth Dunlop
Carlos Dunn
Melissa Dunn
Sarah Eaton
Debra Fagan
Lee Feldman
Rick Ferrer
Arlene Ferris
Dorothy Fields
Audrey Flynn
John Forbes
Scott Galvin
Paul George
Thelma Gibson
Sarah Giller Nelson
Jorge Gomez
Steven Gretenstein
Mark Hampton
Mary Hartley

David Hertzberger
Brigitte M. Hodge
Dawn Hugh
Michael Hughes
Xavier Iglesias
Sarah Ingle
Neisen Kasdin
Pat Kean
Michael Kinerk
Howard Kleinberg
Carolyn Klepser
Randy Koper
Jean-Francois Lejeune
Luly Leon
Nancy Liebman
Hector Lima
Norman Litz
Joanna Lombard
Donna Lubin
Joan Lutton
Becky Matkov
Sherra McLeod
Lilia Medina
Joyce Meyers
Aristides Millas
Thomas Mooney
Gala Brown Munnings
Melanie Muss
George Neary
Lea Nickless
Christy Norcross
Eddie Padilla
Lisa Palley
Arva Moore Parks
Cynthia Paul

Amy Perry
Dana Pezoldt
Elizabeth Plater-Zyberk
John Reed
Julie Reynolds
Judi Ring
Andreina Rivas
Craig Robins
Eugene Rodriguez
Daniel Rojo
Miriam Rossi
Denis Russ
Barron Scherer
Timothy F. Schmand
Shelly Shiner
John Shipley
Bob Smith
Rebecca Smith
Lourdes Solera
Steve Sorensen
John A. Stuart
Anne Swanson
Deborah Tackett
Gene Tinnie
Leonard Turkel
Ellen Uggucioni
Evelyn Uslar-Petrie
Providencia Velazquez
David Villano
Jason Walker
Marvin Weeks
Lynn Westall
Stanley Whitman
Howard Wilkins
Nancy M. Wolcott

Thanks also to the individuals at architectural offices in Miami and elsewhere who provided information from their databases and archives. They include the following, among many others:

Gail Baldwin
Les Beilinson
Robin Bosco
Bruce Brosch
Walter Chatham
Annabel Delgado
Markus Frankel
Jose Gelabert-Navia
Ira Giller
Norman Giller (+)
Thorn Grafton
Donald Grannan
Mark Hampton
Richard Heisenbottle
Cheryl Jacobs
Clyde Judson (+)

Kobi Karp
Tony Leon
Roberto Martinez
Rony Mateu
Peter Menendez
Chad Oppenheim
Anthony Rimore
Raul Rodriguez
Charles Sieger
Kricket Snow
Max Wolfe Sturman
Todd Tragash
Luis Trelles
Thomas Westberg
Dennis Wilhelm
Bernard Zyscovich

The authors are grateful to all the individuals, those listed and those not listed, who assisted us in the development of this guide, but the responsibility for any errors remains with us.

Photo Credits

Photos copyright Robin Hill: Section A (except A9, A42, A53, A62); Section B (except B53, B82); Section C (except C28, C36, C97, C99, C100); Section D (except D27); and E4, E8, E20, E36, E40, E56, E64, E81, E82, F1, F10, F19, F21, F27, F28, F33, F34, F37, F42, F43, F45, F46, F48, F50, F61, F71, F79, G1, G2, G6, G7, G8, G10, G12, G13, G16, H0, H2, H3, H20, H24, H28, H30

Photos copyright Thomas Delbeck: A42, C28, C100, E0, E7, E11, E13, E17, E18, E19, E21, E23, E30, E32, E37, E41, E42, E46, E47, E48, E50, E58, E59a, E59b, E61, E62, E63, E65, E77, F0, F5, F6, F7, F11, F12, F14, F15, F24, F51, F54, F55, G0, G5, H4, H6, H9, H11, H16, H18, H19, H21, H25, H31, H33, H38

Courtesy of Florida Photographic Collection: A9, A53 (William A. Fishbaugh), A62, B53, B82 (Gleason Waite Romer), F80

Courtesy of Spillis Candela DMJM: A140

Courtesy of University of Florida Smathers Libraries, Ken Treister Collection: C36

Courtesy of Giller & Giller Inc. Archives: C97

From *Florida Architecture*, 1956: 124: C99

Courtesy of the Historical Museum of Southern Florida: C111, D27, F64, H26, H37

Bibliographic Essay

James F. Donnelly

Any text of architectural history and commentary rests upon the work of others; *Miami Architecture: An AIA Guide Featuring Downtown, the Beaches, and Coconut Grove* is no exception. The authors have benefited from a variety of sources in history, architecture, and historic preservation. This essay describes how we have used these sources.

For the most part, we have relied on primary sources for factual information about the address, the architect(s), the dates of construction or completion, and the architect and date of any significant renovation. These primary sources include county and municipal records of the time, eyewitness accounts in published and unpublished sources, and other documents or materials of the time. When these were not available even for this basic information, we have relied on secondary sources such as historic designation reports prepared by county or municipal governments, guidebooks for individual cities or sections, newspapers of a later time, articles, monographs, edited volumes, and information supplied by the original architects or the current owners of the properties. There is inconsistency among these sources when describing a building's date. Some list the date the building permit was pulled prior to construction; some list the date the building opened for use; some list the date when taxes were first collected on the new development. When possible we gave priority to the appropriate Building Department or "building card" information. When that was not feasible, we relied on property tax records and other primary sources.

Since the authors began work on this volume, many municipalities and organizations have developed Web sites providing access to primary source documents, photographs, and secondary commentary contributing to a knowledge and appreciation of Miami's built environment. Both the City of Miami and the City of Miami Beach have placed their designation reports online for general public use. These analytical papers, written in support of the recognition of a property or district as historic, have been critical to the development of this volume. The State of Florida's Division of Historical Resources has developed an extensive Web site, including photos and information about historic properties and an interactive Web page on Florida Heritage Tourism. Finally, the National Park Service lists online all properties on the National Register of Historic Places, with basic information about the structures.

Primary sources are the foundation of this volume. From their records, the City of Miami Building Department provided us with the basic information about many of the buildings we have described in Miami: address, date, and architect. The City of Miami Beach offers an online historic property database, and we have used that for the same basic information when appropriate. More broadly, the City of Miami Beach Building Department records provided us with the basic facts about buildings not in the historic database. In some cases, we have been able to utilize the comments of the architects themselves when they made contemporary references to the building's design. While limited, newspapers of the time often had information and commentary about structures as they were proposed, designed, and built. Both the *Miami Herald* and the now-defunct *Miami News* frequently provide significant information and are available on microfilm. The digitally searchable *New York Times* also supplies information about Miami's built environment, reflecting the close relationship between the two metropolitan areas. When confronted with conflicts in these primary sources, we have usually relied upon government records.

When interpreting this factual information, commenting on the architecture, and presenting the significance of the built environment, the authors, of course, are responsible for their own ideas. Anyone familiar with the secondary sources we have used, however, will recognize the intellectual debt the authors owe to them.

First in importance among the secondary sources we used is the Miami-Dade County publication *From Wilderness to Metropolis: The History and Architecture of Dade County, Florida, 1825–1940*, first published in 1982 and again, in a revised version, in 1992. Published in the first light of official preservation consciousness in Miami, *From Wilderness to Metropolis* has inspired many, including the authors, to see and appreciate the role of the built environment in telling the story of the origins and early development of Miami-Dade County.

In the late 1980s and early 1990s, the Historic Preservation Committee of the Junior League of Miami published a series of brochures offering self-guided tours of Coconut Grove, Coral Gables, Downtown Miami, South Dade, and Northeast Dade. Featuring photos and commentary on significant structures, these excellent pamphlets have been extraordinarily useful in achieving the Junior League's goal: "the education of our citizenry in the area of historic preservation." With *Miami Architecture: An AIA Guide Featuring Downtown, the Beaches, and Coconut Grove*, we hope to achieve similar results on a broader scale. More recently, the Greater Miami Visitors and Convention Bureau has published *Miami: A Sense of Place*, a volume of eight essays that link Miami's diverse communities with their equally diverse built environments. Since a sense of place is important to the authors, this small, but useful booklet influenced our thinking about Miami, its buildings, and its people. The City of Miami Neighborhood Enhancement Team (NET) Web site provides extensive contemporary information about Miami's neighborhoods. "Miami Metropolitan Archive," a digital resource managed by Florida International University Libraries, makes available a wide variety of "source materials relating to Miami-Dade County history, management, development, and culture." Most recently, Richter Library at the University of Miami has posted a Web site of special interest developed by Robin Bachin, titled "Travel, Tourism, and Urban Growth in Greater Miami: A Digital Archive."

Among general historical monographs, we have consulted works such as Arva Moore Parks's *Miami: The Magic City* (1981; rev. 1991) and Howard Kleinberg's *Miami Beach* (1994). A very useful bibliography of Miami's history was compiled and published by Susan Weiss in 1995. In time for Miami's centennial, the Historical Museum of Southern Florida published Paul George's *Miami: One Hundred Years of History*, now online at the museum's Web site.

A group of talented historians and social scientists have begun an analysis of Miami's cultural and social history, and we have benefited from the insights of Marvin Dunn's *Black Miami in the Twentieth Century*; Deborah Dash Moore's *To the Golden Cities*; Alejandro Portes and Alex Stepick's *City on the Edge*; and Alex Stepick, Guillermo Grenier, Max Castro, and Marvin Dunn's *This Land Is Our Land: Immigrants and Power in Miami*.

The Historical Museum of Southern Florida publishes two very useful periodicals covering specific topics in time and place: *Tequesta* and *South Florida History*. These publications present material with a specificity and local focus not readily found elsewhere, and cover a broad range of topics and localities within the scope of this volume. Among periodicals, *Florida Architecture*, an annual publication of AIA Florida, provided us with information and images not readily available elsewhere. Specific and more localized histories include Seth Bramson's unique photo collection in his *Miami Beach* and Abe Lavender's *Miami Beach in 1920: The Making of a Winter Resort*, which is a clever use of census data to provide a social history. An important source about the designation, preservation, and development of the Miami Beach Architectural District (Art Deco District) is *Old Miami Beach*, an account of the process originally presented by the Miami Design Preservation League (MDPL) to the State of Florida in 1980, but then published by MDPL in 1994. Barbara Baer Capitman's *Deco Delights* shows the effects of early restoration and redevelopment in the Art Deco District. The more recent past is covered in M. Barron Stofik's *Saving South Beach*, an account of the way Barbara Capitman and others used awareness of architecture and historic preservation as a means to build and develop community. Stofik's book leaves open the question, Is South Beach a model for urban renaissance or an account of a community so unique that its success cannot be replicated elsewhere?

While some sources are generally historical, others specialize in developing an understanding of Miami's architectural history. The pioneering effort was *A Guide to Miami Architecture*, published by the AIA Florida South Chapter in 1963. Aristides Millas contributed *70 Years of Miami Architecture*, a catalogue of an exhibition in 1988 at the Bass Museum of Art, published by the museum in 1991. Millas has been an inspiration to the authors, passing on his enthusiasm for Miami and its architectural heritage. His lectures, offered through the University of Miami's continuing education program and intended for a general audience, are legendary. A monograph on Miami's architectural history, *Building Marvelous Miami*, was published by Nicholas Patricios in 1994. Jean-Francois Lejeune and Allan T. Shulman contributed *The Making of Miami Beach, 1933–1942: The Architecture of Lawrence Murray Dixon*, published by Rizzoli in 2001. In 2005, a revised version, edited by Richard Longstreth, of the 1999 *A Historical Bibliography of the Built Environment in Miami and Southern Florida*, compiled by Malinda Cleary, Richard Longstreth, and Aristides J. Millas, was released on the Society of Architectural Historians' Web site.

Other sources, while paying homage to the historical context, focus more specifically on the architecture of Miami, past and present. Short of a geographically arranged guidebook, *Miami: Architecture of the Tropics*, edited by Maurice Culot and Jean-Francois Lejeune, is a noted survey of Miami's architectural culture. The *Miami Herald* has provided architectural news and criticism from several outstanding writers, including Frederic Sherman in the postwar era, and more recently, Peter Whoriskey, Andres Viglucci, and Beth Dunlop. In particular, Dunlop's critical writing has shaped our understanding of many of the buildings and districts listed in this volume. Dunlop's fluidly and passionately written *Miami: Mediterranean Splendor and Deco Dreams* is enhanced by the stunning photography of Steven Brooke, and documents in words and pictures "buildings worth knowing." The Miami Design Preservation League has published a pamphlet, *Miami Beach: An Architectural Guide*, now unfortunately out of print, that listed and located many of the hundreds of significant buildings on Miami Beach. In addition, Keith Root's *Art Deco Guide* and the Beaubiens' excellent *Discovering South Beach Deco*, also difficult to come by, provide important information about the structures of the Miami Beach Architectural District.

We also relied upon our own earlier work, including Robinson's *MiMo: Miami Modern Revealed*, Donnelly's writings in *South Florida Magazine*, and a number of books and essays on topics related to the architectural and urban history of South Florida by Shulman.

Finally, *Miami Architecture: An AIA Guide Featuring Downtown, the Beaches, and Coconut Grove* is the product of a community with an increasing interest in architecture and with recent—if not fully analyzed— experience in the way architecture and historic preservation can contribute to the cultural heritage and economic development of a community. During the winter and spring of 2004, the nonprofit Miami Architecture Project, sponsor of this volume, led a series of ten community forums throughout Miami-Dade County to present the 2003 Discussion Draft of this volume and receive feedback from the interested public. Preservation activists, architects, public officials, and representatives of Miami-Dade's pioneer families attended and engaged in a series of lively and informative discussions, based on the 2003 draft and, in some cases, source material brought by discussion participants. The authors intend to make, and hope they have made, *Miami Architecture: An AIA Guide Featuring Downtown, the Beaches, and Coconut Grove* truly a product of the community it celebrates.

Reference List of Sources

This is a list of sources used, directly or indirectly, in the preparation of this volume.

American Institute of Architects, Florida South Chapter. *A Guide to the Architecture of Miami*. Miami, 1963.

Armbruster, Ann. *The Life and Times of Miami Beach*. New York: Knopf, 1995.

Bach, Penny Balkin. "To Light up Philadelphia: Lighting, Public Art, and Public Space." In "Critical Issues in Public Art," special issue, *Art Journal* 48, no. 4 (Winter 1989): 324–30.

Beaubien, Richard and Valerie. *Discovering South Beach Deco: Walking Tours in the Miami Beach Art Deco District*. Bolton, Mass.: Domani Press, 2004.

Bramson, Seth. *Boulevard of Dreams: A Pictorial History of El Portal, Biscayne Park, Miami Shores, and North Miami*. Charleston, S.C.: History Press, 2007.

———. *Miami Beach*. Images of America Series. Charleston, S.C.: Arcadia, 2005.

———. *Miami: The Magic City*. Images of America Series. Charleston, S.C.: Arcadia, 2007.

Broton, Jim. *Home on the River: The History of Miami River Residential Development*. Miami: Broton Group, 2007.

Capitman, Barbara Baer. *Deco Delights: Preserving the Beauty and Joy of Miami Beach Architecture*. New York: Dutton, 1988.

Castillo, Greg, and Allan Shulman, eds. *AULA 3: Miami Tropical*. New Orleans: Architecture & Urbanism en Las Americas/Tulane University School of Architecture, 2002.

Ceo, Rocco, and Joanna Lombard. *Historic Landscapes of Florida*. Miami: Deering Foundation and Coral Gables: University of Miami School of Architecture; dist. Gainesville: University Press of Florida, 2001.

City of Miami: Historic Preservation. Sites and Districts. Designation Reports. www.historicpreservationmiami.com/index.html.

City of Miami: Neighborhood Enhancement Teams (NET). www.miamigov.com/NETS/pages/default.asp.

City of Miami Beach. Planning Department. Designation Reports. http://web.miamibeachfl.gov/planning/scroll.aspx?id=25676.

City of Miami Beach. Planning Department. Historic Property Selection. www. miamibeachfl.gov/historic_property/asp/get_prop.asp.

Culot, Maurice, and Jean-Francois Lejeune. *Miami: Architecture of the Tropics.* Brussels: Archives d'Architecture Moderne, 1993; Princeton: Princeton Architectural Press, 1996.

Curl, Donald W. "The Florida Architecture of F. Burrall Hoffman Jr., 1882–1980." *Florida Historical Quarterly* (Spring 1998): 399–416.

Dunlop, Beth. *Miami: Mediterranean Splendor and Deco Dreams.* New York: Rizzoli, 2007.

Dunn, Marvin. *Black Miami in the Twentieth Century.* Florida History and Culture Series. Gainesville: University Press of Florida, 1997.

Federal Writers' Project, Federal Works Agency, Work Projects Administration. *The WPA Guide to Florida.* 1939. New York: Pantheon, 1984.

Florida International University Libraries. "Miami Metropolitan Archive." http:// miami.fiu.edu/.

George, Paul S. "Miami: One Hundred Years of History." Historical Museum of Southern Florida. Online at the museum's site: www.hmsf.org/history/south-florida-hundred-years.htm.

George, Paul S., and Thomas K. Petersen, "Liberty Square, 1933–1987: The Origins and Evolution of a Public Housing Project." *Tequesta* 48 (1988): 53–68.

Giller, Norman M., and Sarah Giller Nelson. *Designing the Good Life: Norman M. Giller and the Development of Miami.* Gainesville: University Press of Florida, 2007.

Historic Preservation Committee of the Junior League of Miami. *Historic Coconut Grove: Self-Guided Tour.* Pamphlet. Coral Gables, Fla.: 1987

———. *Historic Coral Gables: Self-Guided Tour.* Pamphlet. Coral Gables, Fla., 1986.

———. *Historic Downtown Miami: Self-Guided Tour.* Pamphlet. Coral Gables, Fla., 1985.

———. *Historic Northeast Dade: Self-Guided Tour.* Pamphlet. Coral Gables, Fla., 1991.

———. *Historic South Dade: Self-Guided Tour.* Pamphlet. Coral Gables, Fla., 1988.

A Historical Bibliography of the Built Environment in Miami and Southern Florida. Society of Architectural Historians, 2005. A revised version, edited by Richard Longstreth, of the 1999 volume, compiled by Malinda Cleary, Richard Longstreth, and Aristides J. Millas, was released on the Society of Architectural Historians' Web site, www.sah.org/.

Historical Museum of Southern Florida. Research and Collections. www.hmsf. org/history/south-florida-hundred-years.htm.

Kleinberg, Howard: *Miami Beach.* Miami: Centennial Press, 1994.

Lapidus, Morris. *The Architecture of Joy.* Miami: E. A. Seemann, 1979.

Lavender, Abraham D. *Miami Beach in 1920.* Charleston, S.C.: Arcadia, 2002.

Lejeune, Jean-Francois, and Allan T. Shulman. *The Making of Miami Beach, 1933–1942: The Architecture of Lawrence Murray Dixon.* Miami Beach: Bass Museum of Art; New York: Rizzoli, 2000.

Lombard, Joanna. *The Architecture of Duany Plater-Zyberk and Company*. New York: Rizzoli, 2005.

Luna, Ian, and Kenneth Powell, eds. *Kohn Pedersen Fox: Architecture and Urbanism, 1993–2002*. New York: Rizzoli, 2002.

Matkov, Becky Roper, ed. *Miami's Historic Neighborhoods: A History of Community*. Miami: Dade Heritage Trust, 2001.

Metropolitan Dade County, Office of Community and Economic Development, Historic Preservation Division. 1982. *From Wilderness to Metropolis: The History and Architecture of Dade County, Florida, 1825–1940*. Rev. ed. Miami: Metropolitan Dade County, 1992.

Miami: A Sense of Place. Miami: Greater Miami Visitors and Convention Bureau, 2005.

Miami-Dade County, Property Appraiser. http://www.miamidade.gov/pa/property_search.asp.

Miami Design Preservation League. *Miami Beach Architectural Guide*. Pamphlet, 2003.

Millas, Aristides J. *70 Years of Miami Architecture*. Miami Beach: Bass Museum, 1991.

Mohl, Raymond A. "Making the Second Ghetto in Metropolitan Miami, 1940-1960." *Journal of Urban History* 21 (March 1995): 394-427.

Moore, Deborah Dash. *To the Golden Cities: Pursuing the American Jewish Dream in Miami and L.A.* New York: Free Press, 1994.

Nagler, Richard. *My Love Affair with Miami Beach*. New York: Simon and Schuster, 1991.

Nash, Eric P., and Randall C. Robinson Jr. *MiMo: Miami Modern Revealed*. San Francisco: Chronicle Books, 2004.

New York Times. "New York Times Article Archive." www.nytimes.com/ref/membercenter/nytarchive.html.

Parks, Arva Moore. "The History of Coconut Grove, Florida, 1825-1925." Master's thesis, University of Miami, 1971.

———. *Miami: The Magic City*. 1981. Rev. ed. Miami: Centennial Press, 1991.

Patricios, Nicholas. *Building Marvelous Miami*. Gainesville: University Press of Florida, 1994.

Peters, Thelma. *Lemon City: Pioneering on Biscayne Bay 1850-1925*. Miami: Banyan Books, 1976.

Portes, Alejandro, and Alex Stepick. *City on the Edge: The Transformation of Miami*. Berkeley and Los Angeles: University of California Press, 1993.

Raley, H. Michael, Linda G. Polansky, and Aristides J. Millas. *Old Miami Beach: A Case Study in Historic Preservation, July 1976–July 1, 1980*. As originally prepared for the State Historic Preservation Office, September 1980. Postscript added, 1994. Miami Beach, Fla.: Miami Design Preservation League, 1994

Redford, Polly. *Billion Dollar Sandbar: A Biography of Miami Beach*. New York: Dutton, 1970.

Root, Keith. *Miami Beach Art Deco Guide*. Miami Beach: Miami Design Preservation League, 1987.

Shulman, Allan T., ed. *Miami Modern Metropolis: Paradise and Paradox in Mid-century Architecture and Planning*. Miami Beach: Bass Museum and Glendale, Calif.: Balcony Press, 2009.

———. "Miami Beach as Urban Assemblage: A Unique Culture of Housing." *New City: Journal of the University of Miami School of Architecture* 3 (Fall 1996): 26–49.

South Florida History. Miami: Historical Association of Southern Florida.

Sprague, John Titcomb. *The Origin, Progress, and Conclusion of the Florida War*. New York: D. Appleton, 1848.

State of Florida. Department of State. Division of Historical Resources. "Florida Master Site File." www.flheritage.com/preservation/sitefile/.

Stepick, Alex, Guillermo Grenier, Max Castro, and Marvin Dunn. *This Land Is Our Land: Immigrants and Power in Miami*. Berkeley and Los Angeles: University of California Press, 2003.

Stofik, M. Barron. *Saving South Beach*. Gainesville: University Press of Florida, 2005.

Stuart, John, and John F. Stack Jr., eds. *The New Deal in South Florida: Design, Policy, and Community Building, 1933–1940*, Gainesville: University Press of Florida, 2008.

Tequesta: The Journal of the Historical Association of Southern Florida. Miami: Historical Association of Southern Florida.

United States Government. Department of the Interior. National Park Service. National Register of Historic Places. "National Register Research." www.nps.gov/nr/research/index.htm.

University of Miami. Richter Library. "Travel, Tourism, and Urban Growth in Greater Miami: A Digital Archive." http://scholar.library.miami.edu/miami-digital/index.html.

Weiss, Susan. *Miami Bibliography*. Miami: Historical Association of Southern Florida, 1995.

Index of Named Buildings, Structures, Parks, and Art Works

Page numbers in boldface refer to primary entries.

Index of Architects, Designers, Planners, Artists, and City Founders

Page numbers in boldface refer to primary entries. Entries in italics refer to art work.

Index of Places

Page numbers in boldface refer to primary entries.

Allan T. Shulman, FAIA, is assistant professor at the University of Miami School of Architecture and a practicing architect and urban designer. His work focuses on themes of tropical architecture, housing, and historic preservation. He has written extensively on topics related to the architectural and urban history of South Florida.

Randall C. Robinson Jr. works for the City of Fort Lauderdale Planning and Zoning Department and writes about architecture in South Florida.

James F. (Jeff) Donnelly holds a research doctorate in American Studies from New York University and has served as an architectural tour guide for the Miami Design Preservation League since 1987. He is also the chair of the City of Miami Beach Historic Preservation Board.